ONE

ONE FOR THE THUMB

THE NEW STEELERS READER

Edited by
RANDY ROBERTS and
DAVID WELKY

UNIVERSITY OF PITTSBURGH PRESS

Published by the University of Pittsburgh Press
Copyright © 2006, University of Pittsburgh Press
Manufactured in the United States of America
Printed on acid-free paper
10 9 8 7 6 5 4 3 2 1

Permissions and source information for each article appear at the bottom of the
first page on which the article begins.

ISBN 0-8229-5945-3

CONTENTS

ACKNOWLEDGMENTS

Thanking the people who helped in the completion of a book is always a pleasure, and not only because it means that the work is almost complete. It is just nice to acknowledge that what seems to be the work of one or two individuals is really the collective labor of many. One person deserves thanks above everyone else. Niels Aaboe, our editor at the University of Pittsburgh Press, not only suggested the topic of the book but actively participated in its conception, research, and editing. Niels visited the Pro Football Hall of Fame with us, looked through old files, and genuinely shared in the fun and work of finishing this project. We also wish to acknowledge Deborah Meade for her expert assistance in preparing the final manuscript, Ann Walston for coming up with such an attractive design, Marilyn Prudente, and the other staff members at the Press who helped make this book possible. The friendly and accommodating staff of the Pro Football Hall of Fame, and especially Saleem Choudhry, also has our thanks. At Purdue University, Peggy Quirk, Mary Wanger, and the secretarial staff of the history department patiently and good-naturedly put up with our boorish requests to get everything done yesterday. Finally, our wives, Marjie and Ali, tolerated mountains of photocopies, endless chatter about the exploits of the Steelers, and us, altogether not a bad trifecta.

ONE FOR THE THUMB

INTRODUCTION

There was simply no way that William Penn, the founding father of Pennsylvania, and Art Rooney, the founding father of the Pittsburgh Steelers, would have seen eye to eye. Penn believed strongly that self-denial, temperance, and moderation were the proper routes to godliness. Opposed to "frivolous" pleasures, from balls, masques, and plays to cockfights, bullbaits, and gambling, he asserted that all such activities "excite people to rudeness, cruelty, looseness, and irreligion." And the worst were the gamesters, the "most idle and useless people in any government." To nudge the residents of his Holy Experiment along the path toward righteousness, Penn inserted several provisions in *The Great Law* to ban "rude and riotous sports" and curtail the playing of cards, dice, and lotteries. This portion of Penn's legal code, which came to be known as the "blue laws," cast a long, chilly winter shadow over the history of Pennsylvania sports. Though immigrants chipped away at the code in the eighteenth and nineteenth centuries, parts of it survived into the twentieth century like appendixes on the state's body politic. As late as the 1920s and early 1930s, Pennsylvania laws prohibited professional sporting contests on Sundays, causing economic hardship among the owners of the Pittsburgh Pirates, Philadelphia Phillies, and Philadelphia Athletics, and disgusting thousands of baseball fans.

Arthur Joseph Rooney, though he generally tried to observe all good and fair laws, was not inclined toward Penn's rigid world-view. A product of Pittsburgh's First Ward—or simply, The Ward—an Irish-American haven on the north bank of the Allegheny River, a couple of long baseball throws from downtown (pronounced "dahntahn" by true-speaking Pittsburghers), Rooney was the son of a saloon keeper, a natural politician by birth, a gambler by preference, and, like Will Rogers, a man who liked almost everyone he ever met. John O'Hara might have turned his world into fiction. It was populated by large Irish families, nuns, and priests; set against a backdrop of saloons, masses, christenings, and wakes; alive with the sounds of Gaelic, prayers, and oaths.

Rooney probably would have been a politician had it not been for sports. Though there were not quite enough Rooney boys to field a

1

baseball team, Art did have five brothers, and their love of sports was second probably only to their love of their mother. Around the house there was always a set of boxing gloves, and brothers Art, Vincent, and Dan Jr. became accomplished with their fists. They punched each other until they were good enough to win amateur championships and even a few professional fights. And outside their home were ball fields and gyms. "You went on the playground when the sun came up, and you didn't leave till the sun went down," Rooney remembered. Mostly they played baseball and football, joining with friends to organize teams that scoured Pittsburgh and neighboring towns for games. When Art Rooney became old enough to get steady work, he still dreamed of green summer baseball grass and muddy fall football fields. Men's work for men's wages held no appeal. He went to a steel mill once and tried it. When the morning break came, he walked out of the mill and never returned, not even for his pay. "I could see right away that there must be some easier way to make a living," he recalled.

Rooney may have been good enough to box or play baseball professionally, but the fact of the matter was that he did not relish living anywhere but Pittsburgh. After a brief professional boxing career he hung up the gloves and returned to the 'burgh. He signed a contract with the Chicago Cubs, but only played one season in their system. He later inked another contract with the Boston Red Sox, but never reported. Even his stints playing ball at colleges outside Pittsburgh tended to be brief. The only athletic worlds that really mattered to him—the only ones that he wanted to join and conquer—were the sandlot seasons in Pittsburgh. And in Pittsburgh he was not just another player; he was also a coach and an organizer, a ticket seller and promoter.

In the 1920s he became involved in the fledgling world of professional football. At the time, the professional game was something of the seedy underbelly of the sport. The college game was where the action was. Flappers and jazz-agers in raccoon coats and toting hip flasks jammed new stadiums to watch Knute Rockne's Notre Dame, Fielding Yost's Michigan, and Bob Zuppke's Illinois squads. They cheered the Gipper, the Galloping Ghost, and the Four Horsemen— men so famous that they transcended common names. But the professional game was different. Americans, if they thought about it at all (and few did), viewed it as something of a tug-of-war played by steelworkers and coal miners who looked like sure bets to win any fair beer-drinking or pie-eating contest. It lacked glamour, it lacked glitz, it lacked fans, and it lacked money.

At the top of the professional game, which was not very high, was the organization known originally as the American Professional Football Conference. It was created in 1920 in the showroom of Ralph Hay's Hupmobile Sales Agency in Canton, Ohio, and was about as organized as a chase scene in a Keystone Kops film. Representatives from Canton, Cleveland, Dayton, and Akron kicked in twenty-five dollars each to form the Conference and elected Jim Thorpe as president. The Conference quickly grew to include Rochester, Buffalo, Columbus, Detroit, Chicago, Decatur, Rock Island, Muncie, and Hammond, and was renamed the National Football League in 1922. In the decade that followed, owners with more ambition than money or followers formed teams, joined the NFL for a year or two, then dropped out when their losses reached an uncomfortable level. The only thing certain about the league was uncertainty. Schedules were arbitrary and subject to instant revision, games were played on whatever field a team owner could secure, and not all the teams played one another. College players battled under aliases to protect their eligibility, high-school players filled out rosters, and faded stars from past decades ran and hit and spit blood for the sport they still loved.

The NFL's great coup came in 1925 when George Halas of the Chicago Bears signed Red Grange to a professional contract. Grange announced his decision to drop out of Illinois and turn professional five minutes after his final college game, and from November 1925 to January 1926, he proceeded to barnstorm with the Bears. Though Grange himself was not as impressive as he had been at Illinois, the publicity he generated helped to turn the NFL from a small-time Ohio Valley operation to something bigger and grander. He showed that the professional game, played in large cities, could draw twenty, forty, even seventy thousand spectators. Grange's presence announced the future of the NFL; increasingly the small-town franchises disappeared and the league spread to the largest cities in the East and Midwest.

While the NFL was going through its growing pains, Art Rooney became involved in a lower form of football. If the collegians occupied football's top level, and the NFLers the middle, the semi-professionals grubbed at the bottom. They *were* the steelworkers and coal miners, the day laborers and night drinkers who played football because they always had. By forbidding Sunday games, Pennsylvania's blue laws effectively barred the NFL from the state, so entrepreneurs from various cities and towns formed their own squads and played whatever opponents they could line up. Art Rooney found a comfortable niche in this ad hoc corner of the football world. Working out of The Ward, with friends mostly from The Ward, he organized a team called the Hope-Harveys. Hope was the name of The Ward's firehouse that the teams used as a dressing room, and Harvey was the name of a local physician who doctored injured players. There was not much money in the sport, just the nickels and dimes the players picked up from occasional admission fees and passing the hat.

But the Hope-Harveys enjoyed modest success. They battled fairly evenly with a few NFL teams and won more than they lost against other semi-pro and sandlot squads. As the team improved, Rooney recruited a few good college players, and he even upgraded the outfit's name. The Hope-Harveys became the Majestic Radios, after the team's new sponsor. It was a name that combined the ballyhoo of the 1920s with one of the key industries of the decade, and men who remembered the teams—remembered them perhaps more fondly than accurately—swore that they could have played against the best in the NFL . . . hell, could have won the NFL championship. But, of course, the blue laws stood squarely between the Majestic Radios and the NFL title.

All that changed in 1933 when the Pennsylvania legislature, struck by a moment of good sense, repealed the Sunday ban, opening the door for championship football in Pittsburgh. By then, Art Rooney had long since stopped playing the game himself, and his well-earned reputation as a gambler who was uncommonly blessed at picking winners at the track had eclipsed his fading fame as an athlete. But he still had a soft spot in his heart for football and football players—and, in truth, for boxers, baseball players, jockeys, race horses, touts, widows, mothers, children, and anyone generally down on his or her luck; never was it said that Art Rooney had a hard heart for anyone or anything. Be that as it may, in the year that saw both the bottom of the Great Depression and Franklin Roosevelt inaugurated into his first term as president, Art Rooney had the $2,500 necessary for buying an NFL franchise and used it to become the proud owner of the Pittsburgh Pirates—christened after the city's popular baseball team in order to gain name recognition. Although the official repeal of the Sunday ban did not come until after the beginning of the NFL season—forcing the Pirates to play their first four home games on Wednesdays—Pittsburgh had become an NFL town. And for that fine offering, the city had Art Rooney to thank.

The Pittsburgh Pirates, however, were a mixed blessing at best. In their first season the football Pirates played at Forbes Field, wet and muddy from fall rains. Rooney, working out of his office at the Fort Pitt

Hotel, hired Forrest "Jap" Douds to coach the team. But a new name and a new coach could not change the fact that the Pirates still resembled the Majestic Radios—that is, a semi-pro team made up of Rooney's local cronies. It was a "small potatoes" operation, as a former team official remembered, and the team was like Pittsburgh, a melting pot of Irish, Italian, German, Polish, and Hungarian names. But there was hope. After watching the Pirates' first game, NFL president Joe Carr told Coach Douds, "You're not going to win any championship, but you have a fine foundation to build on."

Carr was right about a first-year championship; he was less accurate about the "fine foundation." Neither on the field nor in Rooney's Fort Pitt office did Pittsburgh have anything even approaching a solid base. During the tough years of the Great Depression, players came and went, coaches arrived and departed, fans hoped and grumbled, but the Pittsburgh teams remained at or near the bottom of the NFL. They wasted draft choices, engaged in disastrous trades, scored too seldom, and permitted their opponents to cross the goal line too often. Sunday after Sunday, as they discovered increasingly original ways to lose games, they gave Pennsylvania's legislature reasons to doubt its 1933 blue law reversal. But to Rooney, the optimistic realist, those years of failure were also years of success. Rooney's genius, his son Art Jr. said, was staying in business. He stayed in business by selling high-priced talent and keeping around coaches and players who were not too demanding. He stayed in business by not losing too much money. He knew that playing to win during hard times was a sucker bet.

A new decade produced major and minor changes. At the top, there was some paper shuffling and reorganization: at the end of 1940 Rooney sold the Pirates to businessman Alexis Thompson, who, at least on paper, moved the team to Philadelphia at the same time as Bert Bell's Eagles, again on paper, relocated to Pittsburgh. But before any teams really moved anywhere, the players were reassigned in what can only be described as the Great Pennsylvania Draft. The end result was that a team remained in Pittsburgh under Art Rooney's control, and for the 1941 season it got spiffy new uniforms and a new name that suited their hometown, the Steelers (pronounced "Stillers" by every fan from the western half of the great Pennsylvania divide). They even got a new coach—and then another, and then another. In 1941 everything looked new about the team except the way it played. To Rooney, they still looked like "the same old Steelers." By the end of the year they laid claim to the dubious distinction of having more head coaches

(3) than wins (1), proving very little except that they were not very good.

World War II brought radical changes. In 1942 the Steelers drafted a shifty halfback out of Virginia named Bill Dudley who played distinctively unlike a normal Steeler. Though small and not particularly fast, he had a nose for the ball and a sense of open space. He was an outstanding kick returner, a fine runner, a steady receiver, and a dependable defensive player. Dubbed the "Bluefield Bullet," he injected life and flair into the Steelers offense and led them to a 7-4 record, the first time they won more games than they lost.

But after the season Dudley went into the service and the Steelers confronted the privations of wartime professional football without him. These were, indeed, times to try men's souls. During the war, columnist Walter Winchell lamented an America past:

"Roses are red, Violets are blue,

Sugar is sweet, Remember?"

And for many his words seemed only too bittersweetly true. The steel and aluminum produced in Pittsburgh went into new tanks and jeeps rather than automobiles. In the domestic market there was little rubber for new tires. As for silk stockings, nylons, and furs; whiskey, chocolate, and cigarettes; meat, sugar, and so much more—Winchell was right. "Remember." The slogan across the country was "Use it up, wear it out, make it do or do without."

The slogan certainly applied to professional football. Unlike Major League Baseball, the NFL was far too insignificant for President Roosevelt to consider it essential to American morale, if he considered it at all. The war took a heavy toll on the game. The government gave military uniforms to most of football's finest players, placed restrictions on travel, and rationed supplies of rubber and leather. The league simply had to make do—with 4-Fers and defense workers for players, ever-changing rosters and schedules, worn-out footballs and uniforms, and gate receipts that looked as thin as the coffee. Innovation and improvisation was the order of the day. In 1943 and 1944 the Steelers followed that order by joining forces with the Philadelphia Eagles and then the Chicago Cardinals. In 1943 the combined Pittsburgh-Philadelphia team became the Steagles and played their home games in Philadelphia; in 1944 the Pittsburgh-Chicago squad became the Card-Pitts and used Chicago as their home base. Actually, for Art Rooney, wartime football was not that different from Depression football. The goal was survival. Don't worry about wins, forget the losses; just keep the franchise alive. In the summer of 1945 the war ended, and that fall a professional football team returned to Pittsburgh. It wasn't the Steagles and it wasn't the Card-Pitts. It was the Steelers, playing under yet another new coach, Jim Leonard, who lasted all of one year. During the season the team amassed two wins in its ten games. Still, even the same old Steelers were proud to be home.

On the Pennsylvania Turnpike between Pittsburgh and Harrisburg there is a stretch of road where a motorist moves from Kittatinny Tunnel to Blue Mountain Tunnel with only a brief glimpse of sky in between. The history of Rooney's team between 1933 and 1972 resembles this twin-tunneled highway. The team's Roosevelt years (1933–1945) were the first tunnel, thirteen seasons of futility punctuated only by a player or coach odd enough to trigger a reflexive smile of black humor. The second tunnel was longer but not quite so unremittingly bleak. In the years between 1948 and 1972 the Steelers showed flashes of brilliant mediocrity: an occasional exceptional player, or a rare season when the team won a game or two more than they lost. The patch of light between the two tunnels, that first spring of hope in the Steelers' history, was the short, glorious Jock Sutherland era.

By the 1940s Jock cut a greater figure in Pittsburgh than even Rooney. Rooney was the quintessential man of the people, a product of The Ward who lived comfortably in The Ward, a granite figure chiseled in human size. Jock, on the other hand, loomed over the city, a man equal, some said, to Mellon and Frick, even Andrew Carnegie himself. In fact there was more than a wee bit of Carnegie in Sutherland. Born in Coupar-Angus, Scotland, and raised in poverty by his widowed mother, Jock emigrated to the United States when he was eighteen and settled in Pittsburgh. Going to high school during the day and working as a steel-plant policeman at night, he had no time for sports or any other leisure activity, at least not until he arrived on the University of Pittsburgh campus. Then he flowered into a scholar-athlete, earning All-American honors in football, championships as a heavyweight boxer and hammer thrower, and a degree in dentistry. In 1923, he replaced Glenn "Pop" Warner as Pitt's football coach, a position he held until the University de-emphasized the sport fifteen years later. But in that decade and a half, Jock coached four undefeated teams, two national champions, four Rose Bowl squads, and compiled a record of 111-20-2. A man who had a rock jaw and dour appearance, Jock was stingy with the English language and relentless in the pursuit of excellence.

Rooney lured Jock back to Pittsburgh in 1946 to coach the Steelers, and Pittsburghers responded by filling Forbes Field. In 1946, Sutherland coached the Steelers to a respectable 5-5-1 record, a distinct improvement from their previous year's 2-8 mark. In 1947, the Steelers went 8-4 before losing to Philadelphia in a playoff for the NFL's Eastern Division title. Sutherland's brand of football, scientific football, the strategic use of game films, playbooks, scouting, and classroom lectures, seemed to have a future as bright in Pittsburgh as the Bessemer process. But too often Jock treated his players as so much coke and iron ore, a tactic that worked better in the college than the professional game. He clashed immediately with Bill Dudley, his star player who had always pleased other coaches. In 1946 Dudley led the NFL in both rushing yards and interceptions, and led the Steelers in scoring, but after the season he quit the team rather than play another year under Sutherland. Unconcerned, Sutherland continued to put his system in place, fielding a team of "manageable" players.

What might have been never was. Perhaps Sutherland did have a system that would have raised the Steelers to a championship, or at least made them consistent winners. Perhaps he could have constructed a fine team through the draft and intelligent trades. Perhaps he might have done with the Steelers what he had with the Pitt Panthers. Perhaps. Certainly Art Rooney believed that Sutherland would have brought the Steelers their first championship, and he always insisted that if it had not been for Jock's ability to draw fans to the game, Rooney would have gotten out of the business. But on April 11, 1948, Jock Sutherland died of a brain tumor, leaving the Steelers without a coach or a real vision for the future. The daylight between Kittatinny and Blue Mountain was all too brief. Sutherland's death threw Steelers fans back into the darkness of seemingly endless cellar dwelling, punctuated only every now and then by a period of passable mediocrity. Coaches arrived and coaches departed, and a few coaches even came back again, but the Steelers remained the same old Steelers.

But during the Steelers' Blue Mountain years, in which time seemed to stand painfully still in Pittsburgh, the NFL experienced several upheavals. The first involved the integration of the NFL. Although a few African Americans had played in the early years of the league, by 1934 it had followed professional baseball in drawing an unofficial color line. Team owners, however, were obviously divided on the issue. Some, such as Chicago Bears owner George Halas and Boston (later Washington) Redskins owner George Preston Marshall were determined to keep blacks out of the league. But Rooney and Cleveland Browns coach and part-owner Paul Brown were more racially tolerant. After the war, social and economic pressures forced the NFL to reverse its policies. Not only did Jackie Robinson integrate Major League Baseball, but potential rivals of the NFL, the United States Football League and the All-American Football Conference, moved toward integration. In 1944, Red Grange, president of the USFL, spoke for the new attitude in professional sports: "The Negro boys are fighting for our country; they certainly are entitled to play in our professional leagues."

The great breakthrough took place in 1946 when the Los Angeles Rams (recently relocated from Cleveland) of the NFL signed former UCLA standouts Kenny Washington and Woody Strode to contracts, and the Cleveland Browns of the AAFC invited Bill Willis and Marion Motley to their training camp. All four players were black; each was an exceptional athlete, though Washington and Strode were past their primes. The success of the Browns' black players, and the success of the Cleveland franchise on the field and at the gate, led to the integration of other AAFC teams. Although the NFL lagged behind the AAFC, it too integrated on a wider scale in the early 1950s, especially after the collapse of the AAFC and the absorption of some of its better teams—including the Browns—into the league. Rooney, who had good relations with African Americans in Pittsburgh, adapted better than most of the owners to the new conditions. Eventually the Steelers employed *Pittsburgh Courier* sportswriter Bill Nunn, who covered the black colleges for the newspaper, as a scout. Chuck Hinton, Ben McGee, Ernie Holmes, Joe Gilliam, John Stallworth, Mel Blount, and Donnie Shell were a few of the players that Nunn watched play during his travels. By the 1970s the Steelers would be one of the most racially mixed teams in the NFL.

A second important change in the game during the Steelers' lean years was that the NFL as a whole got fat. Throughout the 1940s and most of the 1950s the NFL struggled financially, fighting off rival leagues and trying to make inroads into the popularity of the college game. Professional football players, wrote one journalist, "are pot-bellies. A bunch of beer swizzlers playing lazy football. And the only thing worse is the bunch of beer swizzlers watching." The fact that college football was "the game" and professional football was stuck somewhere between a curiosity and non-entity was made painfully clear to Frank Gifford early in his professional career. Gifford had been everybody's All-American at the University of Southern California in 1951 and had played on the New York Giants team, one the NFL's premier franchises, in 1952. Returning home to Southern California after his rookie season, he encountered old friends who asked the same question: "Where have *you* been?" For them, Gifford had dropped off the athletic planet, fallen so far from the consciousness of sports fans that he almost ceased to exist.

In the late 1950s, however, the game found its audience and its medium. One game helped to change professional football. In 1958 Johnny Unitas's Baltimore Colts played Gifford's New York Giants for the NFL championship. In the closing seconds the Colts kicked a field goal to tie the score 17-17 and throw the game into the first overtime in NFL history. Some thirty million people sitting in front of television sets, not all of whom were beer swizzlers, watched as Unitas engineered Baltimore's "Thirteen Steps to Glory." Play by play, brilliant pass by well-disguised run, Unitas moved his team toward the winning touchdown, showing America in the process that professional football had something to offer. The game "gave professional football tremendous impetus," commented the director of NBC Sports. Unlike baseball, a subtle and slow game played with a relatively small ball, football seemed designed with television in mind, and it became America's sport as the nation moved into the booming, roaring, tumultuous 1960s.

Although the glamour of television in the 1960s focused on the Baltimore Colts, New York Giants, Green Bay Packers, and New York Jets—on Johnny Unitas, Frank Gifford, Paul Hornung, and Joe Namath—the money from television was spread evenly throughout the league. In 1960 the team owners in the NFL elected a commissioner who knew how to turn the television contracts into substantial wealth. In 1962, Pete Rozelle negotiated a two-year deal with CBS that paid the NFL $4.5 million annually. In 1964, CBS agreed to pay $14 million annually for the next two years. And from there the price for television rights continued to shoot upwards. Owners like Art Rooney and Art Modell, who had been running their operations on shoestring budgets, were suddenly very rich men. No longer could Rooney claim that his goal was just survival. Television had altered the nature of the business for the owners. Now, more than ever, the game was about winning.

In the 1970s the team from the bottom of the pile scrambled to the top. The decade belonged to the Steelers. Two events signaled the change. In 1969, Chuck Noll became the head coach. He promptly led the Steelers to a 1-13 season, the second-worst record in their history (the Card-Pitts of 1944 were 0-10). But Noll brought to the team something that was not obvious from its dismal record. He exuded strength and confidence and, like Jock Sutherland, he had a system and a vision. Linebacker Andy Russell, who was on the team when Noll arrived, remembered, "I was never cynical when Noll came in, because he low-keyed it. He said it would take time. You never lost respect for the guy—because he thought with his brain, not with his heart. He's never irrational, he's never petty, he doesn't talk from a gut emotion. You feel what he's saying is so logical he *should* be saying it." While the Steelers were losing in 1969, 1970, and 1971, Noll was building a team, discarding players with whom he could not win and acquiring players with whom he could. Only six of the 1969 Steelers were still on the team in 1973. Without a lot of fuss or publicity, Noll had constructed a team to his specifications.

Noll insisted on a first-class operation, and in 1970 the Steelers moved into a facility to match his vision. In the 1950s the Steelers had played at Pitt Stadium and practiced at South Park, "whose main function," noted Roy Blount Jr., "was to house a Labor Day weekend county fair. They dressed in the basement of a dilapidated building. It had six showers, four of which worked. The toilets didn't have seats; you had to sit on porcelain." And whether practicing at South Park or playing in Pitt Stadium, the Steelers had to contend with fields that had been chewed up by equestrian contests as well as a wide range of college and high-school football and soccer teams. By contrast, Three Rivers Stadium was state of the art. For the Iron City–swizzling Steelers it was Dom Perignon. "I was so proud," center Ray Mansfield said. "We had a home."

In the 1970s the Steelers had it all—a home, a kindly patriarch, a demanding general, and a locker room full of quirky, interesting, good soldiers. They had Terry Bradshaw's gun, Lynn Swann's hands, Franco Harris's legs, and Rocky Bleier's heart; Joe Greene's mean, Andy Russell's smarts, Mel Blount's bads, and Jack Lambert's toothless grin. They had fans who rallied in Three Rivers behind such banners as Franco's Italian Army, Dobre Shunka (Good Ham), Gerela's Gorillas, and Lambert's Lunatics. And most of all, they had a city, a 'burgh that had been born in smoke and grit, weathered more slights and insults than could be imagined, learned to laugh at heartache, and somehow—in the glory of a football team—had been reborn. One play showed football viewers everywhere that the winds of history had shifted and that the same old Steelers were, unexpectedly, no longer the same old Steelers. In 1972 the Steelers not only had their first winning season under Noll, but went 11-3 and made the playoffs. Matched against the Oakland

Raiders, the Steelers held Ken Stabler's offense scoreless for almost fifty-nine minutes. Then on a broken play, Stabler stumbled and scrambled thirty yards into the end zone, giving the Raiders a 7-6 lead and, most spectators thought, the game. The Steelers had put up quite a fight, but when all was said and done, when the whistle had sounded and the day ended, they were still the same old Steelers. Or that was what most fans were undoubtedly thinking. Then the Steelers got the ball and moved it to their own forty, and on fourth and ten with only seconds remaining, Terry Bradshaw rifled a pass to Frenchy Fuqua. What happened next was a blur of fate. The ball deflected off either safety Jack Tatum's hands or Fuqua's chest, ricocheted backwards above the artificial turf, and fell softly toward Franco Harris's feet. Harris gobbled the ball at full stride and continued on a straight path to the end zone. There followed rounds of confusion, talk, replays, a referee's upstretched arms, and the dizzying, wild, exhilarating, beautiful realization that the Steelers' forty years of futility had ended. So accustomed to finding imaginative ways to lose, they had discovered an immaculate way to win. A fan's 1972 Steelers schedule said it best—December 23: Steelers & God 13, Oakland 7.

During the 1970s the Steelers kept finding ways to win. They had become a team of Midases, and everything they touched turned to gold. Obscure draft picks blossomed into outstanding players, steady veterans played like all-stars, and all-stars performed like gods. And to make matters worse for their opponents and better for their fans, the whole was even better than its parts. Between the 1974 and 1979 seasons they won four Super Bowls, and all of Pittsburgh believed that the fifth title—the one for the thumb—was just a year or two away. It was like an endless summer of perfect days and long afternoon shadows. It helped to ease the reality of Pittsburgh—the mills closing and layoffs and the talk about the rustbelt—and to make the hard times seem almost chimerical.

Then it ended, not with a bang but with a slow, almost imperceptible leak, like a basketball with the smallest of punctures. The veterans got older and slower, then retired. The draft picks fell a little short of expectations. The godlike superstars became just dependable players. Trips to the playoffs ended like they did for most other teams—in failure. Chuck Noll left in 1991, one day after Mikhail Gorbachev stepped down. Two eras had passed. The Steelers appointed Bill Cowher, a home-grown guy with a Pittsburgh heart, to replace the legend. Art Rooney's Steelers—Pittsburgh's Steelers—were changing again.

Cowher's Steelers were not Noll's Steelers. In the age of free agency it would be nearly impossible for any team to remain as consistently superior and dominating as the Steelers of the 1970s. But over the years Cowher's teams took on the personality of their coach. With his magnificent chin, his flame-throwing eyes, and his pyrotechnic tirades, Cowher coached with a passion and intensity that was a throwback to Vince Lombardi. No buttoned-down cool for Cowher, no emotionless, computer-driven, spreadsheet efficiency. His face registered his every emotion, shifting from concern and anger to jubilation and love over the course of a game. He so obviously cared about his players, and even more, about his team. And Cowher's teams were about TEAM. When the Steelers lost players like Neil O'Donnell and Plaxico Burress to free agency, Cowher kept the emphasis on the team, on the Steelers, on Pittsburgh.

Cowher's approach to football seemed to get the best out of his players, summoning surprising performances out of unexpected characters. Some of the best stories came out of Pittsburgh—an XXXXL running back, a Korean–African American wide receiver, a Samoan defensive back. Wide bodies and flowing hair, receivers who threw and quarterbacks who caught—the Steelers consistently delivered the offbeat. And they won, advancing to divisional playoffs, NFC championships, and even a Super Bowl. But at the end of the season their best always fell short.

Then came 2005. For the first half of the season it looked like another disappointing year. After a loss to the Cincinnati Bengals, the Steelers record was 7-5, and even a trip to a wild card game seemed a pipe dream. But then they started to win. Injured players healed, the ball bounced their way, the team pulled together. The national press, focused on the Indianapolis Colts' bid for an undefeated season, paid almost no attention to the reemergence of the Steelers. All that changed when quarterback Ben Roethlisberger made the most important tackle of his life, tripping Colts cornerback Nick Harper and saving the game. After that improbable play, the Steelers became a team of destiny fulfilled. In Super Bowl XL the Steelers won one for the thumb—and for the Bus, and for Bill Cowher, and for Dan Rooney.

It felt like going to Disneyland.

Drawing on some of the best writing about the Steelers from 1933 to the present, One for the Thumb offers a look at the history of the franchise and the personalities who made it special. It is also an examination of how and why the team captured the heart of the city. Cities, like people, develop personalities, and a city's character takes its shape from the interests of its residents. Some towns, such as St. Louis, are baseball towns. Others, such as Indianapolis, are basketball towns. A few, fortunately located north of the border, are hockey towns. And there are even a couple, such as New York and Boston, that are diverse enough to be baseball and football or hockey and basketball towns. Pittsburgh, by any yardstick, is a football town, and even more specifically, a professional football town, a Steelers town. In Pittsburgh, the town and the team have become one in a fashion that few sports franchises ever achieve. Somehow they seem to share a common past, present, and future. The struggles and heartaches, the glory and redemption—those experiences don't just belong to the Steelers, nor do they exclusively belong to the city. In western Pennsylvania, the Steelers aren't just a team, they are family.

The book moves chronologically from the founding of the football Pirates to the present, but it is in no sense a history of the team. Instead, it is an attempt to give the feel of the Steelers, how the team frustrated, enraged, amused, thrilled, and otherwise moved its fans. In selecting the articles, we have been similarly moved—frustrated by the fact that more has been written about the recent than the early Steelers, enraged because we had to eliminate more than a few outstanding pieces, amused by the antics of the members of the Steelers' family, and thrilled by the sheer pleasure of following the team's meandering odyssey to greatness. If we had a single guiding principle, it was to capture who the Steelers were and are, and why they matter so much to all right-thinking football fans. Whoever determined that the Dallas Cowboys were "America's Team" had never been to a bar in western Pennsylvania or in Three Rivers during the 1970s.

When we began considering who to dedicate the book to, the task seemed daunting. Images flashed through our minds: passes by Terry Bradshaw, catches by Lynn Swann and John Stallworth, runs by Franco Harris and Jerome Bettis. Then there were Johnny Blood McNally, Bill Dudley, and John Henry Johnson; Bobby Layne and Big Daddy Lipscomb just carried too much baggage from other teams with them. And then there was Uncle Chuck, who used to watch the Steelers with a bottle of Maalox clutched tightly in one fist and a Terrible Towel in the other. And how many other players and Uncle Chucks deserve mention in a dedication? But on second thought, the choice was obvious. Art Rooney was and is the heart of the team, and it is to him that we dedicate this book.

FROM PIRATES
TO STEAGLES

Art Rooney on Art Rooney

In the late 1960s Art Rooney, Pittsburgh's most famous sportsman, sat down for a formal interview with Myron Cope, Pittsburgh's most famous sports journalist. Of course, the word formal *goes with Art Rooney about as well as caviar goes with peanut butter on a sandwich. Rooney was like his house—old, rambling, and solid. He bought the house during the Depression when it was in a working-class Irish neighborhood and watched unconcerned as black neighbors replaced white neighbors and his street became increasingly low rent. So what, he might have thought. Some things change, others don't. His hair had turned white, his complexion ruddy, his skin wrinkled, but his eyes were still alert and a cigar was still lit in his hand. Looking at Rooney, Cope thought that the Chief resembled "an eastern courthouse functionary from the time, say, of Honey Fitz." He was a type, a John O'Hara–Damon Runyon type chiseled out of granite, unchangeable. And so it seemed in the late 1960s that the Steelers were the same hapless Steelers, losers. But some things do change. In his own words, Rooney gave Cope some sense of who he was, where he came from, and what in life he endured. He also gave Cope a feeling for how the game had changed.*

"WHAT I'M TELLING YOU IS THAT WE'VE TRIED"

Myron Cope

I grew up in what was then the First Ward, but we never called it that. We called it The Ward. All it was ever known as was The Ward. In fact, when I get a taxicab to come to the office, I'll tell the driver, "Well, go down through The Ward." And the old guys, the old cabdrivers, still know where The Ward was.

It was heavily populated. Made up of Irish, mostly. On Saturday nights, when the people congregated, they would speak Gaelic. You would hear pretty much as much Gaelic as you would English, which is unusual because most of the Irish in Ireland don't speak Gaelic. There was a smattering of Polish in The Ward, and a few colored, not

From *The Game That Was: The Early Days of Pro Football* (Cleveland: World Publishing, 1970). Reprinted by permission of Myron Cope.

many, and one Jew. The Jew was an old man named Kurtz, who owned a clothing store and was very highly thought of because he was kind. If anyone ever touched him, it was mayhem.

So that was the makeup of The Ward. The people were poor, and probably the only time a lot of them ever had a ride in an automobile was going to the cemetery when someone died. That was a big event, when someone died. You know, you can go back to the Irish wakes you saw in that movie, *The Last Hurrah*, but compared to the wakes we had in The Ward—well, we had wakes that were tremendous. People would look in the papers to see who died, and they would come from all over town. Of course, some of them were professional moochers, but everyone would be there. It'd last three days, and it would be like a carnival. It was just a gala affair. After those people started in drinking, sometimes they'd put the body outside. One time they put the body outside my father's saloon.

In the horse and buggy days, when I was only a kid, it took all day to get to the graveyard, but in later years we'd borrow a whole string of cars, enough cars for the whole neighborhood. We'd arrive at the graveyard and everybody would scatter all over the place. Everybody would run to the graves where their own immediate people were buried. Then you would hear them hollering the *caoine,* which is the old Irish cry. It was fantastic. It was tremendous. You would hear them hollering the *caoine* all over the graveyard. And in the meantime, nobody paid any attention to the man who was getting buried except his immediate family. Coming back, everybody stopped at least once to get a drink.

When people started taking their dead to funeral homes, that broke up the Irish wake as we knew it. But even today, I like to pay my respects and see the deceased's family. I go to see more dead people than probably anybody in Pittsburgh. I do this because I like to do it. Years ago, in the late 1920s and early '30s, I was a ward chairman, but I'm not a politician now and there's no reason I would be going to visit these people for any gain. But at the office we go through the death notices every day, and when I'm in town it's nothing for me to go to three and four wakes every night.

The Ward was on the north bank of the Allegheny River, across the river from downtown Pittsburgh. I grew up right across from old Exposition Park—Expo Park, we called it—where the Pirates played baseball till they opened Forbes Field in 1909. Later, the Federal League, the outlaw league, played at Expo Park, and all the baseball players loafed in my father's saloon. I knew 'em all. I saw the big fights and top soccer games at Expo Park. It's a funny thing—now they're building a new stadium, Three Rivers Stadium, to replace Forbes Field, and it's on the exact spot that Expo Park was. Which brings to mind the time I almost died there.

In those days, before flood controls, if you spit in the Allegheny River, the flood came up. It wasn't anything unusual for us to leave for school by going out a second-floor window in a skiff. One day there were three of us paddling to school in a canoe—a kid named Squawker Mullen, my brother Dan, and me. We were paddling that canoe right through Expo Park. Right through the outfield.

Squawker was moving around in the canoe, so I said to him, "Sit still, Squawker. You're going to upset the canoe." But he kept moving around, and sure enough, he upset it. Well, we started swimming for the third-base grandstand. Squawker and Dan weren't wearing boots, so they made it, easy enough. But I had on boots and an overcoat. That was the last gasp I had, when I got hold of that grandstand. You see, I was lucky that I lived to see the new stadium being built. I almost got drowned in it.

I played all the sports. You went on the playground when the sun came up, and you didn't leave till the sun went down. It wasn't anything for me when I was fifteen years old—when I weighed 135, maybe 140 pounds—to be playing baseball against the famous colored teams, the Homestead Grays and the Kansas City Monarchs. All of those barnstorming teams—the House of David, for example—they all came to The Ward. Some years, my brother Dan and I would leave town in the summer with a semi-pro team, and we'd travel through Ohio, West Virginia, Pennsylvania, and New York, playing for ten or twenty dollars a game. We'd play in *chautauquas*. You know what a *chautauqua* was, don't you? It was approximately a week of carnival they'd have in small towns.

A lot of those carnivals had athletic troupes that included fighters who would accept challenges from anybody in the house. You'd get three dollars a round for as long as you could stay. Well, that was made to order for Dan and me, because we could lick all those carnival guys. I mean, what kind of fighters would a carnival have? They could handle a farmer, all right, but they were very ordinary fighters. In The Ward, on the other hand, we had a boxing team—St. Peter's Lyceum, they called it—that was the equal of any in the world. A lot of us went to the nationals. So in these small towns the first thing we'd ask was did the carnival have an athletic troupe? But after a while they got to know us and they asked us to stay away. It was a reasonable request, so we did, but that was easy money while it lasted.

I remember a guy in The Ward who "did the buck" on the railroad. You know what that was, don't you? It means he was a scab. The railroad men were on strike, but he went to work. Finally people made it so bad for him in The Ward that he had to leave. Later he came back as a fighter for a carnival, the Johnny J. Jones carnival, and as soon as we heard about him coming back, we got ahold of Squawker Mullen. Squawker was a national amateur champion—just a little fellow, maybe 110 pounds, but, boy, could Squawker fight! We had Squawker challenge the guy.

But the trouble was, Squawker was out of condition and he got tired. He run out of gas. The other fellow got Squawker in the corner and he was getting the best of him. So our Dan, who was a heavyweight, he just reached up over the ropes and hit the fellow—he nailed him like you would nail a bird in midair. Right away, someone hollered, "Hey, Rube!," which was the signal for all the carnival hands to come on the run. The next thing, the whole tent came down, and that ended the athletic events of that carnival. Dan's a priest now. He used to be the father superior at St. Anthony's Shrine in Boston. President Kennedy attended Mass at Dan's church once in a while.

The kind of football I played in the 1920s, I suppose you'd call it semi-pro, but our teams were as good as the teams in professional football. We were as good as the teams in the National Football League, which was just getting started. I was no more than twenty-two when I started up a team called Hope-Harvey. I owned it and coached it and in the important games played halfback. The team was called Hope-Harvey because Hope was the name of the fire-engine house in The Ward and Harvey was the doctor in The Ward. For home games we dressed and got our showers at the engine house, and Harvey took care of anybody who got hurt. So nothing cost us a cent. And a lot of guys in that semi-pro ball got up to a hundred dollars a game—a lot of them got more money than fellows in the National Football League.

I remember we played the Canton Bulldogs and Jim Thorpe in Pittsburgh once. I tried a field goal but it was blocked. Thorpe picked it up and ran for a touchdown, and as I recall, they beat us, 6-0. Oh, I played against Thorpe a number of times. He was certainly very fast, but Thorpe was pretty much at the end of his rope then. Anyhow, the game in those days was just shoving and pushing, compared to what it is now. Not long ago I went to a gathering of some old-timers, just wonderful people. I really enjoy myself loafing with these old fellows that I played ball with and against, but at this gathering they showed a film of one of the football games we played. They thought it was great. They thought it was tough football. But watching it, you know, I thought, "It's strictly shoving and pushing."

In 1933 I paid $2,500 for a National Football League franchise, which I named the Pirates, because the Pittsburgh baseball team was called the Pirates. It wasn't till 1940, when we held a contest for a new name, that we became the Steelers. Joe Carr's girl friend—Joe's been our ticket manager right along—his girl friend won the contest. There were people who said, "That contest don't look like it was on the level."

Anyway, I bought the franchise in '33 because I figured that it would be good to have a league schedule and that eventually professional football would be good. And the reason I bought a franchise at that particular time was that we knew that Pennsylvania was going to repeal certain laws—"blue laws," they were called. You see, until then, Sunday football was illegal in Pennsylvania. This was going to be changed by the legislature. So now I had a franchise, and our schedule was made up. But a couple of days before our opening game, the mayor phoned me and said, "I got a complaint here from a preacher that this game should not be allowed because it's against the blue laws. The repeal hasn't been ratified yet by City Council, and won't be till Tuesday."

"Well," I said, "I never heard of this thing, ratification."

Nobody else had heard anything about it either, until this preacher brought it up. The mayor told me he didn't know what I could do about it but that I should go see a fellow named Harmar Denny, who was director of public safety and was over the police department.

So I went to Denny and I said, "We're in the big leagues now. We can't have a thing like this happen to our opening game." But this Denny was pretty much of a straightlaced guy. All he would say was that he was going away for the weekend. "Good," I told him. "You go away." Then I went to see the superintendent of police, a man named McQuade, and told *him* my problem.

"Oh, that there's ridiculous," he said. "Give them a couple of tickets and I'll go to the game Sunday. That'll be the last place they'll look for me if they want me to stop the game."

So McQuade hid out at the game, and on the following Tuesday the council met and ratified everything. We had three thousand people at the game. Maybe thirty-five hundred.

We didn't draw many people in those days. The colleges got most of the publicity. In Pittsburgh, the University of Pittsburgh was the big wheel. They'd draw thirty thousand people, maybe thirty-five thousand, while we'd draw three thousand, maybe thirty-five hundred. You didn't make a lot of money but you didn't lose a lot. Maybe you made five thousand dollars a season, or maybe you lost a few thousand. All we paid the players was seventy-five or a hundred dollars a game. Professional football wasn't big league, compared to what it is now. Some people say the newspapers pushed us around, but I don't agree. If I was a newspaperman I would have treated us the same way.

In 1938 I did something I thought would bring a little class to the game. I signed Whizzer White out of Colorado University for a salary of $15,800, which was easily the highest salary pro football was paying. White was very hard to sign. I don't remember what the last eight hundred was for—whether it was for exhibition games, or because he had a Rhodes Scholarship and needed the eight to go to Oxford, or what. Anyhow, the fifteen got pro football a lot of publicity, and of course White *was* an asset to the game, an extremely high-class fellow, as you might judge from his going on to become a Supreme Court justice. But I caught some heat from some of the other owners.

A lot of them thought we were out of line. George Richards of Detroit thought it was terrible. He was very successful in the radio business and a fine man, very loose with a dollar, but he thought this was terrible, paying White that kind of money. George Marshall [owner of the Boston, and later Washington, Redskins] phoned me from Washington and said, "What are you trying to do?" I told him I thought it was a great thing for professional football to get someone like White to play the game, which I did believe. I did believe it. Everybody on the team respected White highly. If he had been bigheaded, he could have got himself in a lot of trouble, but he fit in right. He was a fine back, and he was right with the boys. So we didn't mind paying him the highest salary in football. But it's a funny thing—because we've never won a title, a lot of people in Pittsburgh say we're cheap. They say we don't do things right. Well, we don't argue about it. We don't say anything. We just leave it go at that.

Actually, the biggest mistake I've made was that, although I understood the football business as well as anybody in the league, I didn't pay the attention to the business that some of the other owners gave it. I was out of town a great deal of the time, at the racetracks. With me, the racetrack was a big business. And generally I'd have a head coach who was like me—he'd like the races.

I let my coaches have a free hand, but it didn't work. The year we signed White, our coach was John Blood. I still believe that John Blood could have been a tremendous coach, if he would have just paid attention. . . . You couldn't depend on John a whole lot.

The only other thing wrong with John Blood was that he didn't believe in fundamentals. Instead he created a lot of nice sayings and expressions. . . . You know how the players warm up with calisthenics before a game? I don't know if they still count off numbers while they're warming up, but they used to count, "One! Two! Three! Four!" Well, John didn't use counts. He had the ballplayers yell, "Pirates never quit!" John turned everything into a saying.

The players really loved John. But I remember a game in New York when they thought he wasn't helping them. John was a player-coach, you know, and he would put himself into the backfield every now and then. So we're playing the Giants and every time we get down to their twenty- or thirty-yard line, where it looked like we were going to score, John would put himself into the game to call the plays. But we wouldn't score. After this happened a few times, our captain went to the referee and said, "What happens if I don't accept a player coming into the game?"

"Well," the referee said, "in that case, we won't accept him."

So the next time John tried to go into the game, our captain—I don't remember who he was—he refused to accept John. John didn't argue about it much. He waved his arms a little that's all, and then left the field. We immediately scored on a pass and won the game. But after the game, the first thing John did was call the players together and tell them, "You called the same play I went in to call."

Professional football in those days wasn't like it is now. You were much closer to your ballplayers. You loafed with them, and they were your friends. I don't think I ever had a ballplayer I disliked. Elbie Nickel, Jimmy Finks, Bill Walsh, Ernie Stautner—you came to know all those guys. If you didn't travel by bus, you traveled by day coach in what we called "the Sullivans." I don't know how they got that moniker, but that's all I ever called 'em. You'd pull the backs of the seats down and make beds out of them. You were with your ballplayers for hours at a time. And after the ballgame, you might have to wait awhile for the next train, so you'd have a beer with your players. You got to know all their problems. Today you meet a ballplayer when you sign him. Later, when the team flies to a game, you see him on an airplane that gets you there in practically the time it takes to snap your finger.

In the old days I knew newspapermen all over the country. Knew them as friends. A couple of years ago I was spending a week in San Francisco at a time when the baseball season was in the thick of the pennant race and a great many of the newspaper guys were there to cover an important series. I happened to be staying at the same hotel as the newspaper guys. The old ones, I knew. I knew them well, and I was with them every night. They got to telling me their problems, and they said, "Outside of you and George Halas, we don't know the other people in football. You don't get to know them. Even traveling with a baseball club," they said, "you travel so fast that you never get to know the owners like we knew you guys." Now you take the younger newspaper guys. The young newspaper guys today are not really different than those old guys. If they got to know you and you got to know them, it would be a great time all over again. But you don't have the opportunity to know them. It's just an entirely different life today.

The atmosphere used to be more enjoyable among the owners. Although they fought a lot, they were a lot closer to one another than they are now. They were *fans*. The owners today are fans, too, but I think they are also in the game because it does great financially. In the old days you had to be willing to lose your money. Yes, times sure have changed. Today we have nothing to do with making up the schedule. The schedule is sent out to us, and that's it, period. The way we used to do it, we'd have a league meeting and it would last day and night, for maybe a whole week. Everybody tried to get the best schedule. You'd want the teams that drew the biggest crowds. But early in the season you'd want the teams you could beat, so you could start off winning. The owners who had staying power, who were willing to stay in that room day and night arguing, they wound up with the best schedules. The guys who got tired and went home, they got murdered. One time we worked two or three days getting a schedule up there on the blackboard, but when it was just about done, George Marshall got sore. He went up to the board and wiped it all out. We had to go back to work for two more days, because nobody had copied down the schedule.

That Marshall was a man of vision. He probably had more to do with the rulebook and the league constitution, as they're now written, than any other man. He was the father of the player draft. He was the father of the divisions, of the championship game, of player limits. When he wanted to get a piece of legislation passed, he'd get up and talk and talk and talk, but if he saw he wasn't getting anywhere, if he saw he didn't have the votes, he'd suddenly say, "Forget about it. I table this thing." The league meeting would go on maybe five days or a week, all told, and we'd finally be all finished, ready to go out the door, and Marshall would say, "Oh, wait a minute. I forgot about that thing we tabled back there three or four days ago." And everybody would say, "Okay, pass it."

Back in 1938 a fellow named Lipscomb owned the Cleveland club. Cleveland was supposed to play us in Pittsburgh, but we canceled the game because of bad weather. Well, actually we canceled it because there weren't going to be any customers there. Listen, that was nothing unusual. I had other owners cancel games on *me*. This was the only one I ever called off, but this fellow Lipscomb hollered and screamed and yelled that I had to play the game. So then I had to find a place to play the game where it could draw a crowd. Lipscomb said, "Play it in Knoxville, Tennessee. That's my home town." I told him, "People are not going to come out to see *you* play. I'm not about to go to Knoxville."

So I'm looking around for a place to play when a friend of mine named Joe Engle, who was a big shot in minor-league baseball, mentions a guy by the name of Walmsley to me. Coming from The Ward, where you knew politics from the day you were able to speak, I knew who Walmsley was. In The Ward everybody knew about politics, or thought they knew about politics. I knew that Walmsley had been mayor of New Orleans until Huey Long knocked him out of the box. I also knew that a guy named Maestri was now mayor of New Orleans and was a fantastic political leader. Well, as soon as Joe Engle brought up Walmsley's name and gave me his phone number, I got on the phone.

I said to Walmsley, "If we bring this game to New Orleans, will Maestri get behind it?" I knew that if Maestri told the people, "Go!" they went. "Oh, positively. Maestri will positively get behind the game," Walmsley said.

So I gave Cleveland the extra expenses to go to New Orleans and we took the game there. Well, when I got down to New Orleans I accidentally ran into a couple of priests who were teaching at Loyola, and I asked if they were going to the game. They said, "What game?" Then they said, "Nobody in New Orleans knows about it. It must be a secret." Right away I went to Walmsley and told him, "I want to meet Maestri."

So I visited Maestri and I took Whizzer White with me. I figured Maestri might not have heard of me, but everybody had heard of Whizzer White. Well, Maestri and I talked a little bit, but right then and there I knew I was dead, because not only didn't Maestri ever hear of me or know I owned the Pittsburgh club, but he never heard of White either. In fact, he kept getting everything confused. He thought we were a college team that had come down to New Orleans to play Tulane. He said, "I'll see what I can do." I knew our visit to Maestri didn't do us any good.

So on the day of the game I'm sitting with Walmsley in the Sugar Bowl, and nobody's at the game. Walmsley keeps telling me, "Oh, don't worry about it. Everybody comes late to a football game down here." Well, I'd been listening to that kind of stuff as long as I'd been a promoter. I said, "There's nobody going to show up here." And nobody did. The place was empty. To top it off, Cleveland beat us and the New Orleans police called me at the hotel that night and informed me they'd pinched three or four of my ballplayers for kicking over some garbage cans. I told the sergeant, "We got a train out of here at nine in the morning. You keep 'em till it's time for them to get on the train."

Last season I told the story of that New Orleans game to a luncheon in New Orleans. Ed Kiely, our publicity man, had explained to me that a football group down there wanted me to speak, so I said, "All right. But listen, I'm not much of a talker. These people will be disappointed if you're building me up as something big." Well, the speaker ahead of me was one of the New Orleans Saints' coaches, and evidently the Saints were having problems with their quarterback, Bill Kilmer. The people were on the quarterback: They asked the coach a lot of questions about him. Then I got up.

I told them, "Number one, if you're going to ask me any questions I'm going to disappoint you, because I don't know that I'm able to answer your questions. So, better that you don't ask any." But then I said, "There's one question I *could* have answered, because in Pittsburgh we're *experts* on quarterbacks. We had Sid Luckman, we had Johnny Unitas, we had Earl Morrall, we had Len Dawson, we had Jackie Kemp, and we had Bill Nelsen." I said, "Now those are all quarterbacks you know about, and we traded them all. They were all with our ball club, and we got rid of them."

Right after the war we had Bill Dudley playing for us. I believe Dudley was as good as any football player who has ever played in the National League. As a defensive back he led the league in interceptions. Coaches told their passers, "Don't throw in Dudley's territory." He had intuition. He played tailback in the single wing, and as a runner he led the league. He wasn't fast, but nobody caught him. He couldn't pass, but he completed passes. He was one of the top kickers in the game. The best all-around ballplayer I've ever seen. But our coaches used to say to me, "Well, he don't hit the hole."

I'd tell them, "I don't want him to hit the holes. If he starts hitting the holes, he'll turn the game into such a one-sided farce that nobody will come out to see us play."

Dudley was a great guy, although he had his own ideas and he was strong-willed. Our coach, Jock Sutherland, was pretty much like Dudley that way. So he traded Dudley after some sort of an argument they had. I didn't resist the trade too much, because it looked like Dudley and Sutherland were never going to be able to get along.

In the early '50s we had Jimmy Finks on our team. I think there's no telling how great Finks was. Finks might have been one of the great quarterbacks that ever played football. But he played under Walter Kiesling, and Kies had the funniest ideas. He was a big fellow, he'd been a terrific tackle. He was a tremendous coach, and not only that, a great guy. But he was really stubborn. Kies wanted to select the plays, but there were certain plays Finks didn't want to call. Both of them were stubborn. In other words, there was an argument all the time. We had Lynn Chandnois. There's no telling how great a ballcarrier he was, but Kies never thought that Chandnois put out. On the practice field, maybe he didn't. All I know is when it came time in a game, he was great. So one day we played the Giants and Chandnois ran back two kickoffs for touchdowns, over ninety yards each time. And the first thing Kies said after the game was, "Can you imagine that lucky bum!"

We had Unitas in for a tryout, but Kies let him go. He said, "He can't remember the plays. He's dumb." See, you had to know Kies. He thought a lot of ballplayers were dumb. We were arguing about a guy one day, and I said, "I don't care how dumb he is. He can run and he can pass and he can block. If he can do those three things, he don't have to be a Rhodes scholar." But all Kies said to that was "He's dumb." Kies was a great coach, but everything with Kies was that nobody knew football *better* than Kies.

Our players once went on strike over Kies. They were in Boston for a game when I got a call at home. I flew up to Boston and listened to their beef, which was that Kies worked them too hard. I didn't say a word till the ballplayers finished talking. Then I said, "I just want to tell you this—Kies might be tough and all of that, but I want you to know that you are never going to make a greater friend in your life than you'll have in Kiesling." I said, "He's honest, he's sincere, he gives everybody a square shake. He does have peculiarities, like we all have, and he hollers if he doesn't think you're giving everything you've got. But loyalty? I guarantee you that you're going to make a loyal friend of this man and you'll respect and love him for the rest of your life. That's it. I have nothing else to say, only that he is the coach and he's going to stay the coach, and before you're finished, just what I've told you is what you're going to think of this man." Which they did. The majority of them did.

So over the years it's been one thing or another. It's bad that we've never won a championship. I feel terrible about it. There isn't anyone in Pittsburgh or anyone in professional football who hurts as much as I do. But what am I going to do about it? I don't know. I just don't know.

We made trades that turned out bad. I let the coaches make the trades. The only trade I ever made personally was one night in 1939 when I was drinking beer with Dan Topping, who owned the old Brooklyn Dodgers. I traded him Sam Francis for Boyd Brumbaugh, one back for another. It turned out a great trade for us. That was the only trade I ever made, and we made it because we were both drinking beer.

I think that was my whole mistake, letting the coaches have a free hand. I'm positively *sure* that had I run my ball club, like George Marshall ran his ball club, we would have won championship after championship. I was *able*. I was competent. Knowing football, knowing football material, and knowing what was what, I'm sure that if I would have said, "We're not gonna do that, and you can like it or get out"—if I'd have said that, I'm positively *sure* we would have won championships. But I can't change now. I'm too old to change.

Have I ever had any idea of selling the club? No, never. My boys are grown now, and they like the business. Losing kept down our crowds, that's true, but money has never been my god—never. I've had opportunities to move the franchise. I've had tremendous offers. Back in the early 1950s I could have moved to Baltimore, and then later, to Buffalo, Atlanta, New Orleans, Cincinnati. The propositions they made were fantastic. So if you didn't have ties, if you didn't care for your city and its people, if you were just looking for wealth, you could have picked up and gone. But that's not you, not if you care for your city. And I believe Pittsburgh is a great city. I believe if we win, we'll do as good as we would in probably any of those other towns.

Well, when you lose you're so dumb you don't know enough to come out of the rain. All losers are dumb. All winners are sharp. When you win, you know all the answers. I don't know all the answers, so maybe we *are* dumb. But we've tried. We hired Buddy Parker, a top coach. He came to us with a big reputation, not many coaches sharper, and he was a good man. But he was here eight years, and still we didn't win. We hired Bill Austin, who came just as highly recommended as could be, by none other than Vince Lombardi, who we know would tell us the right thing. Okay, we didn't win with Austin. Now we come up with a new man, Chuck Noll, who came from Baltimore, a championship club, with a reputation that's just as good as can possibly be.

We *pay*. I think Buddy Parker, when he was here, may have been one of the highest-priced coaches who ever worked in this league. The papers said eighty thousand a year. It was more. When we make trades, we don't ask what does a player get. Until now—and I don't know how long this will continue, because times are changing—but until now, we've never had a ballplayer here who's played out his option. What I'm telling you is that we've tried. But I want you to know, and I want the town to know, that I'm not alibiing. I'm not crying. I've just told you our side. Who's interested in losers' alibis?

The Stakes

Art Rooney was a legend long before anyone even thought of co-mingling the words "Pittsburgh Steelers" with "championships." He was a local legend, the son of an Irish saloon owner and a product of the Steel City's tough First Ward. Even as a young man he had a way of making things happen. He was an organizer, someone who could bring people together and move them toward a common goal. But Art Rooney was also a legend in gambling circles, known widely as a man willing to take a chance and let a bet ride. Among gamblers on the East Coast, Rooney's winning streak at Saratoga was the stuff of pure envy. The great sportswriter John Lardner here chronicles Rooney's most famous ride.

ROONEY'S RIDE

John Lardner

This is an age of machines in the horse-racing world, of overnight pari-mutuel laws, of jerry-built tracks and daily doubles and dusty stretches and one quick coat of paint—which makes it easy to understand why the old-fashioned gambler points his nose toward the green hills of Saratoga every year, when August comes around.

They take your money just as fast in those mellow surroundings as anywhere else—perhaps faster. Your agent, known up there in the north country as Ace-Deuce Lardner, has paid out money, rather than vice versa, for the privilege of advertising the place where Gates and Arnold stopped Burgoyne. Nevertheless, you keep going back to shuffle the warm bricks of Broadway at noon, to ride to the track after lunch in the hack of an affable bandit, to watch and play the horses, to touch at the lake in the evening for steak and frogs' legs and roulette, to wind up at dawn throwing dice with the frankly predatory mob at the old Chicago Club, hard by the railroad station, which used to be your next stop, if you still had the fare home.

Saratoga, Dick Canfield's town, is the stronghold of the old-fashioned gambler. The old-fashioned gambler is not a guy with a frock coat or a waxed mustache. He is any private citizen who comes along with his private roll to buck the house at the house's game and to stay with it till he makes his killing or takes his licking.

The poolroom and syndicate systems being what they are, few gamblers are known by name any more. The last lone wolf to "make a score" in a free, wide, and purely innocent way was a deadpanned little Irishman from Pittsburgh named Art Rooney, owner of the Pittsburgh professional football club. He made his score at Saratoga, which is only right.

Some people have heard of "Rooney's Ride," but because the Irishman speaks only six words a month in a good year, the blow-by-blow details of his killing were not known until recently, when Mr. Joseph Madden, a literary saloonkeeper, published his third straight undefeated and untied book of memoirs, "Set 'Em Up."

Some seasons ago, Mr. Rooney arrived in New York City accompanied by $300 and the old Pittsburgh light heavyweight fighter, Buck Crouse. Their object was to spend a quiet weekend and get back to Pittsburgh alive. However, on Saturday, at the Empire City track, Mr. Rooney ran his $300 up to $21,000. This seemed to call for a couple of steaks at Mr. Madden's place.

"What's your next move, Artie?" inquired Mr. Madden.

"Back to Pittsburgh," said Mr. Rooney tersely. "First train."

The upshot of this conversation was that Rooney, Madden, and Crouse set out for Saratoga two hours later in Mr. Madden's $150 car, which had four bad coughing spells en route. Mr. Rooney and Mr. Crouse got out and pushed it over the hills, Mr. Madden retaining the helm.

On Monday—opening day at Saratoga—Mr. Rooney sent $2,000 on the back of a horse named Quel Jeu, at 8 to 1. The race came to a photo finish in the rain. Mr. Madden had $2 on this animal and swallowed his cigar when the picture showed him the winner.

"Ain't you happy?" he yelled at Mr. Rooney.

"We were lucky, Joe," said Mr. Rooney solemnly.

There were four photo finishes that afternoon. Rooney's biggest race was the fifth, when he tried to bet $15,000 on another 8 to 1 shot, but could only place $10,000.

"In that race," recalls Mr. Madden, "the four horses came out of the fog and hit the finish line in a heap—looked like a dead heat for all four nags."

"As I had a few clams on this event, I nearly died waiting for the picture to come down. But Artie lit a cigar, got out of the crowd, and went to the men's room, and when I brought him the good news there, he was telling the colored groom the difference between the single wingback and Warner's double-wing.

"'I will finish explaining later,' he said. 'I gotta hot tip in the next race.'"

Rooney won $256,000 that day. He, Mr. Crouse, and Mr. Madden celebrated in the evening with a banana split apiece at a soda fountain.

Has Mr. Rooney still got the dough? Please do not change the subject while I am looking up trains to Saratoga.

A Couple of Firsts

In the summer of 1933, early in Franklin Roosevelt's first administration, the nation turned its eyes to the problems at hand. Banks were ailing, men were out of work, and the economy was in desperate need of something that nobody seemed to be able to put a finger on. Pittsburgh suffered like the rest of America, but in July news from Chicago created a small ripple in the Steel City. At their annual meeting, the leaders of the eight-team National Professional Football League announced that they were considering expanding into two or three additional cities, with Pittsburgh and Cincinnati having the inside track and Philadelphia moving up on the outside. Art Rooney attended the meeting and he lobbied hard for Pittsburgh. The official announcement came the next day. Pittsburgh, as well as Philadelphia and Cincinnati, was voted into the league.

The problem with the Pittsburgh and Philadelphia franchises was that Pennsylvania blue laws prohibited Sunday games. But everyone expected the laws to be repealed on November 7, and until that happy day, league officials made allowances for weekday games in Pennsylvania. So on the night of Wednesday, September 20, 1933, etched against a gray, floodlit September sky, the Pittsburgh Pirates took to Forbes Field under Coach Jap Douds to do battle with Tim Mara's New York Giants.

Pittsburgh reporters did not expect much from their "players fresh from the campuses, untried in the hard bitten ways of the professional game," especially against the Giants' "combination of new blood and experience." Nor did they think that the Pirates could stop Harry Newman, the former Michigan All-American who was now the Giants' quarterback. The scribes were right, but the outcome of the first game was not as important as the fact that Pittsburgh had a team.

A week later the Pirates played their second Wednesday game, this time against the Chicago Cards, led by the great former University of Kansas fullback Jarring Jim Bausch. Sportswriters gave them little chance in that contest as well, but sometimes games did not go as the scribes scripted.

MICHIGAN ALL-AMERICAN GOES OVER WITH A BANG

Chester L. Smith

Has Hand in Two Touchdowns and Kicks 37-Yard Field Goal as Giants Win 23-2 Decision—Local Eleven Displays Promise

Forbes Field was just beginning to recover from watching Carl Hubbell of the Giants throw strikes at the Pirates with a baseball when up popped a chunky little guy who could do the same thing with a football.

Both the gridiron Pirates and Harry Newman, the All-America quarterback at Michigan last year, made their professional bow here last night. Newman was in the uniform of the New York Giants, and he completely stole the show. At the finish he had done everything with the ball but swallow it.

The score was New York 23, Pittsburgh 2, to which the erstwhile pride of Washtenaw County, Michigan, contributed one short sprint past the Pirates' left flank for a touchdown, a 37-yard field goal and a forward pass which arched majestically into the arms of Dade Burnett, who hails from Emporia, Kan., and found that worthy [receiver] entirely free of any hindrance between himself and the goal line.

Big Crowd Attends

Nearly 20,000 spectators whooped and hurrahed first for the Pirates and then, when it was seen they were bound to be beaten, for Newman. They saw a game that was not as one-sided as the score would indicate and enough savage and spectacular football to insure the professional league a permanent home here if it continues to furnish as much entertainment in the future.

President Joe Carr of the National League, who came from Columbus, O., for the inaugural, pronounced the Pirates one of the best first-year entries he has seen in several years.

"You're not going to win any championship, but you have a fine foundation to build on," he told Coach Jap Douds.

Mistakes Are Many

Poor punting by Brovelli and Tesser lost the Pittsburghers many a yard. They displayed marked weakness in allowing pass receivers to sneak behind their secondary and it is questionable whether the two wingback offense they used generates enough power to make headway against the rock-like rush-lines they will be called on to face, but individually, they showed promise at many spots.

The Purdue trio, Oehler at center and Letsinger and Janecek at the guards, was consistently brilliant and only wilted under a terrific pounding because they were not backed up with enough strong reserves. Artman of Stanford was likewise a hard man to budge, and Tony Holm, the ex-Alabama fullback, handled his assignments well.

Pirates Block Kick

The crest of the Pirate attack resulted from a defensive move when Holm exploded a long punt in the third period which Sortet batted out of bounds a foot from the Giants' goal line. Moran went back to punt out, but Artman, Oehler and Letsinger bore down on him and blocked the attempt, the ball rolling out of the end zone for an automatic safety.

That made the score 7 to 2, the Giants having clipped off a touchdown in the second period when Ken Strong, whom Pittsburghers well remember for his appearance here with New York University against [Carnegie] Tech in 1928, picked off a pass thrown by Brovelli and aimed at Moss. Strong was at full speed ahead when he intercepted the ball and he tore off the 34 yards he had to go in no time.

Newman's touchdown in the last quarter resulted from a fumble of a Giant punt by Clark. Reb Russell and Strong punched holes in the tired Pirate line until they had gone to the three-yard stripe. Newman then finished the job.

Tosses Pass for the Score

His field goal, a few minutes later, was on fourth down after he had been smothered in trying to pass. The ball just cleared the crossbar.

The game was almost over when the ex-Wolverine, who had harassed the Pirates with one toss after another, whipped one far to his left which Burnett gathered in.

Harry then place-kicked the extra point, just to make it a large night.

PIRATES RALLY TO DEFEAT CARDS, 14-13

Jack Sell

Kelsch's 2 Goals after Touchdown Clinch Triumph
99-Yard Run by Kottler Leads to First Local Score; Pass from Tanguay to Moss Gives Bucs Second

The man of the hour in Pittsburgh gridiron circles this morning, the fair-haired boy whose name is on everyone's lips, is a gent who never trod a college campus, never cut a lab period or a quiz.

The very latest hero of the pigskin world hereabouts is none other than Christian Kelsch, but to thousands of sandlot football fans throughout the Tri-State district, the burly Northsider is just plain Mose.

Twice last night the Pittsburgh Pirates, local National pro league entry, fought their way from behind to score a pair of touchdowns and overcome a 13 point lead. Coach Jap Douds of the Gold and Black eleven called the big, good-natured Mose from his spot on the extreme left end of the players' bench and rushed him into the game to place-kick extra points.

Boots Perfect Goals

Twice Mose went out before the surprising turnout of 5,000 fans, who forgot the all-day rain and filed into the Forbes Field stands, and booted perfect goals between the uprights, and, when the last whistle sounded, the Pirates had gained their first victory of the season by the narrow margin of 14-13.

There has probably never been a more dramatic moment than after Mose put his second and winning placement through the uprights on the Oakland ball park. Grinning from ear to ear, he ran immediately to the bench, his second half's entire duty done in that one play, and left the boys from Pitt, Stanford, Purdue, Duquesne and other sites of the college grid wars fight to a standstill the rest of the way while he lumbered on to the dressing room, the cheers of the fans and the handshakes of his mates forming a unique chapter in the career of the greatest sandlotter in local history.

From the *Pittsburgh Post-Gazette*, September 28, 1933. Copyright/*Pittsburgh Post-Gazette*, 2001. All rights reserved. Reprinted with permission.

Game Full of Thrills

His unerring marksmanship proved the climax of a brilliant battle, one which kept the crowd in an uproar throughout and rivaled the best of the collegiate attractions for thrills.

Opening up their offense after last week's rather inauspicious opener, the Pirates flashed time after time, but two bad moments when their strategy went haywire gave the enemy a pair of touchdowns and a 13-point lead before the locals dented the scoring column.

The enemy counted one goal in the first period and another in the second before the home entry, displaying the old college try at its best, fought its way to a score in the second quarter and another in the final. Joe Lillard, brilliant colored halfback, missed the first try for extra point by dropkick, and that seemingly insignificant error at the time set the stage for Kelsch's later game winning boot.

Easily outdistancing the other backs on the field, Jimmy Clark, the tough little Greensburg lad, who got his chance because Buck Moore was injured, flashed for the Pirates to balance the brilliance of Joe Lillard, the sensation of the Windy City team. Clark, who played fullback at Pitt, was a consistent ground gainer at right half for the Rooney Regiment, ran back punts brilliantly and hauled down enemy ball toters several times from his safety job early in the game when they appeared touchdown-bound.

Lillard tried his best to equal the performance of Harry Newman one week before. He was a constant threat on the offense, duplicated Clark's fine returning of kicks and added the punting burden to his repertoire. When he left the field midway in the last period after he and Holm threatened fistic exhibitions following a scrimmage, the locals' greatest menace was ended. It appeared that Oehler and Critchfield started the trouble, but Tony was banished along with the ex-Oregon lad. Immediately afterward the home boys shoved over their winning scores.

Kottler Runs 99 Yards

Along with Kelsch and Clark, the names of Butch Kottler, Ray Moss, Ang Brovelli and Ray Oehler must get attention. Kottler brought the locals their first touchdown of the year by intercepting an enemy pass on his own one-yard line and racing 99 yards for the first home score, thereby supplying the spark which sent the locals on to victory.

Moss grasped a pass from Jim Tanguay directly between the goal posts for the last score on the fourth down, just when all avenues seemed closed for an 11-yard gain and the tying touchdown. Brovelli, discredited a week ago, was a star all the way, making his finest contribution by grabbing a forward pass from Holm for a 59-yard gain in the third period for one of the outstanding plays of a thrill-packed battle. Oehler was a ubiquitous figure, moving everywhere, batting down passes, slamming enemy ball carriers to the turf and forming a real Keystone in the center of the Pirate forward wall.

All four touchdowns came through the air lines. The initial score came midway in the first quarter and was a shock to the locals. They had forced the going, rolled up three first downs to none for the enemy, and seemed to be going places when Captain McNally, visiting center, who was good enough to beat Tim Moynihan and Tommy Yarr, both from Notre Dame, out of the center job, bobbed up to intercept a lateral pass from Holm to Brovelli on the 50-yard line and gallop unrestrained for a touchdown. Lillard's dropkick was low and was blocked.

Disconcerted by this sudden turn of events the Pirates evidently thought a jinx was on their trail when the Cards injected their second score in the second period. McNally again was Johnny-on-the-spot to intercept Tanguay's pass on the Pirate 35, and a bit later on the fourth down, although the entire local eleven anticipated a pass, Lillard stepped back and calmly whizzed one on the line to Hal Moe in the end zone and only about a foot inside the sidelines for a second touchdown. Moe went tumbling in a heap on a beautiful play, but it was good and it looked as if an insurmountable obstacle was pushed in front of the Pirate hopes. Lillard made it still tougher with a perfect dropkick for the thirteenth point.

Just before the half ended the Pirates shot their first bolt. With the enemy pounding at the door for another touchdown Butch Kottler, local reserve quarterback from Centre College, picked a pass by Jim Bausch, the ex-Kansas U. fullback, from an enemy receiver's fingertips and ran 99 yards for a touchdown. Kelsch got his initial call and did his stuff, making the score 13-7 at the half, which arrived a moment later.

Lose Ball on Four

The final half started badly for home hopes. Clark made his one mistake of the evening when he ran left end, got confused and heaved a lateral toward Brovelli which Kassel intercepted. The locals took a long time to fight their way into the enemy zone but they plugged away, even unearthing the ancient Statue of Liberty play, a real ground gainer in Douds's day at Wash-Jeff and eventually were as far as the Chicago one-yard line.

At this point 235-pound Keisling, guard of the visitors, who had been injured by a terrific block by Roy Oehler earlier in the game and removed from action, trundled his beef onto the field and helped smear two plays to give the Cards possession on their own four. It looked a dismal ending to local ambitions.

The Douds proteges were not to be denied, however. They came right back in the final stanza and got off to a fine start as Jimmy Clark returned a punt from Lillard from his own 50 to the visitors' 31. Tim Moynihan of Notre Dame fame stopped them by intercepting a pass on the 19, but soon afterward Oehler covered a fumble on the Cards' 20 and the cards were stacked in the Pirates' favor.

Cards Are Outplayed

Nevertheless, they had to fight to the last ditch. Lillard and Holm were caught fighting and banished, whereupon Jim Tanguay uncorked one of those famous New York U. passes to Ray Moss for a first down on the enemy 4, a gain of 16 yards. Repulsed three times on scrimmage plays, Tanguay again went back and cut a beautiful pass through the posts to Moss for a touchdown, barely missing the cross bar, and the ex-Boilermaker hero clutched the ball tightly as discomfited rivals surrounded him. On came the Northsider's Mr. Kelsch and the game was settled.

Pittsburgh had made nine first downs to the Cards' five, completed four passes out of eighteen, to the enemy's four out of eleven. Chicago intercepted four, while Pittsburgh grabbed a pair. Improved punting, with Ray Tesser in the booting role, helped plenty, and from now on, the Pirates are ready for the best of them.

The Legend of Johnny Blood

After going six and six in 1936, Art Rooney hired Johnny Blood McNally—or just John Blood—as the player/coach of the Pirates. As a ball carrier Johnny Blood was something special. He was fast and shifty and starred with Curly Lambeau's Green Bay Packers, leading the team to three championships. As a person, he was equally fast and shifty and was the bane of coaches, managing in his career to run afoul of both Knute Rockne and Lambeau. He drank too much, seemed determined to break every training rule, and spent money like a sailor. Exactly what in that resume Art Rooney saw that convinced him that McNally would be a fine coach is unclear, but in 1937 he brought the "singular talent" to Pittsburgh. As a player, McNally started well, returning the opening kickoff of the first game for a touchdown. But sadly, John Blood was a better player than a coach. He tended toward laxity in discipline and organization. Chester "Swede" Johnston, a fullback and linebacker, recalled that when he was traded from the Green Bay Packers to the Pittsburgh Pirates he knew that he had hit rock bottom. Nothing, Johnston soon discovered, was done according to Hoyle under the McNally regime in Pittsburgh. On one occasion a running play was called for Johnston and he started one direction, reversed field several times, and then in desperation wound up and threw a pass. At halftime McNally said, "That's the way I want everyone to play." To McNally's way of thinking, football was like jazz, the more improvisation the better.

But it didn't work. Johnny Blood lasted two complete seasons as head coach, losing sixteen of twenty-two games. Even so, he contributed to the legend of Pittsburgh football.

NOT A CARDBOARD HERO

Mickey Herskowitz

To an adoring public he was known as Johnny Blood, the grandest, most romantic name ever invented in the entire Technicolored world of sport.

We discovered him the other night in the bar of the Stardust Hotel, a handsome man with steel gray hair and piercing blue eyes, a figure slightly larger than life. He was celebrating his second marriage, at the age of 62, which indicates right there that Johnny Blood has lost none of his competitive fires.

Now, if you ask us what we happened to be doing in Las Vegas, the city that never sleeps, we will retire like a flash upon our constitutional rights and fight extradition. If, on the other hand, you would care to learn a bit more about the most fantastic character pro football ever produced, then read on.

To become acquainted with the legend of Johnny Blood, it is necessary only to put in a minimum number of hours on the sports beat. You keep hearing a reference here, a mention there, a morsel of information that only whets the appetite for the full course. He is one of those people you grow to believe no longer lives, if he existed at all.

But Johnny Blood is real and alive and we can assure you that he is not a cardboard hero created by Walt Disney.

An item about Johnny in one of the local papers caught the eye this week of Sammy Stein, the pit boss at the Stardust Casino. They had been teammates in Green Bay 40 years ago. So Sammy called him at 2 A.M. on his wedding night, and Johnny hurried down to the bar and they talked and laughed and relived the old days until dawn, hoisting many a convivial cup of cheer. A man has got to love football, and treasure his friends, to bring off a trick like that.

When Sammy Stein introduced him his voice sounded like banners waving. "This," he said, with a wave of his hand, "is Johnny Blood."

How the Blood Legend Began

He was born John McNally in a town you never heard of in Wisconsin, but the story—the legend—really begins some years later, in the fall of 1924.

At 19 he had already dropped out of one college and been booted out by Notre Dame, where he fell victim to his own zany impulses. They expelled him after he borrowed a motorcycle one day without the owner's consent, zooming off with a lady friend in the sidecar.

So he was between schools when an offer arrived to play football for a semipro team in Minneapolis under an assumed name. The alias was necessary because he fully intended to return to college, which he did, at the age of 46.

The offer included a pal of his, and together they mulled it over as they strolled that historic night past a movie marquee. John McNally noticed that the feature film starred Rudolph Valentino in "Blood and

Sand." Excitedly, he nudged his companion. "That's it," he exploded. "You be sand and I'll be blood."

Exactly what became of sand no one knows, but thus was Johnny Blood born, and Johnny Blood he remained, all through an immortal career with the Green Bay Packers. For pure swashbuckling color there has never been another like him.

He was an exciting runner and a superb receiver, a complete athlete who lettered in four sports, not including war. In his youth he was wild and unpredictable and wasteful of himself and his great gifts. Sailor, soldier, lover, and intellectual, he was all of them. He had the restlessness of a gypsy, but the mind of a poet.

After he had graduated from high school at the top of his class, and in lyrical mood, he scribbled in his yearbook "Dear God, how sweet in spring it is to be a boy."

The Johnny Blood stories run into the hundreds, and collectors of them are still scratching under the curbstones for more. Sammy Stein remembered the time Johnny, as a joke on his coach, Curly Lambeau, jumped from a sixth story window across a courtyard, onto a window ledge 14 feet away in a driving rain.

"Fourteen feet isn't far," he said, somewhat embarrassed by the gusto with which Stein told the tale. "The hard part about it was the rain, and the fact that the ledge was slippery."

One night a female admirer, of which Johnny Blood had a considerable overstock, dropped by his hotel room to beg an autograph. He excused himself, returned moments later with a razor blade, slashed one wrist and wrote his name in you-know-what. "Blood for blood," he told her, with an obliging smile. He still has the scar.

He Set the Record for Fines

Once he played an entire game with a ruptured kidney, collapsing on the field as time ran out. At 33 he was still swift enough to extend Don Hutson, then a Packer rookie 10 years his junior, in a footrace.

It was never possible to predict what Johnny Blood would do when he stretched his legs across a chalk marked meadow. He might win a game with his brilliance or lose it with his capers. He relished a contest when it was tough. Impossible catches he always made. The easy ones he dropped in lazy indifference.

On one occasion he broke away from a pursuing tackler at midfield on an 80 yard touchdown excursion, but grew bored as he neared the goal line. So he waited at the five for the tacklers to catch up to him, then ambled across. It was more fun that way.

As a consequence of his antics on the field, in addition to his inability to tell time and other forms of Bolshevism, Johnny sometimes wound up owing the Packers more money than they paid him. "I guess I still own one record," he says. "I must have been the most fined player in the history of the game."

He looks upon today's super inflated salaries with wry amazement. "In 1934," he remembers, "I was coaching the Packers [he must mean the 1938 Steelers] and playing 60 minutes and making $2,500. The star of the team, Whizzer White (now a Supreme Court justice), was making $17,000. I've almost gotten over that."

He is retired now, and more than a dozen years removed from any connection with football. But he endures as a relic of a distant and more glamorous time. "The writers keep resurrecting me," he says lightly. "I understand it. They have to dig up skeletons once in a while, so they dig me up. I have more fun pushing the legend around than I ever did living it."

"Life," added Johnny Blood, "is quite a trip."

JOHNNY BLOOD: BEFORE HELL-RAISING CAME INTO VOGUE, HIS "UNFETTERED" STYLE WAS NFL LEGEND

Dan Daly

Sometimes it seems as if pro football has no past, as if the National Football League didn't really exist until the Baltimore Colts, the New York Giants and national television came together in the 1958 championship to produce a sudden-death classic that got everybody's attention. The death last Thursday of pro football pioneer Johnny Blood is a case in point.

Blood should need no introduction to football fans. He's a charter member of the Pro Football Hall of Fame. The five original members of the *Baseball* Hall of Fame—Cobb, Wagner, Ruth, Matthewson, Johnson—are identifiable by their last names alone.

From the *Washington Times*, December 4, 1985. Copyright © 1985 News World Communications, Inc. Reprinted with permission of the *Washington Times*.

But in 1925, Blood's rookie season in the NFL, pro football ran a poor second to college football in the hearts of the sporting public. It wasn't until late that year, when Red Grange did his first galloping for the infant league, that the crowds started to come out.

Shoddy record keeping, moreover, has done much to obscure Blood's considerable accomplishments. One has to dig deep to learn that Blood owns the oldest individual season record in the NFL books, the record for touchdown receptions by a running back. He caught nine TD passes in 1931—there were only 56 thrown in the entire league—and no back in the 54 seasons since has caught more.

So Blood's passing last week at the age of 82 barely caused a stir. Pity, because he was not only one of the game's great players, but also one of its great personalities, a bon vivant whose lifestyle was ideally suited to "The Roaring Twenties." His is truly a life worth reexamining.

Long before hell-raising Paul Horning came to Green Bay, Johnny Blood was tearing up the town—and any other he happened to be in. Red Smith, the late great sports columnist, called him "unfettered," as good an adjective as any to describe Blood's aversion to convention.

"Everything was just fun for him," says Clarke Hinkle, the Packers' fullback in those days and a Hall of Famer himself.

It wasn't unusual for Blood to show up at a social function in Green Bay wearing a tuxedo and tennis sneakers. Once, says Hinkle, he took a prostitute to a ball.

"He still owes me a gallon of Okolehao (a native Hawaiian drink)," says Milt Gantenbein, who played end on those Green Bay teams.

There is a story behind that. One year, Blood helped arrange for the Packers to play a couple of exhibition games in Hawaii after the season. The team spent 22 days on the islands, says Hinkle, "and you wouldn't believe the good times we had."

On the trip back, however, the boat ran into some stormy weather one night. When some players went looking for Blood, they couldn't find him.

"So Milt (Gantenbein) went out again," Hinkle recalls, "and he came back and said, 'Hey, come on, I want to show you something.' So we went to the aft of the ship, and outside the railing, swinging around the flagpole and singing all over the place, was Johnny Blood (drunk on Gantenbein's Okolehao). And, hell, if he'd fallen off, we'd never have found him."

On the face of it, Blood never had a chance. His first NFL team, the

Milwaukee Badgers, had a tailback named Jack Daniels. The next year, 1926, Blood signed with the Duluth Eskimos, who played 21 of their 22 games on the road in the two seasons he was with them. "The Iron Men from the North," sports columnist Grantland Rice dubbed them.

The Eskimos folded, so Blood played a year for the Pottsville (Pa.) Maroons. Then the Maroons went under and in 1929 he joined the Packers, who proceeded to win three straight NFL championships.

Curly Lambeau, the team's legendary coach, was always fining Blood for breaking rules—not that it did any good. Blood came from a wealthy family in New Richmond, Wis., and enjoyed a certain degree of financial independence. Hall of Fame receiver Don Hutson recalls one season when, "at the end of five weeks, he hadn't drawn a dime of his salary and owed Lambeau $400."

The night before one game in New York, Lambeau locked Blood in his hotel room. So Blood climbed out the window, down the side of the building, through a teammate's window one floor below and went on the town.

Then there was the time the Packers' train left for a trip east without Blood. A few miles outside of town, the train came upon a car parked across the tracks and had to stop. It was Blood.

Sportswriters called him "The Vagabond Halfback" because once, to save a little money—and for the sheer sport of it—he sneaked on a train to Green Bay and rode in the baggage car. "I've always had this thing for trains," he told author Richard Whittingham in "What a Game They Played," an oral history of pro football's beginnings. "They bring something out in me."

Lambeau exiled Blood to lowly Pittsburgh for a year after he came to practice drunk one day in 1933. The tipoff came when Blood tried to punt a ball. He missed it and fell on his rear. But Lambeau brought him back to Green Bay in '35, and the following season the Packers won another title.

As a player-coach with Pittsburgh from 1937 to 1939, Blood was no more reliable. He was in Chicago once watching a Packers-Bears game, thinking his team had an open date, when he heard the public address announcer say: "Philadelphia 14, Pittsburgh 7."

"The ballplayers came to me and asked me not to fire him," says Steelers owner Art Rooney Sr. "And I said, 'Well, this is peculiar. I always thought the coach worried about the ballplayers. But in this case, the ballplayers worry about the coach.'"

Such stories, however, hardly tell the whole story of Johnny Blood.

Born Johnny McNally—"Blood" was a pseudonym he used to play semipro football while in college—he graduated from high school at 14 and was an NFL rookie at 20. "He had a brilliant mind," says Hinkle. "When he was sober, he would read Shakespeare and literature like that."

During his one year at Notre Dame, Blood claims in "What a Game They Played," "I used to write Harry Stuhldreyer's (one of the Four Horsemen) English poetry papers for him."

Lambeau sometimes let Blood call the plays. Rooney remembers Blood yelling, "Air mail! Air mail!" on the sideline to signal to his defense that a pass likely was coming.

On the playing field, speed was what separated the 6-foot-1, 188-pound Blood from his contemporaries. Hutson ran the 100-yard dash in 9.7 seconds when he came to the Packers, but he says he only beat Blood, then 30, by "about two years" when the two raced. Blood was at his best as a receiver, where he could use his speed in the open field.

And while Blood wasn't a coaching success, Rooney credits him with getting All-American halfback Byron "Whizzer" White, the Supreme Court Justice, to postpone going to Oxford on a Rhodes scholarship so he could play in the NFL. "I didn't think there was a chance he would play for us," says Rooney, "but John persisted."

Blood tried a comeback with the Packers in 1945, at 40, but just didn't have it. He also ran unsuccessfully for sheriff in St. Croix County, Wis. The main plank in his platform? "Honest wrestling," he is said to have replied.

Johnny Blood. The one and only.

Star-crossed Franchise

The war years of the early 1940s were troubling for Steelers fans. There were doubts as to whether the star-crossed franchise would stay in Pittsburgh. The team had never had a winning season, although it compiled a 6-6 record in 1936. After the 1940 season, even Art Rooney, the eternally optimistic Rooney, was ready to call it quits. But it was at this low point that the Steelers' story became even more interesting. Reports circulated that the team would relocate to Boston, stay in Pittsburgh but be renamed the Iron Men, or join with Philadelphia to form one team to represent both ends of the state. It was more confusing than calculus.

The most improbable of the various scenarios actually took place. After enjoying its first winning season in 1942, the next year, as a sort of concession to wartime conservation, Pittsburgh merged with Philadelphia to form a new team—the Steagles. It was an unfortunate name. It conjures images of a green-and-yellow-feathered Dr. Seuss bird or a discount furniture store—as in, "Come down to Steagles for the best buy on recliners. Nobody, I mean nobody, undersells Steagles." The Philadelphia experiment lasted only one year, but it was not without its moments. Pittsburgh joined forces with the Chicago Cardinals for an abysmal 1944 season that left fans pining for the days of Johnny Blood and the Steagles: zero wins and ten losses, including a final game 49-7 mauling at the hands of the Chicago Bears. But by the 1945 season, Hitler was dead, the war was over, and the Steelers were once again just the Steelers.

ROONEY GIVES UP THE STEELERS

Harry Keck

It Was an Inevitable Decision
City's Pro Football Future in Doubt

Art Rooney's decision to sell the Pittsburgh Steelers' football franchise in the National Professional Football League was not unexpected.

After eight years of trying, you can't blame the guy for giving up when he finds he can't make any money and, indeed, is lucky not to lose a considerable amount.

As Art himself says, it isn't the fault of the local fans or due to a lack of newspaper and radio support that his original Pirates and then his Steelers failed to click. There was only one reason for their lack of appeal at the box office, and that was their failure to be in the running and, frequently, to stack up as formidable opposition for the better teams.

The reason for this is a long story. It revolves about the matters of coaching, finances and opportunity to get the proper players. Art tried out no less than five coaches, starting with Jap Douds in 1933 and running through Luby DiMeolo, Joe Bach, Johnny Blood and Walter Kiesling. He probably missed the boat when he had a chance to get Potsy Clark and the Portsmouth (O.) team back in '34 and turned it down because of a difference of opinion on the matter of salary. Potsy took that club to Detroit and won the championship with it.

One championship season here would have led to big crowds, increased interest, more operating capital—and who knows but that it would have made Pittsburgh one of the league's strongest cities instead of its next to weakest city?

Another grand opportunity was lost during the past season when, with Pitt and Carnegie Tech de-emphasizing, the Steelers started out well but couldn't keep up the pace and finished among the also-rans.

Just what Pittsburgh's future is to be in professional football is problematical. At this writing, there are two possibilities. One is that Alexis Thompson, the wealthy young purchaser, will move the club to Boston, which flopped dismally in the sport some years ago but now is believed to be ripe for a comeback, while Rooney will go in as a partner with Bert Bell, the similarly financially strapped Philadelphia mogul, and jointly operate a team to be known as the Keystoners and split its home games between Pittsburgh and Philadelphia. Another is that Thompson will keep the club in Pittsburgh and pour some money into it in an attempt to make it a winner, while Rooney will go along with the Philadelphia venture. Latest reports are that the club will remain here.

It is said that Greasy Neale, the former West Virginia Wesleyan star, later Marietta, W. & J. and West Virginia coach and in recent years the brains behind what is known as the Yale machine, will be the coach of Thompson's team, wherever it lands, while Kiesling will be retained to coach the Philadelphia squad, with Owner Bell relinquishing the role of mentor.

Developments will be interesting, for the pro game is coming along.

ROONEY SELLS PRO FOOTBALL CLUB TO BOSTON PROMOTER
Staff Reporter

Franchise May Stay Here, According to Report
"Greasy" Neale's Name Connected with Talk of New Coach

Pittsburgh Steelers, local representatives in the National Professional Football League, today were sold by Owner Arthur J. Rooney to Alexis Thompson, wealthy young Boston promoter.

The sale, rumored yesterday as Chicago Bears were humiliating Washington Redskins in the league playoff game in Washington, D.C., was consummated there this morning and ratified this afternoon at an executive meeting of the league.

Rooney, while severing his connection with the local club, which meant the passing here of league football, which has been in existence since 1933, will remain in pro football, having made a connection as part-owner with Bert Bell, Philadelphia Eagles.

May Stay Here for Year

In connection with the sale, it was also reported, but without official sanction, that Thompson, if unable to make necessary plans for operation of the club in his home city, would not be adverse to keeping it here until such time that Boston would be ready for its return to the pro game.

From the *Pittsburgh Press*, December 9, 1940. Copyright/*Pittsburgh Post-Gazette*, 2001. All rights reserved. Reprinted with permission.

Boston was an original member of the league, George Preston Marshall, present owner of Washington Redskins, having started there and continued until shift of his franchise to Washington in 1937.

While official confirmation was lacking, pending the release of the news after the executive meeting of the league, it was said, on good authority, that the new owner has already made overtures to Earle "Greasy" Neale, former West Virginia and Washington-Jefferson coach, to take over the coaching job. Neale at present is at Yale as assistant to Ducky Pond.

Plenty of Headaches

Rooney's local holding has been more or less of a headache since he first entered the league in 1933, when Luby Di Molio was head coach. In his first season, Rooney's club finished in last place, with three wins, six defeats and two ties.

Forest "Jap" Douds succeeded Di Molio as coach in 1934, but failed to better the club standing, again finishing in the cellar with two wins and ten losses. Douds continued in charge during 1935 and moved the club to third place in the Eastern Division, scoring four wins against eight defeats.

In 1936, Joe Bach, former coach of Duquesne University, took over the reins and made the best showing in the club's history, breaking even in 12 games and landing the team in second place, one game behind Boston, which won the Eastern title but was beaten by Green Bay Packers in the playoff.

Blood Replaces Bach

Bach's success marked a new era in the Pirates' history and 1937 saw the club hit its highest point of efficiency and attendance, even though they won only four and lost seven games during the season. Bach that season returned to college ball at Niagara University and his place was taken by John Blood McNally, former backfield star of the Packers and rated as one of the greatest player-coaches in the league.

Signs "Whizzer" White

Blood's failure to keep the club up to Bach's high standard resulted in an unprecedented move by Owner Rooney before the opening of the 1938 season. At the then unheard-of price of $15,000, Byron "Whizzer" White was signed up after having enjoyed an All-America career at Colorado.

Landing the high-priced star made the Pirates the talk of the league and great things were anticipated. But, for reasons which never have been explained, although the burden was laid on the shoulders of Blood, the club won only two games and lost nine and attendance and interest hit a new low here.

THOMPSON WISE CHOOSING TO OPERATE HERE

Chester L. Smith

Because Art Rooney had been approached frequently by Pittsburgh interests wishing to buy the Steelers and had a stock answer in the negative, the passing of the franchise to a Boston combine headed by Alexis Thompson caught nearly everyone unaware. On Sunday night, before the National League meeting in Washington, Thompson's name was heard frequently but not in its present connection. He was, according to the lobby whisperers, to be granted an additional franchise in Boston, with no change here. Rooney's appearance with his coach, Walter Kiesling (who carries a 1941 contract in his pocket), quieted any suspicion that the club was on the block.

Naturally, Pittsburgh felt relieved when it learned Mr. Thompson had decided to operate here. We have the sneaking hunch that he made the right decision. Back Bay and Bunker Hill failed to support George Preston Marshall and forced him to bundle up his Redskins and move them to Washington, while it is common knowledge that all our village needs to show a profit is an eleven of modest winning ways. Mr. Rooney can assure Thompson on this point, for his 1940 team operated in the black although it had only two victories and two ties to offer the customers as a box-office lure.

Earl Neale, who is Mr. Thompson's pick for a coach, is no stranger to Western Pennsylvania or professional football. Here we know him as Greasy Neale, a name he won because he was the slickest end in the district back in his playing days at West Virginia Wesleyan. He is remembered for his record at Marietta College, because he coached Washington and Jefferson into the Rose Bowl and stopped the fabulous California Golden Bears of 1921, and later through his term at West Virginia University. Shortly after he went to Yale as Ducky Pond's

From the *Pittsburgh Press*, December 10, 1940. Copyright/*Pittsburgh Post-Gazette*, 2001. All rights reserved. Reprinted with permission.

assistant, the "Greasy" disappeared from in front of his name, and the word was that the folks in New Haven didn't think it befitting the dignity of the Blue.

Neale also coached at Portsmouth in the years when the National League was struggling to climb to its present lofty estate, and he played there, too, long after he had passed the age when most men can stand the punishment they receive on a gridiron.

As a player, Greasy was a ball of fire and a magnificent leader; at coaching, he was always regarded as more of a clever tactician than a fundamentalist. He has shaped Yale's offense almost since the first day he set foot inside the Bowl. They still chuckle when they tell of his first meeting with the squad, when he delivered a talk in which he didn't want anyone running around in fur coats, which he hinted was a sign of campus softness. During the oration, the door opened and in walked Head Coach Pond wearing a fur coat!

THOMPSON TO KEEP PROS HERE; SAY SALE PRICE IS $160,000

Claire Burcky

Will Hire "Greasy" Neale as Coach
Rooney Buys Into Eagles
BEARS GET HARMON, CARDS GET KIMBROUGH IN DRAFT

A new owner and a new coach for the Pittsburgh Steelers; a new co-owner and a new co-coach of the Philadelphia Eagles, a division of Steeler and Eagle players, some Steelers becoming Eagles and some Eagles becoming Steelers, are the main complications Pittsburgh pro football fans are expected to try to straighten out today.

The new owner of the Pittsburgh pro eleven is Alexis Thompson, persistent and wealthy young New York sportsman who hounded Arthur J. Rooney, local promoter, throughout last season with an offer to buy the Pittsburgh franchise in the National Football League, a Rooney possession the past eight seasons.

Thompson's choice for coach is Earle (Greasy) Neale, well known hereabouts as a former major league baseball player, ex-coach of Wash-Jeff and West Virginia University football, and for the past seven seasons, backfield coach at Yale.

With a part of the purchase price, said to be $160,000, paid him by Thompson, Rooney bought 50 percent of Owner Bert Bell's holdings with the Eagles and took with him Steeler Coach Walt Kiesling, who becomes co-coach of the Eagles, with Heinie Miller, present head mentor.

Rooney is reported to have paid Bell $80,000.

Players Transferred

Under the new setup, Philadelphia transferred Ends Red Ramsey and Joe Carter, Tackles Phil Ragazzo and Clem Woltman, Guard Ted Schmidt, who formerly played for Pitt, and Backs Foster Watkins and Joe Bukant to the Steelers.

At the same time, Steeler players George Platukis, Walt Kichefski and John Klumb, ends; Clark Goff and Ted Doyle, tackles; Carl Nery and Jack Sanders, guards; and Boyd Brumbaugh, Jack Noppenberg, George Klick and Rocco Pirro, backfield performers, were transferred to the Eagles roster.

Perhaps the most definite point in the whole affair today was the announcement out of Washington, D.C., where all these complications came into the news yesterday during the annual business sessions of the professional loop, that a club would operate in Pittsburgh, and another in Philadelphia, next season.

Thompson, an enthusiastic young sportsman of 30, vice-president of a drug company and son of a former director of a steel company, formed a syndicate three months ago, the East-West Sporting Club, to buy a franchise in the league, intending at that time to place it in Boston.

Thompson inherited a $6,000,000 steel fortune at the age of 15.

"I made only $5000 this year, and it was a good year financially at home," Rooney said. "I figured that if that was the best I could do I would have to do something about it. The war situation and conscription, with regard to football players, also had me worried."

Rooney estimated his football losses over the eight years he held the Pittsburgh franchise to be around $100,000. He bought the franchise for $2500.

Will Operate Here Next Year

How long Thompson will maintain the franchise in Pittsburgh Rooney was unable to state.

"All I know is that he has said it will be in Pittsburgh next season," he said.

That much developed at the league executive meeting in Washington yesterday when the transaction was ratified.

Rooney also said that Thompson's Steelers and his and Bell's Eagles would follow the regular procedure in the league draft meeting today, when the clubs are permitted to select 20 graduating collegiate gridders each, players on whom they will have sole negotiation rights.

Neale Best Known for His W&J Teams

Earl (Greasy) Neale, who may come to Pittsburgh next year as coach of the Steelers, is 46 years of age and has spent nearly 30 years in athletics. He is perhaps best known as a major league outfielder and as football coach at W. and J.

He was right end at West Virginia Wesleyan in 1912 and '13, and left college the following year to enter professional baseball. His first baseball connection was with London, Ont., of the Canadian League. From this circuit, he stepped into the majors as outfielder on the Cincinnati Reds world championship team in 1919. Neale also played for the Phillies, and later in his career was a coach of the St. Louis Cardinals.

He began his football coaching career in 1915 at Muskingum College; spent 1916 and '17 as football coach at West Virginia Wesleyan; 1919 and '20 at Marietta College, and finally landed as head coach of Washington and Jefferson College in 1921. That year, the Presidents won 10 consecutive games, received the Rose Bowl bid, and played a spectacular scoreless tie with the mighty California Bears.

Greasy coached the Prexies in 1922, then spent six years as head coach at University of Virginia. It was at the end of his sojourn at Virginia that he returned to baseball as coach with the Cardinals.

After two seasons with the Cards, Neale accepted the head football coaching job at West Virginia, serving the Mountaineers in 1931–'32–'33. When Charles (Trusty) Tallman was assigned the West Virginia job in 1934, Neale moved from Morgantown to Yale, where he has been backfield coach the past seven seasons under Head Coach Ducky Pond.

In 13 years of coaching prior to the West Virginia post, Neale developed teams that won 81 games, lost 13 and tied three. His three years at West Virginia were the leanest in his career, the Mountaineers winning 12, losing 16 and tying three.

PHILADELPHIA-PITTSBURGH FRANCHISE SWITCH

Staff Reporter

'Iron Men' Out, Local Pro Gridders Back to Their Old Steelers Name

Art Rooney and Bert Bell think they have made a pretty good deal for themselves in moving their football club from Philadelphia to Pittsburgh for next fall. They said so jointly as Bell stopped over in Pittsburgh last night on his way back to his home in Philadelphia from the NFL meeting in Chicago. He said: "We have the pick of the Philadelphia and Pittsburgh clubs. Twenty-two good players. For the first time we'll have seasoned players backing up seasoned players at all positions, and we'll be able to put up a battle against rich teams like the Bears and the Giants and the Redskins who always have had this bulge on us. As a matter of comparison, let's see how the situation would work out in baseball. The Phillies and the A's in Philadelphia are tail-end clubs. Neither has enough good players to be in the pennant fight. But suppose they were able to join forces. Don't you think they'd be able to come up with enough good players for one team?"

Rooney revealed how he worked the deal to come back with a club in Pittsburgh after selling his franchise to rich Alexis Thompson and agreeing to go in with Bell in Philadelphia. He said: "It's funny the way it happened. When I sold the Steelers Bell handled all the negotiations for me because I was always missing connections with Thompson, or vice versa, on the meetings we'd arrange. The original proposition was that Thompson would buy the franchise and take the Pittsburgh club to Boston and Bell and I would pool our interests in a Phila.-Pgh. club, splitting the home games between the two cities. Then Thompson changed his mind and said he'd keep the club in Pittsburgh. That made me a partner of Bell's in Philadelphia. A few weeks ago, I asked Thompson when he was going to open his office here and get started on the season and he said he would get busy after the league meeting. Then I got an idea. I asked him how he'd like to make a switch and let me stay in Pittsburgh and take over the Philadelphia territory himself. That suited him, because Philadelphia is so much closer to his New York headquarters and that's how it was worked out. I know we've gone around in circles, but I guess we're settled now. And by the way, the new name for the club, 'Iron Men,' is out. We'll still be the Steelers, and bigger and better, we hope."

STEELERS WIND UP BEST SEASON AGAINST PACKER ELEVEN

Cecil G. Muldoon

With victory still as cherished and as novel to them as a new toy to a youngster, the ebullient Pittsburgh Steelers are no less than an even bet to close out their National League season with a victory over Green Bay this afternoon at the Wisconsin State Fairgrounds Stadium.

However, if Packer End Don Hutson's cartilage separation has not healed sufficiently to permit him to face the Iron Men, then the Steelers aggregation will take the field a decided favorite.

Even though the contest means nothing in the league standings, inasmuch as each team has clinched second place in its respective division and is out of the championship running, the Pittsburghers come up to the game with as much pep and determination as if the championship hung in the balance.

This spirit is easily explained. Whereas the Steelers in previous years wound up either in or just a stone's throw removed from the cellar, this eleven, in achieving the best record of any Pittsburgh team, considers the campaign quite successful even though the championship eludes them.

Anxious to Take Packers

Spurring Coach Walt Kiesling's charges on is their anxiety to become the first Pittsburgh team ever to beat the Packers and because by doing so they'll register their fifth consecutive victory.

Seven of the Steelers' last eight games have been put down on the right side of the ledger. Only black marks on their escutcheon are two defeats by the Eastern Division Champion Washington outfit and another by the last-place Philadelphia Eagles.

Green Bay has a slightly better record, having been beaten only twice, both times by the irrepressible Chicago Bears, and their record also shows a 21-21 tie with the New York Giants. However, even with this record the Packers are somewhat disappointed as they had their hopes on the title.

Individual battles for championships heighten interest in the contest. Bill Dudley, with a 44-yard edge over Brooklyn's Merlyn Condit will be attempting to hang onto this advantage as Condit goes to work against the New York Giants.

Riffle May Pass Farkas

Dick Riffle needs gain only 26 yards to pass Washington's Andy Farkas for third place in the ground-gaining division. The former Albright star is virtually certain to do this as is Cecil Isbell to complete five passes to pass Washington's Sammy Baugh and thereby set a new mark for completions, 133.

Hutson, whose pass-catching record which is certain to stand whether or not he plays, wants to boot two more points after touchdown to break Automatic Jack Mander's mark of 131 set while with the Bears in 1934.

In the all-time series history the Packers have thumped the Steelers seven times, the worst beating last season when they drubbed the Iron Men, 54-7, at Forbes Field. Green Bay has made 248 points to the Smoky City team's 34.

WHEN THE STEAGLES ROAMED ON GRIDIRON

Tom Infield

Only a world war ever produced a football team as odd as the Phil-Pitt Steagles.

It was 1943, the middle of World War II. Most healthy young men were in the military, many off somewhere in Italy or the Pacific. The National Football League was struggling to survive a severe manpower shortage. Good prospects were draft material, all right, but not for the NFL.

President Franklin D. Roosevelt, a fan of the New York Yankees, had declared that professional baseball should continue, war or no war. The national pastime, he said, was essential to morale on the home front. Americans, he thought, "ought to have a chance for recreation and for taking their minds off their work."

But football? FDR had nothing to say about football.

The war had interrupted pro football from its outset. Pearl Harbor Day was an NFL Sunday. Many a cabinet member, general and admi-

From the *Philadelphia Inquirer*, October 26, 1993. Reprinted with permission from the *Philadelphia Inquirer*, Oct. 26, 1993.

ral had heard news of Japan's attack while at Washington's Griffith Stadium, watching the Philadelphia Eagles lose to the Redskins, 20-14.

By then, the '41 season was ending. In '42, 10 NFL teams were able to limp along. Come 1943, 50 years ago this fall, the player scarcity had reached a crisis. The Cleveland Rams folded for the duration of the war. The Eagles and Pittsburgh Steelers didn't have enough players, either.

Elmer Layden, the league commissioner, urged the Eagles and Steelers to merge for that one season, splitting home games between the two cities, which were separated by a 300-mile ride on the Iron City Express. The hybrid would be a two-headed monster, co-coached by Philadelphia's lean Earle "Greasy" Neale and Pittsburgh's fat Walt Kiesling, both future Hall of Famers.

The players would wear the Eagles' green and white jerseys. But what would the team be called? Steelers-Eagles was the unimaginative choice. Fans came up with the catchier name. Thus were the Steagles born.

Jack Hinkle was classified as physically unfit for military service. But that didn't stop him from playing halfback for the Steagles.

"I was in the Air Force, and I was discharged because of ulcers," Hinkle, a second-team all-pro that season, recalled from his home outside Norristown.

Playing a pro sport didn't excuse a man from Uncle Sam's draft. He needed a deferment—or a discharge—for that.

Tommy Miller, an end, "he was in the Navy preflight program, and he had a crack-up, and they discharged him because of an injury that he had," Hinkle said. "He came back and played pro football at left tackle."

Edgar Michaels, a guard, "he couldn't hear," Hinkle continued. "He was practically deaf in one ear because he never wore a helmet. So he couldn't have gotten in the service, anyhow. Then Ray Graves, who was our center, he had one ear. . . . We called him Floppy."

Players who had flunked draft physicals were classified 4-F. Others were 3-A, deferred because they were married and had dependent children. Some were actually in the service, stationed nearby. They played soldier all week, then football on the weekend.

The largest number of players earned deferments by holding jobs classified as essential in defense plants in Philadelphia, where the

Steagles were headquartered. They could work by day and still practice from 6 to 9 each night.

Because of the manpower problem, the NFL owners had considered junking the '43 season. Instead, the league cut the roster limit from 33 players to 28. (Today's NFL teams dress 45 players on game day.)

At the first Steagles workout in July, even 28 players seemed optimistic. Only 19 showed up.

"It's a good thing we merged with the Steelers, or we wouldn't have had a team," Hinkle said.

On the field, rosters might change from week to week. For a player who stayed with the team, it was a chance to demonstrate talent that otherwise might have gone overlooked.

The Chicago Bears—the dominant team of the era—were preseason picks to win the championship. Art Morrow of the *Inquirer* pointed out that they had an edge that applied only in wartime—"more married men than most squads."

But nothing was certain in that season of jumbled rosters. The Steagles opened with a 17-0 victory over Brooklyn's football Dodgers, a Saturday-night affair before 11,131 fans at Shibe Park. Pro football's second-class status as a spectator sport was evident in the press coverage. The Sunday *Inquirer* played up the Penn-Yale game. The *Evening Bulletin*, which had no Sunday edition, gave the game a single paragraph on Monday.

The Steagles won their second contest, 28-14, over the Giants, amid signs of disorganization. They set an NFL record for fumbles: 10 in one game. After that, they dropped two ugly games, giving up a total of 90 points.

To Philadelphia fans, the team began to look like the same old Birds, who hadn't had a winning season in 10 NFL campaigns.

But the Steagles weren't dead. Far from it. It just took time to blend two teams under two coaches.

Francis Joseph "Bucko" Kilroy, described in a press guide as "240 pounds of red-headed fighting Irish-man," was a rookie tackle that season while simultaneously in the Navy College Training Program, better known a V-12. He remembers that Neale and Kiesling couldn't have been more different as men and coaches.

Kiesling, he recalls, was enormous—well over 300 pounds. Neale was lean and elegant, not at all the figure his nickname suggested. He had earned that as a kid when, after calling another boy "Dirty," the boy had retaliated by calling him "Greasy."

A superb athlete himself, Neale had been both a pro football player and major league baseball player. As a Cincinnati Red, he hit .357 in the famous 1919 World Series tainted by the Black Sox scandal.

"Greasy had a sense of humor, and he was a confident, upbeat guy," Kilroy, now vice president of the New England Patriots, recalled. "I wouldn't say Kiesling didn't have a sense of humor, but he was more serious."

It was lucky for the Steagles that the coaches had different interests. Neale was mostly offense-minded, a proponent of the new T-formation, first used in the pros by George Halas of the Bears. Kiesling was a defense guy.

Like most players of the day, Kilroy went both ways. He played offense and defense, and could observe both coaches closely.

He called Kiesling "an innovator . . . the guy who started the basics" of the Eagles' championship defense later in the '40s.

But it was Neale, he said, who altered the game. He picked up Halas' T-formation from film of Bears games and massaged it to perfection. Between them, Halas and Neale "opened up the offense" and "really made" pro football a spectator sport, Kilroy said.

Early in the '43 season, the whole NFL got a scare when the War Manpower Commission announced that it was investigating the Bears' roster for possible draft fraud.

The question was whether Bears who had obtained draft deferments because of their work in defense plants were really war workers, first, and football players, second. The test was money: In which job did they earn more?

Fortunately for the NFL's image, the Bears were low-paid. Most of them earned more in the factory. It would have been a public-relations disaster for professional football to appear to be cheating on the war effort.

All over the league, salaries were as low or lower. NFL players were seen as ordinary Joes, even if they weren't G.I. Joes. That helped alleviate the anger that occasionally arose in public over their draft status.

Of all professional sports, it was baseball that took the most heat. It was simply a bigger sport; the public cared more about it. The two biggest stars of major-league baseball—Joe DiMaggio and Ted Williams—were both booed at one time or another. Both ended up in the service.

Allie Sherman, then a rookie backup to Steagles quarterback Leroy Zimmerman, recalls occasional resentment from football fans.

"There were local tensions, wherever the cities were," he said. "Sure, you had people who were objecting. . . . Why is my son in? Or my nephew in? And why isn't this guy in? He's healthy. . . . You know how people are in time of war."

Sherman would become head coach of three Giants teams that played for the NFL championship in the '60s. Neale called him "the best football mind I ever coached." But in '43, with the Steagles, he was paid exactly $75 a game. Because of a perforated eardrum, a result of childhood scarlet fever, he was classified 4-F and didn't need a defense job. But he took one anyway in the off-season, working at the Navy Yard as a welder.

Like other unmarried Steagles, he lived during the season at the 600-room Hotel Philadelphian, at 39th and Chestnut Streets. He remembers that his roommate, tackle Eberle Schultz, kept his beer cold on the windowsill. Sherman, at 5-foot-10 and 160 pounds, was the smallest man on the team, while Schultz, 6-4 and 250, was the biggest.

Nearby was a Horn & Hardart restaurant, a cheap place to get a filling meal.

"Greasy was a very frugal guy," Sherman recalled. "He was always giving you a lecture. 'Don't call from your room; call from the pay phone in the lobby. . . . And I suggest you eat at the Horn & Hardart. It's the healthiest food, the best food, and it's certainly less costly.'

"So a number of us took him up on it. And then we had a run of diarrhea."

One season the Steagles lasted. But what a season it was.

Neale and Kiesling were able to meld the Steagles into an effective team. Going into their final game, which they lost to the Green Bay Packers, they had a chance to tie for the Eastern Division title. As it was, they finished 5-4-1.

More important, both the Steelers and the Eagles survived. In 1944, the last full year of war, the Eagles were again able to go it alone. The Steelers merged with the Chicago Cardinals. That team was so bad, 0-10, that the writers called it the Car-Pitts—the carpets—because everybody walked all over it.

But the Eagles, it soon became apparent, were putting together the nucleus of a fine football team. In 1944, Steve Van Buren, a future Hall of Fame runner, joined the team, and the Eagles went 7-1-2.

By '47, they were playing in the NFL championship game. And in '48 and '49, they won it all, twice. No other Eagles team has ever won back-to-back championships.

"The old Steagles, that's where a lot of it started," Hinkle said.

PRE-RENAISSANCE STEELERS

Dale Dodrill on '50s Steelers

Dale Dodrill was never a star, but, then, there were very few stars on the Steelers teams of the 1950s. Drafted out of Colorado A&M (now Colorado State University), Dodrill anchored the team's linebacking corps for nine mediocre years before joining the Denver Broncos as a defensive coach in 1960. The 1950s, like the 1940s and 1930s, were lean years for Steelers fans—the team finished above .500 only twice in the decade. It was a era of average squads with little chance of getting better, led by a string of forgettable head coaches like Walt Kiesling and Buddy Parker, who may be best remembered for their short stays in Pittsburgh, their bad drafts, and their ineptitude. In an interview with Stuart Leuthner, Dodrill recalled the misery of training camp, the hopelessness of the teams on which he played, and the revolving-door coaching staff that was supposed to be in charge of it all.

"REF, HE'S HOLDING!"

Stuart Leuthner

It's probably hard for people to believe today, but there wasn't much interest in professional football except in a few specific areas. In those days a lot of people weren't exposed to the game. The Steelers used to train at St. Bonaventure University in Olean, New York, which is south of Buffalo. I had an old Army buddy who lived in Buffalo, and the first year we played an exhibition game in Buffalo I went to see him. We hadn't seen each other since the end of the war, and he wanted to celebrate by having a drink. I said, "I can't. I've got a football game tomorrow." He said, "Oh, come on, for old time's sake. We've got to have a beer." I kept telling him, "No, I can't. I've got a football game tomorrow." He finally said, "You keep mentioning this football. What's football? What do you mean by pro football?"

The Steelers' training camp was terrible. Throughout the league it was said that when guys got cut or traded, they would pray that they wouldn't go to Pittsburgh. Everybody also said if you could last through a Pittsburgh camp you'd make the team. The Steelers were the only club that went two scrimmages a day until the first league game. They also didn't have the best facilities. In fact, some of them were just plain bad. The locker room at Forbes Field had a dirt floor, and the groundskeepers would take a tour about twice a day around the field and shoot the rats that were living in the garbage under the stands.

About my sixth year with Pittsburgh, I got a letter that we were going to train that year at California State Teachers College. I thought to myself, "Boy, this is going to be great. Get out to California, lots of sun, sit on the beach." Then I found out differently. California State Teachers College is in the Monongahela Valley, south of east of Pittsburgh. I never did find out where that school got its name.

The food at training camp was never the best; that was before they had dietitians, and everything was served family-style. There were long rows of tables, and if they started the food at the other end of the room, you never did get a bowl with much of anything in it. Some of those guys could really eat, especially the ones that shouldn't have.

I don't know what it's like now, but there were only thirty-three players on a team, and some of those men had played together for a while and didn't want anybody breaking up their group. Those players really watched out for each other. They like to say that players help each other today, but it's my experience that a guy isn't going to help you any more than he has to, and if he does help you, it may be in the wrong way. It was tough to break into a team and it would take two going on three years before they figured you weren't a rookie.

My first year with the Steelers, we played the [Chicago Cardinals], and I learned what a rookie was in a hurry. We were playing in Chicago, and at that time the Steelers were still using the single wing. I played the middle man in the line and this guy on the Bears was a real veteran. He was an artist. Every time I would give him a forward thrust, he would grab my arms and wrap them up. Then he'd fall over and pull me down with him. Sideways, backward, it didn't make any difference which way he went because I'd go with him. I was getting mad and I told the ref, "That guy is holding. He's holding me every play. Watch him." The ref said, "I'll watch him." The ball was snapped, and sure enough there went the flag. The ref called me for holding. That was my first lesson—keep your mouth shut and don't try to get those old-timers into trouble.

We never had too much to cheer about at Pittsburgh while I was there. Teams didn't like to play us because defensively we'd beat them up a little bit, but they didn't worry about us offensively. We might have ended up second in our division a couple of times, but we never did scare anybody. We had a receiver who would on occasion drop a pass when he was running in the open. I asked him why he did that, and he said, "You make a touchdown and people forget about it. Drop the ball and people talk about it for a long time." If we didn't have at least one or two good fights during a scrimmage, we didn't have a good practice. The guys would get into fights when they went out at night and end up breaking a wrist or spraining something. The next day during practice they'd go into the pile and come out claiming they got hurt, holding that hand or knee they'd hurt the night before.

When we played the Eagles, it would usually get a little rough and dirty. Pittsburgh and Philadelphia were in the same state, so it became a real intense rivalry. They always used to accuse each other of hurting a ball player in the game before, and there would be talk about how next time it's your turn. That's how it went, back and forth.

We had some good players on the Steelers, but they always seemed to be at the end of their careers or just passing through on their way up. Teddy Marchibroda came through there. Earl Morrall, Jack Kemp, Lenny Dawson, Johnny Unitas—I can't remember them all. Bobby Layne was there for a while, and he was a real competitor. Bobby would get it done one way or another. We had both of the Modzelewski brothers, Dick and Ed. Big Mo and Little Mo. Big Mo developed a back problem in training camp, and it carried on so long that he couldn't practice. The Eagles traded him to Cleveland for Marion Motley. Big Mo went to the Browns, and they got him some sort of medication. That straightened out his back and he had some great years with Cleveland. Motley, on the other hand, came to Pittsburgh at the end of his career, and I can still remember the first time I saw him practice. It hurt to see him run [with] the knees he had.

Little Mo wanted to go to Cleveland and play with his brother, so the Eagles obliged him. We had Billy Ray Smith with us for two years and he was sent off to Baltimore, where he became a great one. Jimmy Orr also went to Baltimore. Those were the kind of things that kept happening, and I think it was the reason we never had a really great ball club.

You asked me how it was playing for Pittsburgh in those years, and that's the only reason I'm relating this to you. The kinds of teams we had in those days can be best explained by the fact that for three or four years I was getting the award given out by the Monday Morning Quarterback Club for the most valuable player on the Steelers. Now this is a real successful club when they have to give a linebacker all of these awards and you don't have anybody who can win ball games for you getting any. I'm not putting myself down; I know I was a good ball player, but normally a quarterback, running back, or receiver would be getting those awards if you have a successful ball club, people who can get points on the board.

It really didn't make any difference to me who was coaching. As far as playing, you had to go out there and play, and pro ball was enjoyable because, unlike high school and college, you had one assignment. If a guy does this, you do that. It's the players who make the great coaches, and during a season a coach may win one or two games with coaching. Look at [Browns quarterback] Otto Graham. He wasn't always on target; nobody is. He'd throw the ball behind Lavelli or Speedie, and a defensive guy would have perfect coverage on them. You'd see those receivers reach back with their left hand and just roll the ball in. They were comparable to the receivers Bradshaw had when he won all those Super Bowls. Those are the types of players who create championship teams.

John Michelosen was the coach when I got to the Steelers and was the last man to coach the single wing in pro football. Next they brought on Joe Bach, one of the original Four Horsemen, and I forget how long he lasted and then we had Walt Kiesling. He'd been with Rooney for years and had played with teams like the Duluth Eskimos and Pottsville Maroons in the real early days. Kiesling lasted three years, and when Buddy Parker got there he was going to change everything around. Any time a new coach takes over, he has things he wants to do and certain kinds of players he wants. There's nothing wrong with that, but I wanted Parker to release me because I could [see] that I wasn't going to work into his plans for the future. He told me, "Art Rooney has an investment in you, so you have to stay here. You can sit on the bench for the rest of the season." I said, "I think Art Rooney's got his investment out of me a couple times over." Then I went to see Art and told him I didn't think Buddy was being fair. "Well," Art said, "I'm sorry, Dale, but Buddy's running the show." That was the year of the expansion, and I was sure that if they did trade me it would be to one of the expansion teams. The handwriting was on the wall because every team had to put up so many players, and after nine years in the league I didn't want to go through that so I quit.

While I was playing I worked in a bank in Omaha for a few summers and became interested in the insurance business. It was very difficult to get a summer job if you were playing football because an employer knew you were going to leave when the season started. Companies in those days wanted somebody who would be around forever. Now it's just the opposite, and if they can get a player to work for the company, they're overjoyed because it's great public relations for the time he's there. I started selling insurance in the off-season because it was something I could do on my own time, and after I retired I told my wife to pack up. "We're going back to Colorado." My wife said, "What are you going to do there?" I said, "I don't know, probably the same thing I'm doing here, but I don't want to spend more than two more days in Pittsburgh."

Ernie Stautner

Sometimes, looking back to a time we imagine was more innocent than our own, it seems easy to romanticize the lovable loser, the team that lives perpetually with the promise—the prayer, really—of "wait until next year." But there was little sunshine in the long, bleak autumns of the Steelers' discontent. The few fans who faithfully trudged to the games grumbled and swore and vowed that this season, maybe even this game, would be their last, that the "same old Steelers" were just too painful to watch. And for the players who had pride, the ones who hated to lose, the Steelers resembled a Soviet gulag. Ernie Stautner cared. From 1950 to 1963 he starred at tackle. The son of German immigrants, a World War II Marine, an All-American, and an All-Pro, Ernie played hard and occasionally told reporters exactly what he thought. And they sometimes wrote what he said. The following two pieces give a sense of who Ernie was and how it felt to be a Steeler.

ERNIE STAUTNER RAPS BOOING FANS

Pat Livingston

"I'm not happy playing in Pittsburgh," Steeler vet says, calling town "lousy."

An embittered Ernie Stautner, charging he has wasted his career playing football before empty stands, has characterized Pittsburgh as a "lousy" sports town.

Irked by the booing of his teammate and pal, Bobby Layne, in last Sunday's 30-27 victory over the St. Louis Cardinals, Stautner exploded:

"I'm not happy playing in Pittsburgh, I never have been happy here, and I wouldn't have been here in the first place if I had any choice about it," said Stautner. "This is a lousy sports town and if Art Rooney had any sense he'd get out of it."

Stautner, a veteran of 12 pro campaigns who has been named to the All-Pro team six times, said he lost his patience at a baseball game last summer, long before the football season started.

"I went to a baseball game and what did I hear?" he asked, "They booed Elroy Face. Of all people, Elroy Face! The guy gives you great baseball for six years, wins a pennant for this town and they boo him.

"What's wrong with these people? Do they have an inferiority complex or something?"

Stautner, a 230-pound lineman who carved [out] a brilliant college career as a Boston College tackle, broke in with the Steelers in 1950. He has been a standout since his rookie season, an athlete who rates status in Pittsburgh alongside Billy Conn, Paul Waner, Pie Traynor and other local immortals. This was pointed out to him.

"That doesn't mean anything to me," he added emotionally. "Pittsburgh owes nothing to me. I owe nothing to Pittsburgh. We're all even on that count."

(Stautner's salary is estimated in the $12,000–$15,000 bracket.)

Cites Home Town Fans Elsewhere

A bystander pointed out that if the Steelers were winning, the fans would get behind them.

"Isn't that great?" he asked sarcastically. "Give me a winning team and I don't need Pittsburgh. I can put it in Podunk, Iowa, or Green Bay or even Saranac Lake. Anybody will get behind a winner."

Stautner said it is discouraging to travel from town to town where home town fans are solidly behind the home team.

"The fans have as much to do with winning in New York and Philadelphia as the team does," he said. "A team that gets the appreciation that the Giants and Eagles get has to take pride in its work, it has to put out that little extra effort, that enthusiasm that the crowd starts."

Stautner said that Pittsburgh is a "graveyard for football players."

"There are coaches in this league," he said, "who warn their players about sending them to Pittsburgh. Ask Big Daddy (Lipscomb) or Johnny Sample. Weeb Eubank at Baltimore would tell those guys he'd trade them to Pittsburgh if they fouled up.

"Oh, boy, that would straighten them out in a hurry. You didn't know that, did you?"

Ernie Hits at Criticism of Parker

Stautner also deplored the local fans who, while idolizing Coach Paul Brown of Cleveland, criticize Coach Buddy Parker.

"That's another thing that burns me up about this town." said the Steeler end. "Well, if you think Brown has anything on Parker, just look at the record. See who won the most games when they played each other."

And look at what Brown has to work with. He has the league's leading passer in Milt Plum. He has the league's best power running [back] in Jimmy Brown. He has the league's best breakaway back in Bobby Mitchell.

"How many championships has he won with those guys? I'll tell you, he hasn't won any. Give Buddy two backs who can run like that and you keep Plum. This team would be so far ahead of the pack the race would be over."

Despite his burn over Pittsburgh, would that affect his play the rest of the season? Does he want to be traded?

"I'm a pro. All these guys are pros," replied Stautner. "If it made any difference where I played, I wouldn't have been here in the first place.

"As far as being traded is concerned, I don't care what they do about that either. We're out to win. Sometimes we do. Sometimes we don't. At least we're out there every Sunday taking our knocks.

"Let me tell you something else. I've asked 30 guys who were at the game if they booed Bobby. Luckily, I haven't found one yet who would stand up and admit it."

SENIOR CITIZEN OF THE PITTSBURGH STEELERS

Shirley Povich

The only National Football League player born in Germany's Black Forest is now the senior citizen of the Pittsburgh Steelers' active list. This aborted Prussian type is Ernie Stautner who fled Bavaria at the age of four with his emigrating parents and has been playing defensive tackle for the Steelers for the last 14 years.

That is a long time in the primitive give-and-take that goes on among pro league linemen and there is a dented nose and a couple of warped knees to testify it has not all been pleasant. Nobody who can pre-date Stautner is still active in the NFL, although Sammy Baugh did give it a 16-year fling and Bobby Layne was around for 15 seasons.

"Yeah, but they were quarterbacks," Stautner said, "and they had

From *The Washington Post*, November 15, 1963. © 1963 *The Washington Post*. Reprinted with permission.

to be treated with at least a little bit of dignity. There is no penalty in this league for roughing the right tackle.

"There is a generation of pro league fans who can't remember when Stautner wasn't playing tackle for the Steelers. He admits to being 38. Ed Kiely, the Steelers' publicist, says, "Some people are certain he's 41, they all cheat a couple of years." Joe Kuharich who once coach[ed] Stautner at Aquinas High School in Rochester, N.Y., says 40 would be a good guess.

Anyway, it was a long time ago when Stautner first joined the Steelers as an eager young draft choice from Boston College. Before that there was a hitch in the Marines, an escapist action after being turned down at Notre Dame as "too small." Notre Dame could take another look now at his 245 pounds.

The Steelers were still playing single-wing football under Walt Kiesling, a heritage from Jock Sutherland, when Stautner reported. "Somebody important, I don't remember who, told me 'You have to do more than one thing to stay in this league,'" Stautner said, "so I told Kiesling I was also a kickoff man."

He remembers his first game, against the Giants in 1950, in which he was given the opening kickoff chore. He was understandably nervous, carefully put the ball on the tee, counted off the number of steps for his proper kicking distance, and then before advancing on the ball he counted again to make certain there were 11 Steelers on the field.

"Then when everything was ready, I started my run at the ball and it keeled over in the strong wind. No play," Stautner remembered. "So I started the routine all over again. This time, nothing happened, except to me. I flubbed the kick, dug my kicking foot into the ground a foot in front of the ball, never got it off the tee and was out of the game with a sprained ankle."

Later, Stautner had some success, enough to be named All-Pro league tackle eight or nine times, and apparently is still going strong enough to merit the special attention of the Redskins this week. Redskin Coach Bill McPeak, armed with the films of the Steelers 9-7 victory over Cleveland last Sunday, has expressed a curiosity about Stautner's diet.

"What are you feeding old man Stautner these days?" McPeak asked Kiely of the Steelers. "I've just been watching him chew up that big Shafrath (Cleveland tackle) all day. He acted as if he was still trying to make good, 14 years after he broke into the league."

Stautner now plays not only tackle, but sometimes defensive end for the Steelers. He also is the team's defensive coach and he deployed the Steelers well enough against the Browns last Sunday to hold Jim Brown to 16 yards running in the second half. True, Brown carried the ball only four times in that half, but there must have been something about the Steelers defense to discourage the whole idea.

Stautner says he is going to pack [it] in as a player this year and retire to a full-time coaching career. "The living is easier," he said. "I've enjoyed these 14 years but the old bones are beginning to protest a little."

He said he guessed he made a thousand tackles for the Steelers, not counting the assists he also made. The hardest man to bring down? "There are too many good ones to sort out, but nobody has been tougher than Jim Brown." He said, "You go for Brown's legs and it's like running into two steel beams."

Bobby Layne

Bobby Layne was the stuff of legend, a blue-eyed, blond-haired Texan who loved to drink too much, stay out late at night, swap stories, and play football. He is best remembered for his exploits at the University of Texas and on the Detroit Lions. But Raymond "Buddy" Parker brought Layne to Pittsburgh in 1958 in an effort to breathe life into the Steelers' passing game. With Layne leading the offense between 1958 and 1962, the Steelers won about as many as they lost, but perhaps even more importantly, Layne infused a ton of character into the team. The Steelers who spent time with Layne generally felt better, if a trifle exhausted, for the experience. Indianapolis sportswriter Bob Collins portrayed Bobby's charms.

HARD TO NAME AN EQUAL FOR LAYNE

Bob Collins

"Bobby Layne never lost a game in his life. Time just ran out on him."
—Doak Walker

"When Bobby said block, you blocked. When Bobby said drink, you drank."
—Yale Lary

"I went out with Bobby to get some toothpaste and got to bed three days later."
—Harley Sewell

They still do it because people expect it. But the decisions prior to kickoff are made before the teams take the field.

The National Football League, with a nice touch of theater, uses the pre-game coin flip to honor giants from its past. The ceremony has been handled by George Halas, Mrs. Vince Lombardi, Art Rooney and Red Grange.

And last Sunday before hard-playing, hard-living Joe Montana led San Francisco to victory in Super Bowl XVI, the best man for the occasion was there to start the show. There are many who claim Bobby

From the *Indianapolis Star*, January 31, 1982. © 1982 *Indianapolis Star.* Reprinted with permission.

Layne was the best quarterback who ever lived. It certainly would be difficult to name more than a few who were his equal.

And none, past or present, was more exciting. I can easily conjure up a vision of Layne moving out of the pocket with that waddling gait, his love of the good life hanging over his pants, steely gray eyes probing down field.

Bobby's love of the bright lights is legendary. But he was a relentless driving leader who could carry a team with his fierce determination. He practically invented the two-minute offense.

Despite all the stories, the guy either had to be in shape or own the constitution of a baby blue ox. He played 15 seasons, and when he retired he owned most of the NFL passing records. He took the Detroit Lions to three NFL titles and one runner-up finish. He even led the league in scoring one season.

There are enough Bobby Layne quotes and stories to fill a long evening. When he presided over a press conference at the Dearborn Hyatt there was an unusually large audience, much trading of yarns and plenty of laughter.

The most repeated Layne line came in the 1953 championship game. Cleveland led Detroit, 16-10, with a little more than four minutes to play. So Bobby went to work. A fourth-down pass took the ball to the Cleveland 33. Layne called time, conferred with coach Buddy Parker, called a huddle and grinned: "Gimme a little time, boys, and we'll party tonight."

He threw a touchdown pass to Jim Doran on the next play, then kicked the winning point.

Life is a party to Bobby. And he amassed the means to keep the band playing with oil and gas holdings in Lubbock, Texas. Don Meredith, himself no stranger to neon, once said, "If I'm ever re-incarnated, I'd like to come back as Bobby's cab driver. I'd go to interesting places, stay out late and get good tips."

But, let us not lose sight of the fact he was a great player, respected, even loved by his teammates.

In Layne's day, few players earned more than $10,000. Bobby acted as agent for his teammates, often getting them salary increases. If he thought some were getting the short end, he simply reached into his pocket and made up the difference.

He was a consummate pro who never asked for more than he was giving. And he had that intangible—an ability to make others play beyond their ability.

And the greatest tribute ever paid Bobby Layne was silent. In 1967 when he was inducted into the Hall of Fame, old teammates came from all over the country for the ceremony. They just wanted to be there to share the moment with him.

Layne tried, with considerable lack of success, to bury some of the myths during the press conference. What he got mostly were giggles with lines like, "I didn't fool around during the week, never the night before a game, but, boys, I was burning hell on Mondays. Some people need 10 hours sleep, I only need four. Heck, Mr. Edison only slept two," and "I've been to six Super Bowl games and seen maybe 12 minutes. I get nervous around crowds—'specially when they're drinkin'."

Layne revealed that he has had few disappointments on his trip through life. The biggest was "not winning a championship for Mr. (Art) Rooney at Pittsburgh."

Another was not getting the head coaching job at Texas Tech: "They were afraid I didn't know how to recruit. Heck, there's nothing to that. You just get a mess of $100 bills. You get put on probation, then you win the Southwest Conference."

Layne indicated his highest salary was around $25,000. He also revealed that he never had a contract with Rooney, "Mr. Rooney paid my hotel bill and all my living expenses. It was a wonderful arrangement."

It also may have made Layne one of the highest paid players in history.

Layne took a weak stab at shooting down another much traveled story. Bobby had an accident and was hospitalized the night before his final football game.

Says Bobby, "You guys always made too much out of that. The team had a party for me, but I left early because there was a game the next day.

"I was driving through Pittsburgh when I was hit by a parked swerving streetcar."

It's been a ball and, at 55, Bobby still is living life to the limit.

"I hope I run out of breath and money at the same hour."
—BOBBY LAYNE

John Henry Johnson

John Henry Johnson's mere name evoked the most legendary steel man of them all. And there were times during his long career when Johnson played like he was immortal. Though the Steelers lost often during the years John Henry spent in Pittsburgh (1960–65), he was never a loser, and there were some defensive players who insisted that Johnson was as good a runner as Jim Brown. Like Brown, Johnson was the very prototype of the modern fullback. Big and strong, he was fast, ran with power, and unlike Brown, was an outstanding blocker. He gained over 4,000 rushing yards in five years for the Steelers, but what most of his opponents remembered was the pain he inflicted. Myron Cope, the dean of Pittsburgh sportswriters and a popular radio and television personality, probably knew the team and its players better than any other outsider and penned some of the most perceptive and entertaining pieces ever written about the sport. In the following piece, Myron Cope captured the essence of John Henry's style.

KISS THE GUY OR TACKLE HIM?

Myron Cope

John Henry Johnson is a large and aggressive professional fullback, who tends to break things when he runs. What does John Henry break? A cheek here, a skull there, a jawbone somewhere else. By the grudging admission of opposing linemen, John Henry Johnson is the most rugged all-around fullback in the whole rugged National Football League.

Linemen point out something further, often as they make a tackle. Pro football isn't a one-way street, and he who plays rough gets roughed himself, sometimes inordinately. The game is no place for a passivist nor, despite face masks, is it an area where one can safely turn the other cheek. It is a hard and unflinching sport, peopled mostly with hard and unflinching men. Hit them and they hit back.

Johnson plays hard for a variety of reasons, which we can consider presently. But for now consider an example of John Henry and the N.F.L.'s balance of power.

One Sunday afternoon in 1961 at the Los Angeles Coliseum, the Pittsburgh Steelers, for whom Johnson works, were playing against the

From *The Saturday Evening Post*, October 26, 1963. Reprinted by permission of Myron Cope.

Rams. Well, not playing so much as working. In the fourth quarter Johnson's forearm flashed before the face of Les Richter, the Los Angeles linebacker and captain. "Pop, my jaw was broken," Richter has since recalled.

So then, as always, John Henry—whose play had been perfectly legal—became a marked man, which is to say, the Los Angeles linemen were out to counterpunch, or counterforearm.

Then, unlike always, the Rams got an opportunity right away. A Pittsburgh Steeler pass was intercepted by the Rams Ed Meador, and Johnson ran Meador out of bounds, sprawling across the sidelines as he did. Prone, Johnson looked up to see four Rams running at him single file. He sprang to his feet, grabbed the pyramid-shaped sideline marker and began bashing it against the helmets of the Rams. John Henry survived.

Johnson stands 6-feet-2, weighs 225 pounds, and in his vast hands a football looks no larger than a cake of soap. Last year, at the ripe old age (for a fullback) of 33, he gained 1,141 yards in the National Football League, principally by running over 260-pound linemen. Lugging a football across an open field, he is at once exciting and hilarious to spectators, maddening and painful to tacklers.

He defines his own gait as "a combination of jitterbug, twist and Charleston, with a little rumba thrown in." Once he runs down the linemen, defensive backs charging him low are frequently embarrassed to discover that he has hurtled over them and fled, like a thief gone over the backyard fence.

Cleveland's Jimmy Brown runs hard and fast. So does Green Bay's Jim Taylor. But John Henry not only loves to run; he loves to block. Setting himself to protect his quarterback, Johnson crouches near the ground, his chin less than two feet above the grass. He joins clenched fists at his waist. As linemen drive in toward the passer, Johnson springs at them and, again perfectly legally, bats at them with his forearms. Blockees are scattered throughout the country. Scenes are implanted in the memory of beholders.

When John Henry was playing professional football in Canada, a rapid halfback named Bill Bewley was racing a kickoff up the sidelines during an intrasquad scrimmage. John Henry angled toward him, and Bewley tried to get inside the angle. John Henry block-tackled Bewley at full speed, breaking Bewley's jaw in two places.

"Jeez, John," screamed Bob Robinett, the team's general manager, "was that thing really necessary?"

"Well," John Henry said, matter-of-factly, "what did you want me to do? Kiss the guy, or tackle him?" (Bewley, on medical advice, retired from football.)

When John Henry was established in the National Football League, Ed Modzelewski, a brute of a man playing in the line at Cleveland, crashed through, hoping to block a punt. Instead of the football he ran into John Henry, who bloodied Modzelewski's mouth.

Paul Brown, then Cleveland coach, ran onto the field and shouted at Johnson, "You've hit everybody in the league."

"Then we got a tie game," John Henry retorted. "Everybody in the league has hit me."

Another afternoon Johnson blocked a New York Giant defensive back named Eddie Hughes, fracturing Hughes's cheekbone. "Hughes was real nice about it," John Henry recalls. "He told me 'good block' when I visited him in the hospital."

Johnson's aggressiveness is not always directed against opponents. In a game against the Giants last year he concluded that one of his teammates had cost the Steelers a touchdown by loitering on the one-yard line. "I ever see you do that again," John Henry said, "I'll kill you with my bare hands."

What manner of man is this, when he rips off his helmet, slips out of the jersey numbered 35 and becomes a civilian? Not quite a passivist perhaps, but seemingly peaceful and amusing. John Henry drinks sparingly, never smokes, enjoys conversation, good company and philosophy. Once, when a friend was courting a teenager, Johnson was at his conversational, philosophical best. "Man," he said, "they gonna put you in jail for stationary rape."

His Steeler teammates like him, appreciate his humor, intentional and accidental, and go to some lengths to explain that he is rough, but by no means dirty. "Everybody beats on him," says end Buddy Dial. "Sam Huff (the Giant linebacker) treats him like a dog." Another Steeler adds, "John Henry plays mean, but not dirty. It's a rough game and a lot of the guys play it rough, but they don't have that natural something—the timing or whatever it is—that John Henry has when he whips that shoulder into you."

Whence comes this dedication to such aggressive play? "They jump on me after the whistle," Johnson says, "and they tell me they couldn't stop. They try to snap my neck when I'm running, and if I'm on the ground, they're still choking me. They scratch my eyes—that kind of thing. All them things annoy me a little bit."

Just a Little Riot

Some try to probe more deeply. They maintain that Johnson is an angry man who gives vent to his fury through football. Further, they emphasize that he is an angry colored man, one of that growing body of Negroes who are not inclined to say "Thank you" when shoved. This is not to say that John Henry is anti-white. He has been a good friend of Southerner Bobby Layne, and attributes much of his success last season to the all-white line blocking for him. But, as one Steeler points out, "He reads every word of every integration story he can lay his hands on."

John Henry, agreeing in the slurred way that has earned him the nickname "Mumbles," recalls a game that his high school lost to an archrival. "I played bad," he says. "I cried after the game. I said, 'Next time we gonna beat them.' Next year I made three touchdowns against them and shook up a few people with the usual stuff. Made 'em complain. We didn't have a full-scale riot, just a little small-scale riot."

In the town of Pittsburg, Calif., where he spent his teens, he was an immensely popular football and track star in high school. But John Henry spent his earliest years in Louisiana, and Bob Robinett, who has known Johnson for years, suggests that his rough style of play has its source in his Louisiana elementary schooling. Robinett is today guidance counselor for California's Sequoia School District. "When John Henry came to California," he says, "he lacked proper elementary background, so studies came hard to him throughout high school. He applied himself and tried to become a good student. He was not a poor student. But he wanted to *excel*. And finally, knowing that he could not excel in the classroom, he decided he would on the ball field. That's why he's always played so ruggedly."

After high school, John Henry enrolled at St. Mary's, a California college that played almost anyone, almost anywhere. When St. Mary's abandoned football in 1951, Johnson switched to Arizona State, then moved on for pro football in Canada, where Robinett was general manager of the Calgary Stampeders. Canadian football differs from American football in various ways, among them that no one may block after a punt. The punt receiver stands there, naked in his pads, and as he grabs the ball, everyone grabs him. Canadian coaches frequently discipline troublesome players by assigning them to return punts.

As a collegian, Johnson had led the U.S. in punt returns, but the Calgary coach, Bob Snyder, wanted to preserve his fullback. "I didn't look forward to seeing those tanks coming down and murdering him," Snyder says, "but he kept after me to let him, and I finally put him in for a punt return in a game with Winnipeg. I could see mouths watering on the other side. When the punt came down, all of Canada belted him."

John Henry is durable. In the course of that season he suffered a fractured cheekbone, lost two teeth and endured two broken ribs. He also played both offense and defense in every one of the 23 games Calgary had scheduled.

In 1954 he signed with the San Francisco 49ers, and in a game against the Chicago Cardinals he fractured a rival back's skull with a clean but ferocious downfield block. The Cardinal management protested, but John Henry (a) insisted that he was only playing hard football and (b) that anyone who wanted to try for revenge was welcome to. Later, in another game with the Cardinals, he deliberately carried the ball in front of the Cardinal bench. The moment he was tackled, three Cardinals sprang from the bench to kick him.

Johnson, of course, answers such roughness with a roughness of his own. At times he has continued to churn his feet, even after he is tackled. As a result, piling on him has involved an element of peril—cleat marks in one's forehead.

John Henry has been a professional athlete for a long time. He has been married, fathered five children and been divorced. He has traveled, seen his name in headlines and walked abroad in an exciting world. The one thing he has not done is mellowed. He was born in the Louisiana hamlet of Waterproof, the son of a Pullman porter, and apparently always had most football instincts within him. He was a rough, natural child, and three decades later, he is a rough, natural man.

"When I was raised up," he says, "I played with white kids all the time. But whenever white kids bothered me, we *fought*. I didn't take nothing from anyone. In a football game, though, I hit the colored guy as hard as I hit the white guy, and I don't think about color when I'm playing." Then, in as close to self-analysis as he cares to come, "But it might be a subconscious thing. I've always felt I was as good as anyone else, that's for sure."

Well, he's an athlete, not a parliamentarian or a judge, so his role in the Negro revolution will be no more than a footnote. Perhaps it is best to conclude simply, as one Steeler does, "The rougher they get with John Henry, the rougher he gets with them." Still, one cannot forget another comment uttered by a burly Steeler lineman. "If I had to go into a dark alley," he says, "and I had my pick of one man to go with me, I'd want that man to be John Henry Johnson."

Big Daddy

When Gene Allen "Big Daddy" Lipscomb was eleven years old his mother was stabbed to death by her lover. From then on Gene learned a lot about pain. His grandparents mistreated him, he began to do a man's work in his early teens, he dropped out of school at the age of sixteen, and he signed on with the Marines. But he grew big and strong and surprisingly quick, as natural a defensive lineman as one could find. He is best remembered as an All-Pro member of the championship Baltimore Colts of the late 1950s. In 1961 the Colts traded him to the Steelers, but by then his best playing days were behind him. He lived fast, and often out of control. He drank too much, slept too little, and generally abused his body. In this lyrical article, Edward Linn tried to make sense of Big Daddy's death, and discovered a Greek tragedy in his short life.

THE SAD END OF
BIG DADDY LIPSCOMB

Edward Linn

> John Henry told the Captain,
> "A man ain't nothin' but a man,
> and if I don't beat your steam drill down,
> I'll die with a hammer in my hand,
> Lawd, Lawd,
> I'll die with a hammer in my hand."

John Henry, as any folk singer worthy of his union card can tell you, was a legendary Negro giant who hammered himself into the grave, gloriously, because he was unwilling to live in a world where the machine took the place of nature's muscle and sweat.

Eugene (Big Daddy) Lipscomb was a fun-loving Negro giant who really lived. He was so great and so colorful a football player that he had become almost legendary himself before he died, ingloriously, on May 10, 1963, at the age of 32. According to official records he died of acute heroin poisoning, accidentally, but by his own hand. Daddy lived

From *The Saturday Evening Post*, July 27, 1963. Reprinted with permission of *The Saturday Evening Post* © 1963 BFL & MS, Inc.

grandly, but he died bad. Which proves again that, one way or another, the world has its ways for grinding down the man of muscle and sweat.

> I tell you something true as life,
> And, Big Daddy, you better be believin';
> You lay that needle down right now,
> Or your friends will all be grievin';
> You lay that needle down, boy,
> Or your women will be grievin'.

What the official report omits is that none of Big Daddy's friends, none of the thousands who mobbed his funeral, are willing to believe that he could have stuck a needle into his vein of his own free will, even though the alternative is, if not unthinkable, certainly improbable and unprovable. "Whiskey and women, yes," they say to a man. "But drugs, never."

"I'm a B and B man," Daddy liked to boast. "Booze and broads." And his capacity to handle both was one of the wonders of the civilized world.

Big Daddy worked hard on a football field, and when the game was done, it was time to get around some and have a little fun. "Let's go out and get me a jug," he'd say. "Let's have a taste." A jug to Gene Lipscomb was a fifth of whiskey and he could throw down the fifth the way you or I would throw down a beer.

To no small extent, Gene made himself up. He got his nickname during his early years with the Los Angeles Rams when he was better known for rough, dirty playing than for ability. He took to calling everybody "Little Daddy," which—since he stood six feet six and weighed 285—was a sly way of inviting them to call him "Big Daddy" in return.

It wasn't until Baltimore bought him in 1956 for $100 on waivers that Eugene Lipscomb became "Big Daddy" for real. On the field he wore his uniform sloppily, his pants drooping, his shirttail flapping. He had tremendous speed for a man his size. He was so fast that he could beat almost any halfback in a 50-yard dash. Generally two or three rival linemen were given the assignment of keeping Big Daddy off the passer. The Cleveland Browns usually set four men to harass him. In Baltimore Big Daddy led the Colts to two successive championships.

One of Lipscomb's favorite tricks was to let a blocker make contact with him so that the ballcarrier would be encouraged to skirt him. Then, he'd flip the blocker away and run down the ballcarrier. "Where you going, little man?" he'd say, as he clubbed his arms around him. "This is Big Daddy, and once Big D puts the clamps on you, you're dead."

His real delight, though, was to burst in, his shirttail flying, and flatten a passer.

> Little passer, you better be nimble,
> Little passer, you better pray,
> 'Cause if you get in Big Daddy's way,
> Tomorrow will be yo' burying day,
> Lawd, Lawd,
> Tomorrow will be yo' burying day.

In case he hadn't made his presence known to everybody in the park, he'd linger for another moment to pick up the passer and carefully brush him off. And the smaller the passer, the longer Daddy would linger. With that sure instinct for the dramatic, he was the first professional lineman to take the play away from the backs and become a personality himself.

Off the field he dressed for effect, except here he was dressed not to maim but to kill. Well, when Big Daddy came swinging into a bar with that easy dancing step of his, you could hardly keep from noticing him, what with a diamond ring on his little finger, a white silk shirt like a rock 'n' roll singer, a tie so red that it threw off heat and alligator shoes that crawled right on his feet. And didn't Big D always look pretty grand in that small-brimmed hat with a feather in the band?

> And Daddy would twist to that driving beat
> Till he danced those chicks right off their feet . . .

"Gene didn't need to take drugs for kicks," his cousin Walt Chattman, himself a pro football player with the Philadelphia Eagles, says. "Being Big Daddy was all the kicks he ever needed."

His appetites were gargantuan and insatiable. A typical breakfast consisted of a dozen eggs and a pound of bacon, washed down by a pint of booze. Having learned to cook in the Marine Corps, he would make huge meals, run to the bathroom and throw up halfway through, then come back and finish off the food.

His fondness for variety in women cost him three marriages, as he freely admitted. His favorite story was about the time he passed underneath the room of one of his teammates, just before they were to play an exhibition game in Texas, and caught the echo of a soft and sibilant sigh. Daddy shot up the stairs with a mighty roar, while his teammate, showing quick reflexes, slammed shut the door and tossed the girl into the closet.

Well, now, Daddy went poking around, sniffing at the air until his eyes reached the keyhole and stopped right there. As he always said, and he didn't lie, "All I seen looking back at me was one big eye."

Big Daddy stepped back and Big Daddy was smiling. "Big Daddy is here," Big Daddy cried.

Well, Daddy had a lot of women chasing after him, a lot of the time, and he was never known to run the other way.

Drugs take away a man's appetite for liquor and women both, and that's one reason, his friends tell you, the official story of his death just can't be true. What makes it even more ridiculous, they tell you, is that Gene had escaped from the streets of Detroit, at the age of 16, by joining the Marines. He never knew his father, who died in a CCC camp. When Gene was 11, a plainclothesman came to the house, put his arm around his shoulder and told him his mother had been stabbed 47 times by a boyfriend while she was waiting on a street corner for a bus. Gene was reared in Detroit by his maternal grandfather, who tried to keep him from running wild. Gene rarely talked about those early days, but he would occasionally tell how his grandfather had once tied him to a bedpost and whipped him as punishment for stealing the old man's whiskey. Even here, though, he would tell the story with affection, as if he were trying to show that someone had cared enough about him to go to all that trouble.

Signed out of the Marines by the Los Angeles Rams, he was one of the few pro football players without a college education, a condition that always bothered him. Still, he had a quick, if profane, wit, and after he became so famous and popular, under his magic "Big Daddy" cloak, he would grin and say, "When we're on a football field, man, I got a degree too."

He knew what he had escaped from, and he had a peculiar, all-encompassing phrase for it: "the scum." The phrase, for him, covered the whole condition of the ghetto-ized Negro: the slum itself with its dirt and its crime, plus all of its human oozings—the junkies, the hustlers, the pimps and the bums. He would walk through the worst sections of the cities with his closer friends and he would say, "Doesn't it make you feel great to be able to walk through here like a king, with your head held high?"

Buddy Young, the old Illinois All-American, who became Gene's tutor and conscience, says: "If somebody told me Lipscomb died in an automobile accident or in a fight over a woman, I'd believe it. If it had happened when he first came to Baltimore, a hoodlum and a thug, I'd have believed it. But Gene had grown out of hiding and had come face to face with reality. A man doesn't take away from himself the one thing he has to offer, his ability to play football. Football was his past, present and future, and nobody knew that more than Gene. He knew what his image was, because he himself had made it himself. He wouldn't destroy that with drugs."

Gene was so jealous of that image that he quit the wrestling circuit when he was asked to become a villain. "That ain't Big Daddy," he said.

It has fallen to Buddy Young to protect that image and to protect it, curiously enough, against a man he has never seen, a man as different from himself as any other man could possibly be.

Young, who is now a Baltimore radio executive, exudes good will and sincerity and, if the word isn't too embarrassing, goodness. He has the solidity and conservatism of the self-made man. He can use words and expressions which would sound unbearably pretentious coming from someone else. ("I was often reminding him of his responsibility as a professional football player to be conscious of his actions, of refraining from expressing himself with vituperativeness.")

Buddy Young made himself a sort of den father for a group of Baltimore players, including Daddy, tackle Jim Parker, wingback Lenny Moore and defensive back Sherman Plunkett. Daddy lived with Plunkett in the tree-shaded, middle-class Hanlon Park section of Ashburton, not far from Buddy Young's own home, although Daddy had been traded to Pittsburgh and Plunkett to San Diego of the American Football League.

But still, the Baltimore writers who were closest to Daddy knew that he would grow uneasy around the businessmen Young tried to surround him with, and that, from time to time, he would feel the need to cut out to the "back of town" district where he felt more at home. It was at the Uptown Bar in the "back of town" that he first ran into Timothy Black, the man who saw Big Daddy die.

Timmy Black, 27, is a slim, sparrowy man who came to Baltimore from the South 17 years ago, his left leg withered from a boyhood attack of polio. Even more than Lipscomb and Young, he is a man of his time and his place. His place is in the slums Daddy escaped from. His time stretches back a hundred years.

He is, admittedly, a man who would do his best to get you liquor, women or drugs according to your taste—the functions, he says, he served for Big Daddy. He has, he admits, been in jail, although he balks at revealing the charges. At first glance he seems to be a shy, mumbling, naïve man, soft of voice, quick with deference, apologies and respect. He has a delicacy of language that leads him to refer to the women he has dealings with as "young ladies" and "lady friends."

Survival in the Jungle

"Daddy and I weren't friends," he says, correcting you quietly, as if he is a man who has accepted his curious uses in life. But people close to Timmy Black call him "Hap," and every now and then you see the features shift a little under the slight tilt of his summer straw hat, and you catch a fleeting glimpse of another man underneath, the man who has committed himself to whatever he has to be to survive in his jungle. He is, too, a man with a sick and pregnant wife. Four months ago he got himself a job on the assembly line of a bottling company, a job he still holds.

When Black tells the story of Big Daddy's death, he leaves the impression that it was Daddy who wouldn't let him alone. According to Black, Lipscomb first asked him to get him a "deck" of heroin about six months ago, right after the end of the football season. "No," Black says, not volunteering the information but only answering the question, "he didn't act like it was the first time."

From then on, says Black, Daddy was taking heroin on the average of three times a week, the last time only two or three days before his death. Once, Black says, Daddy even "shot" himself in his car. "All it takes is a whiskey cap to put the stuff in, and a match to boil it up."

Impossible, say Daddy's friends. "He would come to the house never less than three times a week," Young says. "Walk through the door—I can see him now bending his head to get through—and he'd always call out to my wife, 'Hello, Sweetie-cakes. Here's the Daddy.' He couldn't have walked in here and faced me, because I would have known it. He couldn't have lived with Plunkett, day in and day out, and not have him know."

Big Daddy's third wife, Cecilia, who lived only a block away from him, is equally incredulous. "He could never have put a needle in himself," she says. "He was terrified of pain. He got a splinter in the bottom of his foot one time, and the way he carried on you'd have thought he'd lost the leg. He wouldn't even let the dentist pull a tooth without my sitting in his lap. I saw him three or four times a week, and he never could hide too much from me. I could read him like a book."

Young last saw Lipscomb on Wednesday, May 8, a burning hot morning two days before Daddy died. Daddy had come to see him at station WEBB and waited outside until Young got off the air. "He was in brown khaki pants and blue *sleeveless* sport shirt. It was one in which he had torn the sleeves off. His shirttail was out, and he was wearing a pair of—what would you call them?—shower shoes."

Daddy wanted to tell Young he was going to drive to Pittsburgh on Friday morning to sign his contract. Daddy had never made more than $14,000 a year, and he intended to ask for a two-year contract at $15,000 a year, the figure he had always looked upon as the ultimate goal. He had called Buddy Parker, the Steelers' coach, to ask if he'd have trouble getting the raise. He also asked Dan Rooney, a Steelers publicity man, to send him $500 "to meet an insurance payment on my car," the first time he had ever asked the Steelers for an advance.

On Thursday morning he cashed the $500 check at the Union Trust Bank. "Besides the money from Pittsburgh," Buddy Young says, "he had $400 that I know of. He put $200 in his checking account and paid two small bills that came to $40. That means he went out on Thursday with more than $600 in his pocket. Find out what happened to that and you'll know why Daddy is dead."

If there was one thing Gene liked as much as football, it was pitching softball. He played in a doubleheader that evening, and, after the games were over, took a couple of the boys from his team to have some drinks. "When Daddy had a lot of money on him, he'd take his wallet and lock it in the trunk of his car. I talked to the players he was with that night, and before he went into the bar, he locked the wallet in the trunk."

Daddy had another odd habit. Before he was to go on a motor trip, he would always stay up all night. When they were leaving the bar, around 11 o'clock, he asked one of the softball players to double-date with him, but the man already had a date. "If only that guy had been free," Young says, "Daddy would be alive today."

Timmy Black, the sparrow, worked late that night at the bottling plant and didn't get home until eight. After dinner, as was his custom, he went to the Uptown Bar. "I was outside on the corner of Monroe and Edmondson most of the time," Black says. "A guy came by who lived on the next street to me, and I asked if he could drive me home.

But he wasn't going home; he was going the other way. If I'd only went home like I asked to, I wouldn't be in the trouble I'm in today."

Around midnight, Black says, Daddy came by in his big yellow Cadillac convertible—there was another fellow with him—and called him over. "I had an idea he wanted heroin, figuring I might know where to get it, but he didn't say anything about it then, because he didn't want everybody to know."

As soon as Daddy dropped his passenger, presumably one of the softball players, he and Black headed out in search of heroin. Instead, Black says, they ran into two young ladies. Then they bought a six-pack of Country Club, a malt beverage, and took the girls to Black's apartment. At three A.M. the young ladies asked to be taken home. At some time after three o'clock, then, Daddy, according to Black, asked, "You still think you can get down?"

Black could try. "Daddy drove to Pennsylvania Avenue on 'The Block' [Baltimore's large strip-joint center]. We parked near the corner where we could be seen. There was a fellow right up the street in front of a restaurant, just a few yards away. Daddy gave me the money to get down for him and I bought a twelve-dollar bag." A "$12 bag" contains enough heroin for two or three users.

And now Daddy drove back to Black's apartment, at 434 North Brice Street, and from this point on all his movements take on that heavy finality that comes when you know in advance that all of the thoughtless, everyday actions are the last he will ever make.

North Brice Street is small and narrow, little wider than an alley, really, and less than 100 yards long. On either side of the street there is one low, flat continuous row of connected apartment houses, constructed of light brown brick. It is a neighborhood with a reputation second to none for teen-age addicts.

Black's apartment was on the second floor. Daddy walked up a single flight of stairs, so narrow that he must have filled it completely, like a big ship squeezed into a small berth. When he reached the top of the staircase, he was also in the apartment, the bathroom a step ahead, the kitchen ahead to the right.

It was a small kitchen, painted yellow, dominated by a large table against the near wall. Across from the table were a refrigerator and a small stove. At the head of the room, alongside the door leading to the back porch, was an old-fashioned radiator. Overhead hung a bare bulb. A man Daddy's size would have difficulty moving through the open space without bumping something.

It was in such an apartment that Gene Lipscomb lived out his early days in Detroit. It was as if, at the end, the "scum" had reached out to bring Daddy home.

The heroin was cooked up in a wine cap and sucked into a homemade syringe, with a piece of paper providing the neck where the needle and the syringe joined. Daddy, says Black, "shot" himself first and then handed the needle over to him so he could "shoot" himself too.

Heroin is not a stimulant but a depressant. After the first shock it sends the user into a "nod," a sort of semiconscious daydream in which the user sees himself living out the life he would like to be leading. Black's first warning that something had gone wrong, he says, came when Daddy's lips began to vibrate rapidly. Little rivers of foam formed at the sides of his mouth. Black, roused by fear, went to the refrigerator for some ice to press on the top of Daddy's head and underneath his testicles.

At this point, says Black, a third man, Robert Waters, came into the apartment, put a solution of salt water into the syringe and shot it into Daddy's arm, an old-wives' antidote which possibly has some value, though not very much.

When Daddy still failed to come around, Black says, he told Waters to go out and phone for an ambulance. The call was made at about 7:15 A.M.

After Waters left, Black tried to revive Daddy by slapping him across the face. That only served to bring about the final indignity, as Daddy toppled off the chair and fell to the floor, face down upon the worn linoleum.

The police arrived first, followed shortly by an ambulance. Black handed the police Daddy's car keys and $73. "I knew the ambulance would take him away," Black explains, "and, you know, I took it out of his wallet to protect it."

Big Daddy Lipscomb was still breathing when he was carried out to the ambulance to be rushed to Lutheran Hospital. He was DOA— dead on arrival.

"We split the bag in half," Black insists. "I took the same half he did and it didn't kill me. But he was drinking in the bedroom with the young lady and I didn't know it. If I had known . . ."

It is true that alcohol "potentiates" the effect of drugs. But Daddy had not been drinking that much. The autopsy showed the alcoholic content of his blood to be .09 percent. The intoxication level that most states set for their drivers' test is .15 percent. Daddy's drinking through the years did have its effect, though. The autopsy also showed that his liver was somewhat damaged. Since detoxification takes place in the liver, the heroin remained in his system longer than normal.

The autopsy was performed by the assistant medical examiner of Baltimore, Dr. Rudiger Breitnecker. As he explains, it is not the heroin itself that does the damage, because heroin breaks down immediately upon injection. One of the main degradation products is morphine, and morphine is the killer. Daddy had about 10 milligrams of morphine per 100 cubic centimeters of bile, which would correspond to 11.3 milligrams of heroin.

When morphine is used therapeutically, it would be rare for more than a two-milligram dosage to be prescribed. In other words, Daddy's body contained *more than five times* what might normally be considered a safe dosage. "Any dose would have a more serious effect on a beginner," Doctor Breitnecker says, "but, speaking generally, ten percent is a lethal amount. It would take a hardened addict to survive ten percent."

The question that arises, of course, is whether there is any medical evidence that Daddy had ever taken drugs before.

There isn't. A needle mark, as anyone who has ever taken a simple blood test knows, heals completely within a couple of days.

Doctor Breitnecker did find "at least" four needle marks that were only two to four hours old. ("If that's true," Black says, "then three of them would have to be the salt-water injections. He only took one shot of heroin.")

In the course of the autopsy, Doctor Breitnecker also took one very small, very thick slice of skin from the inside of the elbow and, by the use of dyes and high magnification, came across an old needle mark, which was still identifiable only because a small fiber, which seemed to be cotton, was lodged in the puncture. Most addicts filter the cooked solution through cotton or bread as they suck it up into the syringe. Still, one needle mark is just like any other, and no man would be foolish enough to state that a piece of fiber couldn't have become lodged in any hypodermic needle, used for any kind of shot.

And so, while nothing Black says is inconsistent with the findings of the autopsy, it is true that nothing Daddy's friends say is inconsistent either. "There is hardly evidence to call him an addict,"

Doctor Breitnecker says. "We cannot, as a matter of fact, say positively that he ever took more than one shot of heroin in his life." The diagnosis, for the record, is that he died of acute heroine poisoning.

The key question, in the fight to save Daddy's reputation, is whether he could have been knocked out before the heroin was put into his system. To this, at least, Doctor Breitnecker can give a flat reply. "My answer to these attempts by a loyal public to explain away the fact that Big Daddy did take heroin, at this time, of his own free will, is that our tests showed that he was not under any sedative, that he was not intoxicated and that there was not a scratch on him of any kind.

But Daddy's defenders still make out their case. Robby Waters is hardly the passing stranger Black tried, at first, to make him out to be. In their statement to the police, the two young ladies had Waters getting into Lipscomb's car, taking the wheel to drive them to the apartment, and then returning from time to time while they were still there.

What gripes Daddy's friends is that there is only Black's story of the last hours. "Who is this man Black?" Buddy Young asks. "None of Daddy's friends ever saw him or heard of him."

Black was held, at first, on a charge of involuntary homicide, but it was quickly changed to mere possession of narcotics paraphernalia. The original bail of $10,000 was reduced to $3,000.

Black is not an addict. He has not used any narcotics, he insists, since the night of Daddy's death. He is a married man and he has a job. There seems little doubt that when his case comes to court he will be placed on probation.

Black faces the unasked question in his own indirect way. "I was the one who told Robby Waters to call the ambulance," he says. "I didn't want to take Daddy out and throw him in an alley. Right today you pick up the paper and find [people who] die on steps or in an alley. I was frightened. Seeing that happen to Daddy was the worst thing that ever happened to me. I liked Big Daddy."

To which Buddy Young replies, "Nobody knows what happened in that room before the police were called. Nobody knows who was in the room or how long it took to call the police.

"Gene Lipscomb had a soul, he had faith, and I'd walk with him all the rest of my life without believing that he was an addict. I know you can never tell what a person will do, but Daddy wasn't Marilyn Monroe out to commit suicide. He was at the summit of his career, he had come to the place he wanted to be. He knew how big he was."

And then, Buddy Young smiled, and the legend of Big Daddy had taken over again. "He'd have liked to have seen the crowd he drew at his funeral. I could hear him saying, 'See, Young. See, Little Man. You never knew how big Big Daddy really was, did you?'"

> Don't weep for me, Little Daddy,
> Don't bother with no prayer;
> I don't want to go to heaven
> Unless they swing up there.
> Don't take me up to heaven, please, Lawd
> 'Less there's kicks and chicks there.

Hope sprang eternal in Pittsburgh during the early 1960s. Head Coach Buddy Parker kept his team around the .500 mark, and next season always seemed like it would be the Steelers' breakout year. The squad's beer-swilling, uncultured, hard-knock image only made it more endearing to its rugged, blue-collar home town. Here, Myron Cope, in his own unique style, reveled in the team's tough-guy ethos and suggested that winning is not always as important as having fun.

THE STEELERS: PRO FOOTBALL'S GASHOUSE GANG

Myron Cope

Contrary to general belief it was not Y. A. Tittle's passing arm that hoisted the New York Giants to the Eastern Division title of the National Football League in 1963. There is sound reason to believe that the Eastern race was, in fact, decided by a Pittsburgh quarterback's impetuous decision to go on the wagon.

That is precisely what Ed Brown did. On the final day of the 1963 season the Steelers played the Giants in New York, winner-take-the-money. The Giants led the standings by percentage points, but the Steelers, who earlier in the season had humiliated them, 31-0, needed only to win this game to become Eastern champions. To the utter dismay of those who know their Steelers best, quarterback Brown, a strapping former marine buck sergeant, took the big game too seriously. On the Wednesday preceding the showdown battle, he disappeared from his favorite saloon. He went into training.

Now Brownie is not the kind of guy who has to dry out before a game. On the contrary, he is rather a high-class drinker, favoring liquid ensembles—for example, Scotch whiskey on crushed ice with a thin layer of Drambuie added. He has black hair, a chiseled jaw, and broad shoulders and he is a bachelor who can name all the good songs from Armstrong to Kenton. So it is not in his nature to lock himself in a room.

Moreover, although his intentions were good when he decided to train for the big game, he contravened the very motto that had carried

From *True*, September 1964. Reprinted by permission of Myron Cope.

the Steelers to the brink of the title: "Stay loose." He vanished from the nocturnal stomping grounds of his teammates.

Brownie's defection went unnoticed amid the general hilarity with which other Steelers approached the crucial contest. Indeed, the New York press, covering the Steelers' and Giants' workouts in Yankee Stadium the day before the game, was startled by the contrasting attitudes of the two clubs. The Giants appeared grim, high-strung. The Steelers crackled with noisy confidence, tickled by the prospect of kicking the daylights out of all those New York players who pose for Madison Avenue's shirt ads—and then celebrating their victory up and down Broadway.

Sunday came up cold and wet. The field was a great pigpen of mud. But our Steelers—and I say "our" Steelers because I have been privileged over the past few years to spend many a robust evening with the boys—were undeterred. Our pass receivers galloped ebulliently through the slop, leaving New York's defensive backs flat on their muddied faces. Our boys held their hands aloft and yelled, "Here I am, Brownie! Put 'er here."

But Brownie did not put her there.

He threw long yards beyond his receivers. His body well rested, his insides dry as a temperance union president's, his head disgustingly clear, he totally lost his timing and sangfroid. Time and again he overthrew receivers who had no one between them and the goal line. In short, Brownie had trained himself into the most miserable performance of his career. Thus were the Giants able to win the Eastern title.

Now the 1964 football season is at hand. NFL title races being the dogfights they usually are, it is impossible to venture where the Steelers will finish. But red-blooded men must make Pittsburgh their sentimental choice, because in an age of prissy, image-conscious athletes who slip through back doors to do their boistering, the Steelers are men's men. They have refused to resign from the male sex.

"I call them the Gashouse Gang," says Jimmy Brown, the Cleveland halfback. "I hear their coach puts beer on their bus."

"But when you've played against them," Jimmy Brown adds, "your body is sore for days. They leave you black and blue."

That is how they play the game—like cowhands just come off the trail—and their coach, Buddy Parker, does not fret over the fact that they do not wear neckties in public. Parker has been through the mill.

He demands only that his players win; he will deal a losing player if he can get 5 cents on the dollar.

You get a fair idea what the Steelers are like when you see Mike Sandusky, a tubby offensive guard, chug before the TV cameras during the pregame introductions. Already his shirttail is out. He looks like a hoodlum. At the team's annual bowling banquet last season, Sandusky was presented with a trophy designating him "the best-dressed bowler." Ray Lemek, a piano-shaped guard, was moved to remark, "Sandusky is the only man in America who feels well dressed in Texaco pants and a T-shirt."

Nevertheless, Sandusky typifies Pittsburgh's savage offensive line. With the glaring exception of tackle Charley Bradshaw, a 6-foot-6 Texan who has a face like [former Vice President] John Nance Garner's, the line mostly resembles a collection of hot-water boilers. You can best grasp its style of play by knowing that in the offseason Sandusky is a saloonkeeper, center Buzz Nutter is a beer salesman, and fat-boy tackle Dan James is a collector for a finance company. "If you want to punch him," says Buff Boston, a Steeler front-office man who frequently bends an elbow with the help, "the finance company dares you."

It suits Buddy Parker that his ball-carriers are blasters, not sneaky speed merchants. Sneers Parker, "Those fast backs go 70 yards once in a while, but they don't want contact."

Old John Henry Johnson, to name one Steeler back, has so strong a penchant for contact that a few years ago it almost resulted in his being awarded a cement bathing suit by the Chicago branch of the Cosa Nostra. Playing against the Chicago Cardinals in 1955, John Henry roared downfield and hit Charley Trippi with a ferocious blindside block. Trippi's skull was fractured. Two plastic surgery jobs were required to put his face back together. Surgeons had to remove one of his ribs to obtain new cartilage for his nose, parts of which had been left on the playing field.

"Which side of the river you want him fished up from?" Trippi was asked by Chicago fans wearing pearl-gray fedoras.

Fortunately, Trippi insisted John Henry be left alone. "I didn't think it would be in the best interests of professional football," he explains. Trippi's teammates, however, resolved to fix John Henry's wagon in their next meeting, but John Henry quickly let them know he doesn't frighten. He deliberately ran the ball past the Cardinals' bench, inviting them to start a hey-rube. All that happened was that two Cardinals leaped off the bench and kicked him.

No man, however, reflects the essence of the Steelers so much as Ernie Stautner, who doubles as assistant coach and emergency defensive end. Martini for martini, this may be the toughest man ever to play in the NFL.

Stautner may be 39 or 42 or ready for Social Security—it is hard to say, because the records are in Bavaria, where he was born. Note, though, that he fought in the Borneo and Okinawa campaigns even before he went to college. His face, emerging directly from his shoulder without the benefit of a neck, is about as pretty as an auto accident. His philosophy is simple, if chilling: "You got to be a man who wants to hurt somebody. You know where I'm going for? The quarterback's face. It hurts in the face. I want him to know I'm coming the next time. I want him to be scared. Those quarterbacks can't tell me they don't scare, because I've seen it in the corners of their eyes."

Stautner's 15 seasons of pro football are a testimonial to good gin. Not long ago Stautner and a journalist—this journalist, unfortunately—frightened acquaintances by drinking martinis from 5 P.M. till 1 A.M. At noon of the next day, as I lay abed writhing, my telephone rang.

"Hey, dad, you gonna make the scene with me today?" demanded Stautner, fresh as a laundered shirt.

As the reader well may have surmised, Steelers management is a tolerant sort. (Tolerant? Good Lord, the club's official program relates with undisguised glee an occasion when Stautner beat the blazes out of a troublemaker in [an] alley fight.) Club owner Art (The Prez) Rooney—a chunky, beloved Irishman who has a great shock of iron-gray hair atop a ruddy face that clenches a one-dollar cigar—got into the football business 31 years ago because he figured it would be fun. An ex-carnival fighter who made his fortune betting horses, Rooney is depressed to see lawyers overrunning the NFL front offices these days. More to the point, however, The Prez has an easygoing nature that rules out dictatorial methods. At a recent testimonial dinner in his honor, he told a vast audience of Rooney-lovers (ranging from high clergymen to Toots Shor) a story that nicely describes his modus operandi.

"A few years ago," stated The Prez, "I had a coach named Walt Kiesling, who started every game the same way—he sent his fullback into the middle of the line on the first play. The fullback was a little guy named Fran Rogel, and after a while the fans began to chant, 'Hi, diddle, diddle! Rogel up the middle!' It got pretty bad.

"So finally I went to Kiesling and said, 'Listen, Kies. This week I want you to throw a pass on the first play. Don't argue with me. That's an order.'" Kiesling obeyed. On the first play a rangy end named Goose McClairen loped downfield, snatched a pass, and romped to a touchdown. But the touchdown was nullified because a Steeler lineman had lurched offside. "I found out later," said The Prez, continuing his account, "that Kies had ordered that lineman to go offside. Kies told the players, 'If this pass play works, that Rooney will be down here every week giving us plays.' Gentlemen, that was the first and last time I ever tried to send in a play."

In 1964 the New York Giants drafted kicker Frank Lambert out of the University of Mississippi and promptly made him the highest paid punter in the NFL. But his career as a Giant was badly abbreviated when, with only two weeks remaining in the pre-season, Coach Allie Sherman traded him to the Pittsburgh Steelers. For Lambert, this trade was akin to being sent to Siberia—like trading in his new Cadillac for a used Corvair. As he later said, he went from the Big Apple Giants, where—despite a losing record—everything was first class, to the pre-Renaissance Steelers, where everyone was a bit long in the tooth. But in the few years he played for the Steelers he developed an offbeat admiration for the coaches and especially the players on the team. During the week he learned the team lore from his fellow players, and battling with them on Sundays he discovered the heart of the Pittsburgh Steelers. They won a few games, lost more, but always put up a good fight. After Lambert departed the Steelers on good terms, he became a successful businessman, professor, and author of books on American religion.

REFLECTIONS ON THE PRE-RENAISSANCE STEELERS

Frank Lambert

What I knew about the Steelers as a team I had learned primarily from the press. In its inaugural season in the NFL, Pittsburgh had finished last in the Eastern Division with a 3-6-2 record, trailing teams that sounded like they belonged in major league baseball: the New York Giants, Brooklyn Dodgers, and Boston Braves. The Steelers fared little better in recent history, managing winning records in only four of the last fifteen seasons ending in 1964. Firmly established at or near the bottom of their division, the team had never won a division or league championship. In the season before I arrived, the Steelers finished sixth in the Eastern Division, above only the hapless Giants.

From all accounts the 1965 Steelers looked to a sure bet to continue their losing tradition. *Sports Illustrated* picked the team to finish last in the Eastern Division. Veteran NFL sportswriter Tex Maule offered

From *Pittsburgh Sports: Stories from the Steel City*, edited by Randy Roberts (Pittsburgh: University of Pittsburgh Press, 2000).

a preseason analysis of winners and losers. Describing the Green Bay Packers, his choice to win the Western Division and Pittsburgh's opening day opponent, Maule emphasized coach Vince Lombardi's youth movement. Explaining why it had taken a couple of years to revitalize the Packers, Maule wrote, "Lombardi needed time to pump plasma into what was obviously a team operating on tired old blood." On the 1965 team "no less than half the 40-player squad will be men with less than four years' service in the NFL." By contrast, Buddy Parker, the Steelers' "ingenious coach, tries to fill his player needs with sleepers, discards, and trades." Maule observed that Pittsburgh, "often a contender but never a champion, puts no great store in high priced draft choices."

At no position was the point more obvious than at quarterback. The Steelers would open the season again with Ed Brown, the former Bear who in 1964 finished fourteenth among the NFL passers (there were fourteen teams) and had the highest percentage of interceptions. Parker's defense of his decision to start Brown served only to underscore additional weaknesses. The coach explained that "we didn't have the receivers," and Maule added that "rushers often poured through the middle of the Steeler line." Defense was the one bright spot. Perhaps remembering the cover of *Sports Illustrated* featuring a mud- and blood-splattered Y. A. Tittle on his knees after being sacked by Pittsburgh end John Baker, Maule noted that "the Steelers hit and hurt, even when they appear to be badly handicapped."

Coach Parker's assessment was even harsher. Before quitting or being fired one week before the 1965 regular season opened, whichever the case may have been, the head coach walked away, declaring, "I can't win with this bunch of stiffs." As the season unfolded, Parker appeared to be an astute prognosticator, but as much because of injuries as lack of talent. When Bill Nelson, a gifted passer who would later lead the Browns to championships, took over for the aging Ed Brown, he played on battered knees that "made him a sitting duck for every pass-rusher." And our running attack was stymied by the loss of John Henry Johnson, who also suffered from a bad knee.

While banged up and performing poorly, the Steelers were at least colorful. Like the city they represented, the 1965 squad was a diverse lot. We came from every region. The forty players on the roster came from thirty-two colleges in twenty-two states. About two-thirds attended colleges located east of the Mississippi River, and half from schools located on either side of the Mason-Dixon line, extended in the West by the Missouri Compromise line. Thirty-two guys were white and eight were black.

We were a melting pot of ethnic and religious backgrounds. Many of us were newcomers, either arriving to our first Steelers training camp as rookies or via a trade from another team. Altogether twenty-two of us had been in the league less than five years. Others were grizzled veterans like John Henry Johnson, John Baker, Ed Brown, Charlie Bradshaw, and Mike Sandusky.

Off the field, we came from many walks of life and few considered football much more than a brief stop before accepting a more traditional job. Bradshaw was a lawyer, the only attorney in the NFL at the time. Andy Russell held an MBA and looked forward to a successful business career. Ray Mansfield, an English major in college, talked about teaching. Ken Kortas determined to make his fortune while he played. Hailing from Chicago, home of the Commodities Exchange, Ken speculated in the futures markets. He regaled us with exotic tales of the risks and relative merits of corn and pork-belly futures. As the 1965 season came to an end, he informed us that he was seeking more direct profits in hogs. He planned to open a huge hog operation in Missouri, certain of quick, eye-popping profits from animals noted for their prolific breeding and large litters. He left for the off-season talking loud, walking tall, and brimming with optimism. A humbler Ken returned to training camp in 1966. I asked Ken about his porcine enterprise. With a snort resembling that of the animals he raised, he launched into a tirade against the beasts. "You cannot conceive of all the things that can go wrong with hogs," he replied. He then told us of diseases and deformities on the farm and rising costs and falling prices in the marketplace that personally conspired against *his* project. With the new season just weeks away, dejected ex-hog farmer Ken Kortas, wiser though poorer, once again prepared his own 300-pound hulk for rooting out quarterbacks.

The 1965 Steelers also were interested in a wide range of avocations. Many of the guys got caught up in a craze that year: racing little cars guided by remote control. It was quite a sight to see several enormous guys bent over, operating tiny cars flying around a miniature oval and cheering them on with an enthusiasm that increased in direct proportion to the consumption of beer. My own interests took another direction. I happened to enjoy reading, and throughout training camp read a great deal when not at practice or in meetings. At the time I was slowly working my way through the works of the nineteenth-century Russian novelist Fyodor Dostoevsky.

My pastime genuinely perplexed my roommate, a veteran line-backer. A great storyteller and beer drinker, he was frequently at the center of the many bull sessions that players engage in while away long hours during training camp. It mystified him that anyone would select a thick volume, a reference not to the book's content but to its physical measurements, and then devote hours reading it. "Why the hell do you read that stuff?" he queried one day, as if I were ingesting daily doses of arsenic.

I told him that I enjoyed Russian novels and liked to read in succession all the works of a single author, and right now, those were the works of Dostoevsky. But his interest piqued my own. "How about you?" I quizzed him. "What do you enjoy reading?"

Without hesitation, he said that he had read only two books from cover to cover in his entire life. Now that was food for thought. Two books in five years at the University of Minnesota said something of football in the Big Ten, but that seemed to me far less intriguing than the question of the two books themselves. Two books? Perhaps the Bible and a play by Shakespeare? Or *Huck Finn* and *The Hundred Greatest Athletes*? What pair of books found their way into my roomie's hands? I just had to ask.

"The Old Man and the Sea," he replied proudly. "Twice." Though not a long list, I concluded that it had its merits.

Years after leaving the team, I had the good fortune of crossing paths with Byron "Whizzer" White, a former Steeler who also had a passion for reading and who, of all who once wore the Black and Gold, attained the greatest national distinction. The Steelers' first draft choice in 1938 from the University of Colorado, White was appointed Associate Justice of the United States Supreme Court by President John Kennedy. I met Justice White in the mid-1970s when I taught U.S. history at a prep school in Louisville, Kentucky. Each year we took high school seniors to Washington, D.C. Having led several of those trips, I had grown frustrated over the inaccessibility of members of the executive and judicial branches of government to high school students. Representatives and senators were most obliging; after all, kids' parents vote. But I wanted to open doors to the other two branches.

First, with the good offices of one of our parents, Attorney General William Saxbe agreed to spend a few moments with the students in his office. And, as it turned out, through a chance encounter, Secretary of State Henry Kissinger also met with us briefly. Second, I wrote Justice White. I informed him that he and I shared a common experience as former Steelers, and on that common, albeit flimsy tie I asked him if he would talk to the students about the Supreme Court. He promptly and graciously accepted. And then, in an auditorium in the Supreme Court Building, Justice White delivered a brilliant forty-five-minute lecture on judicial review, followed by about twenty minutes of questions and answers. Watching him in that hall that day, I could not suppress a swelling pride in having been with the Pittsburgh Steelers.

Not that all Steeler running backs were Supreme Court material. One of my teammates in particular comes to mind when I think of the sad fact that many players arrive in the NFL with little to show for their collegiate academic pursuits, if indeed knowledge was ever one of their quests. On one occasion, I had a first-hand glimpse at our team's literacy. As part of our intelligence-gathering efforts to learn more about our opponents, on Tuesdays each player would fill out a questionnaire describing the play of one person he had played against during the game on Sunday. For instance, an offensive guard would analyze the tendencies, strengths, and weaknesses of the defensive tackle he had confronted. These assessments would then go into a scouting file that would be available for us to review when we next played that team. At the request of an assistant coach on the day in question, I collated the completed questionnaires prepared after a game against the Dallas Cowboys. As I shuffled through them, one in particular caught my eye. It contained a series of phrases and clauses naked of all capitalization and punctuation. A couple of the statements I remember well. Writing about the Cowboys' tough linebacker, Chuck Howley, one of our running backs had wisely commented, "chuck howley he are hard to knock off he feet." His summary comment was, "chuck howley he are a good linebacker." While one can quibble about the grammar, the analysis was right on target. Indeed, as I recall, the author of those comments had not once knocked Howley off his feet.

In addition to high schools and colleges failing to make sure athletes were also scholars, America had done a lousy job of bringing the races together. Coming from segregated Ole Miss to the integrated NFL I was acutely aware of race. Courageous blacks confronted the country with its shameful record of unfilled promises and discrimination. Race became very personal for me as I joined the Steelers. As a white rookie coming from Mississippi, the state with arguably the most deplorable civil rights record, I wondered how black players would regard me. Specifically, I worried about encountering one particular person. Marv Woodson was a defensive back for Pittsburgh. He had been an All-America performer at Indiana University and then became the Baltimore Colts' first pick in the 1964 draft. I did not know Marv, but he and I knew about each other. We were both from Hattiesburg, Mississippi. A town of about 40,000 in south-central Mississippi, Hattiesburg's schools were rigidly segregated in 1965, more than a decade after *Brown v. Board of Education*. I had attended the all-white Hattiesburg High School. Marvin, an African American, had gone to the all-black Royal Street High School. White politicians had made the patently absurd claim that the schools were "separate but equal," inviting skeptics to look at the two facilities' exteriors: Royal Street was a new brick structure and Hattiesburg High an old, multistory, dilapidated firetrap. The most cursory investigation revealed, however, that when the white school got new, late-edition textbooks, the black one received its discards, filled with torn pages and graffiti. And while I had the best football equipment that our liberal athletic budget permitted each year, Marvin wore what we rejected. Moreover, while Marvin was a far better athlete, I got more attention from local reporters, whose extensive coverage, action pictures, and feature stories of all-white Hattiesburg High dominated the sports pages. Apart from reporting game scores, the *Hattiesburg American* ignored Royal Street High and its players. Finally, Marvin did not have the opportunity to join me at the segregated University of Mississippi.

Perhaps projecting the anger and resentment I believe I would have had if our fates had been reversed, I dreaded our first encounter. As a veteran, he had the power to inflict pain and embarrassment on me, a lowly rookie. Instead, after I arrived, Marvin sought me out, extended his hand, and said, "Welcome to the Steelers. It's great to have a hometown guy on the team." Never before or since has a greeting meant as much to me nor revealed as much class.

In 1965 Americans were deeply divided over blacks' demands for civil rights. My home state of Mississippi had been the scene of some of the worst expressions of racial hatred, particularly in the desegregation of my alma mater, the University of Mississippi. In 1962 James Meredith, an Air Force veteran from Jackson, applied for admission. When he was denied, he sued on the grounds of race discrimination and prevailed. But Governor Ross Barnett intervened, named himself acting registrar of the university, and personally turned down Meredith's application. President John Kennedy and Attorney General Robert Kennedy countered by sending 500 federal marshals and eventually more than 10,000 U.S. troops to the Oxford campus to guarantee Meredith's safe enrollment. I remember the martial atmosphere that prevailed throughout the state on the eve of Meredith's arrival as Barnett, whose defiance was backed by pledges of militia support from thousands of arch-segregationists throughout the South, prepared Mississippians for the impending confrontation with the federal government. We were playing the University of Kentucky in Jackson on Saturday, the night before Meredith was to arrive on campus. Upon returning to the field after halftime, we heard 50,000 fans singing not the school's fight song or alma mater but a piece newly commissioned by Barnett, a state battle hymn. Before that night I had not associated football with political and social issues. But during the awful days that followed, when two people were killed on our campus, scores injured, and hundreds arrested, I came to realize that society's hopes and fears and politicians' power and authority were sometimes settled on fields of play.

Having grown up in Mississippi, where de jure segregation was securely in place despite *Brown v. Board of Education*, I was unprepared for the de facto segregation we encountered in Pittsburgh. The city had a particularly tight housing market when my wife and I first arrived in 1965, in part because in a consolidation move U.S. Steel had brought many of their people back to the city. Quite by accident we found an apartment in the South Hills at a location convenient both to South Park and Pitt Stadium. Many less fortunate teammates holed up in motels and hotels hoping for apartments to come available. Shortly after we moved in, the superintendent stopped me one morning as I left for practice, proudly announcing that a unit was coming on the market and telling me to spread the word among the Steelers. I was delighted and immediately thought of Marv Woodson. Before I got out the door, however, the super called and said, "By the way, no colored are allowed here." Stunned, I replied in my naivete, "How can that be in Pittsburgh? In Mississippi, of course, but here? How can you do that?" As if sensing that I might defy him by bringing a black teammate to look at the unit, he took me to the vacant apartment and pointed to a stack of paint cans in the corner. "If anyone we do not want here comes around to look at the vacancy," he explained, "I just point to the paint cans and tell them the place is still being repainted and is not available." That, I realized, was how the color line was painted north of the Mason-Dixon line.

I soon discovered that professional football softened the hard edges of racism. There is a degree of equality on a football team not seen in the rest of society. Players, black and white, have similar educational backgrounds, earn money based primarily on performance, and perform as equals in a game that demands teamwork and cooperation. To be sure, the National Football League had been slow to recruit black players and coaches, reflecting a similar lag in college football. Before the 1960s, although many outstanding African Americans played in universities across the country, none had been selected as a Heisman Trophy winner. Then, in 1961, Ernie Davis of Syracuse won that cherished award. More important, in the 1960s the NFL drafted the nation's best football players regardless of race, and black athletes immediately demonstrated their talents, dedication, and hard work.

Regardless of race, professional football players engage in a brutal sport, and the 1960s Steelers were past masters of violence. From reading popular sports magazines, I knew something of the Steelers' reputation as tough guys, on and off the field. The issue of *Sport* on the newsstands when I was traded carried a feature story on "Those Hell-Raising Steelers." I soon learned that "hell-raising" was a long and revered part of the team's culture. The pre-Renaissance Steelers were a hard-living, hard-hitting lot whose antics off the field often reflected their ferocity on the gridiron. When Big Daddy Lipscomb arrived in Pittsburgh in the early 1960s, the 300-pound giant found a home where he could sate his enormous "appetites with unbridled zeal." As one sportswriter put it, "In quarterback Bobby Layne and other Steelers roughnecks, Lipscomb had new drinking pals. After practices they would repair to the South Park Inn, where Layne would buy everyone except Lipscomb a drink." He bought Lipscomb a whole bottle of V.O.

One of my teammates, Brady Keys, remembered Big Daddy's Pittsburgh adventures. He said that when he arrived at the giant lineman's place each morning to pick him up for practice, "an orgy was often in progress." Keys recalled that "there would be three or four women, and they would be half naked." He continued, "Big Daddy had enough energy for them all. He was always drunk. And he always had cash lying all over the place. Big Daddy did three things: he drank, he screwed, and he dominated football games." The first two of those activities fit many of my teammates. Regrettably, the latter applied to only one or two.

Steeler lore reinforced the team's image. An important part of a team's culture are the stories that players and coaches circulate about the past. Players select and repeat those stories that current team members find amusing, entertaining, and relevant. The stories amuse and instruct, teaching new players what it takes to be a man in the NFL. At the core of the 1965 Steelers' culture was hard-hitting, hard-drinking, blue-collar masculinity. Not only was that a self-image, it was a widely held perception among those who followed professional football. In fact, a year before I joined the Steelers in 1965, a *Sports Illustrated* cover made graphic the team's hard-nosed style of play with its famous photograph of Y. A. Tittle. Many viewed Pittsburgh as a team that played "dirty" football. My guess is that if one considered the matter with some degree of objectivity, rarely possible when discussing sports or politics, the facts would reveal that the Steelers had no more personal fouls or player ejections or fights or brawls than other NFL teams. That said, sometimes because of insufficient talent to make plays, our players committed infractions. Defensive back Brady Keys had a reputation around the league for holding pass receivers that he tried to cover. I rather thought that he simply knew his own limitations, and when he could not cover a young, fast receiver he grabbed the guy's jersey to prevent a sure touchdown. True, some of his offenses were so blatant as to bring a chorus of boos from fans, but teammates saw those as prudent choices by a wily old veteran. On such matters perspective was everything.

In 1965 the two figures who loomed largest in Steeler lore were ghosts of the past—former quarterback Bobby Layne and recently fired coach Buddy Parker. Both had had long, colorful, and successful careers in the NFL. And both were known for their off-field antics as much as their performances on Sunday afternoons. Veterans trafficked freely in Layne lore. He was a Steeler's Steeler—tough, talented, and competitive, with a decided emphasis on tough. His teammates said that while his passes were "ugly," meaning that they rarely had the classic tight spiral, they were accurate. He played the game hard and expected everybody else on the team to do the same, never shrinking from publicly berating those who missed assignments. Lacking the physical size and power to lead by intimidation, he relied upon his good friend and offensive tackle Ernie Stautner as an enforcer. On more than one occasion Layne ordered offensive linemen who failed to provide adequate pass protection to leave the field, knowing that the miscreant would obey because Ernie would enforce the edict. Perhaps the 1965

Steelers loved to repeat Bobby Layne stories because we desperately wanted players with his passion for excellence and winning.

The most oft-repeated story about Layne said as much about the Steelers as it did about the celebrated quarterback. It seems that Layne and his sidekick, running back Tom "the Bomb" Tracy, were out on the town "unwinding" late one Saturday night before a home game the next afternoon. By the wee hours of Sunday morning, the pair was thoroughly relaxed as they sped through the streets of Pittsburgh, a city that still had streetcars in operation. Unfortunately, Tracy, the inebriated driver, plowed into the side of a parked trolley car. It was at this point that the person relating the story always warmed to the telling, enacting how Layne with his inimitable cockiness left the car unscathed, staggered over to the streetcar, and shouted at the operator for not watching where *he* was going. Then, after a pregnant pause, the storyteller would inform his listeners that Layne went out that afternoon and "played a helluva game." It's difficult to say what about the story resonated with players. Perhaps it was triumph despite one's own self-destructive behavior, or the ability "to soar with the eagles after hooting with the owls." I do not recall much analysis after those stories, but it was hard not to share an imaginary swagger with old Bobby.

Buddy Parker tales dribbled toward the dark side, kind of football horror stories. He had made his bones as a top NFL head coach during the 1950s as coach of the Detroit Lions, who regularly challenged Paul Brown's Cleveland Browns for the league championship. When he came to the Steelers in the late 1950s, he brought with him such top players as Bobby Layne and John Henry Johnson.

He reduced the game to bare essentials. The team that made the fewest mistakes (measured by penalties, fumbles, interceptions) and who maintained the best field position (determined in large part by the kicking game) usually won in the NFL. He had little toleration for mistakes. According to one story veterans repeated often, Parker once fired half a dozen players at halftime. It seems that the Steelers' play that Sunday had been particularly hapless. In the locker room, the livid coach paced in front of the players, pausing from time to time to point to an individual and shout, "You!" When he had so identified five or six guys, he said, "Don't bother coming out for the second half, you're cut."

Before I first heard that story and knew better, I managed unwittingly to cross Parker. I had joined the Steelers at training camp at the

University of Rhode Island on the Wednesday before a Saturday pre-season game against the San Francisco 49ers. Parker devoted much of Friday's meetings to the kicking game, going over blocking assignments and return schemes. Then during practice we went over each aspect carefully. When it came time for the punting team to go through its drills, I assumed my place. Parker again talked about assignments, walked us through what we could expect from the 49ers' punt blocking and return tactics. Finally, he glanced in my direction, said, "Okay, punt a couple," and turned his back on me to watch the proceedings unfold. Speaking to his back, I said, "I do not punt on the day before a game." Far from being insubordinate, I was merely informing him of a longstanding preference, maybe part superstition, for abstaining on the day before combat. Parker spun around and glared at me in disbelief and, I thought, contempt. For what seemed like minutes but actually only a few seconds, he fixed me with a stare that penetrated my soul. Finally, probably sensing that athletes were a superstitious lot, he shook his head and shouted, "Well, throw the goddam thing!"

Our team added its own propensity for outrageous behavior to the folklore. The most memorable incident requiring a cover-up involved a bit of after-hours fisticuffs between two of our players. It occurred, ironically, after we had attended a dinner promoting Catholic Charities in Pittsburgh. The Steelers had very close ties to that wonderful organization that did much good in the community, especially in working with youth. First, Art Rooney's brother was a priest and head of Catholic Charities. Second, we players contributed our fine money to that particular charity. I do not recall if that designation resulted from a vote or from executive fiat, but we all considered it a sage strategy. Throughout the season, coaches fined various players for a variety of infractions, such as practicing or playing without having one's ankles taped ($50), losing one's playbook ($500), or failing to reach a target playing weight ($50 per pound). Poor play or faulty judgment during a game could also cost a player money. Coach Mike Nixon threatened to fine me after one game when we were penalized five yards for having too many men on the field. As punter I was responsible for counting our players to make sure we had eleven. Fortunately, the kick after the penalty was assessed resulted in our having decent field position, and I escaped without financial damage. At the Catholic Charities dinner in question, we dutifully attended and basked in the warm glow that our indiscretions on and off the field would help fund worthwhile initiatives for others. The idea that our failing and our penance would benefit mankind—or childkind—struck me as properly Catholic. Afterwards, we went spiritually our separate ways.

It is safe to say, however, that two destinations attracted most guys. A significant number returned to their apartments and homes to be with their wives or girlfriends. A larger group repaired to the team's favorite watering hole: Dante's Bar. A blue-collar bar on the south side of Pittsburgh, Dante's was the sort of bar where guys went without their spouses. It attracted groupies who wished to make it with football players, and we had plenty of accommodating guys. I went home.

The next morning Coach Nixon convened a special meeting before our regularly scheduled prepractice film session. From his somber demeanor it was apparent to all that something was amiss. Some players shot questioning glances at one another. Others avoided all eye contact as they stared at their hands. After a long pause, Nixon finally spoke, informing us that after the charity dinner two of our teammates had an altercation that rendered one incapacitated for the upcoming game because of a, well . . . crushed cheekbone from the fist of the other. It seems that the two, fullback Mike Lind and guard Ray Lemek, had shared a ride to the previous evening's event. Afterwards, the former looked for the latter for a ride to a bar. Apparently, however, Lemek left without Lind, understanding that his rider had made other arrangements. Highly offended and sorely angered, the aggrieved Lind went in pursuit of Lemek, bent on redress for the slight. Professional football players, like other males of the species throughout history, live by a code of honor. Any word or deed, no matter what the intent behind it, can trigger an immediate demand for satisfaction by the offended party. Unlike eighteenth-century gentlemen, however, twentieth-century NFLers choose to settle things with fists, elbows, knees, feet, and other manly anatomical weapons as opposed to sabers, pistols, or swords. Upon finding Lemek at the aforesaid watering hole, Lind demanded immediate satisfaction, and upon receiving something less than what he deemed acceptable to assuage his fevered spirit, he proceeded to pummel Lemek's face with a savagery characteristic of people who make their livings from such bellicosity, albeit governed by rules intended to make the violence just. Nixon, a former Pennsylvania state representative, assured us that he had contacted local officials and sympathetic members of the press to keep the affair from public attention. Most of us gave the incident little thought. Having been in the sport at some level for decades, I knew this sort of behavior was not unusual. When I was playing at the University of Mississippi, a similar incident occurred on the practice field. The second-team center landed a brutal blow between the interstices of the face mask of the first-team center who was playing middle linebacker at the time. After the injured party left for the hospital—also with a caved-in cheekbone—the head coach said simply, "Gentlemen, let's keep our hands to ourselves." He then told the survivor to put on a first-team jersey, and we resumed practice as if nothing had happened.

Unfortunately our ferocity was matched by our fecklessness on the field. We approached each Sunday with optimism and believed that we had a solid game plan that could produce a victory. But we managed, through penalties, fumbles, and interceptions, to beat ourselves. One game in particular stands out in my mind as representative of how we self-destructed. In preparing for a home game against a hapless Philadelphia squad, our coaching staff noticed that the Eagles' punt-return team left itself vulnerable to a pass because the players moved quickly to set up a running lane for their returner. Therefore, we installed a fake punt and worked on it all week. With Roy Jefferson playing end on our punt-coverage team, we had our best receiver in position to pop open over the middle for a pass that I would toss after beginning the motions for a punt. After executing the play successfully all week long, we were confident it would work and were eager to try it in the game. Our game plan called for us to use the play the first time we had to punt. But, on that cold December Sunday afternoon, we reached new levels of ineptitude. In the first quarter the Eagles intercepted three passes and returned them for touchdowns, a new NFL record. By the time we faced our first punting situation, we were down 35-0. As I left the sidelines, I asked Coach Nixon if he wanted to go with the fake punt. "Hell, no!" he replied, "Punt the goddamned thing." So many of our balls had been intercepted I feel he suffered from shell shock.

Frustrated by our ineptitude, Art Rooney replaced Nixon after the 1965 season. In 1966 the Steelers started the season with high hopes fueled by a new head coach, Bill Austin, one of Vince Lombardi's assistants at Green Bay. He brought to the task a great deal of energy and a determination to transform us into a more disciplined football team. Toward that end, he imposed a grading system for position coaches to evaluate the performance of each player under his tutelage. To illustrate, consider the play of a defensive back. If that player did his job on a given play, say prevented a completion, he received a zero (0). If he did something exceptional, say made an interception, he got a plus one (+1). And if he really excelled, say, ran an interception back for a touchdown, he was awarded with a plus two (+2). Conversely, if the back got beaten for a completion, he received a minus one (-1), and if he got beaten for a touchdown, he got a minus two (-2). An overall grade of 0 meant that the player did his job consistently. Cumulative scores above or below 0 reflected exceptional play either positively or negatively. On Tuesdays after reviewing films of the previous game, the ratings were posted for all to see. Players congregated at the bulletin board to see how they and their teammates performed. Usually, however, mistakes had been highlighted twice previously: once during the game itself and again during the film session. The posted ratings served as a visual, permanent record of one's performance.

Illustrative of the gap between Austin's expectations and our performance was the occasion when one of our guys received a -2 for the game without leaving the sidelines. One of our captains, defensive end John Baker, had missed several games because of an injury. As we prepared for a home game against the Cowboys, however, Baker worked out and was deemed ready for limited action. Defensive coach Lavern "Torgy" Torgeson decided to use John only on the goal-line defense, that is, when the opposing team had the ball inside our five-yard line. Throughout the week, sportswriters and sportscasters had trumpeted John's return, unaware that he would see only limited duty. They conveyed the notion that his service would no doubt end our losing ways. I remember the day well, a cold, wet Sunday in late November. When not playing, parka-clad players milled about perpetually searching for a measure of warm, dry comfort. The Cowboys got their offense going, and quarterback Don Meredith drove them down the field. A pass resulted in first and goal at our two-yard line. Clearly a situation calling for our goal-line defense, our big guys lumbered onto the field all, that is, except John Baker. Meredith came to the line of scrimmage, noticed that we had no defensive end on one side, called an audible, and walked the ball into the end zone. Austin was livid. His anger turned to head-shaking bewilderment, however, when Baker explained his failure to enter the game because he was unsure if first and goal from the two-yard line constituted a goal-line situation. The "Jesus Christ!" that Austin roared transformed Pitt Stadium into an evangelistic crusade for a brief moment. On the following Tuesday, we all saw Baker's score posted by his name: -2. And he never removed his parka.

The following year, after I had left the team, Austin again sought to transform the Steelers into a finely tuned, winning machine. This time he brought to training camp a team of psychologists to administer a battery of tests. It was a scientific experiment. The idea was to see if there were any personality quirks that threatened team solidarity and, if so, to deal with them in a way that promoted cohesion. In a team meeting introducing the testing, Austin expressed his belief that the Steelers could go all the way this year and that he wanted to take every measure to ensure success. Hence, the psychological testing. My old roommate was still on the team, and he is my primary source for what happened during the testing. He said that the exams consisted of such questions as "When did you stop wetting the bed?" and "Do you love your mother?" Because the instruments were designed to be taken at the examinee's own pace, players finished at different times and left the room. My ex-roomie said he finished in fifteen minutes, and that virtually everyone else had completed the task shortly thereafter. After turning in his paper, he remained in the room and conversed for thirty minutes or so with a couple of the assistant coaches. As he started to leave, he noticed that three teammates, hulking defensive linemen, with pencils dwarfed in their outsized mitts, were still taking the test. Curious as to what could possibly be taking so long, my buddy walked undetected behind the trio and peered over their shoulders. To his surprise, they were all on question number 9 of the 100 or so total. He watched silently as the three sat motionless, hovered over their papers. Finally, one said to another, "Hey," calling one of his pals by name, "what do you think the answer is?" My narrator thought in disbelief, "My God, we are in deep trouble. These guys are cheating on personality tests!" Unfortunately, the screening program failed to improve performance on the field: the Steelers' record fell to 4-9-1, one less win than that of 1966.

At the end of the 1966 season, I decided to leave professional football to pursue other interests. While the won-loss results of the pre-Renaissance Steelers were frustrating, the challenges, competition, and camaraderie of those Steeler teams are memorable. We simply lacked the talent and leadership to bring a championship to Pittsburgh. It would take a new coach and new players, perhaps best exemplified by another player named Lambert, for the Steelers to enjoy the kind of renaissance befitting the city they represented.

Rocky Bleier

In 1968, the Steelers selected Rocky Bleier, but their summons was superseded by a different draft, this one from the Army. Uncle Sam sent Bleier to Vietnam, where he was caught in an enemy ambush and shot in the left thigh. As he crawled back toward his platoon, a grenade rolled in his path and fired shrapnel into his right foot. Doctors gave the fullback little chance of ever playing football again. But after three operations and countless hours of rehab, he returned to the Steelers and, defying all expectations, went on to have a stellar career, both as a blocker and a ballcarrier. Rocky Bleier's inspirational story and rigorous work ethic made him one of the most popular of all the 1970s-era Steelers. His 3,865 career yards are unusually strong for a fullback, and he averaged 4.2 yards per rush. In this excerpt from his auto-biography, Fighting Back, *Bleier spoke frankly about making the transition from captain of Notre Dame's Fighting Irish to lightly regarded NFL rookie. He also provided an insider's account of the coaching misadventures of Buddy Parker and Bill Austin and explained the rather unorthodox training methods of the 1960s Steelers. He opened with his impressions of Pittsburgh as he reported for his first camp in 1968.*

PITTSBURGH

Rocky Bleier

Two minutes into downtown Pittsburgh, I was rudely introduced to the fact that none of the streets run parallel. God's three rivers made the land a triangle, so man constructed the streets the same confusing way. And left me hopelessly lost in search of the Steelers' offices.

Finally, I found them, parked across Sixth Avenue, and checked into the Roosevelt Hotel. Next morning, I met the coaches, took a physical, weighed in at a beefy 205 pounds, and agreed to arrive at training camp in the evening. I walked across the street, and lo and behold, there in the parking lot was an empty car. Mine.

Devoid of my belongings. Everything I once owned was stolen. I mean everything, including all my football shoes.

Bad as that was, there was worse news awaiting me at St. Vincent's

From *Fighting Back* by Rocky Bleier with Terry O'Neill (New York: Stein and Day, 1975). Reprinted by permission of Rocky Bleier.

College, our training camp in Latrobe, about seventy miles east of Pittsburgh. The Steelers were trying to field a squad for a rookie scrimmage with Cleveland in two weeks. They were short on receivers, so they made me a flanker. I was bulked up to 205, thinking I'd be a running back . . . and here they were looking for the quick cuts and deft moves of a receiver. The extra weight had slowed my forty-yard time to five seconds flat. There was no way I could make the team as a flanker.

I got a break within a few days, however. One of the rookie running backs, Jay Calabrese of Duke, had stepped on a piece of glass in a swimming pool the week before we reported. Now it was bothering him, so the coaches substituted me for Jay. I was the leading ball carrier in the Cleveland scrimmage and scored a touchdown . . . offsetting one by my old teammate, Tom Schoen, for the Browns.

But I was still light-years away from making the team. There was a superquick rookie named Byron McCane running beside me. And the veteran backs were coming in—Dick Hoak, Willie Asbury, Earl Gros, Don Shy.

The arrival of the veterans also meant the resumption of a fine old Steeler tradition . . . happy hour before dinner. During two-a-day practices, we were off the field at four-thirty, with dinner scheduled for six. So, if you showered in about a minute and fifteen seconds, dressed on the way to the parking lot, and drove the country roads of Latrobe like Jackie Stewart at Monte Carlo, you'd have exactly one hour of heaven in a little pub called The Nineteenth Hole.

It was Paul Martha, a defensive back and off-season attorney, who first explained it to me. He said, "Bleier, I like you. You're a good kid. You worked hard out there today, and I think it's time you replaced some of your natural body fluids. Besides, the biggest hell-raisers in the NFL have consistently come from Notre Dame—great names like Paul Hornung, Monty Stickles, Myron Pottios, Mike Lind. I'd like to see you uphold that tradition. I never met a man from Notre Dame who couldn't drink beer, and drink it well, in large quantities. I'm betting on you this afternoon at the Nineteenth Hole."

The veterans would bet each other which rookie could drink the most beer. (You can imagine the pressure it placed on us rookies.) But in Martha's case, this was an act of sympathy. The first day he saw me, he was convinced I couldn't make the team. He thought I was too slow, top-heavy from all the weight lifting and prone to muscle pulls in my legs. He was just trying to show me a good time before I was cut.

What he didn't know was that I hadn't had more than one drink per evening since my little spree on the night the Steelers drafted me. I guess I was still inhibited by my ideal of the Notre Dame captain. It was simply understood that he didn't smoke or drink in public. My good friends Tom Schoen and John Pergine would hide beer under their beds and crush out cigarettes when I'd come into their room. That's how strong the captaincy image was.

But I didn't feel I could explain it to Paul Martha. So I dutifully drank every beer he placed in front of me that first evening. Which was thirteen. (Another night, a big rookie tackle named Ernie Ruple of Arkansas drank that many shots of whiskey, and favored us with a like number of "sooooooooooooooooey pig" hog calls before passing out in a contest with Ben McGee.) I was also assigned to take the little aluminum ring-top from every veteran's beer can and fasten them into a chain. They cut my fingers a thousand different ways, but I was too drunk to care.

Martha told me that when he was a rookie, in 1964, the place to drink was Iggy's in Warwick, Rhode Island, near the old Steeler training camp at the University of Rhode Island in Kingston. Bobby Layne, the grizzled quarterback, would load his rookies into the back of a pickup truck for a night on the town. Then, after they'd drunk to Layne's satisfaction, he'd drive them back to camp, as they barfed over the sides of the truck.

We heard lots of stories about those great old days in Rhode Island. Martha told me that, if anything, they were understated. The coach, Buddy Parker, told his players he didn't care what they did off the field. And the players took Buddy at his word. They were on campus with thousands of URI coeds, and fifteen minutes away from a beautiful summer resort, Narragansett Bay. It was an early night for Bobby Layne if he found his dorm room by 4:00 A.M.

On the field, things weren't much different. Parker insisted the team run a two-mile trail through the woods every day after practice. The veterans would run until they were out of his view, then sit down on tree stumps and pull out the cigarettes they'd hidden under their jerseys. After the rookies had run the outlying section of the course, the vets would get up and rejoin the pack as it headed back toward Parker, who stood with stopwatch in hand, screaming for a final sprint. Layne would pant breathlessly, "Goddam, Buddy. That gets tougher every day."

Not even the rookies got in shape in those days. In 1966, Pittsburgh's first draft choice was a fullback from West Virginia, Dick Leftridge. He was a local boy, and supposedly the big, fast back who would give oomph to the offense. Well, Dick showed up in Rhode Island plenty big, all right. He was 250 pounds, thirty pounds over his playing weight.

After a hot afternoon practice, he'd always be the last man staggering off the field. By the time he got undressed, everybody else had showered. And as the drinkers sprinted off to Iggy's they would stop for one final look at the spectacle of their No. 1 draft choice. Leftridge would have all the shower nozzles pointed to the middle of the floor, the water turned as cold as possible. He'd be lying on the floor in the midst of this torrent, his great, oversize body gasping for air and moaning with relief.

Pittsburgh never won anything in those days, of course. In fact, until 1972, the Steelers had been in the league forty years without winning so much as a division title. They came close however, in 1963. Entering the final game, they were 7-3-3, a bizarre record befitting a bizarre team.

Parker had spent the season shuffling his personnel in fits of rage and superstition. For instance, he cut a very good offensive guard, Lou Cordileone, on the flight back to Pittsburgh after a defeat. Somebody told Lou a joke, Buddy heard him laugh, and he was gone. Eventually, players took to hiding in lavatories under blankets to avoid Parker's tantrums. But for Lou, it was too late. The next day, as the Steelers watched the film, Buddy spotted several good blocks and asked, "Who was that?"

Each time came the answer, "Cordileone."

Somehow, despite all that, the Steelers had only to beat the Giants in New York to win the Eastern Division. But their quarterback was not up to it. Ed Brown was thirty-five years old by this time . . . a nervous type, a bachelor, and a drinker of no small capacity. He'd had several bad games late in the season, so he decided to go into serious training for the Giant game. He went "on the wagon," and his system couldn't take the shock. By kickoff, his hands were shaking visibly and he was feeling slightly irritable. Bobby Layne, the quarterback coach that year, called down a play to him from the press box in the first quarter, and Brown knocked the headset off Bobby's ears by screaming, "That's the dumbest play I ever heard of." Pittsburgh lost the game, 33-17.

Parker did not have what you would call a strong staff. His receiver coach, for a prime example, assigned to convert Martha from a college running back to a pro flanker, handed him several thousand feet of film.

"What's this?" Martha asked.

"Film of Buddy Dial, the best receiver we ever had here," the coach replied. "You study those films and you'll become a great one, just like him."

"But, but, but," Martha stammered. "Aren't you going to show me some moves and techniques on the field?"

"Oh, no," said the coach. "I don't know any more than you do about this stuff. We're going to have to learn it together."

Layne, meanwhile, would disappear Sunday night, after each game. Parker would tell the team he was scouting college players. When Layne reappeared on Wednesday, *he* would tell the team what a great time he'd had in New York raising hell with his good buddy, Mickey Mantle.

Layne and Parker were amusing, but of all the characters of that era, they tell me the Hall of Famer was Bill Saul. He was a kid from a coal-mining family in Butler, Pennsylvania.

Saul was simply bigger than, was stronger than, was tougher than, smoked more than, drank more than, played cards better than, shot pool better than, and buried his helmet in your numbers harder than anybody around. We don't have people like Saul in the NFL any longer. He could, literally, drink a case of beer and smoke a pack of cigarettes until two in the morning . . . then come to practice at ten o'clock and perform better than anybody on the field.

That first night at The Nineteenth Hole, Bill showed me his famous no-hands trick. He fit his mouth firmly around a glass of draft beer. Then, without using his hands, he raised the glass, opened his gullet, and chug-a-lugged the whole thing. Incredible!

It was an incident with Saul, they told me, that led to the demise of Bill Austin, the Steelers' head coach from 1966 to 1968. Late in the preseason of 1967, Austin exploded at an afternoon practice. It was hot and humid, threatening rain, and the players were weary of two-a-days. Austin raged, "Goddam it, we'll run 'live' goal line till I see something I like." He pitted his No. 1 offensive unit against his No. 1 defense for a series of running plays. In the National Football League, that is positively unheard of. Forty-five minutes later, everybody knew why.

The first man injured was Saul. He tore up his knee so badly that he never played again with any effectiveness. Then Ken Kortas, a defensive tackle of huge dimensions and potential, hurt his ankle. Then Jim "Cannonball" Butler injured his knee, and the team had lost its outside threat on offense. Then Martha made a hit, and the suspension in his helmet collapsed. The helmet split, leaving him with a concussion and a bad cut over his right eye.

Finally, Austin put an end to this "game." But the damage was done. It was too late to replace any of the four injured, especially Saul. He was a true leader and the hub of a defense that had jelled near the end of '66. With that defense and Austin's abilities as an offensive coach, the Steelers had come to camp in 1967 thinking they might have a good year. But after the senseless carnage of that scrimmage, the feeling was gone. And so was all respect for Bill Austin.

When I arrived in 1968, he was in the last season of a three-year contract. It seemed the players sensed his vulnerability and exploited it. Roy Jefferson, in particular, used his leverage as player representative to defy him.

One evening in camp, several guys had a playful battle with water buckets and fire extinguishers. Austin was infuriated when he heard of it, but Jefferson persuaded him not to discipline the players involved. The next day at a team meeting, Austin said, "I know about last night. I know some of you don't have the maturity to handle professional football, but I wish you'd try. I think you should stop acting like little boys. Isn't that right, Roy?"

Jefferson jumped up and screamed, "You said you wouldn't mention this. I thought we agreed to handle it man to man."

Austin was silent for a second as his face flushed. Then he said, "Talking back to the head coach will get you a hundred-dollar fine."

Jefferson screamed again, "Why don't you make it two hundred?"

Austin said, "Okay, two hundred dollars."

Jefferson bid one more time. "Make it three hundred."

Austin screeched, "You got it." But nothing was ever done about the fine.

Jefferson got the best of his coach another time. In a film session, Austin ordered several replays of Jefferson dropping a long touchdown pass from Dick Shiner. He said, "With performances like this, we'll never win in the NFL. These are important plays. These are plays we have to make if we want to win."

Jefferson finally snapped, "Go to hell. I couldn't reach the fuckin' ball. Nobody could. If you were a better coach, you wouldn't have to rely on me to catch the bomb every down."

Ironic, isn't it, that they're together again with the Washington Redskins.

Jefferson wasn't the only player who flaunted Austin's authority. Don Shy listened to a critique of his running one afternoon in the locker room, then turned away from Austin and said, over his shoulder, "What the fuck do you know about it?"

That sentiment was completely foreign to me, after playing for Ara Parseghian. He was a man of such passion for winning that our respect for him was automatic. At squad meetings, he'd lionize teams like Iowa and Army, making us feel we'd have to play the game of our lives to beat a thirty-point underdog. And in pregame speeches, he'd fire us like a blast furnace. Ara would cock his head to the side, work over his chewing gum, and pace among us. I don't remember many of the words he used, because they didn't seem important. It was his tightly drawn posture, the cords that stood out in his neck, the desire that seemed to run through his fibers and fuel his body. If Ara had a fault as a coach, maybe it was this intensity. Sometimes he'd get us so high and so tight before a game that we didn't relax and play naturally until the second quarter.

With Austin and the Steelers, however, no such danger existed. The first time I started in a training camp scrimmage, I rushed into the huddle, bubbling, "Come on, guys. Let's go, let's get after it."

One of the veterans looked at me and said, "Cut out the college rah-rah shit. Just do your job, kid. That's what you're getting paid for."

There was also a big difference in technique between Notre Dame and the Steelers. Pagna and Parseghian had analyzed and refined their offense so thoroughly that they had a method for everything.

Not so with the Steelers. One morning in camp, Heinrich, the backfield coach, asked me how we ran an off-tackle play at Notre Dame. So I showed him: crossover step, step, plant, and hit the hole. Each was a precise movement.

Heinrich then told the backs, "Try Rocky's method to see if you like it. We don't really care how you run it. Just do whatever feels natural."

I liked the new freedom to express my creativity as a runner. In an exhibition game at San Diego, I actually reversed my field on a sweep and gained thirteen yards . . . something I never would have done at Notre Dame. I suddenly realized Ara and Tom had made me a mechanical, rigid, structured runner. While there may be a debatable merit to that, it cannot be argued that their teaching made me the Steelers' best-prepared rookie in 1968.

None of the Steeler receivers, for example, could take their three-point stance left-handed. Coach "Bones" Taylor once tried to explain how they could save a step by taking a left-handed stance when throwing a crack-back block from the right. But none of them could do it. "Bones" asked if anybody on the team could, and I was the only guy who raised his hand. That's the first thing we learned in freshman year at Notre Dame. And it's a technique I still use—lined up on the right side of the center, I take a left-handed stance; and vice versa.

Those kinds of fundamentals, probably more than anything else, are what helped me make the team. I got a big chance during that preseason game in San Diego when Shy hurt his shoulder on the first snap. I played the rest of the game and outgained all the Charger rushers combined, with sixty-one yards.

I started the next week against Cincinnati. Then, against Washington, I scored my first professional touchdown on a marvelous evening. I felt quick—diving, twisting, jumping—and fast in the open field. One run, I broke for thirty-six yards. I had a nothing-to-lose attitude as the final cut drew near, so I played with the kind of abandon that reminded me of my high school years.

Alas, once the season began, I found myself on the bench. If this was to be Austin's last year—and it was—he was going down with veterans. Rookies were strictly for the special teams, in his view. Even more frustrating was the specter of Earl Gros, our starting fullback. Rightly or wrongly, I felt I could fall forward farther than he was running.

It was a dismal year. While the players spent their time pointing fingers at each other, Austin lost trust in all of us. They say the ultimate, in that regard, was Joe Schmidt, the Lions' coach, who once accused his players of talking about him in the huddle. Well, Austin was not far behind. He charged that some players were not putting out intentionally . . . as a means of getting him fired.

Bill was from the Vince Lombardi school of coaching, which favors ranting and raving, pushing and cajoling. With Lombardi, there was a loving personality under the crust, which came through to his players. With Austin, there was nothing. Often, we'd see him after he'd had several drinks, scratching the middle of his chest in a nervous habit. That '68 season, he nearly scratched a fracture in his breastbone.

The first victory of our 2-11-1 year came in the "O. J. Simpson Bowl." We entered the game 0-6 against Philadelphia, which was 1-5. At that time, it seemed the loser would finish with the NFL's worst record, and therefore earn the right to select O. J. in the college draft.

The game was just what you might expect . . . sloppy tackling, poor execution, and stagnant offense directed by two of the greatest dinkshot passers of our time, Dick Shiner and Norm Snead. It was humiliating to be a party to it. We finally won, 6-3, on two field goals by Booth Lusteg, our eccentric kicker.

Booth warmed up for his game-winning boots by kicking paper cups around the sideline. One of his practice kicks, in fact, took with it a glob of mud and struck Ben McGee in the face. Ben would have killed Booth, except we didn't have another field-goal specialist. So we beat the Eagles, which prompted some fans to complain. "The Steelers can't do anything right. They can't even win O. J. Simpson by losing."

Awe-Inspiring Futility

These three newspaper columns capture the awe-inspiring futility of the Pittsburgh Steelers at the onset of the Chuck Noll era. A two-win season in 1968 spelled the end of Bill Austin's short tenure as head coach. His replacement, Noll, brought new hope to the team by leading them to victory in the 1969 season opener against Detroit. His squad then dropped the next thirteen games and again finished in the basement of the NFL's Century division. It was not, as the San Francisco Chronicle and Examiner's *Prescott Sullivan pointed out, a team that inspired fear, dread, or even interest. Even the hometown fans had grown tired of their eternal losers. Reports from the* Pittsburgh Post-Gazette *and the* Pittsburgh Press *sounded more like summaries of Pop Warner games than of the NFL.*

A BREAK FOR THE 49ERS

Prescott Sullivan

The San Francisco 49ers are in Pittsburgh, Pa., this weekend for a National Football League confrontation with the Pittsburgh Steelers.

It is well for Coach Dick Nolan and his men that we aren't back there with them. Our presence couldn't help and it might prove harmful to their cause.

It's like this: Where today's game is concerned, we have a potentially dangerous attitude. That is to say, we are taking the Steelers lightly. Very lightly. Try as we might, we just can't think of them as anything other than soft touches.

You might call it over-confidence. And you know what over-confidence can do to a football team. Well, that's just it. That's why we didn't make the trip to Pittsburgh.

We were afraid that our over-confidence would, upon close contact, rub off on the 49ers and ruin their chances. Of course we couldn't have that on our conscience.

At this distance, however, it won't hurt to say the Steelers aren't much. The 49ers should win with ridiculous ease, provided, of course, they don't get wind of this in Pittsburgh.

From the *San Francisco Chronicle and Examiner*, November 24, 1968. Reprinted courtesy of the *San Francisco Chronicle and Examiner.*

We are counting on you to keep it from them. Scout's honor. Not a word. No tricks. We'll know if there have been any leaks. They'll show up in the score.

The Steelers have been losers for years. They have yet to win a NFL championship and they've been in the league since 1933. We don't say this contemptuously. It really isn't anything against them.

We don't hate them for it. Quite the contrary. The Steelers are our kind of people. As one who hasn't won any championships either, we feel a kinship for them.

The Steelers are humble. You'll find no balloon heads in their ranks. So far this season, they have won two of ten games. For them, that's a good record, but you don't hear them crowing about it.

From top to bottom, the Steelers are just plain folks. Football isn't their strongpoint, but, after all, does it matter? . . .

HEIGHTS OF MEDIOCRITY

Al Abrams

In Philadelphia, we are told, some sports fans are so crude they boo nuns and passing funerals.

In Pittsburgh, our equally disgusted athletic supporters boo losers.

If, by chance or arrangement, all these boo birds would merge, they could fill the Pitt Stadium to its 57,331 capacity next Sunday.

Why next Sunday?

That's the day Pennsylvania's Pro Football Futility Championship will be played when the Steelers (0-6) meet the Eagles (0-6).

If the schedule makers contrived to go all out they couldn't have come up with a heights of mediocrity pairing such as this.

On a clear day yesterday afternoon you could hear the booers forever. They not only gave the razberries to the Steelers' opening lineup as it was being announced, they yakked so loudly at one stage in the game they changed the strategy. And, they were right.

This came in a fourth down and one situation. The field goal kicking team romped out but the boos were loud enough to give Coach Bill Austin a second thought. The Steelers went for the sticks and made 'em with yardage to spare. From there they went in for a touchdown.

Someone in Section 32 thought out loud that the crowd should take over the coaching chores.

We doubt even this would help. In the end, the score was New Orleans 16, Pittsburgh 12.

There's no way, it seems, for losers to change their course. Ask the Pirates. Ask Pitt. Ask the Steelers.

The Steelers only have themselves to blame for blowing a game they should have won. It was the same last Sunday against the Washington Redskins.

They had a dozen or more chances yesterday to grab off the elusive victory and couldn't. There were times when we felt more pity for them than censure. We doubt if the fans did judging from the mutterings we heard on the way out.

The fans were put through a ringer again. They started out booing, cheered when Dick Hoak tried valiantly to turn the tide, then ended the day on a raucous theme when the home boys couldn't score in the final minutes when they had the ball on the Saints' four with a first down.

From the outset it looked like a loser's day. The Steelers tried an onside kick which didn't work. Loser's onside kicks seldom do. The Saints got the ball and marched in to a 3-0 lead.

THE BATTLE OF GLOOMSDAY

Roy McHugh

Above the stadium's rim, on Herron Hill, a grimy layer of snow covered the graveyard. It was one of those bad Sundays, late fall at its worst, rain pelting down on the 25,000 plastic-encased lunatics and the umbrellas that sprouted like mushrooms on a hillside.

The officials made their first mistake before the game started. They had the teams all lined up for the kickoff when here came the Sto-Rox high school band, marching onto the field in beautiful array, marching under the goal post to the 10, the 15, the 20, the majorettes lifting their knees. About to kick off to the Steelers, the Dallas Cowboys turned around and stared. Voices cried out, the band came to a halt. Still in cadence, it marched off the field backing up.

A Cowboy moved to adjust the ball on the kickoff tee, but at that moment the public-address announcer reminded the officials that it was time for the National Anthem, thus calling attention to the flag, a leftover, apparently, from the Battle of Gettysburg, its tatters bravely flying in the wind.

The football game, when it started, resembled the static trench warfare of World War I. Drenched with rain, plastered with mud, both teams were pinned down and immobilized much of the time.

They were ignorant armies on a darkling plain. Terry Hanratty, the Steelers' rookie quarterback, threw an occasional accurate pass, but when he did, the receiver usually dropped it. Orientation was the difference between Hanratty and Craig Morton, the Cowboys quarterback. In the second quarter, Hanratty ran past the line of scrimmage and then threw a pass. Morton ran past the line of scrimmage and kept on going for the six points.

Roundup Time

At the start of the fourth quarter, with the score 10-0 and the rain turning to snow, Dick Shiner took Hanratty's place. Shiner has been on the bench most of this season. Last week against the Cardinals he came out of limbo, but the critiques of his performance, after a 47-10 defeat, were less than enthusiastic. Now, with what appeared to be cold anger, throwing and completing four passes, he took the Steelers 90 yards to a touchdown.

The Steelers had the Cowboys headin' for the last roundup. A bloodthirsty roar went up from the crowd. Also aroused, the Steelers fought through the slush to the Cowboys' 37-yard line, where Shiner handed off to nobody and Dallas recovered.

"It was my fault," Warren Bankston said later. "I was supposed to veer in, but I went straight to the outside. I wasn't there when he handed me the ball."

But again the Steeler defense kept Dallas from moving. "You can't deny their defense is one of the best," Morton acknowledged in the locker room—and on fourth-and-one at their own 37 with five minutes left, the Steelers did not punt. Dick Hoak, butting into the line, just made the first down. With that, the Steelers proceeded to another first down on the Dallas 39.

Shiner called a time-out. In the murky December twilight, he consulted with Coach Chuck Noll. "What's our best running play?" Shiner asked. Noll gave Shiner the Steelers' best running play and it lost a yard.

Counted Out

On second-and-11, Shiner sent Hoak up the middle for three yards and a fine spray of water and mud. The two-minute warning sounded. In the press box, a man from UPI said, "The Steelers are establishing their running game."

Shiner threw passes on third down and fourth down, but both were incomplete. When he explained the running plays, he would say, "The counter had been working all day, good for four and five yards a crack. With 2:50 left, I thought I'd see if I could keep the clock moving. If we scored a touchdown there wouldn't be time to do much when Dallas got the ball, and if we didn't score a touchdown we'd be in field-goal range.

"But they must have read the first play pretty good. On the second one, the hole was there for a split second, but Bob Lilly got back and made the tackle.

"It was just a great play by a great football player."

The Cowboys accepted their victory, which gave them the championship of the Capitol Division, about as raucously as the Steelers accepted their 11th straight defeat. Owner Clint Murchison made a speech, but it was only one sentence long. He said, "We're not gonna break out the champagne."

On this Sunday, the champions were drinking tap water.

Broeg on Rooney

The 1969 Steelers were a disaster by any yardstick. Although several players later claimed that new coach Chuck Noll's attitude and method inspired confidence, anyone watching the Steelers limp to a 1-13 record must have felt that the latest version was still the same old Steelers. Rooney's bunch were still losers. Of course, Noll's approach did produce championship teams that bathed Art Rooney in glory. St. Louis Post-Dispatch *sportswriter Bob Broeg surveyed Rooney at the team's latest nadir. The "same old Steelers" would change, Broeg concluded, and Rooney would not.*

ART ROONEY: HE'S A WINNER WHO ALWAYS BACKS A LOSER

Bob Broeg

The Pittsburgh Steelers, perennial also-rans in pro football, probably won't be back in St. Louis for some seasons after 1969 because, like the Cleveland Browns and Baltimore Colts, they're transferring next year to the American Conference of the amalgamated league.

If the luck of the inter-conference scheduling doesn't bring the Steelers to St. Louis for considerable time, sure, a guy will miss Andy Russell's linebacking, Bruce Van Dyke's blocking, Roy Jefferson's pass-catching and Dick Hoak's deftness with the halfback running pass.

Mainly, though, he'll miss Art Rooney, the extraordinary person who owns the team that will be at Busch Memorial Stadium to play the football Cardinals this afternoon.

Thirty-five years ago, a season after he paid $2500 for a franchise that became first the Pittsburgh Pirates and then the Steelers, Rooney arrived in town with a loser. The 1934 Pirates fell by a 6-0 score to the St. Louis Gunners, who were in the National Football League briefly that season.

A generation later, still losing ball games if not money, Rooney is the man who never won a championship, but never loses a friend. He practices what others preach when they talk about sportsmanship.

From the *St. Louis Post-Dispatch*, November 30, 1969. Reprinted with permission of the *St. Louis Post-Dispatch* © 1969.

The general manager of the Minnesota Vikings, Jim Finks, who played quarterback for Rooney U. starting in 1949, talked about his old boss and friend the other day.

"He always was at his best when things were tough, after the team had lost a close game," said Finks. "He always reacted in the right way."

"He's a very religious man—attends Mass daily—and doesn't swear or lose his temper. If I ever had a problem, I went to Art Rooney. He was like a father to me."

A Team of Tragedy

Closing in on 70, Rooney seems as far away from his first championship as ever. Fact is, the Steelers have had only nine winning seasons in 37. They haven't threatened since they were 8-6 in 1962 under Buddy Parker and 7-4-3 the next season.

If ever the Steelers looked as if they would roll, the occasion was a couple of decades ago when Rooney lured Dr. John Bain (Jock) Sutherland back to Pittsburgh.

The Scottish dentist who had built the University of Pittsburgh into a powerhouse was dismissed in an athletic retrenchment and coached pro football at Brooklyn before he took over the Steelers at the end of World War II.

The Steelers, 8-4 in 1947, lost the Eastern Division Championship in a playoff to the Philadelphia Eagles, who then bowed to Jim Conzelman's Chicago Cardinals in the Big Red's last title success.

Shortly thereafter, Coach Sutherland, on a scouting trip, was found wandering in a field near Cairo, Ill., stricken with a brain tumor that became fatal. And tackle Ralph Calcagni, key man on the double-duty Steeler line, died unexpectedly after an appendectomy in training camp.

Often dangerous, usually respectable, but seldom successful, the Steelers have been over .500 only five times since. And, ironically, just when they came the closest again in '62–'63, their top lineman, 290-pound Eugene (Big Daddy) Lipscomb died tragically, allegedly of an overdose of narcotics.

Honesty's Reward—Defeat

Art Rooney didn't come up from poverty. It just seems that way because he's so charitable, humble and loyal to his old friends and neighborhood.

Art and his wife, Kate, raised five sons in the same big house in the same area where his father first operated a saloon, then a brewery. The Rooneys remained even when the neighborhood ran down, but Art's loyalty was rewarded because Pittsburgh's new Three Rivers Stadium, opening next year, will be practically in his backyard.

Art and his brother Dan, a Franciscan priest who was a missionary in China and then became athletic director at St. Bonaventure, were good athletes—good and rough.

Art boxed as a middleweight and mixed it with his ring idol, Harry Greb. He attended Georgetown and Duquesne universities and had tryouts with the Boston Red Sox and Chicago Cubs as an outfielder. He later managed Wheeling, W. Va., in the Mid-Atlantic League.

Somewhere along the line, Rooney made a killing at the race track. Now, he only owns the Steelers and plays the grain market, but he has a thoroughbred farm called Shamrock in Maryland and conducts a harness-racing meeting just outside Philadelphia.

Although son Dan and Art, Jr. have relieved him of much of the responsibility, Rooney still carries his office in a little black book, trying in a day of multimillion-dollar computerization to run his business as he did in the old days when a simple handshake was enough.

A Republican whose closest friends are Democrats, Rooney was persuaded to run for public office just once. In 1939 he was put up as a candidate for Register of Wills in Allegheny County. He made just one short, unforgettable speech.

"Frankly," he said, "I don't know where the office is located or what the duties are, but if I win, I'll employ some people who can handle the office."

The honesty was applauded, but not enough to overcome a Democratic landslide against the real-life Frank Skeffington, who, like the focal figure in "The Last Hurrah," is the last of his breed.

Of Johnny Blood and Winnie the Weeper

Rooney is a soft-spoken, easy-going Irishman who attends more wakes than a politician running for office. And he's got a politician's gift for remembering names and faces, but he's even better known for his slow horses and losing football teams.

"If I ever get a truly great horse, I'll name him 'Johnny Blood,'" he said in admiration for one of his favorites, the legendary Johnny (Blood) McNally. Other players he idolized as well as paid included Bill Dudley and the Supreme Court justice with whom he corresponds—Byron R. (Whizzer) White.

Short, chunky, thick-notched, his iron-gray hair brushed back so that it looks like a tall, thinning crew cut, Rooney sits silently in a corner of the pressbox, teeth clamped on a dead cigar, quietly rooting for his team in black and gold.

"I'd love to have a Kentucky Derby winner," he said, "but nothing would match the thrill of a championship football team."

Rooney, generous and kindly, has given away more money than his teams have given away games over the years, but with the true spirit of charity he'll recount only one act of compassion.

"I was coming away from the cashier's window one day at Narragansett and happened to have a winner," he said. "I noticed a little old lady dressed all in black. She was standing against a wall, crying bitter tears. I walked over and said, 'Ma'am, are you ill? Can I do anything for you?'

'No, sir.' she said. 'Nobody can help me now. I've lost my rent money and the medicine money for my little grandson who's lying there in our furnished room and getting weaker by the minute with the whooping cough. I came out to the track, praying that I would have a winner to buy medicine for the little tyke. But my horse lost by a lip, and now I don't know what to do.'

'But it's all right, sir. Don't you mind. You're a fine gentleman and you just go ahead and enjoy your winnings with a champagne and lobster dinner somewhere. I'll get by somehow.'"

Rooney, pausing, smiled around his cigar stub and said, "Well, I reached into my pocket and pulled out a $100 bill, 'Take this, my dear lady,' I said. 'Pay your rent and get the medicine for the little boy. Say a prayer, and I'm sure something will turn up for you.'"

En route back to his hotel, Art found he'd been taken by Winnie the Weeper, an old doll who had been hanging around the $50 cashier's window and working that act with strangers for years.

"I still think," Rooney recalled, the smile widening, "that The Weeper deserved the money. She gave a great performance."

Which Art Rooney hasn't always been able to say over the years about his slow horses or losing football teams.

Andy Russell saw good times and bad times in his twelve seasons as a Steeler linebacker (1963, 1966–76), and he wrote about both in A Steeler Odyssey. *Like most ex-players and fans, he credited Chuck Noll, who began his twenty-three-year tenure as head coach in 1969, as the key to turning the franchise into the marquee team of the NFL. Noll came to the team with an impressive resume and no head coaching experience. After playing both offense and defense at the University of Dayton, the Cleveland Browns drafted him to play linebacker. He retired from legendary coach Paul Brown's squad at the age of twenty-seven to serve as defensive coordinator for Sid Gillman's Los Angeles Chargers. From there, he moved on to Baltimore to work under the tutelage of Don Shula. In his sixteen years prior to joining the Steelers, he was a member of eleven division champion teams, five of which went on to win an NFL or AFL title. In his 1998 book,* A Steeler Odyssey, *Russell explained the teaching techniques that made Noll great and breathed personality into a cold and firm, yet deeply caring man.*

CHUCK NOLL

Andy Russell

The Steelers hired Chuck Noll in early 1969 after the team had had a series of disastrous losing seasons from 1964 through 1968. Despite feeling an allegiance to Bill Austin, his predecessor, who had been good to me, letting me make mistakes, allowing me to learn the game, I was still excited about having a new coach. Maybe he could diagnose what was wrong with us and turn us into winners.

We had read that Noll was extremely bright. He had trained under some of the great coaches in the business, Paul Brown in Cleveland, Sid Gillman in San Diego and Don Shula in Baltimore. I realized, however, that Coach Austin, despite learning from the legendary Vince Lombardi, still hadn't been able to find that elusive formula to post a winning season.

It was my eighth year in the league (with two out for military service in Germany) and I was the team captain. Having played in my first

From *A Steeler Odyssey* (Champaign, Ill.: Sports Publishing, Inc., 1998). Reprinted by permission of Sports Publishing, Inc.

Pro Bowl after the 1968 season, I was excited when the new coach called me into his office during the off season, fully expecting that he wanted to give me a pat on the back. Instead he carefully explained to me that I wasn't as good a player as I should be. He said I took too many chances, was frequently out of position, blew too many assignments, and my techniques needed to improve.

He admitted that I made a lot of big plays (sacks and tackles behind the line of scrimmage) but also made far too many mistakes. He said he doesn't want any heroes, just consistently competent players. Despite knowing that some of these criticisms were valid, I was extremely resistant when he told me he wanted me to change. My seemingly insatiable ego loved making big plays—could I still make them without guessing and taking chances? I doubted it.

Later, at St. Vincent's College in Latrobe, Pennsylvania for our first Noll training camp, waiting to hear his first speech to the team, I wondered if he would have the ability to analyze our weaknesses and mold us into a winning team. The players at that time, having come off a series of terrible years, were close, bonded through fire. We had lost game after game in the final seconds, in ways so bizarre that they were almost humorous, unless one's job, and pride, were on the line.

Once when punting on fourth and long, Cannonball Butler, having forgotten to come into the game, coming from our bench on the left, had crossed behind the long snapper, Ray Mansfield, to get to his upback position on the right side of the formation. Unable to see Cannonball, Ray snapped the ball at the very moment Butler crossed behind him. The ball ricocheted off Butler, 30 feet up in the air and was eventually recovered by our lucky opponents who, of course, went on to win. Being the fullback of the punt team, I was blamed for that little fiasco because I hadn't counted the players on the field prior to setting the offense. As a last resort, I should have called time out.

There were so many weird things that had happened (strange fumbles, deflected balls into opponents' hands, disastrous sacks at key moments, penalties nullifying game winning plays, missed tackles, missed blocks, missed opportunities), that we consistently dominated the annual NFL Bloopers film. Johnny Carson told Steeler jokes on Monday nights. "One Steeler to the other, 'Do you think we'll ever start winning again?' second Steeler, 'What's winning?'"

We had frequent team meetings to discuss what was wrong with us. Why did these things continue to happen? Were we losers? Were we chokers? Why did we continue to make these bonehead mistakes?

We had all been successful college players, many from winning programs. Why then weren't we winning? None of us had a clue but, since we had all made our share of mistakes, we all felt responsible. I suspect we felt like we had let the owners, the coaches and the fans down, but most of all, let our teammates and ourselves down. We were failures at something we loved and had always done well. By the time Chuck Noll arrived, our team psyche was very seriously damaged.

We had more excuses than the fans had criticisms. Our jerseys, embracing a golden triangle on the shoulders, were too ugly. The coaches couldn't lead us properly or our game plans were old-fashioned, etc., etc. Some players blamed the Rooneys, claiming they were too tight with the finances and weren't willing to pay what we deserved.

Despite our failures we were very close, bonding through our adversity. In fact the players on those losing teams were closer off the field than those on the Super Bowl teams. Apartment owners didn't want to lease to the Steelers. There were few speaking engagements and those that we did attend we were bombarded with questions like, "What's wrong with you bums?"

We felt like we embarrassed our neighbors and many of us avoided interaction with the public. Later, when we became champions we were embraced by the fans and invited to functions all over the city. Losing had made us feel isolated and we stuck together more. It has been said that it is lonely at the top. Believe me, it's more lonely at the bottom. Maybe a player has to have been at the bottom before truly being able to appreciate the top.

Our mood at Latrobe was subdued despite not having seen each other in months. Most of us were anxiously waiting for the new coach to tell us what was wrong. When Chuck Noll entered the room it went dead silent. Could he heal us? Was he tough enough to handle all the strong egos and flighty temperaments in the room?

At first glance he looked more like a college professor than a professional football coach. He was only 39 years old, not much older than some of the veteran players in the room. Many of the veterans, in fact, were taking a wait-and-see attitude. Some had joked earlier that, "We were here when he came and we'll still be here when he leaves." Little did they know.

The new coach got right down to business. He told us that he had spent the months since he'd been hired reviewing our game films and he could tell us why we had been losing. You could have heard a pin drop in the room. Here was the man who could enlighten us, tell us what was wrong with us, give us new hope, provide us with redemption.

He then outlined our weaknesses. We weren't winning games because we were not executing our techniques properly, we made far too many mistakes, and we weren't disciplined enough. He assured us that our losing was not because of a fault in our character or a lack of motivation.

"If your strategy and your techniques are flawed it doesn't matter how hard you try, you're destined to fail," he explained.

In short, we weren't doing the right things and part of his job would be to bring in some additional talent to help us win. To me the speech rang true and I don't think there was a veteran player in the room who didn't silently agree with him. We just weren't good enough.

He told us he would teach us how to win. He wanted smart, disciplined players who stayed within the system, not trying to make big plays in somebody else's territory. Since proper techniques and non-gimmick schemes are more difficult to execute, he predicted that we would get worse before we got better.

He expected us to motivate ourselves. If he found that any of us needed to be inspired by him we would be "let go," to go find our "life's work." He would not tolerate anyone who didn't put the team's interest in front of his own.

There were approximately 50 veterans in that room and probably another 40 rookies listening to Chuck Noll's first speech. Some were forced to retire because of injuries; a few didn't fit into the system; others were traded; many were cut. Six years later, the year we won our first Super Bowl, there would be only four of us left—four gritty and lucky survivors who made it to the promised land: Ray Mansfield, Sam Davis, Bobby Walden, and me. It would be a difficult but fulfilling journey, one that we would all cherish forever.

There were many reasons I respected and admired Chuck Noll. First and foremost he was a teacher who had an unrelenting belief that if he had enough eager, intelligent pupils who were taught properly, success would follow. It was not uncommon for Chuck to stay late after a hot afternoon practice at training camp to teach techniques to some bright-eyed rookie who Chuck knew he was going to have to cut the very next day. He loved to teach and he was good at it. He was patient. He believed that an inferior athlete could outperform a better athlete if he had superior techniques and an attitude that combined a refusal to quit with doing "whatever it takes (within the rules, of course)," paying the price, doing the hard things to get the job done correctly.

He dealt with the players in a straightforward and fair manner. For the most part he treated all players the same with a few exceptions. We could all see the wisdom in allowing Joe Greene to have his occasional temper tantrum when others might not have been allowed to vent their frustration in the same fashion. He may have allowed Terry Bradshaw to make mistakes that could have gotten other QBs benched.

He set strict but fair team rules and told us that if we violated them he would get rid of us. He certainly got our attention when he traded our best offensive player, Roy Jefferson, to Baltimore when he continued to defy Noll's authority by ignoring bed check.

He was demanding in the sense that he constantly reminded us that it didn't matter what we had accomplished the previous week, let alone the previous years. He demanded perfection today and tomorrow. It wasn't enough to make the tackle. He wanted it to be executed perfectly, with one's face in the opponent's number, hitting a rising blow, knocking the runner backwards. He was interested in NOW! How good are we today? Would we be better tomorrow? He wanted to see constant improvement. He liked nothing better than to see old vets working hard to master new techniques (like teaching me how to perfect the bump and run coverage of running backs, or teaching Ray Mansfield how to pass block by mastering the mirror-dodge drill with the arm extension blocking technique).

He wanted athletes who had a voracious appetite for the finer points of the game: memorizing the other team's tendencies, understanding minute positioning (alignment) advantages; perfecting the ability to read one's keys; and reading [an] opponent's body language and positioning. The magic is in the details.

He humbled rookies who had made collegiate All-American by teaching them how to get in a stance, something they thought they had learned properly in little league. He took veterans like me and taught us how to think. "Andy, don't just react—think about the opponent's tendencies before the ball is snapped and then process it in relationship to your keys." It was exciting and we could slowly see how it made a difference. His logic seemed irrefutable. Most of us became believers. Those who remained cynical departed.

He was unlike any coach I had ever had. I had been blessed by always having strong coaches to show me the way. Bob Davis, my St. Louis high school coach, taught us Bud Wilkinson's Oklahoma innovative offense, enabling us to win most of our games by 30 points or more, going undefeated my senior year. When I went to the University of Missouri I had a leg up because my techniques were sound. Dan Devine, at Mizzou, was one of the all-time great motivators—our teams consistently played better than our talent, surely a mark of a great coach. Under Devine, we only lost four games in my three years, playing in two bowl games, Mizzou having the best won/lost record for the decade of the sixties of any Division One team.

Buddy Parker, my first coach at the Steelers, was an offensive genius who could be counted on, nearly every game, to find a weakness in the opponent's defense, take advantage of it, and get a gift score. Bill Austin understood, as well as anyone, how the running game worked. But Chuck Noll was uniquely different—a technician, a professor who loved to teach, possessing an all-consuming, unrelenting pursuit of perfection.

During our first practice, when Chuck first called the team together, we went through the usual macho shouting, trying to get ourselves psyched up.

He had held up his hands, demanding our attention and said "Look, I don't want to hear any of this 'pseudo chatter.' Save your energy, you're going to need it. You don't play better by faking enthusiasm— you play better by doing the right things. I don't want you to have to get psyched up to play well because no one can sustain it. I want you on an intense, focused, concentrated level that never changes, no ups and no downs." We were all stunned—No rah-rah stuff, this was unheard of.

Later during that first year, when I made my first big mistake under Noll, allowing a running back to beat me deep for a touchdown, I had come off the field expecting some significant verbal abuse. I was humiliated and angry—I hated getting beat. No one, including Noll, felt worse than I did about letting the team down. Chuck didn't say anything as I walked by him. He was letting me cool off. A few plays later, he walked down to where I was standing at the end of the bench, still fuming at my error. After a quiet moment, he turned and calmly said, "Andy, on that play action pass, where they scored, what were you thinking?"

I was stunned. I had expected to be yelled at or at least receive some harsh criticism. I felt tremendous relief. He wanted to know why I had reacted incorrectly. He knew I had been beaten by my brain, not my body.

"Coach, over the last three years they have only shown that formation 40 times," I said. "Only ten times did they threaten my position from that formation and they ran only two plays: one play, the off tackle run, they ran nine times and the other play, the play action pass, they ran only one time. Coach, I can't believe they ran the play action pass, first, without setting me up first with the run?"

Noll just stared at me for a long time. You could almost see his brain turning. Finally he smiled, as if appreciating my logic or, perhaps, the cleverness of the opposing coach, and, almost whispering, said, "It's good to show tendencies, Andy, but don't bank on them 100 percent. Don't guess—read your keys after the ball is snapped."

He was telling me that if I had noticed the offensive tackle's stance before the snap, and his one-step pass block after the snap, I would have known it was a pass instead of the run. Based on their tendencies, I had assumed it would be the run and, therefore, was easily beaten.

As he walked away from me, I realized that this was a coach who understood. He hadn't called me names; he hadn't ridiculed me in front of the team; he respectfully had wanted to know my thought process. I knew then that I really wanted to play for him, not just for myself and the teammates.

Perhaps his strongest contribution to the Steelers' success was his uncanny ability to evaluate and develop talent. He drafted Joe Greene, Terry Bradshaw, Jack Ham, L. C. Greenwood, Jack Lambert, Lynn Swann, John Stallworth, Mel Blount, Franco Harris, Mike Webster, all elected to, or soon to be in, the Hall of Fame. The Steelers didn't draft a Hall of Famer from 1950, when they picked Ernie Stautner, until 1969 when they picked Joe Greene. Then suddenly the team picked ten, seven who are already elected, in six years. Granted Chuck had help from his scouting staff, but, in the end, he had made the final decisions.

More importantly, his ability to develop the talent of these superstars, without screwing them up (destroying their confidence by harping on relatively minor weaknesses), enabled these players to blossom under his tutelage. He kept his own ego out of it. He combined his ability to instruct, whether it was how to develop physical techniques or mental tactics (key reads—pre- and post-snap tendencies, positioning, and anticipation), with allowing the athlete the freedom to develop his own style, to have the courage to gamble on occasion, to not be frozen by fear of making mistakes.

He definitely made me a better player. I came to understand that his early assessment of my gambling style—sometimes right, often wrong—was correct. He taught me to play within the scheme of the defense in a more disciplined manner that made me a far more consistent player. True, I didn't make as many big plays as I had but he improved my techniques, both run and pass. My reads were more fundamentally sound and my anticipation based on my knowledge of tendencies improved dramatically. I became a smarter, sounder technique-wise, better prepared, and, therefore, a more successful player in my thirties than I had ever been in my twenties.

In 1974, preparing to play Oakland in the AFC Championship game, Chuck gave his most inspirational speech. At the time we weren't exactly a team overflowing with confidence since we had lost to an average Houston team the second to last game of the season at home, when needing a win to clinch our division. Joe Greene had been so upset over that loss that we had to talk him out of quitting and going home. After clinching the Central Division title in a lackluster game in New England and getting past Buffalo too easily, we were about to play away, an Oakland team that had beaten us badly in the previous year's playoff game and had just come off a last-second win over the previous year's champion, Miami. It was Tuesday, our first meeting to prepare for Oakland. Chuck came into the meeting room visibly irritated, barely controlling his anger.

He spoke quietly, but was nearly shaking with rage. Talking between his teeth, he said, "You may have seen the quote by John Madden in yesterday's paper about their victory over Miami." It came out more like a hiss than words. Trying to control his anger but clearly losing the battle, with his voice rising, "Coach Madden, describing the Oakland win over Miami, said that 'when the two best teams in the NFL play each other it is going to be a super game.'" He paused for a moment, struggling to maintain self-control, and then, apparently giving up, a violent expression on his normally passive face, he shouted, "Well, he hasn't seen the best team in this league yet because it's sitting right here in this room and they are going to have to deal with us."

Joe Greene, sitting next to me, had risen to his feet slowly, like some volcano about to blow, standing there, shaking with fury, with the school desk chair still wrapped around his huge legs. Raising his fist in the air, his eyes closed, all Joe said was, "Yes!"

After the meeting I worried that Chuck had made a mistake. He had gotten us ready to play on Tuesday. Could we sustain the emotion until Sunday? We did and beat an excellent Oakland team in probably the biggest Steeler win ever.

Chuck had gone to the Super Bowl with the Baltimore Colts when they had been embarrassed by Joe Namath's upstart Jets. He believed the Colts were uptight. He was not going to make the same mistake. When we arrived in New Orleans he told us "to go out and get the city out of our system—there will be no bedcheck." By Wednesday, we were begging for a bedcheck.

Confident that we were superbly prepared, his speech right before kickoff was classic Chuck: "We came a long way to get here. Just maintain your intensity and execute the way you know how. This game is our reward for a good season and it is important that we enjoy the experience. Now, I want you to go out there and have some fun." End of speech.

We went out and beat the Vikings. The pressure was intense and, although fun was the furthest thing from my mind, somehow we prevailed. The whole team played with the controlled abandon, focused confidence, intensity and concentration that the Coach demanded. He had made us believers in his system and we were able to aggressively use our athletic talent to execute it.

Of course, Chuck is human. There were times when he didn't control his temper but we all knew that he just wanted us to realize our potentials—to perform well so we could be proud of ourselves. Winning would follow. Make no mistake about it. Chuck Noll is one tough guy who ran his Steeler teams with an iron will. It is like the difference between a parent who disciplines the old-fashioned way by a spanking versus the parent who, with controlled anger, talks to you about your failures. Which one causes the most anxiety?—the latter I think. None of us wanted to have to debate his fierce logic.

Chuck believed in change. Every year, regardless of our success or lack thereof, Chuck came up with some new idea. One year he told us how it had been proved by the Olympic athletes that we could improve our speed by running down steep slopes. When we tried running down hill most of us pulled our hamstrings and discontinued the effort.

Another year he wanted us to run five laps around the football field (approximately one-fifth of a mile), and keep our heart beat at approximately 180 beats per minute. After each one-fifth of a mile lap, we would count our pulse (with our finger against our neck's main artery), and see if we were 30 beats for 10 seconds. If we were less than that we should speed up, if faster we should slow down—it was all done on the honor system. The theory, discovered by the astronauts' training, was that if your heartbeat was below 180, you wouldn't maximize your training.

After one particularly hot summer practice, when my heart had no trouble sliding above 180 heart beats a minute during this one-mile run, I asked Chuck, "Do you think it is logical that my heartbeat, when I'm 35 years old, should be the same as Lynn Swann's at 24 years old?"

"Just get it done, Andy, regardless of how old you are," was Chuck's reply. "If you're too old it might be time for you to seek your life's work."

He was a demanding, controlling, and sometimes irritating perfectionist. One year Chuck nearly drove Jack Ham and me crazy trying to force us to use a coverage technique that we believed was inherently flawed. When responsible for covering the halfbacks on pass routes, he urged us to drop three to four yards and "settle" before "jamming" the back off his route. Jack and I knew the technique was vulnerable (to the back, making you miss) which was a real problem because it created a situation off the missed jam where we were going north and the halfback was going unfettered south, which, of course, could easily result in a touchdown. Time after time our Steeler backs would beat Jack and me, trying desperately to execute this new coverage technique. When even Rocky [Bleier] could beat us, I knew something was very wrong.

After fifteen minutes of failing to execute his technique properly during our backs on backers drill after weeks of frustration, I approached Chuck and knowing the answer to my question, said, "Coach, do you think Jack Ham is a good pass coverage linebacker?"

Staring at me with his icy blues, he said, briskly, "Yes, of course."

"Then why is it that every time Jack tries your coverage technique he gets beat?"

He didn't say anything, just kept staring at me, like he's thinking 'Russell this better be good.' Too far into my complaint to change direction I continued to dig a hole.

"Can you show me any linebacker in the league, on film, that executes this technique successfully? Bobby Bell can't do it; Chuck Howley, Chris Hanburger, who?"

Perhaps equally frustrated he snapped, "Just keep trying—we've got to find a better way! We can't let the opponents move the sticks with those easy possession passes."

In the end, even when Chuck was wrong, he was right. Frustrated by my inability to execute his coverage technique I devised my own bump and run strategy that worked like a charm. Instead of dropping off and settling at three or four yards deep as Chuck proposed, I would penetrate up field, allowing no room for the back to release inside between Dwight White and myself and then jam him to the outside, giving him only one way to go. I would then funnel him further to the outside and insert myself into the passing lane. We called it the "hug 'em up."

It worked perfectly and Jack Ham and I were able to nearly eliminate the halfback option pass from our opponent's game plan. Chuck's insistence that there was a better way had ultimately caused us to create a technique that truly frustrated such great receiving threats as O. J. Simpson, Jim Kiick, Ed Podolak, Floyd Little, and Lydell Mitchell. After viewing my "new" technique, Chuck remembered that he had used a similar technique in the under formation while playing linebacker for the Browns many years before.

He demanded our total concentration through every practice. He controlled, or attempted to control, our most basic techniques. He was a tough taskmaster and we all feared his anger but, mostly, we didn't want to disappoint him or let him down. He was our mentor, our spiritual leader.

Under his guidance, the team developed a work ethic, a chemistry, an unbelievably supportive culture, where players voluntarily chose to stay late to work on their techniques or to help a teammate do so. Others would lift weights, take a sauna or get treatment for their injuries. Afterward, we would return to the classroom to watch films of our practice that day. Coach Noll had molded a group of young men who enjoyed each other's company, who respected one another, and who competed informally to see who made the least mistakes. This was truly a group that without Chuck's mentorship might have gone a different direction. Instead we collectively chose to blend our individual egos and skills with our teammates, which produced a new level of team perfection.

REASONS
FOR HOPE

The following trio of veteran sports reporters revealed a different attitude emerging around the Steelers. After the debacles of 1968 and 1969, the team's 5-9 mark in 1970 and 6-8 campaign in 1971 offered hope for the future. Noll seemed to have the team going in the right direction. Unlike his predecessors, he had drafted wisely, stocking up on young, talented athletes like Terry Bradshaw and Joe Greene. His team was inexperienced, but it played with enough heart and determination to win back many disaffected fans and win over many new supporters. The pendulum, as long-time Pittsburgh sportswriter Pat Livingston noted, was definitely on the upswing. In 1972 the Steelers went 11-3 and made it to the playoffs for only the third time since World War II. Super Bowl glory was not far away.

FOOTBALL'S POVERTY POCKET NO MORE

Bob Ortman

For years this was the poverty pocket of pro football. You never asked who won or lost if the Steelers played the game. They spent so much time in the league basement, they acquired the pasty look of cave-dwelling grubs.

An optimist was identified as a Steeler coach who took a long-term lease on a house. Most of them never even bothered to unpack. Art Rooney had more coaches than Mickey had wives.

So when he sent out a call for another one last year, it sounded like a warning to hide, but Chuck Noll thought it was opportunity knocking and opened the door. He leaped at the chance, like a fellow swan-diving out of a 10th story window.

If coaching is in your blood you're in the same situation as a king with hemophilia. But you can't die happy until you've tested yourself and your theories as head man.

To the undiscerning, the Steelers looked like the same old sad sacks in Noll's first season, but Chuck, who served the San Diego Chargers as aide to Sid Gillman before joining Don Shula in Baltimore, professed to detecting evidence of advancement.

From the *San Diego Evening Tribune,* June 4, 1970. Reprinted with permission of the *San Diego Union-Tribune.*

Progress, Record Two Different Things

"We made progress," he maintained, "although it doesn't reflect in the win-loss column. It was progress in areas that are not convertible to win-loss."

After completely remodeling the Steeler machine and replacing most of its parts, Noll is hopeful of progress that can be convertible, but he's reluctant to make any promises.

"There are so many ifs," he noted. "We've made so many changes in personnel—if they come through. We still have holes to fill. If we keep getting better every week I'll be pleased."

Happiness at the moment is improvement. A baby is elated when he advances from crawling to toddling. But eventually Noll will be happy only if the Steelers are racing at the head of the pack.

"Our ultimate goal is the championship," he declared. "There is talk [about] 'if we can just be respectable,' but we'll not be satisfied with that. Our goal is the championship, but I don't know when we'll realize it. It's hard to put a time schedule on it."

Duration of Contract Is Something Else

Certainly it will take longer than building Rome, and what are Chuck's chances of still being on the scene when the Steelers scale football's Everest for the first time?

"I have a three-year contract, one of which has passed, " he said unconcernedly. "I can't allow that to affect my judgment.

"We're proceeding with the idea of making the right decisions. Can these people win for us? Are they [of] the caliber to give us a championship? If you make the right decisions, you're headed in the right direction. Other problems will take care of themselves."

Because of their 1-13 record, the lowly Steelers were awarded first pick in the draft and they grabbed a "championship caliber" quarterback from Louisiana Tech, Terry Bradshaw.

"We felt he was the very best athlete in the country," said Chuck. "We were somewhat concerned about his competition, but when he got down to the Senior Bowl, he exhibited leadership qualities. He was not awed by the competition."

Effort Applied to Developing Support

"A quarterback, though, is only as good as his supporting cast," Noll pointed out. "This is what we're working on, getting the supporting cast in shape."

Pittsburgh is moving this year from the National to the American Conference in Pete Rozelle's amalgamation, an item of news that was not greeted here by dancing in the streets. Even though the fans figured the Steelers already had hit bottom, they viewed this shift as another step down.

But victory by the American's New York and Kansas City clubs in the last two Super Bowls erased some of the frowns.

"I'm sure the unconvinced will be converted before another season ends," said Noll. "I had great respect for the AFL when I was with San Diego. It was just a matter of maturing. Now they have matured. It is a state of mind more than anything."

"Now we look at these films," he shuddered, "we're awed by the talent we have to face."

Spoken like a true head coach.

FASCINATION IN FRUSTRATION

Joe Stein

Rooting for the Pittsburgh Steelers is akin to writing a thesis on the strong points of the Italian army. You state your objective and then fall back and wait for the laughter to subside. Still, I must plead guilty. To the Steelers, that is, while acknowledging that the Italians have nicer uniforms.

Yes, I unabashedly admit the Steelers are my favorite professional football team, if you want to use the term professional loosely. I became indoctrinated with the Steelers' losing spirit as a child in Pittsburgh and it stuck. Perhaps it's because I'm loyal to my old hometown or because the fan club is so exclusive.

Then, there's a certain fascination in frustration, and the Steelers are the Harold Stassens of football. They have been the butt of more jokes than Poland—most of them true, unfortunately. Maybe it's this macabre fascination that keeps Steeler fans going, a captive audience to comedy at its blackest. There's some doubt whether the team's a victim of misfortune, inept handling or a combination. Decide for yourself:

Item—The Steelers have never won as much as a divisional title in 37 years.

From "Inside Sports," *San Diego Evening Tribune*, September 22, 1970. Reprinted with permission of the *San Diego Union-Tribune*.

Item—The Steelers were the last pro team to abandon the single wing.

Item—The Steelers originally owned the rights to quarterbacks Sid Luckman, Bobby Layne, Johnny Unitas, Len Dawson, and Bill Nelsen and gave away all one way or another.

Layne, who was traded by the Steelers for a tailback named Ray Evans, later returned to Pittsburgh when he was well past his prime for two high draft picks and a quarterback. That quarterback was Earl Morrall, who led Baltimore to the National Football League championship two years ago.

Item—In 1953, when Walt Kiesling coached the Steelers and Joe Schmidt was a senior at Pitt, the sons of team owner Art Rooney badgered Kiesling to draft Schmidt. "Worst thing you can do," said the senior Rooney, who refused to interfere with his coaches' policies. "You're talking him out of it." Kiesling drafted Black Cat Barton, an offensive tackle from North Carolina, in the seventh round with Schmidt still available.

Detroit took Schmidt that round and came up with one of the great pro linebackers. At training camp the next summer, Kiesling cut Black Cat inside of a week because there was too much competition. "In those days," says Dan Rooney, one of the sons, "the draft went 30 rounds, and Kies would draft 29 offensive tackles."

Item—The Steelers had the choice of any college senior at the 1955 draft and shocked the NFL by taking the defensive back Gary Glick of Colorado A&M. Glick lived up to his lackluster reputation.

Item—Both Pittsburgh and Cleveland desperately wanted Purdue quarterback Len Dawson at the 1956 draft. Since the teams tied in the standings, a coin flip was necessary to determine which would draft first and take Dawson.

Pittsburgh "won" and the Browns had to settle for a Syracuse running back named Jim Brown. Dawson never got a chance at Pittsburgh , but drifted to the American Football League and became a star with Kansas City.

Item—All-Pro defensive tackle Gene (Big Daddy) Lipscomb died tragically of a drug overdose while a member of the Steelers. The team was a contender at the time and barely missed winning the Eastern Division title even without Big Daddy. With him, who knows?

Gary Glick among Illustrious Draftees

In a sense, the college player draft is more responsible for the Steelers' plight than any other single factor. Their first round list, even ignoring

Glick, is a study in futility. There are names like Ted Marchibroda, Art Davis, Mike Taylor, Dick Leftridge and Bob Ferguson (the Steelers won a bidding war from the Chargers for him and San Diego had to content itself with signing Lance Alworth and John Hadl that year.)

Much of the time the Steelers didn't have to worry about the draft. Coach Buddy Parker traded draft choices en masse for washed-up veterans during his regime.

[For] two years the Steelers didn't own a pick until the eighth round. When Pittsburgh did bumble into drafting a good player here and there, some sort of disaster seemed to befall them.

Johnny Lattner, a No. 1 from Notre Dame, had a promising rookie season for Pittsburgh and then entered the Army. He injured a knee playing service ball and never recovered.

Lowell Perry of Michigan was a strong contender for NFL rookie of the year in 1956 until Roosevelt Grier of the New York Giants sandwiched him on a kickoff return. Perry suffered a fractured pelvis, the type of injury usually associated with an auto accident, and never played again.

Things Look Up, then Old Tex Strikes

This season there appeared to be a brighter outlook for the Steelers. The team moved into brand new Three Rivers Stadium and the American Football Conference. Chuck Noll, the energetic young coach, doesn't appear to have the foibles of Kiesling, Parker and other past Steeler coaches.

He plucked a gem from the draft in Joe Greene in 1969 and this year landed Terry Bradshaw, a quarterback described as a clean-cut Joe Namath. Bradshaw led the Steelers to four victories in five exhibition games. Then disaster struck.

First, Tex Maule of *Sports Illustrated* picked the Steelers to win their divisional title. This is the ultimate hex, like breaking 13 mirrors while walking under a ladder, for teams usually go to pieces after Maule puts the evil eye on them.

Sure enough, it was a disaster Sunday when the Steelers opened the regular season at home favored over the Houston Oilers. Bradshaw completed only 4 of 16 passes. Pittsburgh lost, 19-7, and the crowd put out the S.O.S sign—same old Steelers.

A Steeler fan looks back in anger and asks, "Why Tex?"

NO ANCIENT HISTORY, PLEASE

Pat Livingston

As a sportswriter who has been covering losers for more years than I care to recall, it raises the hair on the back of my neck to be reminded that the Steelers haven't won a championship in 39 years.

It is particularly hackling this year, tarring the best personnel the Steelers have ever had with the failures and weaknesses of their predecessors. The architects of the Steelers' ignoble past are gone, many of them before the oldest veteran on the team, John Brown, was even born.

It strikes me as being eminently unfair to attribute to the 1971 Steelers—class players like Joe Greene, Lloyd Voss, Dwight White, Terry Bradshaw, Mel Blount, Andy Russell, Jack Ham, Dave Smith, Chuck Allen, the whole collective squad—the stigma of failure. This, in truth, is a team that hasn't failed, despite what critics may think of its record.

How could one expect more than the Steelers have given?

It would be a travesty for professional football should Terry Bradshaw, a baby-faced kid of 22, walk into the season and show the Morralls and Brodies and Dawsons and Gabriels and Nelsens how pro football should be played. Quarterbacks, even at age 25, rarely have the poise or maturity of judgment to win big, pressure-packed games when they count.

Strong young quarterbacks can win games, but it takes wise and experienced heads to win titles.

My confidence in this Steeler team isn't shaken by its losses to Denver and Houston. Wasn't it Bart Starr, 26, with the Packers' Team of the Decade behind him—not Norm Van Brocklin—who failed in the Packers' 1960 showdown? And in another year, it was Dallas' young quarterback, Don Meredith, who threw victory into the alien arms of Tom Hart in the Green Bay end zone.

Pity the Q-Back

In no sport is the pressure so intense as it is on a quarterback in football. In baseball or basketball, teammates are there to take up the slack; a loser in golf answers to no one but himself; in tennis and

From the *Pittsburgh Press*, December 9, 1971. Copyright/*Pittsburgh Post-Gazette*, 2001. All rights reserved. Reprinted with permission.

boxing, it's man against man, one on one. But in football, the man who gets the snap from center controls the game, or the game controls him.

The pressures on quarterbacks are intensified because so many depend on so few. Aside from game pressure, quarterbacks face economic tensions because underpaid players expect so much of overpaid passers, and they face racial aggravations because whites depend on blacks and blacks depend on whites, and everybody looks into other lockers when there is a search for a scapegoat.

The Steelers lost in 1971 because their fine young quarterback, Terry Bradshaw, had not stewed in the kettle of pressure long enough to come out as a full-fledged pro.

They did not lose because Art Rooney paid Tex Mayhew only $100 a game. They did not lose because their tailbacks, Johnny Clement and Morales Gonzalez, were sidelined with injuries for the playoff with Philadelphia, nor because Lynn Chandnois cracked his ribs, correcting the mistake of Johnny Lattner who had fumbled at the one. It wasn't because Walt Kiesling cut Johnny Unitas or Buddy Parker traded Lennie Dawson to Cleveland, nor because Bill Austin lost control of his team.

The Steelers did not lose because their coach is low-key, for compared to the Vikings' Bud Grant, Chuck Noll is a hopping jack-in-the-box and compared to [the Rams'] Tommy Prothro, a blabbermouth. The Steelers lost for the same reason Green Bay lost, because they didn't have a Bart Starr to absorb the pressure.

Absorbing pressure is an important course in the curriculum of a quarterback, just as it plays a part in the making of a golfer. Even as fine a pro as Jack Nicklaus spent three years on the tour, an acknowledged master of the game, before he became golf's leading money winner.

Try Pat on Back

The Steelers' failure to win must not be permitted to demean the accomplishments of a 40-man squad. This is a fine football team, a team perhaps on the threshold of excellence, and to equate it with incompetent teams of another era introduces McCarthyism to sports. Guilt by association is scarcely the sporting thing.

For the first time in a decade, the pendulum is on the upswing for the Steelers, a team more deserving of support than slander. Impressionable, brimming with the confidence of youth, the Steeler kids are at an age where a pat on the back is more effective than a kick in the teeth.

It accomplishes nothing to accentuate that the Steelers, over the last 25 years, have been the worst team in football. In the first place, that's not true. Since the end of World War II at least, the Washington Redskins' record is worse than the Steelers'.

Or do we revert to the days of the [1920s] Pottsville Maroons to evaluate the Steelers of 1971?

Rust-Belt Rivalry

Except for a short time during the 1990s, in which Cleveland mourned for their beloved, departed Browns and awaited the beginning of a new Browns' era, the Pittsburgh Steelers and the Cleveland Browns have played each other twice a year since Cleveland entered the NFL in 1950. The rivalry was a natural one not just because of proximity, but also because both cities prided themselves on their gritty, rust-belt images. A Steelers-Browns game was not just about gridiron supremacy, it was a contest to determine which town was tougher, manlier, superior. A pair of articles by Phil Musick suggested the importance of the rivalry to both camps' fans and depicted the holiday atmosphere that surrounded the biennial tradition. Musick's pieces also reflected the Steelers' changing fortunes. Cleveland was clearly the dominant team in 1969—Musick's report followed a 24-3 drubbing of the Steelers—but it was equally obvious that 1972 was a special year for Pittsburgh, when the Black and Gold stomped the hated Browns 30-0 on their way to capturing the AFC Central title.

FANS (HIC) TOAST VICTORY BY BROWNS

Phil Musick

Mostly, Red drinks beer, but like a good Browns' fan, he will improvise when necessary. "If you can pour it, I can drink it, " he boasts. Red's biggest bag is the Browns and yesterday he was numbered among the 4500 or so Cleveland fans who came to town to watch the Steelers calmly absorb another full measure of humility.

Between sips, Red admitted that the 12 cases of beer that traveled with him and 39 buddies had not held out as well as expected. Calling on the reserves—a plastic flask of bourbon—Red watched a little slice of Ohio wend its way up Allequippa Street towards Pitt Stadium.

"We let it all hang out when we come to Pittsburgh, it's really a one-day blast," he said, pouring down a triple and then sucking in the crisp air blowing up Centre Avenue past the 75-odd chartered buses which had hauled Brown fans to the blood-letting.

More buses—another 30 or so—were parked up on the rim of the stadium, making the field easy to find for those bleary of the eye.

If Red isn't typical of the Brown fans who annually invade Pittsburgh under a full head of Scotch, the mold wouldn't have to be bent much to accommodate him.

It's a crowd full of broken fingernails and leather jackets; guys who carry lunchpails and would be embarrassed if they had to lug a briefcase a block. But mainly they come to laugh, to drink and to go home a winner.

"They're just having fun—so far," says a harried traffic cop, laboring to keep Clevelanders out from under the Greyhounds. "There will be a few scuffles, a coupla bloody noses, but it's just the booze."

One Brown fan, wearing a white straw skimmer and a blank stare, lurches into the traffic, puts a shoulder fake on a blue Buick and ricochets off a parked car onto the sidewalk. Having safely negotiated the crossing, he proceeds to fall headlong into an ashcan full of ice and beer cans, and it takes two friends to extricate him.

"I got news for you," sneers a guy in a wool mackinaw. "I ain't carrying you up that hill." The drunk regroups his dignity and struggles up Avalon Street at the tail end of a weaving line.

Not all are hitting the jug. Solid citizens also scurry toward the arena. A husband and wife argue. He has forgotten the extra blanket; she has mislaid the thermos of coffee. They mediate the quarrel and push on.

"We're here to whomp the (bleep) out of the (bleep) Steelers," a man shouts, precipitating a pennant-waving, screeching verbal duel between himself and a Steeler fan. They prod each other until the Steeler supporter slips on the ice. Cheers. The Browns win again.

Most of the women in the tumbling mass of well-bundled humanity are shapeless in heavy corduroy or wool. A tight, pink pants suit, forsaking warmth for admiration, draws a cheer and a statuesque blonde brazens it out, staring back at the leers. But mostly the women peek out from under mufflers and scarves and lopsided hats of all shades and shapes.

Fighting into the stadium, guys from the Garfield Heights Eagles, and Teddy's Bar, and Tom's Bar, and Tillie's Tavern, quickly find seats and break out the six-packs some have slipped past the cops whose numbers have been tripled to approximately 130 because of the Cleveland invasion.

Before the day is over a haggard police sergeant at an Oakland station will admit there have been "arrests too numerous to mention. We haven't quit counting." Mostly it's the booze. But one fan is hit by a snowball and pulls a gun. The Tactical Police Force patrolmen hustle him off without a shot fired.

Meanwhile, barrels of fried chicken and a flood of ham-and-cheese on rye appear. Fat-cat Cleveland fans are in a more festive mood than their Pittsburgh counterparts, which is, of course, to be expected.

When the game begins, they offer advice unabashedly. "Run the curl!" they scream. Gary Collins runs a curl pattern and scores. Accepting a Brown win as inevitable, the visitors recharge their batteries.

Bottles come out of brown paper bags; gym bags and blankets and at least one full-sized suitcase surrender beer cans. An argument breaks out, the cops move in. A 5-8 patrolman snaps his billy in a short arc and a 6-6 Clevelander grows humble, his nose suddenly a fountain of red.

A T.P.F. cop finds it thirsty work. Sneaking a quick belt, he tells a friend, "If I can get one of those down to my toes I'll be all right."

Down on the field six policemen give the bum's rush to an inebriate, who emulates his heroes and tosses a neat downfield block which sends two of the cops slithering into the gooey slush.

As the sun beats down, the hooch starts to take a heavy toll. Good-natured humor is lost when a drunk drops his Cleveland pennant and follows it down the concrete steps breaking his glasses. He scuttles away to hide his embarrassment. At halftime the band plays John Philip Sousa when "How Dry I Am" would have been more appropriate. "Get a basehit," screeches a late-arrival who has been sleeping it off in the back of the bus. His six-pack is immediately confiscated and added to a stack beside Gate 23 that would have turned on half of Oakland.

The game becomes a rout in the fourth quarter, ending with Cleveland reserve quarterback Jerry Rhome knocked down by three fans. The cheerful lads from Sgro's Bar on the East Side of Cleveland— pelted unmercifully by snowball-smoking Steeler fans when they carried their bed-sheet pennant around the stadium before the game—fold it up and trudge toward the buses.

Back on Centre Avenue the lampposts are festooned with those who have misjudged their capacities. But loyalty dies hard and, like the Marines, the Clevelanders carry their wounded from the battlefield.

Here and there a body dots the snow, an outflung arm pillowing a head unbothered by thoughts of frostbite or overexposure. The mighty Browns have prevailed, uninhibited camaraderie has been displayed, the bottles are all empty.

Can a Cleveland fan ask for more?

STAND UP AND CHEER
Phil Musick

You don't root. It's part of the job; like you being in Atlanta and your suitcase being in Toledo. It's unprofessional to root. Under the influence of a little booze, most of us talk with pride about how when 50,000 people are tearing at their clothes and otherwise going out of their minds, we've had the mental presence to note that while the fullback was running 99 yards for the game-winning touchdown, the center was holding the other guys' middle linebacker by the seat of the pants with both hands.

No, you don't root. Last week a reporter who covers the Steelers jumped up at a critical juncture. Another writer told him to sit down. "Don't root," said the guy.

And you don't write about not rooting. You go over to the stadium and you talk to a player about the game. You don't write about rooting, pro or con; it's unprofessional, too. Like writing in the first person.

Today I'm going to root. Further, I am going to write about why I am going to root, and if that upsets you, the funnies are up front someplace. Today I am going to root for a town. This one. Paris [made] hard by the pollution; Vienna as interpreted through the eyes of architects scared early in life by an erector set. Birmingham of the North.

I am going to root for all the times I played hooky to watch Pat Brady loft those incredibly high, twisting punts into the cold, blue sky over Forbes Field. And the times my old man and I sat in the end zone, sipping a little sour mash and learning something about this complex business of father and son. And I am going to root for all the Jobs of this town who feel the Steelers somewhere just under their sternums.

From the *Pittsburgh Press*, December 3, 1972. Copyright/*Pittsburgh Post-Gazette*, 2001. All rights reserved. Reprinted with permission.

No town should harbor a loser for more than 40 years; to do so would be corrosive to the spirit. We have smoke and unemployment and teachers with picket signs in their book bags and not long ago we had plumbers being chauffeured to faulty spigots, but four decades of disaster we do not deserve.

So today I am going to root for justice. The Cleveland Browns have won 25 assorted championships; the pointy-headed Pittsburgh Steelers have won 25 less. If that blindfolded old broad on the scales is not a phoney, the Steelers are going to trim the Browns today.

They are going to win it mostly for a guy I know. He works with his hands, which is to say he doesn't make a lot of dough; he also works split shifts, so he's never quite sure if it is time for breakfast or Archie Bunker.

Most of the time he sleeps on the couch after dinner because at 5:30 his wife is going to start elbowing him in the ribs. He takes his work to lunch in a metal box, and while he's eating chipped-ham-on-rye-with-mustard and Tuesday's leftover cake, he talks with his buddies about the Steelers because, like the mortgage and the car that overheats and kids with colds, they belong to him.

He talks about the Steelers a lot, because this is a football town. The Pirates win all the time and that's fine. But this town has thick wrists and hot blood and men who when they bump one another on the street say "Watch it, Mac" instead of "pardon me," and in a place where some of the women even wash down their whiskey with beer, the gut game is football.

This guy I am talking about is a football man. He's behind at church and the grocery store and half the other places in town, but he'll lay down $7.15 today because, even though he's scared, he figures this is the year he's been waiting for since he can't remember when.

He likes "Gerela's Gorillas," the guys from Port Vue who cheer for placekicker Roy Gerela. When they put up bedsheets trying to psych the other team's kickers, he laughs. It might not be considered the epitome of wit some places, but he thinks it's funny.

He was there last week when the Steeler offense kept overloading the defense, and he was one of the guys Andy Russell was talking about when he said, "These fans are really something else. We kept holding and holding, but after a while you get to thinking, 'This is futile; we're going to lose the damn game 3-0.' But every time we came off the field we could hear them yelling for us. They wouldn't let us quit."

My guy has been screaming and booing and cussing for years. And on some cold, gray Sundays when they've waited until the last few seconds to blow one, he's walked out of the stadium hoping someone would cross him so he could punch them in the mouth.

This guys sounds familiar, you say? Maybe he is. Maybe he's you.

The Immaculate Reception

A case could be made that the most perfect play in the history of the NFL—and perhaps of all sports—occurred on December 23, 1972, when the Steelers hosted the Oakland Raiders in an AFC playoff game. On a purely athletic level, the Immaculate Reception was a fluke, a long shot that in any mathematically just world should not have happened. The physics were just too improbable. Considering the score when it happened, the time remaining in the game, the position of every player on the field, the rules of the game, and the unpredictability of a bouncing football—it just should not have happened. But it did. And every sports season, one or two such flukes take place. A Hail Mary pass, a last second fifty-foot basket, a lucky punch in the fleeting moments of a fight—they happen.

What elevates the Immaculate Reception above the other flukes, what lifts it to the realms of poetry, was the fact that it also marked a moment—the exact moment—when the Pittsburgh Steelers quit being the same old Steelers and became something very special. It formed a double-hinge in Steelers history, closing one door and opening another. In addition, it came when the town, the entire region, needed it most; when the steel mills were closing, workers were losing their jobs, and the Rust Belt was taking shape. When hope was at a premium, a football settled into Franco Harris's hands.

There were numerous views about what happened that day. Quarterback Terry Bradshaw recounted what it meant to him, and Red Smith, one of America's finest sportswriters, suggested what it meant to the Steelers. Finally, sportswriter Tom LaMarre provided Oakland's bitter read on the play.

A GOOD ROAR

Terry Bradshaw

I arrived in Pittsburgh as a rookie so naive about life that I wanted to walk up to people on the street and lick their faces like a big puppy dog. I was scared to death they would discover that I was only little old Terry Bradshaw from Shreveport, Louisiana, who didn't know a zone defense from a zip code.

From *Looking Deep* by Terry Bradshaw with Buddy Martin (Chicago: Contemporary Books, 1989). Reprinted by permission of Terry Bradshaw.

A flip of a coin had decided my fate this time and not the bounce of a football. Like the Steelers, the Chicago Bears had won only one game that season, and, ironically, that was 38-7 against—do you believe it?—the Steelers. Chuck Noll won his first game as a rookie coach, 16-13, and lost all the rest. So the two teams flipped a coin for the first pick in the 1970 draft. The Steelers won and chose me. The Bears picked tackle Rufus Mayes of Ohio State.

Three seasons after that draft, my dreams and the hopes of generations of sports fans in Pittsburgh converged into one unforgettable magic moment.

Three Rivers was rockin' that famous day in December. Each star player had his own little cult among the fans. There was Gerela's Gorillas, a group of devotees to placekicker Roy Gerela, some of whom actually wore gorilla costumes. There was Franco's Italian Army, followers of our great running back Franco Harris, who wore combat fatigues long before Rambo made them popular. Franco's Army came to the games with grenades, green berets, machetes, combat boots, and I swear, I think half of them parachuted into their seats from helicopters. The guards at the back gate even wore combat helmets. Franco was our Italian Stallion, a kind of Rocky Balboa of the Steelers, and if he had chosen to lead his troops to war, I have no doubt they would have followed him straight to Southeast Asia.

Then there was the other Rocky—Rocky Bleier, the Vietnam veteran, the tough little guy with the big heart. Rocky was a star running back, the captain of his Notre Dame team, a brave soldier who had part of his foot shot off in Vietnam. He was a favorite of our owner, Art Rooney, who kept Rocky around on injured reserve and, I believe, paid for the surgery on his foot. Then we had Kolb's Kowboys, the disciples of Jon Kolb, the big offensive tackle from Oklahoma State. And there was Jack Ham, the Polish linebacker from Penn State. Polish people would send him Polish hams.

Mean Joe Greene's fans were in fine form and so were the supporters of Ernie "Fats" Holmes, who was just a rookie. There might even have been a few Terry Bradshaw fans, but not many, because I was still struggling just to keep my starting job. It was an incredible collection of spectators. And they were primed for this stirring moment in Steeler history, what I like to call—with tongue in cheek—"The Immaculate Reception."

The Steelers were coached by Chuck Noll, a little-known assistant from Baltimore who had come to them from Don Shula's staff in 1969.

After winning just five and losing nine my rookie season, Noll's team won six and lost eight in 1971, showing little improvement. But the Steelers of 1972 surprised the league by winning nine of their last ten games for an 11-3 record, and the city of Pittsburgh got hotter than the foundry at U.S. Steel. The good people of Pittsburgh were simply not prepared for what they were about to witness. Nor was I.

Trailing 7-6, we were all looking for a miracle in the last seventy-two seconds of our first-round American Football Conference playoff game against the Raiders. Unaccustomed as we were to the circumstances at hand—being in a position to still win but not really knowing what it would take—there was little hope that we could escape what appeared to be inevitable defeat.

The Raiders had put a clamp on our star rookie Harris, who had gained a thousand yards rushing that season, and at the half it was a scoreless tie. Oakland quarterback Daryl Lamonica was suffering from a bout with the flu, so he was replaced in the fourth quarter by a young left-hander named Kenny Stabler. I finally completed a couple of passes and we got two field goals out of Gerela for a 6-0 lead with just under four minutes to play. There probably weren't many fans there that day who believed we could hold on to win against the mighty Raiders. And I guarantee you there was not one who thought we could come back to win it after Stabler caught us in a safety blitz and scored. George Blanda kicked the extra point to put Oakland ahead by one. There was no chance to return the Raiders' kickoff because Blanda hit the goal posts, which in those days were still on the goal line.

If the Steelers would have told the truth, we would have admitted to being ready to pack up our gear and leave the field, because all of us thought we had already heard the all too familiar refrain of The Fat Lady. We had no shot. Our offense had been stuffed by the Raiders' defense all day. The chances of our scoring on the Raiders at that point were about as likely as Johnny U. showing up in our huddle, wearing Steeler black and gold again, and asking: "Can I help, guys?" We were an unproven commodity, a young team without an identity or a winning tradition, directed by a quarterback who had always been long on dreams but short on big-time credentials.

The worst sin a football player can commit is to confess he is a realist in the face of trouble. Athletes learn at an early age to ignore the facts and deny the inevitable. You may be scared to death, totally uncertain about the next few seconds of your life, but you don't ever admit it for fear of being branded a quitter, non-believer, and a lousy team player. Here in the last minute of the most important football game played to that date in Pittsburgh, I was glad the Steeler coaching staff didn't ask me to take a loyalty oath, because I would have flunked.

Quarterbacks are supposed to be brash, cocky field generals with tunnel vision and a strong sense of purpose. It's the quarterback's job to inspire the ten other men around him in the huddle, and coaches say if that quarterback wavers just a tiny bit, the team's confidence will erode. I was a little short on confidence at the moment. So I had to fake my coolness. I had my walk down to perfection and could swagger in and out of the huddle like a show horse. As long as the fans didn't see my knees shaking, they probably said: "Look at that Bradshaw boy! He's in total control." I had very little confidence that I could move the Steelers the final eighty yards for the winning touchdown against the Raiders. Fact is, I was just trying to get us a first down.

I was a young quarterback who'd never been in that situation before, never had to carry such a load, and here we were on national TV, playing these mean, nasty, spiteful Raiders, who not only had a Commitment to Excellence, but a Commitment to Kicking Our Butts. They had already played in one Super Bowl and probably viewed this game as a minor inconvenience on their way to the AFC Championship Game.

I had spent most of the day handing the ball off left or handing it off right, with an occasional pass, because that's the kind of offense Noll ran then. I wasn't doing much to help our cause. And although I did get the Steelers up to the forty yard line, two of my next three passes were knocked down by the Raiders' great defensive back Jack Tatum, who was to be a central character in the drama that was soon to unfold.

You can see why my confidence was lacking as we got in the huddle, looking downfield at sixty yards of green artificial turf between us and the end zone. So far that day it had been virgin territory to the Steelers, except for Gerela's two field goals.

In the hurry-up offense, or two-minute drill, time can be your best ally or worst enemy. Everything is in high gear. Quarterbacks generally call two plays at a time in the huddle, and it takes a savvy veteran to use the clock exactly right. Unitas was a master at it. You throw an incomplete pass out of bounds to stop the clock, regroup, and call two more plays. We were regrouping in the huddle. Our big tight end from Clemson, John McMakin, had been telling me all day that he could get open and so I fired one off to him, incomplete, and we scampered back to the huddle in search of something else that might work. On the second play, I threw it over the middle to McMakin again, incomplete, almost right into the hands of a Raider. Tatum knocked it away. The first lucky bounce. Time was running out and I was feeling more pressure every second. I tried one more pass to my left, this one to wide receiver Al Young, but Tatum was there again.

It was fourth down and ten with twenty-two seconds to play and Chuck sent in a play. We had not produced a single yard in three tries. I had completed just ten of twenty-four passes for a mere 115 yards. How was I going to complete a fourth down pass against the Oakland Raiders when I had been playing terribly? All of a sudden I was faced with throwing the greatest pass of my life. The fans were screaming so loud that I could hardly hear the play Chuck sent in as it was repeated in the huddle. I was supposed to hit Barry Pearson, the receiver from Northwestern in his first season as a Steeler, somewhere over the middle.

It was fourth down with a long, long way to go when I took the snap from Ray Mansfield and dropped back, feeling the heat of the Raider rush like a blowtorch in my face. Oakland's two defensive ends, Tony Cline and Horace Jones, had arrived in the pocket almost as quickly as I did. Across the field, big John Madden was on a rampage, yelling at the Raiders to play deep in the prevent defense and watch for the long pass.

No matter how tall a quarterback is—and I'm 6'3"—you only feel about 5'6" when you stride and stretch out to throw the football with giant 6'8" defensive linemen coming at you. I felt like a midget as I looked for a crack of daylight, hoping to see a Steeler jersey somewhere in the clear.

The final twenty-two seconds had all but evaporated. I couldn't see Franco, but he was downfield waving and yelling for my attention. I thought I saw Frenchy Fuqua over the middle and figured I could throw a deep post route. A huge figure in silver and black was bearing down on me from my left side, so I moved to the right in the pocket. When I cocked my arm, I wasn't sure where I was going to throw the ball because I couldn't see downfield, but I knew the worst thing for me to do was get sacked. One guy was grabbing me; I shook loose and had to push another guy off with my left hand. I was swinging the ball, about to throw, and another Raider came barreling at me in mid-air, so I ducked and he went flying over my shoulder. When I came up I saw people all around me, and I knew I had to get rid of the ball in a hurry. So I gunned it. And when I gunned it, I got gunned. Knocked flat on my ass.

When you get knocked to the ground on a football field and can't see the action, you listen carefully for telltale sounds. You learn to read those noises the way an Indian reads bear tracks. There's a good roar and bad roar. I was on my back and couldn't see anything but gray sky overhead, green artificial turf, and black and silver uniforms on top of me. The ball was somewhere on the way toward Fuqua—I thought— because as I unloaded it, I thought I saw a number 33 in the middle of the field. So I turned up my hearing to listen for a clue as to what had happened.

Of all the roars I have ever heard, there's never been one to compare to that one. As I picked my head up off the turf, knowing instinctively that all but a few seconds had expired on the game clock, I had the feeling something wonderful had happened. The fans were going nuts. And as I jumped up, I saw something truly miraculous: Franco crossing the goal line and going into the end zone. Art Rooney, Sr., had left the owner's box before the end of the game, thinking we had lost, and was waiting in the dressing room to console us. He heard the unexpected noise and asked an attendant what had happened. Stunned, Mr. Rooney couldn't believe the news. The attendant told him to listen to the crowd noise—it was a good roar.

Fans streamed onto the field, some of them mobbing me. I realized we had won, but I still didn't know how. "This is unbelievable! Unbelievable!" I said. "Somebody tell me. What happened?" They just kept hollering, "You did it, you did it!" And I kept asking, "Did what? Somebody please tell me!"

Then I got a grip on myself and said, "Terry, you quarterbacking demon! You must have threaded the needle right in there amongst all those Oakland Raiders and hit Frenchy and then he lateralled to Franco who went in for a touchdown." I started feeling pretty good about myself. And I knew it was time to get my quotes down. As a pro athlete you learn early to get your quotes down. When you talk to the press after a big play or big game, you need to sound a little bit hip, throwing in a few technical terms so that they never totally understand what you're saying. And always act humble while taking credit for something that you really don't deserve.

You'll still get different opinions from each side about what actually happened on The Immaculate Reception. Here's the Steelers' version: Tatum of the Raiders, going up for the ball at the same time as Fuqua at the Oakland thirty-five yard line, knocked it back in my direction about twenty feet as he collided with Frenchy. The ball caromed toward Franco, who was standing at about the Raiders' forty-two yard line, hoping to get my attention. Franco had taken off running toward Frenchy after seeing the ball was thrown to him, looking to throw a block. Harris later said that as he ran toward Frenchy, he saw the ball pop out. "The ball kept coming straight at me," he said, "and from there it was all instinct." Franco reached down below his knees for the ball and I swear it was no higher than a half-inch off the artificial surface. He took off running with Jim Warren of the Raiders chasing him and scored with five seconds left in the game.

Speaking as an observer of game films and not an eye witness—I was only an "earwitness"—I think the ball must have been hit first by Tatum, the defender. Coming from his defensive backfield position, Tatum knocked the ball backward toward me. I don't think I threw the ball hard enough for it to hit Frenchy and bounce backward twenty feet to the spot where Harris made the catch. If it had hit Frenchy in the chest at the angle he was running, the football would have veered off to the right instead of straight backwards, because of the ricochet factor. See what I mean? Frenchy is moving laterally across the field, Tatum is coming from his safety position, they converge on the ball, and Tatum's momentum carries the ball backward. There has never been conclusive evidence as to whether it hit Tatum or Fuqua first. All we can do is speculate. It may have hit them at exactly the same time.

You can understand why Raider fans still get emotional about this call, because if it was wrong, their team might have been screwed out of going to the Super Bowl that year. If Frenchy *did* touch the ball first, then the play was voided. In those days, it was illegal for a ball to be touched first by another offensive player, as the Raiders claim Fuqua did, before being caught. Frenchy has said in past years that he didn't, but now when you ask him he likes to play coy. The only people who really know for sure are Frenchy and Tatum. I never see or hear from Jack and don't expect to. Frenchy, who now works in the *Detroit News* circulation department, doesn't want to say and is either going to take his secret to the grave or write a book about it himself someday.

I'm not even sure Frenchy could settle the argument anyway, because no one is going to convince those irate Raider fans that we won fair and square. So we can forget that. However, we shouldn't let that controversy taint the historical significance of The Immaculate Reception or diminish Franco's great effort—he pulled off a spectacular catch. No matter how many times experts looked at tape and film, they could never really get the real truth. Even the still photos of Franco clutching the ball just above the artificial turf were slightly blurry, so you couldn't see for sure if he had possession—although there's no question that he did. Twilight Zone stuff, man.

There was no such thing as use of instant replay by the officials back in 1972, although the networks were using it in their telecasts. Madden reminded me one day years later that referee Fred Swearingen did not signal for a touchdown right away. First, he went to the sideline and conferred by phone with Art McNally, chief of NFL officials, in the press box. Swearingen's crew didn't know who touched the ball first, so they had ruled it was touched simultaneously and wanted to know if there was anything revealing in the replay. They even rigged up a special TV for Swearingen on the sideline so he could watch the replay at the same time. McNally concurred: no conclusive evidence to reverse the call. This was the first time in NFL history that TV was used to aid an official's judgment. Instant replay was born.

I don't think Madden will ever forgive us for winning that game, especially the unorthodox way we did it. He was stomping along the sidelines, trying to figure out what happened like everyone else. And Madden would never let his team forget the bitter defeat, which set the stage for the great Steelers-Raiders rivalry in years to come. We paid for our good fortune: the next season the Raiders whipped our tails, 33-14, in the AFC playoffs. But over the next four seasons it was pretty even: the Raiders and Steelers met in four straight postseason contests, with each team winning two games.

So many lives were affected by what happened in Pittsburgh on December 23, 1972. The seeds of the Steelers' dynasty years were planted right there in the artificial turf of Three Rivers Stadium when the football took such an incredibly bountiful bounce for us. Some men went on to become famous and few even made small fortunes. Nobody benefited from it more than Chuck Noll, who was still there long after the dynasty years ended, picking up the pieces.

HOW FORT DUQUESNE
REPELLED RAIDERS

Red Smith

In the raucous streets, Frenchy's Foreign Legion honked at Bradshaw's Brigade, Gerela's Gorillas hailed Ham's Hussars, and foot soldiers in Franco's Italian Army waved red, white and green flags. Back in the bowels of Three Rivers Stadium, Frenchy Fuqua's muttonchop whiskers twitched rapturously. Art Rooney's cigar was limp. The first postseason football game in Pittsburgh history was over and not since Braddock was ambushed at Fort Duquesne had the town known a day like this.

Forty years ago little Arthur Rooney, 135-pound playing coach of the Majestic Radios, the Hope Harveys and the James P. Rooneys, paid $2,500 for a franchise in the National Football League. Never in all the cold autumns since then had the Steelers got the whiff of a championship of any kind, and now here they were: half-champions of the American Conference with a date to play again next Sunday for the conference title and a chance to earn $25,000 a man in Super Bowl VIII. And of all the 478 games they had played before last Saturday, none was more gaudily theatrical than the 13-7 conquest of the Oakland Raiders that had brought them to this plateau.

Five seconds this side of defeat, the victory was accomplished on a busted play in which the Oakland defense performed flawlessly.

With fourth down, 10 yards to go, on the Pittsburgh 40-yard line, 22 seconds remaining on the clock, Oakland on top by 7-6, and a horde of predators clawing for Terry Bradshaw's eyeballs, the Steelers' scrambling quarterback threw a pass that Oakland's accomplished safety man, Jack Tatum, deflected out of Frenchy Fuqua's reach. The play was designed to gain about 18 yards—enough to get the ball into field goal range for Roy Gerela—and Fuqua became the target only because the defense wouldn't let the primary receiver, Barry Pearson, get downfield.

Electronic Judgment

Blocked by Tatum around the Raiders' 35-yard line, the ball flew back about 7 yards to Franco Harris. The rookie runner fielded it at his knees and crossed the goal line 42 yards away with the clock showing five seconds to play.

"We'll take those little crumbs," said Chuck Noll, the Pittsburgh coach. His tone was devout.

The Steelers reached their dressing room in a daze. Fuqua, who had been knocked down in a collision with Tatum, had thought the pass was incomplete. "When I got up I saw Franco [at] about the 5-yard line."

"I didn't see the ball bounce away," Bradshaw said. "I just saw Franco take off. I thought, 'Man! It must have hit him right on the numbers!' I've played football since the second grade and nothing like that ever happened. It'll never happen again. And to think it happened here in Pittsburgh in a playoff!"

"We're putting the play in tomorrow," Noll promised.

Before Fred Swearingen, the referee, ruled the touchdown official he checked with Art McNally, the NFL supervisor of officials, who had watched the televised replay in the press box and confirmed Swearingen's observation that a defensive player (Tatum) had indeed touched the ball and the pass had not gone illegally from Bradshaw to Fuqua to Harris.

Jim Kensil, the league's executive director, hastily denied that the decision had been made in the press box for fear such a precedent would be cited forevermore by coaches and players demanding that officials consult the instant replay before rendering judgments. However, Noll, who had huddled on the field with all the officials and John Madden, the Raiders' protesting coach, already had reported that the referee had agreed "to check upstairs. I didn't know how."

Dr. Jock Was Smiling

Heightening the melodrama of the finish was the primeval stodginess of the defensive struggle that preceded it. For 58 minutes the teams played antediluvian football. After a scoreless first half, witnesses were saying, "It took the Steelers 40 years to get here, and they're setting the game back 80." Somewhere in the gray nothingness overhead, Dr. Jock Sutherland must have been watching with a smile of benign approval. When that dour Scot, that rock of conservatism, coached the Steelers, he considered the forward pass a crime against nature.

Harking back to the days of the Minnesota shift and the flying wedge, the Steelers smothered Oakland's attack so effectively that a 6-0 lead on two field goals by Gerela seemed safe until, with a minute and 13 seconds left, Ken Stabler slipped around end for a 30-yard touch-down run and George Blanda's conversion put Oakland in front, 7-6.

Now Chuck Noll remembered that on fourth-and-two on Oakland's 31 in the first half he had ordered a line plunge that failed instead of a placekick by Gerela. The 3 points he might have got but didn't would have meant a 9-7 lead now. "If I'd had a third leg I would have kicked myself," he confessed.

With a kicker like Gerela around, that would have been another mistake.

MADDEN: RAIDERS WERE ROBBED

"TATUM DIDN'T HIT BALL"

Tom LaMarre

Coach John Madden is positive Jack Tatum didn't touch the ball on Pittsburgh's freaky 60-yard pass play that killed the Oakland Raiders' season two days ago.

If he didn't, it should have been ruled an incomplete pass for bouncing off Frenchy Fuqua right to Franco Harris, who ran the last 35 yards past the stunned Oakland defenders. It meant a 13-7 Pittsburgh victory in the final five seconds.

But Madden was most disillusioned by how the call was made.

Apparently, the National Football League officials in the pressbox established a precedent by making the decision from the television instant replay.

High NFL officials Jim Kensil, Art McNally and Val Pinchbeck were sitting just above the press row.

"The officials told me they didn't know what happened," Madden said, "and they were going to check upstairs to see what it was. The referee (Fred Swearingen) went in to use the dugout telephone, and when he came out he called it a touchdown.

"I saw McNally at the airport and he told me there was no doubt. Tatum touched the ball. But then I saw Jay Randolph of NBC Television and he told me there was no way to make a positive decision off the TV replays. Those are the same films McNally saw."

Madden spent part of Christmas Eve viewing the film he brought

As originally published in *The Oakland Tribune*, December 25, 1972. Reprinted by permission.

home from Pittsburgh and now is certain the Raiders were had.

"What Jack did was give him a good shot from behind," Madden explained, "Jack never touched the ball, which hit Fuqua on the shoulder pad. And then after the ball went to Harris, they clipped Phil Villapiano.

"But there was no way they were going to call it the other way with all those people out on the field. They only called one penalty on them all day as it was, and it was just a little five-yarder. I just think we were bleeped."

Steeler public relations director Joe Gordon told reporters in the press box that the NFL officials had made the decision from the replay, and even Pittsburgh coach Chuck Noll said it.

But when Kensil and Pinchbeck were confronted, they denied it.

"The decision was made on the field," declared Pinchbeck. "The referee was just phoning us to inform us of his decision."

He could have done it much easier by just signalling a touchdown.

"That's like an explanation I get from my little boy," said Madden, "when I catch him with his hand in the cookie jar.

"It's just so disappointing. It doesn't make any sense to come down through a whole season and have it end like that. It's unfair.

"If they would admit they set that precedent then maybe we could get a recall on this game and look at those films again. But it'll never happen."

It happened so quickly, most people didn't know exactly what took place.

Frenchy Fuqua?

"I cannot tell a lie," Fuqua said when asked if Tatum touched the ball. "No comment."

Later, Frenchy was overheard telling a Pittsburgh writer, "I'll tell you after the Super Bowl."

Madden didn't really expect to get the call.

"They couldn't have any other decision with all those wild people on the field," the coach said. "Something would have happened. Those people might have killed them."

The twin shocks of the Immaculate Reception and the prospect of the hapless Pittsburgh Steelers making it to the Super Bowl were too much for Jim Murray to handle. Writing in the Los Angeles Times *several days after Oakland's unlikely exit from the playoffs, he expressed his disbelief that a circus act like the Steelers might win football's highest prize. Forty years of futility were nicely boiled down into two columns as Murray minced no words and spared no feelings in this uproarious masterpiece of invective. The Steelers did what they could on game day to preserve Murray's peace of mind, dropping the AFC title game to the undefeated Miami Dolphins, 21-17.*

FOOTBALL WON'T BE SAME IF PITTSBURGH GETS IN SUPER BOWL

Jim Murray

If the Pittsburgh Steelers get in the Super Bowl, the world of football couldn't be more shocked if Harvard made it, contact lenses and all.

This is not a team, it's the football version of the old Flatbush Follies. It's a Warner Bros. frolic (pigskin parade) starring the Ritz Bros., the Meglin Kiddies, F. Hugh Herbert and Jack Oakie. Someday we're going to find out it's just a set for "The Road to the Super Bowl" starring Hope and Crosby and Dorothy Lamour.

No other team would get into the playoff on a pass that ricochetted off two colliding pass catchers into the arms of a half-black, half-Italian halfback who would run for a touchdown with five seconds to go. Tell me that isn't right out of Frank Capra's "Mr. Harris Goes to Town." "It happened one day." Print it. It's a take.

The team wasn't founded, it was, so to speak, foaled. Art Rooney, a race track punter and carnival fist fighter, broke the windows at the Saratoga Race Track one day in '33 and with his winnings bought a football team or, rather, he bought the Steelers. It's not the same thing.

Jim Butler, the L.A. advertising man, was on the phone in near tears the other day. He's an old Pittsburgh Steeler buff and, to them, achieving respectability is the saddest thing that's ever occurred to the Steelers. They view it like Jackie Vernon playing Hamlet, John Wayne

From the *Los Angeles Times*, December 29, 1972. Reprinted by permission of the Los Angeles Times Syndicate.

doing Camille. It's Frenchy Bordagaray picking up grounders with both knees off the ground, Babe Herman catching fly balls on the first bounce. For years, this team went around getting the custard pie in the face. It quit at the quarter pole, kept unseating its rider.

Some of the great all-time characters wound up on the Steelers. A Supreme Court justice once played in its backfield. So did a lot of guys whose cases will come before him.

Pittsburgh was never one of those "Take it in, John!" teams, Butler points out. It was more of a "well, what'll you clowns do wrong next?" type of team.

Take, for instance, Butler's favorite character. That would be Pat Brady the left footed kicker. Pat could kick a ball 100 yards but in a line drive. This usually meant the punt returner brought it back. Brady had a lower net than a crooked businessman with a double set of bookkeeping. So, they encouraged him to kick it high. Pat did. Pat had the highest kicks the league has ever seen. They came down with snow and eagles on them. The defensive end would signal for a fair catch as soon as they started up.

Pittsburgh was always a team which could play down to its capacity. They had an "attack" one year which consisted of Fran Rogell who was the master of the one-yard sweep. He ran to daylight, so long as the daylight was only inches away.

Their draft procedures they borrowed from a little old lady who plays the races with a hat pin. Pittsburgh always got the bonus pick (a "so so season" for them meant 4-10) and they picked up such all time all pros as Gary Glick, Johnny Lattner, Paul Cameron and Bob Ferguson. None of them could move fast enough to get away from a glacier. Pittsburgh had the distinction of having passed up such nonentities as Jim Brown, Paul Hornung, Bart Starr and Gale Sayers to get them.

They got their coaches out of "situation wanted" ads and their players out of the Street G. Smith Football annuals. Myron Cope, the Pittsburgh telecaster, once noted the Pittsburgh interior line looked "like a collection of hot water boilers. Just about as agile." Ernie Stautner, who anchored the defensive line, once went into the front office and demanded half the offensive team's pay. "Sometimes we don't have time to get off the field before they cough up the ball. I ain't sat down on the bench in years," he said. Some years, the offense has the ball five minutes a game. Including timeouts.

They brought Bobby Layne in from Detroit to play quarterback, and

Bobby, who scouted after hours joints as if they were defensive half-backs promptly hit a streetcar with his automobile one night. Since a streetcar does not have too many moves, this was not easy to do, but the club ticket manager was able to explain. "The streetcar," he said, "was wide open."

You can see where this lovable crew doesn't belong in the Super Bowl. They'll start coming out in women's hats. It'll turn out to be Flip Wilson, Jack Lemmon and Tony Curtis. It's a Billy Wilder script or Busby Berkeley will walk out in the middle of a huddle and blow a whistle and say, "okay, places everybody for the Hawaiian number!"

And, of course, if they get blown out of the tube by Miami, they've always got that great Joe E. Brown punchline: "Nobody's perfect."

Offensive Linemen

Everybody knows that offensive linemen are not quite right. They are the dirtiest, the most long-lived, the most clannish of all football players. They labor in anonymity, absorbing devastating hits from massive defensive linemen, opening holes for better-paid and better-known running backs, and protecting quarterbacks who soak up the lion's share of the attention. If you hear an offensive lineman's name during a game, it is probably because he has just committed a costly holding infraction. But linemen are people too, as seen in this selection from Roy Blount Jr.'s remarkable study of the Steelers, About Three Bricks Shy of a Load. *Blount, a writer for* Sports Illustrated, *spent the 1973 season with the team and produced one of the most candid, humorous, and heartfelt books ever written about football. In this chapter, he profiled Ray "The Old Ranger" Mansfield (Center, 1964–76) and Bruce "Moosie" Van Dyke (Guard, 1967–73), two of the starters on Pittsburgh's offensive line.*

MOOSIE AND THE OLD RANGER
Roy Blount Jr.

This football business is like a day off compared to what I did on the farm as a youngster. You don't get patted on the back or written up in the press for picking cotton.

—LEE ROY JORDAN, DALLAS COWBOYS

The road to easy street goes through the sewer.

—FAVORITE EXPRESSION OF OAKLAND HEAD COACH JOHN MADDEN

Mansfield and Van Dyke were indeed humorous company, but they didn't see football as any kind of joke. "Well, Bruce and I laughed our ass off about this," Ray said, when I asked them for a funny game story. "We were playing the Baltimore Colts. We were backed up to the 1-foot line, it's cold, we were losing bad, we wanted to get the game over. They're booing us, throwing snowballs at us, at home. Guys were ducking snowballs in the huddle. Well, in those days we had girls called the Steelerettes doing dances and shit behind the end zone. Larry

From *About Three Bricks Shy of a Load* (New York: Ballantine, 1974). Copyright Roy Blount Jr.

Gagner looked over there at them and said, seriously, 'Come on, you guys! At least the girls are still with us.'

"The girls are still with us! Great! But even that wasn't a laughing matter at the time. Only later. At the time it was a chuckling matter."

"You're not in a humorous mood," said Bruce, "on the field."

I talked to Moose and the Old Ranger for two or three hours one afternoon, trying to get an idea of what it was like in what are known as the trenches.

One of the things defensive linemen hate is to be "cut"—hit low, around the knees, and cut down. "I don't let nobody get my knees," Fats Holmes had said. "Come in and cut me, I say, 'Pleeze don't do that again.' Come in again, cut me, I got on him and hold him down, grab his old balls and twist 'em and say, 'Don't you do that again.'"

"Yeah, well," Van Dyke said, "they're embarrassed by being cut. It's sort of humiliating. But Joe Greene will chase an offensive lineman around kicking him. I wouldn't let Joe intimidate me like that. I cut Curly Culp once, he jumped up and got his cleats in my back, and made sure he stepped on my hand. But usually they don't do anything."

"What did you do when Curly Culp did that?"

"I hurt."

"Ray and I have different philosophies. He provokes guys, makes them mad. I try to stay friends with 'em, because if you don't they're going to hurt you more. They've got those great big forearms and they can beat the shit out of your neck. Once Walter Johnson beat me on a pass and Ray came across the middle from three or four yards away and stuck his helmet in Walter's ribs. Then Ray said, 'Way to hit, Bruce.'

"Well, there was Walter Johnson with veins just sticking out of his neck and forearms, and on the next play he just beat the shit out of me. It's a difference in philosophy. A sleeping giant like . . . We better keep personalities out of this. Don't want to make 'em mad. A sleeping giant, you don't fuck with him."

"Alex Karras," said Ray, "would have a personal vendetta against you. He'd come after you to the point sometimes he forgot about doing his job. Course he never could see. He saw objects, but that's about all.

"In the days of the 4-3 defense the center was the intimidator."

"Ray could sit back there all day and take those cheap shots."

"That's why you could be a 225-pound center. Now, with these uneven fronts, you've got those 280-pounders right over your head most of the time. But still . . . Karras—I used to like to get him mad. Some guys I like to mouth off to. Say 'Old Cunt. You must be having your period.' The defensive guys have to do a job. If the ball carrier's there they've got to get him, not you. But we can seek them out.

"I'll tell you a case when somebody got me, though," Mansfield said. "When we opened against the Bears in '67, our receiver caught a pass and I went flying downfield and blindsided Butkus. He was screaming the whole game, and I was cutting his ass down the whole time. Then there was a fumble. I fell on it. Butkus landed on me and his forearm caught me across the back of the neck. I got up. I couldn't tell which end of the field was mine. I said, 'Dick, I didn't even feel it.' They penalized him 15 yards. Course it didn't help my neck any. I would go after a guy like Joe Greene. I wouldn't let him intimidate me. I'd go after him till they threw me out of the game. I'd blindside him, whatever it took. When I meet my match and more than my match, I've always had the dogged attitude, I don't care how overmatched I am, I'm going to make it as hard as I can on that guy."

"I've been intimidated," said Bruce. "Before they changed the rule on clubbing. Now the defensive guy's supposed to be able to hit you with his arm only once, on his first step. It used to be—Walter Johnson would slap me in the head like a sledgehammer. Left, right, I was dizzy on my feet, I'd start to worry."

"I've been humiliated," Mansfield said. "By Bob Lilly, when Dallas beat us 56-14. But I've never been intimidated."

"I remember sometimes Walt didn't even rush the passer," said Van Dyke. "Just come across the line and wham, wham. Nothing I could do but put my hands up. He found it pretty easy to beat me after that. In the last exhibition game . . . no names . . . a guy complained, said I hit him a cheap shot. I said 'You motherfucker, you're not that good, that I have to cheap-shot you. You better watch your ass, cocksucker.'

"Then he said, 'Oh . . . Well . . . I didn't mean . . . '"

"It doesn't really get so intense, as far as the animalism of the attack," Mansfield said. "You can't just be an animal on the offensive line. You've got to be calculating and cunning."

Bruce: "You're graded on consistency. You've got to approach it as a business."

Ray: "You're playing a psychological game with these guys."

Bruce: "In your mind, you're trying to make yourself perform. To think the right things at the right time. I go over the play as I go to the line. First I look at what defense they're going to be in. Then I think of the count the snap's going to be on. If it's a trap play I think of my route real quick, or if it's a pass I think to myself, I'll have to set up real quick. Then I listen for an audible. Then if there's no audible at the snap I uncoil and do it.

"Everything's in my mind. All the plays and my assignments. All I do is flash back in my memory and make sure. If I don't sometimes I'll mess up. If I don't think 'I've got to set,' I'll mess up on the pass-block. It's easy to get complacent about your assignments. You're wired for it all but you've got to remind yourself every time."

Ray: "I think harder on the number the snap's going to be on. My primary responsibility is to get the ball up on time. I keep saying '2, 2, 2' or '4, 4, 4' to myself going up to the line. Once in a while I've forgotten it. Once in a while the quarterback forgets it. Thank God most quarterbacks anticipate a little bit by pushing their hands up. So I've got to think about the snap. Then the play and my blocking assignment. I see myself using the type of block I'm going to use."

Bruce: "The snap. It's like a sprinter getting off. Everybody has to get off at the same moment. Exact. Everybody anticipates just a little bit, everybody together."

Ray: "It's a relative thing. It amazes me, really. When is the exact time everybody gets off? It's not on the number, really. Say the snap is on 2. 'Hut 1, Hut 2 . . .'"

Bruce: "Usually it's just before the second 'hut.'"

Ray: "Yeah. I guess so. 'Hut 1, Hut . . .'"

"Then, too," Ray said, "sometimes the center has to make an adjustment. The guy who was supposed to be over me may be over Bruce. After the audible, then the center may make a blocking call. Sometimes a tackle or tight end will repeat it, so the whole line hears it. It's hard to hear down there. Guys will be saying, 'What? What?' I may call 'Stack' or 'Solid' or 'Gap.' Change the blocking assignments. A 'Gap' call can mean so many different things, according to what the play is. We have a gap call just about every play. We used to just have two calls: even and odd.

"Then the defense is trying to react. They can tell when the quarterback's calling an audible, by his voice. And they can see guys in the line picking their heads up."

Bruce: "You know we used to have a play on defense called the Fake Fake-the-Blitz Blitz. We would fake a fake blitz, and then blitz."

"Did it work?" I asked.
"I don't know," Ray said. "That's why we didn't win then maybe."
"What do you see and hear down there?" I asked.
"You're not aware of noises," Ray said.
"Everything flashes by," said Bruce.
"I always see eyes," said Ray. "I'm looking at eyes down there, not so much at faces. I'm looking to see where they're looking."

Bruce: "It's funny when your eyes do meet. You think, 'Wow, this is some kind of freak, looking right at me.' You feel guilty. You think you're going to do something wrong."

Ray: "I eye-fake. If I'm going to block a guy straight ahead I'll look down the line."

Bruce: "Lot of times if I'm going to the right I'll look to the left first. Then to the right. You've always got to look in the direction you're going to go."

Ray: "You know, I don't even know what guys on other teams look like."

Bruce: "Yeah. I remember seeing what somebody looked like recently, after a game. I was shocked. I never thought he looked like that. Guys look different in helmets."

Ray: "Hanratty looks like Yosemite Sam in his. Big nose sticking out of his helmet with a big moustache under it."

Bruce: "If you're on the field with the other team afterwards you may shake their hands. But not some games when you lose. Some games, there's no way I'm going to talk to any of 'em. No damn way. But last year after the Oakland game, after the Miraculous Reception, I felt compassion for those guys. They were down on the field with their hands down, their heads down, like they were praying to the East. I knew how I'd felt a few seconds before. I walked up to Art Thom. I thought he was Tony Kline. I said, 'Good game, Tony.'
"'How soon we forget,' he said."

"How do you feel when a teammate makes a big mistake, that costs you a game?"
"It's like when your little kid hurts you accidentally," said Ray.

"Like when Jimmy kicked me in the ribs two days after they were broken. You want to hit him, but your reason takes over."

"You know it could've just as easily been you," said Bruce.

Toward opponents their feelings were more complicated.

Bruce: "We were telling Bill Bergey, for Cincinnati, that we were going to get him for giving Hanratty a cheap shot. He was saying, 'Bruce, watch the film, it wasn't a cheap shot. You'll be wrong, you'll see. Bruce, that's publicity, you don't believe that, do you? They're trying to get me!'

"I said, 'You're a good football player, why do you do that stuff? You just piss people off.' He said, 'Well, I don't mean it. Bruce, you're always giving me the hard-ass.'

"You get to know guys. It makes it tough for me to play guys two games. Only way to play a good game is intensity—you've got to get mad. I'm not vindictive, I don't carry a grudge. But you've got to want to hurt people.

"But maybe you like the guy. He talks on the field to you. And I really want to hurt him because we're losing the game. How can I have these feelings? But they're temporary feelings."

Ray: "The impulse is to hurt a guy while you're out there. Then if you do hurt a guy you feel like a horse's ass."

Bruce: "I remember Lou Cordeleone said, 'Bruce, why'd you have to do that?'"

Ray: "Et tu, Bruce."

Bruce: "It was in LSU stadium. We were running a sweep the other way. I've got to take two steps and jump toward Cordeleone's legs. His knee is sticking out . . . 'Bruce, you hurt me bad,' he said. He never played again after that. I knew the guy. I'd been to his bar.

"Reid'll talk to you. Instead of jumping around me on a pass he'll try to run over me. Then he'll say, 'God damn Bruce, it's like trying to climb out of a fifty-foot deep well.'

"Bergey's a clothesline guy. Like Mel Blount. He does little goofy shit. A guy recovers a fumble and Bergey'll push him, for no reason. 'Oh, knock it off,' you say."

Ray: "I admire a guy who never gives a cheap shot. Bob Lilly. I always watched and admired him. He'd taken all kinds of cheap shots and never retaliated. We were playing Dallas last year. I came over and caught him with my helmet right under his chin. He pulled back and gave me a punch in the head.

"'Bob,' I said. 'I never thought you'd do something like that.' I think it embarrassed him that he did. But he was frustrated. He had a bad ankle, a bad instep. For thirteen years guys had just been double-teaming his ass. Same thing Joe Greene has to put up with. I'd like to see what Joe could do if he went one-on-one with a guy.

"You know," Ray mused, "when some guy gets blindsided, they run the films of it back and forth, back and forth. I got blindsided against New York last year—I just saw people's faces and lights flipping over and over. But it's sort of . . . *firing*. It *fires* you when you see a hit like that. That's what football's all about. See some poor defenseless guy get blindsided, and you just feel the emotion run through the crowd.

"When the guy getting hit is your quarterback, it's a cheap shot. But a cheap shot is a relative thing. I'm a cheap shotter in a way. Those guys are going to be diving on the pile when I get there. Sometimes I have to jump over the pile to get to a guy— stick him and knock him over."

Bruce: "When we're losing, I like to see a guy really crumple some people."

Ray: "I stepped on a guy in high school once. I didn't like it then, and I'll never do it again. I remember my cleats crunching into his back."

Bruce: "Wally Hilgenburg, the Vikings, is a cheap shot."

Ray: "Yeah. He'll go out of his way to hurt somebody. He stepped on Moon's back. He went out of his way to step on Moon's back.

"But you know, everybody always laughs, watching the films, when you get hurt. Even when I saw my ribs getting broken, in the films, I laughed."

Bruce: "I remember once I was going full speed and hit the defensive end. He hit me in the head. I go down on my knees. I just go down on my knees and fall over. It's really funny in the films. Even when the quarterback gets hurt, it's funny."

Ray: "It's sort of like a nervous laugh."

Bruce: "We all know we could get it any time. If you laugh at it, it keeps it on a lighter plane. And it makes it . . . tougher."

Ray: "You don't want sympathy. You don't want guys saying 'Aw, Ray, you got hurt man.' I'd rather they laughed.

"I remember when Bradshaw jammed his finger against Houston last year. It wasn't funny at the time, looked like we'd lost our quarterback. He came off the field, on national television, acting like he'd really been killed. It was funny in the films because he was acting too dramatic for it to be the injury it was. I remember Gary Bleeker, our quarterback in college. He gets up off the ground, starts spinning around, falls down. He jammed his thumb. We all thought some sniper had got him from the lower deck.

"At [the University of] Washington they never helped you off the field. I saw guys making it off with broken legs. The only guy who I saw just laying in the mud, staying there, was a guy who'd split his spleen. It was in practice. I'd just seen a movie of Wild Bill Elliott dying in the mud. Bleeding from the mouth. I said, 'This guy's shot!' He damn near died. But they wouldn't help him off. They just moved practice further down the field. The school nearly got sued on that. I wish they had.

"They used to tell us wild-ass stories. We'd imagine the superguy, playing with his neck broken, coming off under his own power after the game with the bone sticking out. Guys laugh at stories like that today. We thought it was great. Today they say the guy musta been nuts. 'Hey man, funky dude.' Look at you like you're a weirdo if you do things like that. A guy like that is a short-haired guy, too far to the right. 'You've only got one body,' they say today."

Bruce: "We were brainwashed, maybe: it should feel good to get pain. Like my little kid—he sees blood on his finger and likes it. Feels tough."

Ray: "Yeah. I don't think it's good, even now, to be sissy. But it's not good to be stupid either. I've got hemorrhoids. The urologist said it was from stress."

Bruce: "Younger guys ask you, how can you put up with the pain? As you get older, bumps and bruises bother you more. The artificial turf, age, playing against bigger guys."

Ray: "Pro football is a different animal from college. In college it was animalistic. The only thing in the world that mattered was the fucking win."

Bruce: "Well, that's the same in the pros."

Ray: "Yeah, that's not different. But it's . . . There was a purity between the players and the fans in college. I rarely remember a

Husky being booed. The fans were part of you. Here you're a fucking pro. You're not part of them. Still you're somebody to be admired, though."

Bruce: "Yeah, I think football's a good and just and nice and reasonable thing to do."

Ray: "And booing. When the Pirates are fucking up I'm sort of booing down inside. I knew some of them, guys like Giusti and Blass. But it's not Giusti and Blass, the guys you know, when they're playing. It's the Pirates.

"It used to piss me off that people didn't recognize me. Now I hate to be recognized. The other day a little skinny guy came up to me and wanted me to feel his shoulder separation."

The conversation swung back around to hitting. "The only reason we like to hit people," said Bruce, "is because we've been conditioned to. We know we're going to be commended."

Ray: "The things I do I don't try to put 'em in any perspective. Whether it's right or good . . . I don't want to figure it out. I don't want to know myself. I like myself the way I am."

Bruce: "But that's rationalization."

Ray: "No, it's not."

Bruce: "I try to figure . . ."

Ray: "I got thinking after reading Gent's book and talking to Gent. I don't want to put it on a plane where I have to justify it."

Bruce: "But you have to justify it, when the coach is screaming at you, and . . ."

Ray: "But then I justify it because I was brought up under the old system. That's what coaches have to do. I really do enjoy hitting. More for approval than for anything else."

Bruce: "Yeah, that's what I said."

Ray: "But not from the coach. From teammates more than anything else."

Bruce: "And from the guy you're hitting."

Ray: "Right. You want respect from the guy you're hitting. And if you're really good, attention is going to come. When Tinglehoff got All-Pro center all the time—he's getting respect from guys he's hitting. I'm not."

Bruce: "Well, but the way people vote for All-Pro. Guys get reputations off the field. Like Ben Davidson in Oakland."

Ray: "Yeah. Ben is the most publicized third-team tackle ever. He played behind me in the Rose Bowl. I remember when Tim Rossovich went to the Pro Bowl as a defensive end. Hear how tough this guy is. Huh.

"But you always question yourself. No matter how good you are, you wonder, is this real? Always worrying. I'd like to have one summer of happiness. There was a movie called that.

"Maybe we're a dying breed. Maybe football will become flag football."

Bruce: "I remember you and I used to be the only ones who liked training camp."

DYNASTY

The Most Feared Man in Football

It's odd how time works on the mind. We remember "Mean" Joe Greene as the gentle giant on the Coke commercial, the man who lovingly tossed his game shirt to the little kid—not so mean at all. And perhaps there were times when he wasn't, but on the field he was the most feared man in football. Greene was a player who changed the position of defensive tackle, forced even Dick Butkus to back down, and approached each game of football as if it was a war—no prisoners, no compassion, no quarter. His play also spoke eloquently about the racial changes in sport. When Jackie Robinson integrated Major League Baseball he was forced to accept insults and maltreatment; expected to perform on the field but not to fight back. African Americans were held to a different—and higher—standard of conduct than white athletes. The media viewed black players as representatives of their race, while white players were just players. Joe Greene and other black Pittsburgh Steelers refused to be racial representative models. They insisted on their right to be distinct individuals.

And no one was more unique than Joe Greene. Teammate Andy Russell considered Joe Greene's particular contribution to the Steelers. Terry Bradshaw reminisced not only about his friendship with Greene, but about the education he received as a young, white quarterback playing for the first time on an integrated team.

JOE GREENE

Andy Russell

In my opinion, Joe Greene was unquestionably the NFL's best player in the seventies. No player had a greater impact or did more for his team. But when he came to the Steelers in 1969, as our number-one draft choice from a small school, North Texas State, we veterans, having seen many highly touted draft choices come and go, were skeptical but hopeful he'd be the savior we needed. We'd wait and see.

Joe was supposed to be an impact player, a franchise player, someone who could single-handedly change the course of a game. His first

From *A Steeler Odyssey* (Champaign, Ill.: Sports Publishing, Inc., 1998). Reprinted by permission of Sports Publishing, Inc.

unique move was to be the first Steeler rookie to ever hold out for more money, signing in time to make the second day of training camp.

Walking to his first practice at St. Vincent's College in Latrobe, Joe was approached by Pat Livingston, the veteran *Pittsburgh Press* writer covering the team. Angry that Livingston had criticized his holdout, Joe proceeded to get into a heated argument with Pat right in front of a large crowd of spectators. When Livingston defended himself, Joe angrily stalked off—not a good way to ingratiate yourself with the local press on your first day. Clearly this was an unusual rookie and the veteran players weren't thrilled with his act.

His first full-speed "live" drill was to participate in what's known as an "Oklahoma Drill," where the defender lines head up on an offensive player, tries to defeat his block, release and make the tackle. It's normally more difficult for the defender because the offensive player has some advantages: he knows the snap count; he often has the strength and weight of the running back to help him, making it two against one; and a stalemate is usually a win for the offensive player (because despite stopping the offensive lineman's forward movement the defender still can't release quickly enough to make the tackle).

All eyes were on the number-one draft choice when he lined up against Ray Mansfield, the team's most wily old veteran offensive lineman, whose knowledge of technique and tricks was unparalleled. As Ray came off the ball, positioning himself between the hole and the new rookie, an extraordinary thing happened. Greene stopped Ray's forward momentum with only his left arm and threw him aside as though Ray were a puppy attacking a grizzly bear. He then proceeded to crush the ball carrier with his right shoulder. For a moment everyone was too stunned to speak but then the coaches began shouting encouragement and patting Joe on the back. Joe seemed oblivious to their encouragement, apparently needing no one's praise to validate himself.

Joe's next turn was against Bruce Van Dyke, a future Pro Bowler, and one of the best offensive linemen to ever play for the Steelers. Joe swatted him away like a lumberjack dealing with a bothersome mosquito. We veterans knew right then that the Steeler drafters had finally brought home a winner—this young man was going to be a force.

Apparently he'd always been that way. There was the time in high school, when, after a particularly bitter loss at home to their biggest rival, Joe was at the local Dairy Queen, trying to soothe his disappointment. When the winner's bus pulled into the lot, the opposing players began heckling and challenging Joe from the bus.

"Hey, Greene you aren't so bad—we just kicked your butt," and, "You're not so mean."

Joe, never one to back down from a challenge, attacked, going in the front door of the bus all by himself. The entire opposing team, coach included, escaped out the back door. Even in high school Joe was a legend.

Once, during his rookie year, when he was particularly frustrated late in the fourth quarter of a humiliating defeat at the hands of the Vikings in Minnesota, Joe lost his temper and was penalized for his rough play. As he came off the field, two respected Viking veterans, Carl Eller and Alan Page, huge defensive line stars whose bench was on the same side of the field as ours, made the mistake of berating our furious rookie. Without responding to their taunts, Joe, in a total rage, went directly to the trainer's tool box and pulled out the first tool he could find—a pair of nasty looking scissors. With weapon in hand, spinning toward his hecklers, looking totally insane, he charged toward the Viking bench, making wide swipes of the scissors in the general direction of Eller and Page. We were all so stunned that none of us moved.

Eller and Page, convinced they were dealing with a madman, both turned and sprinted toward the railing into the stands, perhaps hoping that their fans could protect them. I'm sure that Joe had no intention of actually hurting anyone. It was the ultimate bluff, an act. Had Eller and Page stood their ground I'm sure that Joe would have dropped the scissors but his whole life experience told him they would turn and run.

He apparently wanted our opponents to know that he would not tolerate any insults. They would learn to respect him and his team. Despite losing by 38 points, I got on the bus to the airport after the game, thinking "Man, this guy is something—he will absolutely not accept that we are losers." Many years later, in our first Super Bowl, those same Vikings would learn big time that they had taunted the wrong man.

Later that year, we played in Chicago against the Bears who were also struggling, despite having a couple of real superstars, Dick Butkus and Gale Sayers. Our defense was playing reasonably well but our offense was being destroyed by Butkus, who was having an All-World day, frequently sacking our quarterback, Terry Hanratty, stopping our ball carriers behind the line of scrimmage, causing and recovering fumbles, and knocking down passes.

It was one of the most impressive performances I had ever seen—Butkus was single-handedly humiliating our offense, making plays all over the field. It was an unbelievable defensive tour de force.

At one point Butkus even put himself on the kickoff team wanting to humble us even further. But this time he went too far, crushing Joe's pal, L. C. Greenwood, a blocker on the kickoff receiving team, right in front of our bench.

Seeing his friend writhing in pain was too much for Joe. He charged Butkus, from not ten feet away, and grabbed him by the shoulder pads, pulling his face up towards his own—they were face mask to face mask, Joe's 6'4", 295 lbs versus Butkus 6'3", 255 lbs. Since the face masks were apparently preventing the level of intimacy Joe wanted in this private, little conversation (only in front of the entire stadium) he tore off his own helmet and drew it back as though he intended to use it as a club to bash Butkus. I could hear Joe mumbling something and just knew it was highly insulting. Joe was clearly challenging Butkus to a fight, wanting badly to provoke him into a one-on-one confrontation and destroy the one man who was embarrassing our team.

I could see Butkus' eyes blink in disbelief. It was as though he was asking himself, "Do I die now or do I die later?" With that decision made, Butkus turned and ran back to his side of the field. None of us could believe it. Joe had just backed down the baddest man in the league.

Seeing Butkus in a bar later that year at the Pro Bowl, I cautiously baited him about the incident.

"Dick, with respect, how could you let Joe Greene's challenge, his 'in your face, confrontational, let's you and me finish this thing right now' attitude go without retaliating? I was sure you'd draw a line in the sand."

Butkus paused, as though he was trying to remember the incident and then, smiling, said, "I was having too much fun destroying your offense to get kicked out of that game—for fighting with that wildman rookie of yours."

I walked away thinking it was a pretty good answer but I realized that Butkus was no longer the baddest dude in the league—Joe had definitely replaced him.

But the story that, to me, best shows his unbelievable talent, his complete outrageousness, and his absolute refusal to accept losing, happened in Philadelphia, in the last game of his second season. Having won only five games, we were about to lose our ninth game, in a humiliating fashion, that some of us veterans were getting entirely too familiar with.

Our offense had played very well with Frenchy Fuqua about to set the Steeler all-time rushing record for a single game, 218 yards. Despite his success running the ball, our defense, except for Joe who had four sacks, had played terribly and the Eagles were up by a couple of touchdowns and were about to score another when I heard Joe, in his deep, resonant baritone calmly tell the man playing across from him, "Man, if you hold me one more time, I'm going to have to hurt you."

Two plays later it was third and long and I knew the guard playing across from Joe was in trouble because the only way possible to block him was to hold him. The guard had two options. Either hold Joe and get hurt if he meant what he'd said, or not hold him which would mean a sack or the potential of getting his quarterback hurt.

Well, he made the courageous choice and chose to hold Joe. I heard a loud thump and a whooshing noise, as the guard lost all the air from his lungs. The player was lying there on the ground, writhing in pain with Joe, standing above him, quietly telling him, "Man, I told you not to hold me again."

The officials, missing the infraction, had a stretcher brought on the field to carry the injured player off. Moments later the Eagles put in his backup, a third-year man, not exactly relishing his "opportunity." Before the first play, I heard Joe again explain the consequences of holding.

The backup, apparently deciding he'd rather be hurt than humiliated, also chose to grab Joe. Again I heard the cry of pain and there he was, lying on the field, clutching his stomach. Soon the second teamer also had been helped off the field and they sent in a rookie, also not particularly thrilled by his big chance to show his stuff.

I heard Joe say, "Hey, Home. Good to see you, man. How you been?"

Realizing the rookie was from North Texas State, Joe's alma mater, where they had been teammates together, I listened as Joe continued, "Now, don't you be holding me like those other dudes. You know how I hate that."

Of course, a few plays later, Joe's ex-college teammate was also forced to hold Joe but Joe refused to hurt his old friend. I could see that

Joe was now extremely frustrated, as he began to pace back and forth between the Eagle huddle and ours.

As the Eagles broke the huddle and approached the line of scrimmage, Joe picked up the game ball and walked toward our bench, telling the official, over his shoulder, that, "if you can't see these guys grabbing me, this game is over."

With that he casually flicked the game ball over towards our bench and then stood, legs wide apart, with his hands on his hips, staring at the officials. The officials, not believing what they were seeing and hearing, trying to maintain control of the game, got another ball from the Eagle's bench and placed it down, expecting to resume play. Obviously, they didn't understand as Joe picked up that ball and held it away from the official, repeating his position.

"I told you, man. You either start calling this holding or this game is over."

"Give me that ball or we'll be forced to call delay of game, and eject you," the head linesman answered.

The official nearest to me, obviously bending over backward to be sympathetic to Joe's position, said to me, "Captain, would you please talk to Mr. Greene—he's obviously not responding."

Reluctantly I walked over to Joe, put my arm around his huge shoulders and whispered, "Joe, you can't do this. Why don't you just give me the ball and let's finish the game." Feeling doubtful, I continued, "We can still come back and win it."

Looking at me menacingly, as though I were in cahoots with the officials, he said, "This game is over, Cap'un—unless they start respecting the rules."

About this time, the 55,000 people in Philadelphia's Franklin Field, realizing that something unusual was going on, had started to boo and roar their disapproval of the delay in the Eagle's exciting comeback win. When Joe heard the fan's anger, seeing them standing and shaking their fists at him, still holding the ball, with the officials threatening to throw him out of the game, he walked away from us, over to the hash mark at about the 30-yard line, and, holding the ball above his head in one hand and waving the fans towards him with the other, Joe yelled back at the crowd,

"Come on, you want this ball—come and take it."

Fifty-five thousand people had just been challenged by one man, a rookie, clearly testing their city pride. It was the mob against a single man. Despite a few drunk hecklers, the stadium grew quieter and no one, regardless of how drunk, made a move to come out of the stands. When it was clear to Joe that there were no takers to his challenge, he suddenly reared back and threw the ball high up into the second tier of the stadium, at least 100 feet off the stadium floor. It was a throw that even Bradshaw couldn't have duplicated. The crowd, understanding the unbelievable, raw power that it would take to throw the ball so high, sat back down in stunned silence.

Before the officials even had time to throw him out, Joe turned and walked off the field. Joe, certain the game was over, two touchdowns behind with only seconds left, had made his protest. He would not continue to play whether they threw him out or not. He was still furious, shaking his head back and forth, as though he was dealing with a bunch of incompetents, not capable of doing their jobs properly. Chuck Noll didn't say a word to him, probably secretly applauding the statement the young rookie was making—his absolute refusal to accept losing.

On the bus to the airport, despite my ambivalence about Joe's behavior, I recognized that we had in our midst a remarkable person, a man capable of extraordinary physical greatness, matched with a powerful will to win, with a pride that was all consuming.

Knowing that the game was already lost, Joe had made his statement—the officials must call the game fairly. He didn't care that his temper tantrum might be viewed as childish or irresponsible. He didn't care what people thought about him. All he cared about was winning and his angry eruption was a protest for all of us to deal with an unbelievably frustrating year. This is the man, I thought, who we can finally build a team around. Despite losing our ninth game in a row I suspected that our long journey to a championship had just begun—we were on our way.

Of course, his actual play on the field was far more important than these extraordinary incidences when his anger got the better of him. Most of the time he let his performance speak for him and he was absolutely unstoppable.

In 1974, our first Super Bowl year, frustrated by his inability to cause the kind of havoc he wanted, he developed a totally unique positioning technique that caused our opponents real problems. Instead of lining head up across from the guard he would jump in the gap between guard and center at the last second before the ball was snapped. Lining up nearly offsides, with his shoulders instead of being parallel to the ground tilted almost vertically to the ground, he would penetrate across the line of scrimmage, making it virtually impossible to block him. He experimented with it in practice during the year but, despite our offense's inability to block him, the coaches remained skeptical and refused to let him execute it during the season. Finally, Joe was allowed to try this unique new positioning in our first playoff game against O. J. and the Bills. It quickly became clear that his new technique destroyed many of the plays Buffalo wanted to run and we won easily, with O. J. getting only 48 yards on the ground.

The following week against Oakland in the AFC Championship game, the Raiders, a strong rushing team, were only able to generate a total of 29 yards on the ground. In the Super Bowl, Minnesota managed a total of 17 yards. All three of these teams based their offense around their strong running games.

The Vikings made the big mistake of running at Joe, the old Lombardi theory of running at the opponent's strength. Joe was finally doing what he had always wanted to do—dictating the action, forcing the opponent to react to him, making things happen.

Later that year at the Pro Bowl, Joe and I, basking in the glory of having won our first Super Bowl, sat in the Orange Bowl locker room, and were approached by the AFC Pro Bowl coach John Madden.

"Congratulations! You fellas sure did a job on our running game. Do you think we might have been more effective trying our counter traps against that new defense?" Madden said.

Thinking that Madden surely didn't expect us to answer him truthfully, but doing it anyway, I said, "Coach, it wouldn't have mattered what you ran. It was just our day."

Madden, clearly upset, shaking his head, said, "What about our 'wham sucker'—that might have taken advantage of Joe's penetration."

"I'm telling you coach," Joe answered. "You could have run every play in your play book and they were going nowhere. We were in that zone and there was no saving your Raiders."

Madden walked away, shaking his head, sure there would be some way to attack our new scheme with Joe in the gap but from that moment forward the Raiders never really ran the ball effectively against us. In retrospect, I must admit that Madden did figure out a way to beat us, but never by running the ball—they did it in the air.

There was the time, years later, in Houston, with the season on the line, at the most pivotal point in the game (third down, twenty seconds left, on our twenty-five, when a field goal would beat us), when Joe told us in the huddle,

"This game is over. Trust me—I'm gonna take the ball away on the next play."

Lining up for the next down I gave little credence to Joe's prediction. We were in trouble. If they didn't turn the ball over, they would probably win by kicking the field goal. When the ball was snapped, Joe, knocking the double team off him, penetrated into the Oiler backfield and crushed the runner. When the officials sorted out the resulting pileup, there on the bottom of the pile was Joe, grinning up at us, with the ball. The game was over. I walked off the field in awe, wondering how it was possible for a man to make a call like that—to predict a game stopper—talk about positive imaging.

Over those years, Joe's personality changed from the wild, uncontrollable rookie to a more responsible, less explosive, almost fatherly figure. Once, later in his career, sitting next to me on the team bus, he asked, in total seriousness, "Captain, why do you suppose they call me 'Mean Joe Greene?'"

Without hesitation I replied, only half serious, "Because you're mean! You've got a real ugly streak, Joe, and you've got to try and control it."

He stared ominously at me for a long time, probably trying to decide if he should show me how really ugly he could be but then he smiled and said, "That's not true—I'm just misunderstood."

Later, of course, he would do the Coca-Cola TV ads winning the heart of America by throwing his jersey to the little kid. Actually, Joe was always nice to children. When leaving the stadium he would always be surrounded by youngsters asking for his autograph. Hating autographs, Joe would say, "I don't give autographs but why don't you kids get on the bus and talk to me." He would then sit, as we waited for the last stragglers from the locker room to board, and talk patiently with these kids, answering their questions and showing interest in their lives and aspirations.

The year after I retired, Joe was made the team Captain for the last exhibition game in Kansas City. Acting as the color man for the TV broadcast back to Pittsburgh, I had noted that Joe, playing with a back injury, was called for a roughing penalty late in the game, keeping the Chief's final, winning drive alive.

Afterwards, noticing Joe sitting dejectedly in the locker room, knowing how much he hated to make mistakes, I approached him, patted him on the back and said, "Joe, don't worry about it—it's just an exhibition game. It's not that important." But it was to Joe.

Shaking his head, with his eyes showing the emotional turmoil he was feeling, he said, "I'm not sure I want to be the Captain. It isn't me—it might get in the way of my natural instincts. I don't want to be worrying about how things look to the rest of the team—got to be my own man."

Realizing that he was totally conflicted and upset, I said, "You're right, Joe, just be yourself. You are a very special person. You don't need to change—do it your way. Your contribution to the team is far more important than being the Captain. You are the person everyone relies on to get the job done."

Joe, nodding his head in agreement, said, "Yep, I don't want to be acting like some gentleman, sportsman out there—it just wouldn't feel right."

With that he got up and limped into the training room. Watching him go, I realized that unless his back got better, that his best games were probably behind him. Unfortunately, it didn't and they were, but he did learn to control that temper and, unquestionably, became a very important leader in that locker room.

The young guys looked up to him and he set the tone. He would help the team win two more Super Bowls and be elected to the Hall of Fame. He was the best ever. Joe Greene was truly the player whose refusal to give in to defeat, unwillingness to accept anything but a total commitment to excellence and brilliant individual performances started and finished the Steelers' long journey, first to respectability, then to competitiveness and finally all the way to Super Bowl glory.

CORNERSTONE OF A DYNASTY: MEAN JOE GREENE, FOOTBALL MACHINE

Terry Bradshaw

The Pittsburgh Steelers of the '70s were a rare collection of men. We had great pride, reveled in the "nasty" image, and never failed to remind our opponents that we were tough guys from Steeltown. Once we got a taste of the pie, we wanted it all. It's difficult to stay on top, as NFL teams discovered in the '80s. But the Steelers' hunger pangs were boundless and that's why we won four championships in six short

From *Looking Deep* by Terry Bradshaw with Buddy Martin (Chicago: Contemporary Books, 1989). Reprinted by permission of Terry Bradshaw.

years. Like the Los Angeles Lakers of the '80s, Green Bay packers of the '60s and New York Giants of the '50s—teams that were able to keep generating championships back-to-back—the Steelers remained motivated throughout the mid and late '70s.

Pro teams in today's world seem to lose sight of their goals from one season to the next. As the years go by and I see teams trying to repeat, I almost chuckle to myself. The more Super Bowls I see, the more I say to myself "Uh-huh, you boys are making all the money, doing all these commercials, getting all this fame, but when you try to do it again, it's not so easy, is it?" Then the modern players try to say, "Well, it's not as easy to repeat as it was back when you played." And I say, "Okay, that's cool. But it wasn't the same for us as it was for the Green Bay Packers, either." So you can't say that.

In my travels around the country, I sense it's beginning to dawn on pro football fans just how remarkable the Steelers' accomplishments really were. When they are reminded that we won four titles in six years, sometimes it completely blows them away. Only now, nearly a decade later, are people beginning to realize just how dominant we were.

One of the reasons for our dominance was Joe Greene, the cornerstone of the Pittsburgh dynasty.

When I look back on my first year at Pittsburgh, with all the many things that I had to learn and endure, the one person that comes to mind first and foremost is Joe Greene. I'll never forget the first time I laid eyes on Joe coming down the hill to practice: socks down around his ankles, huge thighs, big Afro, jersey hanging out, looking like he had been up all night. What a sight! He was called "Mean" Joe Greene because he earned the name. He took cheap shots at quarterbacks, driving them out of bounds and into the bench if he could. He was ferocious. He couldn't be blocked because he was so overpowering. Joe Greene was something that the NFL had never seen before—he redefined the position of defensive tackle.

Early on in his career, Joe Greene worked hard at being a bad actor on and off the field. As the first real star on Chuck Noll's team and the number-one draft choice the year before I arrived, Joe already had a niche for himself. And, in some respects, not a very good niche. The first time I saw Joe, he weighed more than three hundred pounds and couldn't even jog around the goal posts before we did our calisthenics. We were worlds apart. I had my shirt tucked in, looking prim and proper, saying "yes, sir" and "no, sir," and here comes Joe Greene, AFC Rookie of the Year. We were all running around the goal posts and Joe was barely making it, saying nothin' to nobody, because he is not just Joe Greene, he is "Mean" Joe Greene.

Joe wasn't wearing knee or thigh pads. When practice started, he was so out of shape from not taking care of himself and smoking tons of cigarettes that he could hardly do anything physical. Then one day I found out why they called him "Mean" Joe Greene. He got angry because the cooler was out of Gatorade and the ball boys were slow in bringing in refills. So he took his foot and knocked down a huge door with welded trim, just to prove his point. Joe wanted him some Gatorade. And he got it. Plus a five-hundred-dollar fine for knocking the door down.

I was dazzled by the media, afraid to say the wrong thing, always trying to please them. Joe took a different view: he treated the media with complete disdain. He actually spat on Pat Livingston, veteran *Pittsburgh Press* columnist—spat right in his face—during one of the early NFL players' strikes.

This man was mean, nasty, vile, tough, dirty—all the things I wished I could be and wasn't. After all, I was Terry Bradshaw, All-American boy, trying to be perfect in every way. And he was Mean Joe Greene, who didn't give a damn if anybody liked him. I guess that's why Joe became one of my heroes and best friends right off.

"Mean" was a way of life for Joe, and the name fit. He had a terrible temper on the field. When an offensive lineman would hold him, Joe would warn him: "Don't do that again." And if the offensive lineman held him again, Joe had his own way of dealing with him. He punched Paul Howard of the Denver Broncos in the gut right on national TV and it was shown on instant replay. Howard doubled over with pain and had to leave the game. I figure Joe said something to Paul like, "Now, Howard, don't hold me again. I know we're in Denver and I don't want to have to punch you in the stomach and knock you out, so don't hold me again." Paul held Joe. Joe knocked him out.

During the regular season at Philadelphia, Joe took the helmet off an Eagle and started swinging it like he was Samson with the jawbone of an ass. He kicked the center's tail, then took on a few more and nearly wiped out half of the Eagles team. The referees chased Joe around Franklin Field before they finally caught and ejected him. Joe came running back on the field, stole the football from the referee, ran into the end zone, and threw it into the stands. Later that year, Joe did the same thing in Cleveland. "Mean" Joe Greene. Get it?

When Joe became successful, he dropped the "Mean." He became this classy guy who was still a great football player but had a different public image. It seemed to change about the same time Joe did that Coca-Cola commercial with the kid, the one where he tossed his jersey to the boy as he was walking through the tunnel. (That commercial, incidentally, won a Clio Award as one of the year's best.) Deep down, he had always been a pussycat, but we didn't know that. Joe just wanted everybody to fear him, because fear was one of his tools. And his tool sure worked on me.

The tools worked on offensive linemen, too. Among the stories about Joe's intimidation was this one, written by Pete Axthelm in a 1981 issue of *Inside Sports*, about how he intimidated five-time Pro Bowl guard Joe DeLamielleure of the Buffalo Bills:

"The evening before Joe DeLamielleure was to confront Joe Greene for the first time, the Buffalo guard (later traded to Cleveland) dined with reserve center Willie Parker, a college teammate of Greene's. Parker related how Greene had once bludgeoned an All-American lineman, ripping the player's face mask off his helmet at one point. 'Joe turned white as a sheet and went up to his room,' Parker remembers. 'He was up until three in the morning throwing up.'

"A year later, in a well-known incident toward the end of a game, DeLamielleure learned about Greene. When Buffalo broke its huddle, Greene had his foot on the ball. He said, 'I'm going to teach you white boys how to play.' DeLamielleure turned to center Mike Montler: 'Is he talking to you or me?' 'Both of us, I think.'

"The next two plays, Greene kicked the hell out of both of them. He kicked Montler in the groin. He kicked DeLamielleure in the lip. It was third down and three and DeLamielleure told the quarterback, Joe Ferguson, 'Throw the ball out of bounds. Please!'"

You can see why I was glad to have Joe Greene on my side. But another reason why I will always love Joe Greene is that he came to my rescue when I was a rookie. I was scared to death and needed somebody to reassure me of my place on this Steeler team, because it was going to be a bumpy ride. Joe must have seen something in me, because he showed his faith by saying: "Hey, man, you're going to be all right. You are our leader, the man we are going to win it with. Don't worry about what all those stupid assholes say. You are going to take us all the way. You are going to lead us. I just want you to know that." Joe warned all the reporters to get off my back the first few years and for a while they did. He always defended me for some reason.

Joe was my best friend on the team, even though we hardly did much together off the field except play a little poker together during the week. I loved Joe Greene. There was no other player on that team that I felt quite the same way about, although I actually spent more time with other players. My buddies on the Steelers team were Calvin Sweeney and Jim Smith, whom I played golf with; John Stallworth; and Ray Mansfield. It's funny now looking back at it, but only Mansfield was white. For a kid coming to Pittsburgh from the deep South, that was quite a revelation.

The scariest person I met in Pittsburgh—contrary to what people may think—was not Ernie "Fats" Holmes or "Mean" Joe Greene. The scariest person was wide receiver Roy Jefferson, whom I met in my first few days on the team in 1970. Ernie, also known as "Arrowhead" because he shaved his head in an arrow, merely shot at helicopters and grabbed reporters by the collar. Jefferson petrified me because he hated whites. Or, at least, I thought he hated whites. At my first Steelers' practice, fellow rookie quarterback Bob Leahy found out about Jefferson's temper when he accidentally threw a ball behind him in a warm-up drill. Jefferson turned to Leahy and growled: "Don't you ever throw a ball behind me again!" I said to myself, "Bradshaw, you're in trouble, because you've got to throw passes to this guy." I could see myself dropping back in a game, spotting Jefferson in the open and my arm locking up with fear. When a quarterback strings out his receiver by throwing behind him, he becomes vulnerable to a shot in the ribs or the head by a defensive back.

Sure enough, Jefferson got open against Miami in a preseason game. I threw to him three times and he dropped all three. In a matter of days, Jefferson was gone. Roy went on to the Redskins to have a great career. But it was best for us he leave because, among other things, Roy had a bad influence on our superstar, Joe Greene, the first player ever drafted by Chuck Noll in 1969. And Joe was already regarded as the baddest man east of the Mississippi River.

Whether Roy really did have that much impact on Joe or not, I'm not sure, but in the eyes of Steelers management he did. I have talked to Roy since then and we laugh about it now—him being a black militant and me a redneck from Louisiana. Roy has changed, much for the better, and hopefully so have I.

Pittsburgh. An integrated city where blacks and whites socialize, play together on sports teams, and work side by side in the marketplace. It was a fact that never occurred to me until I moved there in my rookie season. Sometimes you need to experience a little pain in order to grow. My own prejudice came as a surprise to me, although maybe it shouldn't have. Racism exists today at every level in the NFL: against black coaches, black quarterbacks, potential black owners, right down to the black fans who can't afford the big money for high-priced season tickets.

For the most part, even the players discriminate among themselves—cliques on a pro football team are almost exclusively black or white. One of the characteristics of the Steelers championship teams is that we were able to bridge that racial gap and had no real cliques. Sometimes it's a case of black players wanting to be among blacks, so it isn't always the whites doing the excluding. We may have broken down some of the obvious racial barriers in our society, but there are still so many subtle ones. And I wonder sometimes if we even notice anymore.

If I learned nothing else playing football, at least I can say my black brothers and sisters taught me about their race. They must have gotten a kick out of observing my learning experience, because this was the first time in my life that I ever played on a team with blacks or was around them socially.

I simply had never experienced black culture. When I hit Pittsburgh as a rookie quarterback, it must have been like Opie from Mayberry getting off the train the first time in the big city. It didn't take me long to figure out that I was prejudiced. The first back teammate I ever talked with was Jon Staggers, the wide receiver from Missouri. This was the early '70s, when black militancy and Afros were very much in vogue; I think old Jon had been lying in the weeds waiting for a honky like me to come along. I was always terribly impressed by any player who went to a major university—regardless of his skin color—so whatever Jon had to say was going to bowl me over. I can just imagine what Jon was thinking when I arrived: " Hey, we got this redneck coming in from Louisiana today. I don't know what he's going to be like, so let's go down to his room and hear what he's got to say." So he did. And he found this very shy, naive kid who had lived a sheltered life in Shreveport, a small-college player who traveled mostly by bus to all his college games, hadn't been anywhere or seen anything, had no clue about the big-time media or how to deal with it, and was completely awed by this black wide receiver who had gone to a major school on a football scholarship.

I immediately became Jon Staggers's project. In a matter of minutes, I was picking up his jive talk and feeling confident that by dinner I'd be shaking hands with a black person, locking thumbs, and hanging out on the street with all the brothers. I wanted everybody to accept me and if I could act like Jon Staggers, my new black friend, maybe they would. Being straightforward, I just admitted to Jon right off I didn't really know very much about "coloreds."

"Hold it right there!" Jon said, and I could tell I'd already done something wrong. "Hold it! We don't say 'coloreds.' We say 'black.'" So I learned my first lesson about blacks, and clearly there were going to be many more for me. I'm embarrassed about it now, but the truth is that I was learning about my prejudice, something that is ample in the rural South. Since we didn't use the word "nigger" in my house and never thought the Bradshaws were better than anybody else, it just never dawned on me that I might have even the remotest racist thoughts or feelings. I think Jon sensed my innocence and knew that there was nothing malicious about my racism. So, hoping I could be salvaged, he set about to tutor me on black culture. I thought I was the only person in the world north of the Mason-Dixon line who was prejudiced.

Years later I learned just how rampant racism is in sports. And I cringe today at the incidents involving Al Campanis of the Dodgers and Jimmy "the Greek" Snyder, my former fellow CBS-TV broadcaster. I can honestly say that the times I was around Jimmy at CBS, I never heard him make any racist comments, but clearly he made them in front of the camera in 1987 and action had to be taken by the network. Do I think Jimmy the Greek was a racist? No. Do I think he made racist comments? Yes. And he paid the price for it. All of us are a little guilty of such indiscretions, however; I shudder to think what I must have said or thought about blacks before my enlightenment the first year I went to play football in Pittsburgh.

Today when I am stopped on the street in New York, Chicago, Pittsburgh, or some other NFL city and asked for an autograph, the chances are pretty good that the man or woman will be black. Why? Because I was a member of one of the greatest football teams in history, a team that happened to be predominantly black. The Pittsburgh Steelers of the '70s were much like the Brooklyn Dodgers of the '50s in that they had many black role models for young people to follow. You could go down the list of Steeler stars and more than half of them were black: Joe Greene, Franco Harris, John Stallworth, Lynn Swann, Mel Blount, etc. Consequently, as a member of that team, I am probably more recognizable in more black communities than white ones.

Over the course of the years with the Steelers, a good many of my best friends were black. I know that's a cliché, but for me it was true. In the beginning, however, my lack of knowledge about black culture made me very uneasy. My black teammates knew I was struggling with my personal growth and development in this area and they would set me up. At team parties, the black guys would send their wives over to ask me to dance. I know Joe Greene was behind this. I can see him hiding behind a pole somewhere and saying: "Honey, go over there and make Bradshaw dance with you. Heh, heh, heh, heh." And I'll never forget the night a black woman kissed me on the lips for the first time. I turned completely scarlet. Didn't know how to deal with it in those days. What if somebody saw me? I am ashamed to admit some of these things, but, remember, in those days, I just had never been exposed to blacks or black families in a social setting.

As a child, the only black person I really knew was a maid who came to our house. I couldn't understand why blacks were treated like inferior people. I remember that they couldn't drink at the same water fountains that we did and couldn't go into the same stores or restaurants. I felt sorry for black people. Why could I walk into a store and buy candy, but a black child had to walk in the same store through a back door? Even I knew that wasn't right. When we took a trolley to downtown Shreveport, we sat up in the front and the blacks had to sit in the rear. My first experience playing against a black would not have been until my junior year in college when we played New Mexico State. But when I arrived at Pittsburgh, I never even thought about having blacks as teammates. It was intriguing to me. But it was as simple as this: if you've never had a can of Coca-Cola before and you drink one, now you've had Coca-Cola. So what's the big deal?

Generally, whatever racism that exists in our society is simply caused by a lack of exposure. Racism will never really be wiped out until our children have had a chance to grow up together and share each other's cultures. Black and white babies play together without recognizing any differences. That's the only hope for the two races to be completely compatible. That's one reason I don't want my daughter, Rachel, or any future children of mine to attend private schools—most of them are racially segregated. I want my children to grow up with black friends so they won't fall into the trap of racism that I did.

White people don't realize how fortunate they are. That was made clear to me as a child when I rode with my mother down to Cedar Grove, Louisiana, a predominantly black community, and saw these "shotgun" houses where they lived and wondered, "Why do they have to live like this? Why are they pushed all the way out here? Why do we have most everything we need?" From a human standpoint, it just didn't seem right to me. How would you like to be dumped on all your life, or kicked around, or have jokes made about you?

No wonder I felt uncomfortable when I first went to Pittsburgh. It was like starting my life over again. My ignorance wasn't by design; it was because of the environment I grew up in, and I struggled to overcome my background. Today, I think I understand the plight of the black man better than a lot of white people do because Jon Staggers, Joe Greene, Calvin Sweeney, Jim Smith, and other black teammates were willing to invest time in me as a human being. As a result, I have genuinely warm feelings for them.

So as difficult as those first few years as a Pittsburgh Steeler were, it was still a tremendous education. What better lesson in life can there be for a person than learning how to get along with another race? Dealing with my prejudice and overcoming racism was probably my greatest triumph as a pro football player.

Joe Greene has a loving, sensitive spirit that I appreciated in a special way. When I needed support, Joe gave it to me. And I will never forget that. People often want to know: was Joe Greene really that good? He was the very foundation of the Steelers' success. You build teams with defense, and Joe Greene was the bedrock of the Steel Curtain.

Sports and Race

"What better lesson in life can there be for a person than learning how to get along with another race?" As Bradshaw made evident in the preceding piece, the intricate link between professional sports and race was growing stronger during the 1960s and 1970s. The unabashedly black Muhammad Ali was the Champ. Upraised fists on the medal stand at the 1968 Mexico City Olympics were silent but powerful reminders of black pride.

The idea of a black sports star was relatively new to Pittsburgh—other than John Henry Johnson, most of the Steelers' stars had been solidly white—but this had changed by the 1970s, as Roberto Clemente, Dave Parker, and Willie Stargell emerged as the most prominent figures on the Pittsburgh Pirates and Lynn Swann, John Stallworth, L. C. Greenwood, Joe Greene, and other African Americans became the leaders of the Steelers. Art Rooney himself lived in a predominantly black neighborhood. If mainstream newspapers saw a significance in the increasing number of black faces in Pittsburgh sports, they generally kept it to themselves. But black newspapers like the nationally distributed Pittsburgh Courier *hailed changing athletic demographics as a clear sign of black equality, if not superiority. At a time when cries for Black Power rocked the country, the* Courier's *James David offered his own racially tinged explanation for the Steelers' win over the Oakland Raiders in the 1975 AFC Championship game. David went on to propose a blueprint for guaranteeing future victories, beginning with one in the Steelers' upcoming Super Bowl matchup against the Minnesota Vikings.*

SUPER STEELERS: ALL OVER FOR OAKLAND BEFORE TERRY'S RAID

James David

It was all over, really, before the Raiders and the Steelers took to the field.

The din that was set up during the introduction of Oakland's defensive unit reached and pierced the sky, seemingly, through which the sun poured, spottily, down upon the field of play, was fierce. But not enough.

That Franco Harris stutter-stepped, danced, darted and rambled for 111 yards, and Rocky Bleier struck up the middle and swung around the ends of an additional 98 yards, was devastating; that Joe Greene inspired the defense to rise to every occasion and sparked Jack Ham and J. T. Thomas to make key interceptions, was awesome. But it was finished before that.

Despite the psychological warfare waged by the Raiders, despite Oakland Al's smart remark that, "it was a shame that the Steelers had to take the long trip only to lose," it was done and finished before the opening whistle.

The closing of the coffin came with Franco's streak to pay dirt late in the fourth quarter to end the scoring 24-13. The Steelers had won.

With less than a minute to play, Chuck Noll called his embattled troops off the field. They soul brother–slapped each other with grimy and sweaty palms; a tall stringbean-like player firmly shook Terry Bradshaw's hand and slapped him on his rump as he (Bradshaw) trotted off to find a seat; Ron Shanklin wrapped his long arms around Bradshaw and gave him a bear-hug, holding him every bit of ten seconds. A faint smile creased Bradshaw's face.

At that point, Bradshaw's mind must have wandered back to Monday, October 28, 1974. It was that night that he led the Steelers to a 24-17 win over the Atlanta Falcons on ABC's Monday Night Football.

Bradshaw was a different quarterback that night. Subtle. But a subtlety that was [a] signal that he had learned something. He set up to pass not nearly as far back as he had done previously. He looked for secondary receivers, instead of just firing, come what may, to his primary target. He kept his cool. He did not panic. He even ate the ball, occasionally.

The blond had learned from a Black. That same "tall stringbean-like player that had firmly shook his hand and slapped him on the rump" moments earlier.

They call that player by the name of Jefferson Street Joe, who prefers his surname to be pronounced "Gil-lum."

Yes, Terry Bradshaw learned something that Monday night in October. And he improved with every game thereafter. He learned to be a better quarterback as he stood on the sidelines and looked at Joe Gilliam execute for six games.

Now the Steelers have arrived. They should be a power in the National Football League at least another three or four years. However, there is a big "If": If the Rooneys and Chuck Noll give due financial respect to their Black players.

With the exceptions of Joe Greene and Lynn Swann, most of the other Black players were acquired from Black colleges. Skills notwithstanding, most Black players going into the NFL from Black colleges still remain in a weaker bargaining position than those from the major universities.

Gilliam, though, may not be too concerned. A reliable source informs this writer that he is seen quite frequently with Joe Namath during the off-season. It is rumored that the New York Jets are interested. However, Gilliam is undecided, it is said, and that Namath is telling him to "cool it" until he does make up his mind.

But there is no indecision about Bradshaw's fate. He is in, and will remain the Steelers No. 1 Quarterback until he is too old to throw and run. Mr. Bradshaw knows this.

It was finished for the Raiders after the Steelers trounced the Buffalo Bills. Terry Bradshaw, quietly, knew this. He knows, too, about the Minnesota Vikings. It is all over.

A Win for Pittsburgh

Victory. Victory after forty-one years as a laughingstock. Victory af-ter decades of blowout losses, imbecilic trades, and great players that got away. Victory in Super Bowl IX once and for all time established the Pittsburgh Steelers as a real NFL franchise, not a joke. Pittsburgh Post-Gazette *columnist Vito Stellino, and the entire city, celebrated the team's 16-6 win over the Minnesota Vikings and took the oppor-tunity to banish all the years of frustration, now ghosts of the past. It was not just a win for the team or for Art Rooney, it was a win for Pittsburgh.*

IT'S SUPER!!! STEELERS BOWL OVER VIKINGS

Vito Stellino

Light a cigar for Art Rooney. Open a bottle of fine wine for Chuck Noll. Pour a drink for Johnny Blood and Bobby Layne. Tell Leo Durocher that nice guys don't always finish last.

And sing no more sad songs for the Steelers. Never again will they be known as pro football's loveable losers. The Steelers finally won the championship of Pete Rozelle's universe yesterday for the first time in their 42 years of existence.

Before a television audience of 75 million people and a chilled crowd of 80,997 at dilapidated Tulane Stadium—including a large con-tingent of enthusiastic Steeler fans—on a raw windy day, the Steelers won the Vince Lombardi Trophy for themselves and Art Rooney with a 16-6 victory over the Minnesota Vikings in Super Bowl IX.

Imagine, the Steelers are the super champions. Yes, the Steelers.

"Winning this game for Mr. Rooney was the big thing," beamed oft-maligned Terry Bradshaw, who directed an offensive attack that chewed up 333 yards, including 249 on the ground.

Offensive guard Jerry (Moon) Mullins, who helped anchor an offen-sive line that blew the Vikings off the ball the entire game, agreed, "I'm just honored to be on the team that won for Mr. Rooney," he said. "We get the money but he gets the prestige."

It's typical that 73-year-old Art Rooney, who founded the team in 1933, tried to duck the spotlight. "I didn't want to accept the trophy (from Rozelle). Dan Rooney (his son) and Chuck Noll deserved it. I guess they just wanted me to be a big shot for a day."

It was the kind of day when the Steelers had more heroes than they could count. There was Dwight White coming out of a hospital bed to play an inspired game, Franco Harris breaking Larry Csonka's Super Bowl rushing record, L. C. Greenwood batting down three passes and helping to set up a safety, Ed Bradley and Loren Toews coming off the bench to play so well when Jack Lambert and Andy Russell were injured.

And there was Joe Greene, who was Joe Greene and even intercepted a pass besides recovering a fourth period fumble that Chuck Noll labeled the turning point of the game.

It was typical that the Steelers won it the way the Steelers usually win. Their defense was, quite simply, awesome and they completely stymied the other team—holding the Vikings to just 21 yards rushing—until the offense finally came up with the big touchdown when it was needed.

The first half seemed to be a replay of the Oakland game. The Steelers dominated it entirely but led only 2-0, just as they dominated Oakland in the AFC title game two weeks ago but left the field with a 3-3 deadlock.

As center Ray Mansfield, who joined the club in 1964, noted: "Chuck told us at halftime to keep doing what we were doing and we'd win." The Steelers kept on truckin' in the second half but only had a 9-6 lead with 10:33 left in the contest when Matt Blair blocked a Bobby Walden punt and Terry Brown recovered it in the end zone.

Bradshaw then engineered a 66-yard drive in 11 plays that chewed up seven minutes and two seconds and put the game out of reach. The key play was a 30-yard pass from Bradshaw to Larry Brown on a third-and-2 play on the Steeler 42. Brown fumbled after making the catch and the Vikings recovered but the officials, despite bitter protests from the Vikes, ruled he fumbled the ball after he was tackled. That was only one of several controversial calls by the refs, who seemed to have a worse day than the Vikings.

The touchdown came on a four-yard pass to Brown, a play that was suggested by Joe Gilliam, and that made the final score 16-6.

The Steelers' first score came on a safety with 7:11 left in the second period. Tarkenton botched a pitchout to Dave Osborn, Greenwood hit the ball and it bounced into the end zone where Tarkenton fell on it. White touched him for the safety.

The Steelers got a big break on the second half kickoff when Roy Gerela got off a poor kick that bounced at the 30 and was fumbled by Bill Brown. Marv Kellum recovered and four plays later, Franco Harris swept nine yards for the touchdown. Franco, who went around the left end for 24 yards two plays previously, wound up rushing 158 yards in 34 carries to win the MVP award. He'll get a car in New York this week from *Sport Magazine*.

In last year's Super Bowl, Csonka shredded the Vikings for 145 yards in 33 carries.

The way the defense was playing, even after Lambert and Russell limped off, the Steelers looked like a good bet for the first Super Bowl shutout. But they had to survive two scares in the final period when they lost the shutout.

The first one came when Paul Krause recovered a Harris fumble on the Steeler 47 and Mike Wagner was called for interference on the Steeler five on another one of those controversial calls that seemed so prevalent in the game.

But on the very next play, Toews and Ernie Holmes hit Chuck Foreman to knock the ball loose and Greene recovered it on the seven to kill that threat. Four plays later when Bobby Walden punted from his own 15, Blair broke loose to block the punt that set up Terry Brown's touchdown and cut the score to 9-6.

The Steelers came right back for the touchdown that wrapped it up and then all that was left was the celebration.

The team was almost subdued in the locker room after it was over. They seemed to feel all along they were going to beat the "first time" jinx in the Super Bowl and hand Minnesota its third loss in six games in pro football's championship game.

"You only get excited when you surprise yourself," said the low-key Noll.

"We've been pretty loose. You don't have to juice anybody up for a game like this," Noll said. "I think Dwight playing is indicative of the attitude of this team. The doctors told me there was no way he could play but he said he could, so we figured we'd let him run around in the warmups and he'd keel over."

Instead, it was the Vikings who keeled over.

The players celebrated with a private party after the game and are looking forward to the trip back home today where the big welcome-home celebration is planned.

"The burg may be in ashes," grinned Jack Ham. Mansfield smiled, "I wonder if there'll be a town there when we get back."

Steelers-Cowboys

The most famous of football rivalries still strikes a receptive chord in every Pittsburgher's heart. They were clearly the two best teams of the 1970s and, Steelers fans would argue, the Black and Gold's two Super Bowl victories over Tom Landry's squad, first in 1976 and again in 1979, established without a doubt who was the better of the best. Phil Musick's article, written the day before their second title contest, clearly delineated what was at stake. The game on the field, he implied, would not just determine the better team, but also the better lifestyle. Super Bowl XIII became a war of North vs. South, blue-collar vs. white-collar, the hardworking vs. the pampered. Musick's piece was indicative of the tensions between the two teams. Dallas was still smarting from the three-year-old memory of the Steelers' 21-17 win in Super Bowl X. The Cowboys resented the brutally physical, yet unpenalized, play of the Steelers's defensive backs, and Dallas linebacker Thomas "Hollywood" Henderson only fanned the flames with his pre-game assertion that Terry Bradshaw "couldn't spell 'cat' if you spotted him the c and the a." But after all the talk, there was still a game to be played. Under the warm Miami sun, the Steelers and the Cowboys staged one of the best NFL Championship games ever, a seesaw affair that featured dramatic turnovers, a stirring comeback bid, and one heartbreaking dropped pass that has haunted Cowboys fans and tight end Jackie Smith ever since. When time ran out, the Steelers celebrated another triumph over "America's Team." Three Super Bowls, three victories.

SUPER BOWL FANS CONTRAST IN STYLE

Phil Musick

As everyone not residing in a cave in the Mojave Desert must realize by now, Super Bowl XIII is a matter of matchups. The big one, of course, is Pittsburgh vs. Dallas. The cities and the fans, not the football teams.

Even the combatants acknowledge the differences: Grit vs. gaudy, Perrier water vs. Carstairs-and-a-draft, kolbassi vs. escargot. "Pittsburgh," laughs Joe Greene, is "brick and cobblestones, Dallas is neon and monogrammed shirts."

So Super Bowl XIII has come down to basics . . . a difference in style. Steeler fans here are betting 10 bucks and fretting over the point spread; Cowboys fans are wagering $1,000 and ignoring the spread. The Cowboys are wearing white hats; the Steelers are Darth Vader.

"You look at Roger Staubach," Rocky Bleier says, considering the scene here, "and he's squeaky clean. Tom Landry is squeaky clean. All Dallas is squeaky clean.

"We wear black uniforms."

The Big Matchup. "Dallas is like a crisp $50 bill," Bleier warms to the comparison. "Pittsburgh is a crumpled 20."

It sounds implausible that teams and their followers could be so unlike each other. It isn't. Super [Bowl] XIII affords a superb matchup. Iron City vs. Chivas Regal or chablis; Guccis vs. brogans; Cardin vs. Kaufmann's; where it's been vs. where it's going.

The Dallas fan flew here in a Lear jet, arriving well ahead of the domestic driving his Cadillac in for the weekend. He's staying over at Le Club in Ft. Lauderdale or at the Doral . . . in a suite. The Steeler fan got in late last night in a van with decals on the windows after working the split shift, and he's staying in a room for two with seven other people in a motel two light years from the Gold Coast.

Dallas fans are on expense accounts. Steeler fans are blowing the rent money and the savings bonds. There have been 50 movies made about Dallas, one about Pittsburgh. It was called "Unconquered."

Dallas is Cowboy linebacker Thomas Henderson's mouth vs. Jack Lambert's observation that "with all the media down here, a chimpanzee could get a lot of attention." Dallas is superfan Whistling Ray and a hat that sprays the unsuspecting with water; Pittsburgh is a guy in a Gorilla suit who'll stove five of your ribs if you laugh at him.

Miamians say they can't distinguish Dallas fans; they can't miss their Steeler counterparts. They make noise, while Cowboy fans are reading stock quotations. In the Orange Bowl Sunday, the sound from the Steeler side will probably make the stadium tilt.

"That's because Texas Stadium is in a dry city," Cowboy defensive end Harvey Martin sniffs. "Put a few six-packs out there and you'd hear some noise."

Not if it rains on Sunday. The Cowboy fans will hunker back under the Orange Bowl overhang, used to the roof at Texas Stadium. If it rains, the Steeler fans will take off their shirts and open another beer.

They may not even notice, the way they didn't seem to two weeks ago at Three Rivers when the Steelers were up, 31-3, at the half and only 26 people went home.

"In Pittsburgh, we live tough, we work tough," explains Dwight White, a Dallas native. "After a while, it gets to be part of you. It's no picnic in Pittsburgh.

"There are a lot of mill workers, honest people. The work ethic is important. In Pittsburgh they work, go to church, have babies and go to football games. That's all."

Is the comparison between things in Dallas and things in Pittsburgh a valid one?

The Cowboy hotel overlooks a beautiful beach; the Steeler hotel overlooks a Miami Airport taxiway. The Rooneys are staying at the team hotel. Cowboy owner Clint Murchison is roughing it at Spanish Cay, an island he owns in the Caribbean which has its own landing strip and his-and-her yachts.

The people here from both cities have stylish hair; the Pittsburghers have theirs covered with baseball caps emblazoned "Super Steelers." At the Cowboy post-game party, it will be ultra-suede and $300 denim; at the Steeler party you can bet the ranch there will be a few yellow hardhats with red lights revolving around on them.

"There's a difference in style," Dan Rooney agrees.

There is that. The Dallas Cowboy cheerleaders are here; the Steelers abandoned cheerleaders 20 years ago because the players liked them better than football.

The Cowboys will wear white and say Pittsburgh is cheap because *their* decal is painted on both sides of their helmets; the Steelers will wear black and say the Cowboys are gauche because they have stars all over *their* helmets.

Dallas fans wear hats to keep the sun out of their eyes; Steeler fans wear them because they're black-and-gold and make a statement. Dallas party types drink Alka-Seltzer and stay in bed until noon; their Pittsburgh counterparts drink Bloody Marys at 8 A.M. and suffer with a smile.

Pittsburgh has to be back at work Monday; Dallas is trying to get home by Valentine's Day. If Dallas fans had a flight delayed en route here, they tried to buy the airline; if the same thing happened to a Pittsburgh fan, he probably tried to wreck the airport.

"Our fans will win their game, too," Greene says.

"Dallas?" Dwight White ponders the Big Matchup. "Dallas is flashy, modern, streamlined, barbecues and big Texas egos. When I think of Dallas, I think of El Dorados and Sevilles.

"We have El Dorados and Sevilles in Pittsburgh, too. But the salt on the roads has eaten big holes in them."

Fourth Time's a Charm

The final score, 31-19, looks more lopsided than Super Bowl XIV really was. In Pasadena, only a stone's throw from their home field, the lightly regarded Los Angeles Rams gave the aging Steelers all that they could handle. Untested starting quarterback Vince Ferragamo staked the Rams to an early lead, and it took a sterling fourth-quarter performance by Terry Bradshaw, whose 309 passing yards netted him a second Super Bowl MVP award, to put the Steelers over the top. Sports Illustrated's "Dr. Z," Paul Zimmerman, caught the jubilant mood surrounding the team's fourth Super Bowl win. Beneath his buoyant prose, however, lurked a suspicion that this championship run might be the last hurrah for the team of the 1970s.

THEY WERE JUST TOO MUCH

Paul Zimmerman

It was an emotional Super Bowl and easily the best of the XIV played so far. It was the way Super Bowls are supposed to be played, but haven't been. The score changed hands six times before it ended Pittsburgh 31, Los Angeles 19, but only the guys who laid the 11 points with the bookies read it as a 12-point Steeler win. The Rams made it that close. They stayed in it because of a sustained intensity that brought them great honor, because of an unexpectedly brilliant performance by young Quarterback Vince Ferragamo, and because of a tackle-to-tackle ferocity that had the Steeler defense on its heels much of the afternoon.

But the Steelers aren't exactly virgins in this type of warfare, and when they needed the great plays they got them—two Terry Bradshaw-to-John Stallworth passes worth 118 yards in the fourth quarter and a deep interception by Jack Lambert on his own 14 that cut off the Rams with 5:24 left to play and Pittsburgh ahead 24-19. The Steelers routinely make the great plays, and when you get all excited about those feats, they'll look at you level and say things like, "I've made better catches in Super Bowls . . . a couple of one-handers one time" (Stallworth); or "It's part of our basic coverage . . . it's on the films" (Lambert); or "I really didn't think it would work . . . I hadn't been completing it in practice" (Bradshaw).

Which is why the Steelers have won four Super Bowl rings in the last six years, and why Joe Greene can say, "This game was an invitation engraved in gold."

"An invitation to what?" someone asked, on cue.

"To immortality . . . along with those tremendous pacesetters, the Green Bay Packers," Greene said. He thought for a moment and then added, "Next year it'll all be forgotten. It'll be, 'What have you done for me lately?' A vicious, vicious cycle."

As the Steelers discovered on Sunday, it's getting tougher and tougher to stay on top. Two weeks before, Houston was supposed to roll over—but hadn't; the Oilers had hung tough until the fourth quarter of the AFC Championship Game. This time it was the Rams who were supposed to lie down. The betting was even money that Ferragamo, making only his eighth start, would not be in at the end. The only Ferragamo interview of note that had appeared in the papers during the week was a piece about his malapropisms: "How they arrived at their conclusions behooves me," etc.

But Ferragamo was clear-headed in Pasadena, and he led a very spirited team. As the clubs changed ends to start the fourth quarter with the Rams leading 19-17, a significant thing happened. The Rams had intercepted Bradshaw—for the third time—at the L.A. four-yard line, and Wendell Tyler had broken one for 13 yards, out to the 17, behind a big block by his fullback, Cullen Bryant. Then the whistle blew, and next thing you knew, the Rams were sprinting for the other end of the field.

"We talked about doing it," said Left Tackle Doug France. "It was a very good psych. It let them know we were ready to go. We had 83 yards to cover, and we had to show them we had the strength to do it. We were saying to them, 'Hey, we're not that tired.'"

The Steelers took their time switching ends. No sense getting all excited about a change of quarters.

"No, I didn't see it," said Greene of the L.A. sprint, showing a tiny bit of annoyance for the only time during the post-game interviews. "I had other things on my mind."

"I think the Rams were just excited," said Cornerback Mel Blount, like Greene a veteran of Steeler Coach Chuck Noll's eight playoff teams. "You know, it's the Super Bowl and all that."

If Hollywood, not Pasadena, had been hosting XIV, the Rams would have driven those 83 yards and put the game away and the losingest team—9-7 on the regular season—ever to come into a Super Bowl would have tasted the golden bubbly. But what happened was that the Rams ran three plays, gained six yards and had to punt. And it was a terrific punt by Ken Clark, 59 yards, one yard short of his career best. The Steelers got the ball on their own 25, and, hey, the Rams were still on top of this game.

First-and-10: Jack Reynolds stuffs Franco Harris after a couple of yards. Second-and-eight: Sidney Thornton drops a screen pass, but the play is messed up anyway because Gerry Mullins, the Steeler right guard, is 10 yards downfield. Hang on, Rams, the champs are coming apart. Third-and-eight at the Pittsburgh 27 and what to do? Normally, the Steelers would have gone into a three-wide-receiver set and tried to work something underneath the zone defense for the first down, but they didn't have three wide receivers left.

Lynn Swann had given the Steelers a brief 17-13 lead in the third quarter with a leaping catch of a 47-yard touchdown pass, but he had been knocked out of the game one series later as the result of a very bad decision by Bradshaw. Bradshaw had rolled to his left, looking for help, and had dumped the ball to Swann, curling to the left side. Throw late over the middle and you run the risk of getting either an interception or one of your receivers killed. Bradshaw got the ball high to Swann, who got a very rough ride from Cornerback Pat Thomas. When Swann came to, his vision was blurred and one whole area was totally blank. "Lower right quadrant," he said. "I couldn't see anything at all in that area. The doc told me I'd had it for the day."

Theo Bell, a backup receiver for the Steelers, had been removed from the game after taking a vicious shot by Linebacker George Andrews on a punt, and now, with third-and-eight on their own 27, with a little over 12 minutes to go and trailing by two points, the Steelers had only two wide receivers left on the roster. Bennie Cunningham, the tight end, split wide left. Jim Smith, Swann's backup, was wide right, and Stallworth was in the slot inside him. Chuck Noll sent in the play "60 Prevent Slot Hook and Go." A pass to Stallworth, who would make a little hitch inside and then take off.

"I didn't like the call," Bradshaw said, "but you know, the coach sent it in. I hadn't been hitting that pass all week. It's a matter of building confidence. You don't build confidence in things that don't work. Maybe it was our ace in the hole. I don't know."

It hadn't been a good week for Bradshaw. He was beat, having slept only four or five hours a night. The night before the game he went to bed at midnight but woke up at 3 A.M. "I couldn't get back to sleep," he said. He had dragged through the practices, the interview sessions, the pre-Super Bowl madness that turned the Steelers' Newport Beach hotel into a zoo. Meanwhile, the Rams were practicing on their home turf over in Anaheim and going home to the wife and kiddies at night. On Thursday, Bradshaw gave one of his zillion radio interviews of the week. His answers were mechanical.

"You certainly seem laid-back going into this game," the guy with the mike said.

"Yeah, well, you know, we've been here before," Bradshaw said, giving stock answer No. 435.

"Laid-back, hell, I'm tired. Tired," he said later. "I'm not sleeping. I just can't sleep . . . I don't know what it is. Pressure, I guess. Tension. I've never felt it this bad. I haven't thrown the ball well in two weeks. I'm just tired of football. Drained."

Ray Mansfield, the old Steeler center, dropped by the hotel to visit with his former teammates. "I could always look at Terry before a game and tell you what kind of a day he was going to have," Mansfield said. "If he was a little glassy-eyed—you'd be talking to him and he'd look through you like you weren't there—I'd know it was going to be a long afternoon."

"How does he look today?" Mansfield was asked.

"Don't ask," he said.

And now the coach is telling Bradshaw that his arm is going to win it. Bradshaw's first interception, which had set up a Rams go-ahead field goal—13-10—in the second quarter, had brought back visions of the interception Houston's Vernon Perry ran back for a TD in the AFC title game. His first interception against the Rams had been a late throw over the middle to Swann; Bradshaw had tried to force the ball through double coverage, and Dave Elmendorf had picked it off. Bradshaw's second interception had been a ball that got away from him, a bloop throw to Smith on a deep pattern. His third one had been a force to Stallworth over the middle, deep in Ram territory, with the Steelers behind 19-17.

There had almost been a fourth one. In the third quarter, with the Rams still on top 19-17, Bradshaw had tried to find Swann inside and Nolan Cromwell, the L.A. free safety, had roared up like the Duesenberg that had transported Steeler patriarch Art Rooney out for the coin toss. "The only thing that could have stopped him," said Steeler Center Mike Webster, "was a .357 magnum." But Cromwell dropped the ball.

Third-and-eight on the 27. Your game to win, Terry baby. The Steelers' running game? Forget it. Thirty-seven carries for only 84 yards on the day. "The Rams did their homework," Webster said. "When we'd audible, Jack Reynolds would call the correct defense for the play we audibled to. They knew us."

"I could see them doing research on the sidelines," Ram Defensive End Fred Dryer said. "I think Terry was having trouble reading us."

There are not many ways a human being can throw a football better than Bradshaw did to Stallworth on that third-and-eight play. Stallworth got inside Rod Perry, the cornerback, and behind Elmendorf, the strong safety, and took it 73 yards for a 24-19 Pittsburgh lead. Two series later Stallworth did it again—15 yards on the same play— only this time he didn't bother to throw the little inside fake. It set up Franco Harris' one-yard touchdown for the 31-19 margin that rewarded the Steeler bettors.

"God-given ability," Webster said. "You just can't beat it. Terry had enough ability to overcome the mistakes, the three interceptions, the bad week he'd had. He had the courage to go with that long stuff."

In the Rams' locker room Perry answered the same question over and over: "Inside-outside coverage. I had the outside. I did the best I could. Hey, haven't you ever seen a perfect play?"

Emotions were running high in that dressing room. On his way in, Tyler had turned to the writers and said, "I didn't fumble in the game. Put that in your paper!" Tyler never fumbled. No one did. The Steelers banged Tyler around plenty, too. Knocked him out of the game five times. Count 'em. But he kept coming back.

"We wanted to gang-tackle him because he has a reputation for fumbling," Lambert said. "We wanted to make him know he'd been in a football game."

It went both ways. On his third carry Tyler broke a 39-yarder, which set up the Rams' first score and gave them a 7-3 lead. Faked two guys off their feet on the slippery sideline turf.

"It set the tone," Greene said. "Put us in the tank, so to speak."

In a corner Ferragamo was trying to describe what it had been like to face 103,985 fans and 11 Steelers in his first Super Bowl. "I tried audibling one time at the noisy end of the field," he said. "No one heard me. I was a little leery about audibling after that. There was a 30-second clock, but it was kind of concealed. It was tough to see until it started getting dark. It was there for you, though, if you could make it out. Hell, you'd better make it out."

Ferragamo was asked a technical question. "I tried zooming—and motion—they took me out of it," he said. No one knew what he was talking about. Ferragamo stopped for a moment and looked up. "It just hurts to know you're that good and you can't win it," he said. "It's a hurting feeling inside."

"Ferragamo was the better quarterback today," Webster said in the other dressing room. "Overall, I'd have to say he did the better job."

It was a strange role-reversal for the clubs. The Rams were the muscle team, not the Steelers. L.A. established a running game very early and worked it. The Steelers went big play, big gamble. Three big plays, three interceptions.

"Anyone who calls us dogs," Jack Youngblood, the Rams' defensive end said, "well, let him call me that to my face."

"We gave it everything we had, we went out there with everything in our hearts," Dennis Harrah, the L.A. right guard, was saying. "We picked up all their stunts, all their defensive-line games. I think we surprised them with our guts and determination."

He was looking at the floor. When he looked up, you could see he was crying.

"I'm sorry, but I just can't talk about it anymore," Harrah said.

Jim Jodat, a reserve running back, put his arm around Harrah. "C'mon man, the bus is leaving," he said.

"I'll be all right," Harrah said.

"I said a few nice things to Joe Greene after the game," Harrah said. "I hugged my buddy (Steeler defensive tackle) Gary Dunn. I just . . . I'm sorry. I can't say any more."

There were times when the Pittsburgh defense looked shaky, when it looked as if the Steelers were barely hanging on. They reached Ferragamo for four sacks, but they had to use multiple blitzes to do it. Linebackers, safeties, cornerbacks—the Steelers threw it all at the kid. Ferragamo said, "On one of them—when we were down on their 13 and they put 11 men up on the line and sacked me—well, maybe I should have called time out before I ran the play. Maybe it's inexperience. We'll be back here again."

The Rams fooled the Steeler secondary on their last touchdown, a 24-yard halfback option pass, Lawrence McCutcheon to Ron Smith, that gave them the 19-17 lead. L.A. did a number on Ron Johnson, the left corner, on that play. Johnson had been having words with Billy Waddy, the Rams' wide receiver. Then Waddy, on an underthrown ball, had caught a 50-yarder on Johnson, the kind of catch that drives cornerbacks crazy. The book says you don't let crazy cornerbacks off the hook, so the Rams swept McCutcheon to Johnson's side, and when Johnson was drawn into the net, it was time for McCutcheon to stand and deliver to Smith. Six points.

"You could see we were getting to them," said Gordon Gravelle, the reserve L.A. tackle who used to be a Steeler. "At times they looked a little confused out there. I haven't seen that on a Pittsburgh team in a long while."

"Jack Lambert hollered so hard in the huddle in the first half that I got scared," said Steeler Strong Safety Donnie Shell. "I can't repeat what he said, but he got real red in the face. He said we were sleep-walking out there."

The final chapter is that the Steelers' big-play people—Bradshaw, Lambert, Swann, Stallworth, the guys who had done it so many times before—rose up one more time.

"The real fact," Greene said, "was that we just had too many good football players. It had to show today because the Rams were so high emotionally and they were executing so well."

He looked at his audience. "You can't beat talent," he said.

Jack Lambert

Sam Rutigliano, former coach of the Cleveland Browns and NBC/ESPN television commentator, knew football inside and out. He knew football talent, and he had a fine sense of what made a few players great. What he saw in Lambert went beyond the player's physical abilities, beyond what coaches could measure, time, and quantify. It even went beyond Lambert's All-Pro heart. It had to do with the quality of the linebacker's mind and character. The Steelers drafted Lambert in the second round of the 1974 draft, and he became the only rookie on Pittsburgh's first Super Bowl team. Between 1974 and 1983 Lambert led the Steelers in tackles every year, and when he retired he said that he just wanted to be remembered "simply as someone who played the best he could." He is remembered for that—and for much, much more.

WINNERS MAKE PLAYS: JACK LAMBERT

Sam Rutigliano

Jack Lambert was the quarterback of the Steeler defense. He was the hub in the wheel with ten spokes revolving around him and one of the very best ever to play linebacker. Jack was a second-round draft choice from Kent State who will join his teammate, Joe Greene, in the Hall of Fame. We had many confrontations with Jack because we played the Steelers twice each year. I got to know Jack pretty well when I coached him in the Pro Bowl in 1981.

When you sit down and talk with him man-to-man, he's very different from Jack Lambert the linebacker. He left pro football prematurely because of a very bad toe problem. He simply wouldn't continue to play unless he could play up to his own high standards. That made Jack different. Some players felt they could evaluate and apply their own degree of intensity as the situation dictated. Not Jack. He went all out, all the time. As a coach, I loved to see that in a player.

Every year, from 1978 on, Jack was a tremendous thorn in our side. Not only was he a great physical player, but he was very bright. Many a time I heard him from where I stood on the sideline, yelling and

From *Pressure* (Nashville: Oliver-Nelson Books, 1988). Reprinted by permission of Sam Rutigliano.

screaming at linebackers and defensive backs to make adjustments in their positions. Countless times he broke up our big passes and important runs. Lambert always seemed to be there to stop the play from being a big one. As a result we often had to kick a field goal instead of scoring 6 points that would have won the game. He was a very cerebral football player.

I remember our game in Pittsburgh in 1983 when Brian Sipe had dropped back to pass and he couldn't find an open receiver. He rolled out of the pocket and came toward our bench, but Jack Lambert caught him as he was going out of bounds and knocked him cold. Brian was finished for the day.

Ben Dreith, the referee, threw the flag and also threw Lambert out of the game. Ben Dreith is one of the best and most animated officials in the league. I was always happy to have Ben referee our Steeler games. His job as a referee is to protect the quarterback. Because of the Steelers' pass rush and intimidating style, Ben called many "roughing the quarterback" penalties. I kidded Ben when I met him on the field before the game. I told him, "Hey, Ben, if you're going to referee this game, I've got to call my wife and tell her to call the doctor. She'll need some tranquilizers if you're going to ref this game."

Lambert came right over to our bench and said to me, "Sam, that was not a cheap shot." After the game, Lambert came into our locker room to talk with Sipe. He really didn't intend to hurt Sipe. But when Lambert was involved in the heat and emotion of a game, that game to him was bigger than life, and he gave no quarter. Once the game was over, however, Jack was a very private person with a tremendous sensitivity.

We played another game against Pittsburgh in Cleveland in 1983 when Lambert did the same thing to Sipe and knocked him into our bench again. All our guys jumped him and hit him, and he finally ran out into the middle of the field. The referee threw him out of the game. He had caused Sipe to throw an interception, but the referee threw a flag and we kept possession of the ball. Whenever Lambert got thrown out of a game, it was a big help to us. When we were on the offense and Lambert was on the sideline, it was a comforting feeling. He had the respect of all the players.

Watching Lambert from the sideline as I did many times, I saw a physically tough and mentally alert player. Someone has said that deaf-mutes play the game of football with tremendous intensity and are great hitters. One of the reasons is that they can't hear the noise. Hearing the sounds of contact from the sideline is sometimes scary. You can also hear the sounds of people going after each other, screaming and groaning. Jack was an intense player who wasn't distracted by all that.

He was contagious. Young rookies who played with Jack played as much to please him as they did the coach. They knew they would hear from Jack if they didn't play up to the level that he felt was necessary to win. Even veteran players would feel his scorn at times. Jack played almost a decade with that great Steelers team.

I always felt that even if Jack Ham or Joe Greene or Donnie Shell or Mel Blount was out of the game, so long as Jack Lambert was there, the rest of the players would play to their optimum level. Coaches always talk about having a player who is like a coach on the field. That was Lambert. I always knew the Steelers would never beat themselves so long as Lambert was playing. Jack was both interesting and ominous to watch on the field because he was so animated. Every coach wants players like him. They don't come along every year.

When Lambert came out of college, many people didn't think he would make it because he appeared to be too long and tall but not heavy enough. He was about six feet five and weighed about 210 pounds. His great innate strength gave him tremendous leverage, and he always seemed to be at the right place at the right time.

The moment a game started, Jack was like the conductor of the Cleveland Orchestra as he organized the line in front of him and the defense behind him. The defensive line and the linebackers always handled the running game while the defensive backs and the linebackers handled the passing game. For most of Jack's career he played in a four/three defense where he was the middle linebacker. He was the guy who orchestrated everything defensively and made the adjustments on each play. If we came out in an unusual formation or used a man in motion or anything exotic, Jack was the guy who had to get the word to the rest of the defense. And he almost always did.

The defense must respond as one. Communication is important. If there was a situation with third down and 6 yards to go and we threw the ball to Gregg Pruitt, Jack somehow got there to knock the ball down. If we had a back run out as a pass receiver, Jack seemed always to be able to run with him step for step and make the play. Or if we had a crucial third-down-and-one situation where we needed the first down to continue our drive, kill the clock, and get into field-goal position to win a game, Jack was always there on the line of scrimmage to stuff the play. He always made the big plays at important times. He shouldn't have been that good. He wasn't big enough. He was a throw-back, the kind of player who should have played at Notre Dame in the 1940s. The guy simply loved to play football.

Jack didn't have much to say off the field. He was a private person. Sure, he had to negotiate his contract and got quoted in the newspaper once in a while. Seldom did he say anything negative. Once when he was asked what he thought about all the new rules to protect the quarterback, he replied, "From now on they oughta make sure the quarterbacks wear skirts!" But on the field he was as serious as they come. He didn't say things to please people; he said what he believed and felt strongly. Although I never had the pleasure of coaching Jack, I probably had more respect for him than most other players I ever watched. He's in a select category in my book.

The Steelers have lost a lot of great players in the last few years. Mel Blount, Jack Ham, Andy Russell, Dwight White, L. C. Greenwood, and Mean Joe Greene are gone. But what hurt them the most was losing Jack Lambert, future Hall of Famer. In all my years in professional football I never played against a guy, in any position, who was more of a dominating force than Jack Lambert, both physically and mentally. Jack was the complete player. If you could bottle what Jack Lambert had, it would be illegal! Yes, the Steelers were the best team of the 1970s. Four Super Bowl wins! They may go down in football history as the best team ever. Jack was selected on the second round. That's why the draft is a crapshoot. Sometimes it's better to be lucky than good.

During the 1970s, the Steelers prided themselves on being a unified team rather than an assortment of individuals. Despite their cohesion, the franchise had a number of standout personalities—the fluid Swann, the bombastic Greene, the homespun Bradshaw. But Franco Harris, in many ways the heart of the potent Steelers offense and the third running back in NFL history to rush for over 10,000 yards, remained a largely private figure. In the words of Roy Blount Jr., Harris, who rarely sat for revealing interviews, was "an enigma." He was a famous man who shunned the limelight, a physically punishing back with a not-unwarranted reputation for avoiding pointless hits. In this piece, first published in 1982, Blount showed that Harris was also a humanitarian whose charitable endeavors often went unnoticed— mainly due to his own reticence—by the community he thrilled on Sunday afternoons.

THE ASCENT OF AN ENIGMA

Roy Blount Jr.

Franco Harris, who once worried that the National Football League would blackball him, has now run with the league's football more times that anyone else, and has won its humanitarian award. One of the many people he has shown humanitarianism toward is himself. Which has something to do with the fact that he is frowned upon by some people, and a great deal to do with his being able to carry the ball so many times.

Harris has enormous presence. This is partly because he is enormous, partly because he has the face of a sheikh or a Moorish prince or a young Old Testament prophet, and partly because he doesn't seem to be entirely present. He looks *almost* as if he just woke up and isn't sure whether he slept well enough or not and is determined to make up his own mind about it. But there is something unfulfilled about the way he walks that suggests he is mulling a matter of more general interest than that.

"On a football field you don't have time to stop and think," says Harris' former teammate Joe Greene. "But Franco thinks about every-

From *About Three Bricks Shy . . . and the Load Filled Up: The Story of the Greatest Football Team Ever* (New York: Ballantine, 1989). Copyright Roy Blount Jr.

thing. You watch Franco run, he's not dancing. He's making decisions."

You watch Franco walk and it's as if he doesn't really believe in walking, he's beyond it: running is true discourse, walking is small talk. Yet he's notoriously in no hurry. In season and out he walks with the pained, stiffish amble of a powerful but sensitive and banged-up centurion, or a reflective cowboy just out of two weeks in the saddle.

His carriage suggests that his shoulders are connected to his feet by elastic cords that can only with effort be stretched. "Breaks down better than any big man I have seen," wrote a Steeler scout, on the plus side when Harris was at Penn State. To break down is to maintain in action a good football position: balanced, gathered, cocked fluently at the knees and hips. Franco walks as if on the verge of that (and perhaps also the automotive) kind of breakdown. Or it may be more as though his body is a horse that feels like itself only in the strain of a full stride, and his mind is a rider broodily aware that it's a long while between times to burst out.

Then on the field he does burst, and you'd forgotten that he, or anybody else, could flow as complicatedly but smoothly as that.

Harris is one of the few sports figures—Oscar, Wilt, Reggie are among them—whose first names suffice, and his is one of the most recognizable sports faces. Fans may think they have him summed up: Immaculate Reception, all those Super Bowls, half-black-half-Italian. But his wife and Penn State Football Coach Joe Paterno have called him "an enigma," and this season vicariously hard guys in Pittsburgh bars will once again be watching Harris step out of bounds to avoid being needlessly crunched and will crunch their beer cans and exclaim, "What's his *story?*"

"There are no Franco Stories!" says Lynn Swann, his Steeler roommate, with an air of illumination. "That's Franco. Franco likes to do things alone. Or with a few people he knows well. He's quiet."

"But then . . . you go somewhere and see him *surrounded*. Kids, all kinds of people, *flocking*."

And Harris mixes well with them if they're celebrities, lends a hand if they're a charity, signs autographs ad infinitum. "His motto," says Swann, "is 'A man's gotta do what a man's gotta do.'"

Harris weighs anywhere from 220 pounds (his reckoning) to 240 (tacklers' estimates) and stands at 6' 2", and yet his running style has been described as "dainty." Which is why he has been able to play in 157 of a possible 166 games in 10 years, tie Jim Brown's record of seven 1,000-yard seasons, run for more yards and score more touchdowns in postseason games than anyone else ever, and gain more regular-season rushing yards (10,339) than anybody but Brown (12,312) and O. J. Simpson (11,236).

In 1972, when the Steelers first made the playoffs, Harris was AFC Rookie of the Year and came from nowhere in the first round of the AFC playoffs to grab a deflected pass just before it hit the ground and carry it 60 yards to beat Oakland in the last five seconds and go down in history as the Immaculate Receptor. In the Steelers' first Super Bowl, IX, in 1975, in which they beat Minnesota 16-6, he rushed for 158 yards and was named Most Valuable Player. In 1976 he was named NFL Man of the Year, and after last season he was presented the Byron R. (Whizzer) White Humanitarian Award.

Like others of the 12 still-active members of the Steeler dynasty that won four world championships in six years, Harris may, as they say, have lost a step. Or a fraction of one: He ran 40 yards in slightly under 4.8 seconds (from a bad start) in camp this year, compared to slightly more than 4.7 seconds as a rookie. But, at 32, he's still quick and sound, he still moves in his own mysterious ways, and he may well have enough steps left to pass O. J. and Brown. He makes an estimated $350,000 a year from a Steeler contract he negotiated himself. So he no longer rides a municipal bus to Three Rivers Stadium and hitch-hikes home the way he did when he was a rookie. Now he drives a Toyota that is always in the shop because he doesn't like to shift gears. Harris isn't a run-of-the-mill guy.

"I always say Franco is the one person I know of who's going to go straight up to heaven," says Dana Dokmanovich, the elegant Eastern Airlines flight attendant who has been an item with Harris since college, has been living with him for several years and is the mother of Franco Dokmanovich Harris, three, called Dok. Harris introduces Dana as his wife, but they have never felt compelled to make their union official, which is why Bess Dokmanovich—who lives with them in Pittsburgh and helps take care of Dok and serves as Harris' secretary—refers to herself amiably as "Franco's mother-in-law-so-to-speak."

"Franco and the Pope," says Dana, thinking of one other who will go straight to Glory. "Because of what Franco does for other people. To me he's a pain in the butt. He lets *anybody* in the house."

Franco, Dana, Dok and Bess don't live in a house you'd expect a football player to have. "When Franco first showed it to me, I thought it was a joke," says Dana. But that was when it was boarded up and in terrible shape inside. Now it's the kind of townhouse a well-fixed San Francisco lawyer might have, with imposing marble mantels, rich-grained wainscoting, corkscrew balustrades, great hardwood floors and high ceilings. Franco walks around in it and says, "Feels *solid*." The house stands in an old part of Pittsburgh called the Mexican War Streets area (because its streets were laid out during that conflict), which is gentrifying, but not by leaps and bounds.

"It's an interesting neighborhood," says Harris in his deep murmur. "Not everyone would like it, but I like it. It has some interesting people." It reminds Bess of places she used to live. Dana, who doesn't remember that far back, would like to move somewhere "away from things." She says, "I'll tell you why he bought this house. Because it's so close to the stadium. Otherwise he'd never get there on time."

Near the house is a park. Steeler patriarch Art Rooney, who lives a few blocks away, once located Harris by going to this park, hailing the first little kid he saw playing basketball and saying, "Find Franco."

In this park, a young man comes up pushing a bent-limbed woman in a ramshackle wheelchair. Both of them look as if they've been down on their luck all their lives. "Here he comes again, with his mother," says Dana. "You should hear her holler at him when he hits a bump." The pair hails Franco, and Dana rolls her eyes.

"Did you find a place to live?" asks Harris in an elder-brotherish tone of concern. The last time he saw them they were on his doorstep under the impression that his house, like most of the large dwellings in the vicinity, contained apartments for poor folks. Harris counsels with the pair for several minutes.

Meanwhile Dok, less reserved than his father, is dashing about like a Serbo-Italo-Afro-American butterfly.

"Dok goes up to people and says, 'Do you know who I am? Do you want to meet my daddy?'" says Dana (who's of Serbian descent). "When Franco signs autographs, Dok signs too—scribbles—on the same paper. We went to McDonald's and he saw Franco's picture on the glasses they're giving out. 'Give me my daddy's glass!' he yelled. Fortunately, he's hard to understand."

Harris is resigned to moving out of the inner city for Dok's sake, but he points out that no one has broken into the house.

"How would anyone break in?" says Dana. "They'd have to time it just right. There's always someone ringing the bell.

"He's never here, he's always away doing charity work. And I only know three-fourths of what he does for people. There are parts of himself he just won't share, and that's one. I don't think he wants to admit how much people get him to do for them."

One day Pittsburgh sportscaster Myron Cope got a call about a local kid who'd been hit in the head by a line drive in a Little League game. The kid couldn't speak and could barely move. He had to do therapy on special walking boards to keep fluid from gathering in his lungs, but he couldn't get motivated. Would it be possible for Cope to arrange for the kid's No. 1 sports hero to visit him in the rehabilitation center? Cope said he'd try. He called and called but could not get the hero to call back.

"Who was the kid's No. 2 hero?" Cope inquired. Franco Harris. "Oh," said Cope, relieved. "No problem." After one call Franco was at the center with a huge bundle of coloring books and comics for the kids there.

"I sat down to wait while Franco and the doctor went into a room with the kid," says Cope. "I figured it'd be 10 minutes or so. I sat there for an hour and 15 minutes. Finally Franco came out. He'd been helping the kid on the walking boards. As we left he was telling the doctor, 'I'll be back with Swann and some other guys.' Franco is one guy who *really* does charity."

"Franco will go out of his way to help *anybody*," says Greene, "but he isn't concerned with what anybody thinks. He's not concerned with what *I* think." Greene, who until his retirement at the end of last season was the most authoritative of Steelers, and the only one other than Swann who could be said to know Franco well, adds, "Franco answers only to Franco."

He won't dispute anything with Dana, though. "We have plenty of arguments," she says, "but I'm the only one arguing. He will not argue. He has his own pace, and you can yell at him but it doesn't make any difference."

That led to some problems during Harris' in-and-out career at Penn State. Steeler scouting reports said things like, "Can cut, slide, stop and go. Will lower the boom. Lots of movement and wiggle." But also things like this: "Has all needs (scout talk for requirements) of a great pro but is not a hustler."

"Not a hard runner for his size."

"Question his top competitiveness."

And, finally, "Could be a great pro but might not even be a good one. However, I feel he is worth the gamble."

The Steelers took that gamble after considerable internal debate, but Harris didn't blow people away when he came to camp as the team's top draftee in '72. "I didn't think he could make the team," recalls retired Center Ray Mansfield. Rocky Bleier, who, with Franco, produced the Steelers' most effective running attack, and now does sports news on Pittsburgh TV, says his first impression of Franco was "lazy."

Bleier's second impression: "I sat next to him in meetings and thought, 'Little thin arms . . . he's undeveloped. . . . What does he have that I don't have?'" Bleier was a committed weightlifter who had built up his chest, arms and legs enormously. "Franco's not all chiseled," observes a friend. "He's just sort of there." By the time Harris joined the Steelers he thought of himself as being into serious lifting, but that was by his own standards. People who were in camp then recall that he didn't seem to know how to handle weights. Harris started lifting weights alone. About halfway through his rookie year the Steelers realized Franco was neither lazy nor weak but just unconventional.

As recently as 1979, however, Jack Tatum, then a feared Oakland defensive back, said in his book, *They Call Me Assassin*, "I have never seen a more imposing physical specimen of an athlete with less drive than Franco. . . . If Franco doesn't run for the sidelines, slip and fall, or cake out before anyone gets near him, then . . . someone else is wearing his game jersey."

Of course, being criticized in those terms by Tatum is like being called effete by Stalin. But the kind of thing that Tatum exaggerated is what makes Harris such a refreshing fullback. Most backs, says Bleier, would be embarrassed to run the way Franco sometimes does. "But you know Franco," Bleier says, "He could give a damn. And look what he's accomplished."

It all began in Pisa, Italy, where Sergeant Cad Harris of Jackson, Miss., who never talked much, met Gina Parenti, whose village had been destroyed and whose brother, an Italian soldier, had been chopped to pieces by Nazis, but who talked a great deal. She married Cad and went with him to Mount Holly, N.J.

Franco's father stayed in the Army, at Fort Dix, N.J. after World War II, and Franco grew up in a firmly disciplined family of nine children. "He took after our father, because he was into his privacy," says Harris' younger brother Pete, who tried out unsuccessfully as a defensive back with the Steelers this year. "But I never saw Franco much when we were kids. He was always at Fort Dix shining shoes and bagging groceries. Too many kids to support."

Franco was also starring in baseball, basketball, and football. But "nobody in our house talked about careers," he says. "In the seventh grade I got put in an A-track class, and the teacher went around the room asking whether we were going to take commercial or college prep, and everybody else said, 'college prep, college prep,' so I said, 'college prep.' But I never thought about going to college until my older brother Mario went to Glassboro State."

Franco did even better: made high school All-America and went to Penn State, where he wore a T shirt, khakis, and high-top black tennis shoes and hung out at the hoagie shop just like back home. But he also took his grades seriously. At the end of the first term, Harris had a 1.9, a tenth of a point under a C average. Many a jock would have been pleased, but Franco says, "I was *sick*. I couldn't get over it. I wasn't going to let *that* happen again"—possibly because he remembered the time that one of his sisters came home with a bad grade "and my father tore her *up*. Whooo. A lot of times I didn't cross the fine line into getting in trouble because of fear of my father."

Which isn't to say that he toed every line. "The late '60s and early '70s was an era when I guess a lot of people didn't look at authority as very good no matter where it came from," Harris says. "Being in college then, you learned to read between the lines. Kent State, I think, was the most tragic thing in the history of our country. I couldn't believe our own countrymen shooting and killing. . . . If there were demonstrations or takeovers, I liked to go see what was happening. But I wasn't one to overthrow the university. At times I felt a lot of pressure from people who thought it would be great to have a football player visible in a lot of things. But I still was kind of a punky kid from New Jersey and I didn't want anybody to tell me what to do, especially college kids.

"After I got to Penn State I heard that there had been a discussion among the coaches about whether I should shave my mustache. I'd never had gone there if I'd thought they'd tell me that. I never thought of my mustache as being a mustache. I thought it was just part of my face. I had hair on my lip at a very early age."

He also had a sense of how to play football at an early age, and in college he didn't test that sense enough. He was an All-America honorable mention his sophomore year, but tailed off after that. It's often said that Penn State relegated Franco to blocking for his friend and classmate Lydell Mitchell, who was a consensus All-America their senior year, but the situation wasn't that simple. John Morris, who was sports information director at Penn State then, says he promoted Harris and Mitchell equally as Mr. Inside and Mr. Outside, with the twist that Harris, the bigger of the two, was Mr. Outside. Their senior year, Harris got hurt and took a long time to get back in shape, and Mitchell became the primary ballcarrier. Years later, Morris says, "Franco told me, 'I wish I knew as much about conditioning then as I do now. I'd have been unstoppable.'"

As it was, he made pro scouts doubt his mettle, and he ran afoul of coachly authority. Paterno was hollering at his troops trying to get them psyched at the beginning of practice one day when Harris, who had characteristically been the last player to get taped, came trotting up a few minutes late. In front of everyone, Paterno told him that if he did that again he'd be demoted to second team.

The next day, Mitchell recalls, "I told Franco not to do it, but he did it anyway. Franco is the type of guy that I don't know how people cannot like him. But once he makes up his mind to do something, usually he does. Actually, Franco wasn't at practice late. But once we took the field, he sat inside. He came out late. He called Joe's bluff, and meanwhile Joe called his bluff."

Later Paterno blamed himself for challenging Harris in such a way, but the upshot was that Franco didn't start in the Cotton Bowl, and that raised questions about him in the pro scouts' minds.

"I always thought I was an all-right guy," says Harris. "But there was talk that I might be blackballed from the NFL. Joe was on vacation, out on a boat somewhere. I tracked him down and called him, asked him if he was saying anything negative about me. He assured me he wasn't."

"But it was going around that I might have been a problem. I remember wanting to send the Steelers a telegram not to draft me, because I didn't want to go where the fans threw snowballs at the players. But the guy who was my agent then told me not to send the telegram because I probably had a bad rap now, and it would just make it worse. I got a call that I'd been drafted by the Steelers, and I was in shock."

However, he was ready for the pros. For one thing, he was tired of trying to live on $15 a month laundry money. "I never did understand that," Harris says. "How is somebody from a poor family supposed to get by? You're not supposed to scalp tickets. You're not supposed to get money from anybody else. You couldn't have a job. Somebody who doesn't have any rights is the college football player. Fortunately, I was able to scalp a few tickets."

And he'd had the maturing experience of working for Walter Conti, who has since become president of the Penn State board of trustees. Conti owns a restaurant in Doylestown, Pa., and he was prevailed upon to take Harris on as a summer worker because he was majoring in hotel and restaurant management.

"Around his junior year," says Conti, "Franco had become lax about some things. He was supposed to show up for an interview at six. He showed up at 11. He said he'd be finished with school on the 17th of June. So I told him to call me on the first of June and I'd arrange for a place for him to live. On the 16th of June at 1 A.M., after I'd given up on him, he called. So I found him a nice place to live. He didn't like it. I found him another place. The first three days of work, he was supposed to be here at eight in the morning. He'd show up at 5 P.M. I told him, 'Either you come or you're done.' And the guy responded."

"Now I say Franco's my third son. He asked me questions that had more depth to them than I'm asked by professionals.

"And he had a desire for perfection. I could see that with my liver. Every calf's liver has to be peeled, or when you cook it, it curls up. Peeling liver is not one of the better jobs that people like to do. Franco Harris cleaned my liver better than anybody else has."

Harris also played in the Senior Bowl and in the College All-Star game, "and I realized I was a better athlete than those other guys. Why had they accomplished more in college?" I went to some of the weightlifters at Penn State and they taught me how to lift. I developed a total commitment to getting in shape. It made all the difference in the world. I told myself, when the other guys are tired, that's when you do it. I felt stronger, smarter, my feel for the game was sharper."

And the Steelers thought he was lazy. "I'm still trying to figure that out," Harris says. "After the first exhibition game the coaches came up saying 'Good game,' like they didn't expect it from me. It was hard to believe they were disappointed in me the first week of practice. Maybe it was because I didn't allow people to beat on me."

Ah. The crux of Franco's peculiarity and strength. "I always feel that the easiest thing you can do," he says, "is run into somebody."

Call it common sense or call it elitist, such unabashed thinking is surprisingly rare in football. When asked how he responds when people accuse Harris of not running hard enough, Steeler Middle Linebacker

Jack Lambert, headknocker nonpareil, doesn't say, "I wrench their torsos off." He says, "That's Franco's problem."

Of course, defenses and offenses have ever been uneasy allies. It's entirely possible that the Steeler defense would feel more comfortable if the team's mainstay running back were Chicago's Walter Payton, who says, "My running style is that I attack the defender."

Franco isn't the kind of humanitarian to take that approach, which, in the long run, is playing into the defenders' hands. It's like throwing fastballs to a fastball hitter so he'll respect you more.

"When I went to Buffalo in 1969," says O. J. Simpson, "I thought I had to show my macho, to go out and play fierce. I did it for two or three games, and then I realized I wasn't going to be long for the NFL if I kept that up. Franco didn't have to prove himself, either. He's used his athletic gifts with discretion."

He has, in fact, been flagrant about it. Dana says that, although he has traditional notions about the roles of men and women, he's never shown any macho, and so do friends who've been in places where people told him he'd never be half the man Jim Brown was. Harris is so secure that he isn't afraid to say things like, "If it's a matter of winding up in the same place, I'd rather not get hit than get hit, chicken as that may sound."

Defensive players would like runners to define themselves in terms of contact with the defense. But Harris knows what he's interested in, and it isn't being pounded by tacklers.

"I will always watch the runners run," he says. "We're studying films, supposed to be watching defenses, and I find myself running along with the runner, putting myself in his shoes. Lots of running backs are faster than I am on a straight-ahead run, but not in the first 10 or 15 yards, dodging people and being quick about it. I'm watching where other backs' feet are, how they move their hips. I see a certain move I like, and I run it over and over in my mind, and I'll try it.

"Every play is different. I can run 19-Straight 10 times, and every time get a different read." He doesn't just read, he peruses: gliding laterally along the line, scanning it for a breakthrough. And if he winds up in the margin, he doesn't apologize.

He couldn't get away with that fancy stuff if it didn't work for the team, of course. For one thing, as Greene points out, "Franco is brushing a lot of people aside with a lot of authority. He just does it in such a smooth manner it doesn't look like he's bowling them over."

For another thing, Greene says, "The Pittsburgh style is the cut back style. Partly because Dick Hoak, our backfield coach, was that kind of runner, looking for the opening, using his blockers. But. . . . gliding, waiting for something to happen. . . . Franco perfected it."

And the Steelers learned that, as Harris says, "I take my shots. On first or second down, maybe I don't get an extra few feet that we didn't need, but if it's a third down situation, I go as hard as anybody else."

"After a game," says one of the Steelers' physicians, Dr. Paul Steele, "Franco has big raw welts all across his back, as if someone has beaten him with a truncheon, and he just gets up and goes again."

"When I first saw him," says Greene, "he reminded me of myself. He didn't like practice. Franco had a wonderful sense of timing; he could gauge the tempo of a play without going full speed in practice. He wasn't sloughing off. Every time he ran a play, he'd run the ball all the way to the goal line."

And if Harris didn't pump iron as lustily as some of his mates, he did do regular weight work, for tone rather than bulk, and he has habitually been the last Steeler out of the locker room after practice. He jumps rope, he lingers in the whirlpool, he kids around with the locker room boys, he does odd exercises no one else does, such as jumping up and down on a mat to develop his spring from a surface with no bounce.

When most of the other Steelers were in the showers after practice the first day the veterans reported to camp, Harris was catching short passes from a rookie quarterback, over and over and over—trying to snag the ball *perfectly*, with no element of bobble whatsoever. He would make little catching faces and catching noises, with a faraway look in his eyes, like a kid imagining himself a pro football player. When he dropped one he would go, "Awwww," and grimace and shudder with almost histrionically real feeling, as if in a pass-dropping-and-reaction drill. When he caught one he would hold the freshly received ball in his hands like cupped water, scrutinizing it, dwelling on it, as if it were a liver that had to be ideally peeled. ("The only thing about it," says Conti, "is he would take 3½ hours to peel one liver.")

"In the midst of our so-called dynasty," says Greene, "it was an era when if you couldn't run, you couldn't play, and we ran, and we ran with Franco. Ninety percent of the offense then was Franco."

"You can see the frustration sometimes," says Swann. That is, you can see [Coach] Chuck Noll on the sidelines "wanting to say, 'Franco, run over the guy!' And Franco is getting up and. . . .'" Swann does an imitation of Franco moseying, preoccupied, with his back to the bench. "But Franco plays Chuck's offense. He does the job."

"If you want to get Franco jacked up," says Quarterback Terry Bradshaw, "just try to embarrass any one of us." In Super Bowl XIII, the Cowboys' Hollywood Henderson jostled and taunted Bradshaw between plays. Harris snatched Henderson away. On the next play Bradshaw picked up a safety blitz, called a trap, and Harris boomed through the hole for the deciding touchdown.

Harris still does things for his own reasons, though. Over the years there have been stretches when the team wondered when Harris was going to get going. There has been talk among the coaches of sitting him down to jolt him into intensity. In his career he has run for 100 yards or more in 44 games, only 13 of which have been made in the first half of the season. "You don't really get into the thick of things until the last half," says Harris. Even during the juggernaut years, he could sometimes cut the thick awfully close.

That's because Harris isn't an automaton. He's a humanitarian. He has to have a certain kind of inspiration. Some players stoke their fires with amphetamines, but not Harris. Nor would he ever let anybody shoot him up so he could play hurt. In fact, well, he and Swann were working out at the University of Pittsburgh before camp this year and Swann found him in the locker room holding bloody ice on the back of his hand, where he had cut it on a light fixture. Swann talked him, with difficulty, into going over to the infirmary.

"He didn't want to. Didn't want them to take a stitch. And, when they put antiseptic on it, he *screamed*," says Swann. "There was a little kid sitting in there. He'd probably been sewed up a dozen times; he couldn't believe it.

"Then they had to put antiseptic on it again because Franco kept touching it, and then they put the stitches in and Franco is going like this. . . . " Swann makes a series of tight-lipped faces.

"Franco's saying 'Is that all? Is that all?' And the doctor said he thought he ought to get a tetanus shot. Franco didn't want to. I told him *I'd* take one, I hadn't had one in a long time and we get those carpet burns on the turf. Franco still didn't want to. He said, 'How bad is it if you get tetanus? The doctor said, 'You get like this. . . . '" Swann makes a series of tight-lipped faces just like the ones Franco was making when he got stitches.

"I'm saying, 'Franco, just go ahead and get the shot.'"

"'Well, what are the warning signs?' Franco wants to know. 'I could wait and get the shot if I start having them.'"

"The doctor says, 'Put it this way, Franco, nine out of 10 people who get the warning signs don't make it.'

"'What if I get nauseous?' Franco says. 'Could I get the shot then?' He's still trying to talk the doctor out of the shot. Then finally he sits down, and he's like a high jumper crouched waiting for the wind to be just right. 'Got to get ready. Ah-right . . . mmm. Ah-right-ah-right-ah-right—wait a minute.'"

So. Maybe Harris *is* chicken. Maybe that's why he's so sympathetic to kids in hospitals, and why he has preserved himself so admirably, and even why he suddenly gets those sudden bursts. Walter Conti says Franco told him, after making his first long NFL run, "All of a sudden I saw a hole, cut through it, and saw these two big fellas coming after me. I was so scared I burst out fast, and the next thing I knew I was 10 yards downfield. I don't like getting hit."

Maybe that's not the kind of humanitarianism Whizzer White seeks to foster, but you have to take humanitarianism and breaths of fresh air and great running backs where you find them. One thing Harris has learned in his years of reading is this:

"The hole is never where it's supposed to be."

Lynn Swann

Lynn Swann, a 2001 inductee to the Pro Football Hall of Fame, did not project the typical football player image. He was a graceful ballet dancer who absorbed brutal hits over the middle; he was a fluid acrobat whose hard-nosed play resulted in 336 career catches and 5,462 receiving yards, securing third place in both categories on the Steelers' all-time list.

Frank Deford's 1976 profile captured the contradictory image that the wide receiver offered Steeler fans during his nine years with the team. In this wide-ranging piece, Swann discussed his on-field persona, his struggle to transcend traditional racial perceptions, his role on the dominant Steeler teams of the early 1970s, and his feelings for the city of Pittsburgh. In Final Confessions of an NFL Assassin, *the autobiography of the hard-hitting Oakland Raiders defensive back Jack Tatum (1971–79), a short and stinging perspective on Swann's play was offered from the other side of the line of scrimmage. But as the Deford article illustrated, Swann, and his unforgettable achievements on the field, had the last word.*

RATING MY PEERS: LYNN SWANN

Jack Tatum

I realize that some people might think I overlooked Lynn Swann for personal reasons. After all, he did write some nasty letters to Pete Rozelle in my behalf and has sounded off to the press about my tackling style. But Lynn Swann has not been overlooked. I believe that Lynn is truly a superb athlete. He is graceful, has quickness and speed, and he can catch the ball like few, if any, other receivers can. Lynn Swann could be the best if it were not for his one major weakness. There have been several times when I sincerely believe that Swann has been intimidated. Sure, he has played some great games, unbelievably great games, but I have often been on the field when Lynn has actually quit. His concussion during the 1976 game at Oakland was questionable. I know that he went to the hospital, but I remember seeing him running up and down on the sidelines after Atkinson had blasted him. He

From *They Call Me Assassin*, in *Final Confessions of NFL Assassin Jack Tatum* by Jack Tatum and Bill Kushner, contributor (Coal Valley, Ill.: Quality Sports Publications, Inc., 1996). Reprinted by permission.

seemed okay to me then, but when I got Stallworth, and Lynn Swann was asked to go back into the game, he suddenly fainted on the sideline. Maybe he was actually injured; I really don't know. It's just hard for me to believe that George's "semi-Hook" was that devastating. I've watched the films of that action and in my estimation the hit did not look that awesome. Quite frankly, since that incident, Lynn Swann has continually been ineffective against the Raiders. In fact, one hardly realizes he is in the game with us. I know most teams take special precautions when defensing the Steelers wide receivers but we don't. If Lynn Swann was truly a great receiver, we would be extremely cautious when playing against him. Instead, we concentrate more on Stallworth and Cunningham because they have a tendency to stick their noses into the action, whereas Lynn will not.

I give Swann all the credit in the world and sincerely understand that self-preservation is a very important part of football. Maybe if I were the receiver and he The Assassin, my reasoning would be the same as his. Maybe! But at the same time, I rather doubt it. You see, I realize that football is a contact sport and people must get hit. I'm sure Lynn Swann also realizes this, but at the same time, he is trying to play the game without actually getting involved in the serious contact. Lynn will probably continue to hide from the contact and survive playing in the NFL for many years to come. He will play many more great games and pile up his statistics against the passive teams, but he will cause little concern for the physical teams.

CHAMPAGNE, ROSES, AND DONUTS

Frank Deford

Well, it certainly is a Barnum & Bailey world, and wouldn't you just know it, it turns out that the last romantic left on the face of the earth is working for a living in Pittsburgh, P-A. Or, the punch line for the movie version: *Hey, I've got a great idea—Lynn Swann*. That's something of an in joke you'll understand better as we go along. But for the present: Lynn Swann wears his own poetry inscribed in gold about his neck; he sends six dozen yellow roses when he falls in love and buys donuts for his teammates; he prefers white tie and tails if you are dressing, and champagne if you are drinking; he tap-dances his way into your heart, honeymoons in Paris and firmly subscribes to the old ad-age that it is the inalienable right of every American boy to grow up and play Robin Hood in the movies.

Usually we live in our own times and dream of others. How strange that Swann is a child of olden days whose dreams focus on the savage reality all about him. He has, in fact, one recurring nightmare. When it begins, he is standing in the Bank of America branch on B Street in San Mateo, Calif., where he grew up. He glances up and sees that a menacing robot has just entered the bank. Everybody, Swann included, runs like hell out the back door. But the robot follows Swann and chases him into a store. There the robot turns into a gorilla. The ro-bot-gorilla keeps changing back and forth and chasing after him as he weaves in and out of stores. He has this nightmare often.

An authority on dreams told Swann that the robot represents logic, the gorilla emotions, and that the two are competing with each other for control of his being. Sometimes, if Swann is with a person who knows about his nightmare and does something reflexively and natu-rally, Swann will smile and say, "That's the gorilla in me," which sounds very confusing, because we are hardly accustomed to gorillas standing for blithe images. Shouldn't the gorilla in the nightmare be the defensive backs and linebackers who pummel Swann, who supply him with concussions, who drove him to the brink of retirement when he was only 25?

You would think so. But Swann was never a sports fan, and perhaps his subconscious refuses to acknowledge that he has become an ath-lete, a pro football player, the very best at what he does, catching passes. It is mostly a fluke that he has become what he is. Swann is listed officially at 6 feet, 180 pounds, which is small enough, but, in fact, he is no more that 5'11" and weighs only 173. He wears high school-model shoulder pads. He has suffered three concussions, and he is known in the trade by the ugly cretins who play it brutally as a "paperhead." Which simply means that his skull crushes with ease—fair game.

Yet, in his sixth NFL season, age 27, there are almost no marks upon his ginger skin, and he appears nearly—if the word is fair—dainty. Encountering stylishness where you least expect it will give you that impression. Swann's face has the aspect of a cute Disney animal—a chipmunk, perhaps—with tiny ears, a coiffure carefully shaped so that every hair is in place, gleaming brown eyes, teeth so flawless that Swann cannot deny, though he's loath to admit it, that they must be largely a testament to the talent of some dental artist. His cheekbones are high, affirming the Cherokee blood that courses through him from both sides of his family, and directly below are, naturally, a pair of dimples, apt quotation marks for his happy, regularly employed mouth.

Even in Pittsburgh, where Swann is a demigod, his face as well recognized as his number 88, fans meeting him for the first time are invariably amazed at how petite he is. Of all the most popular Steelers—Bradshaw, the rugged bellwether; Harris, sturdy and reliable; Greene, Mean Joe; Ham and Lambert, the hard-nosed Jacks from next door; Bleier, the doughty veteran—little Swann is the one most esteemed for his courage. *He goes over the middle.* Those burghers who run into him about town will offer up the obligatory "nice game," but an inordinate number of them also feel a need to cite his bravery to his face: "I just want to shake your hand, sir"; "God bless you, Lynn"; "I admire you so"; "You're one helluva man, is all I have to say."

Although Swann is a black man in a city with a small black population, the citizenry identifies as much or more with him as with any of its heftier and lighter-skinned heroes. "Well, it's a workingman's town, the shot and a beer, all that," Swann says. "That's not me, but maybe they see me as one of them anyway, because I'm the little guy who goes over the middle."

Ah, once again: over the middle. There are certain itineraries we expect football players to follow. The quarterback, as every mother's son knows, drops back; the fullback bulls ahead; the defensive backs, we are advised, rotate, while linebackers are crab-like beings, ever displaying the vaunted lateral speed. And the wide receiver is, of course, the creature of the down-and-out. We never visualize him as anything but his archetype, Raymond Berry: playing footsie with the boundaries, tapping toes down in sideline Morse code as he reaches out for the pigskin, high, wide and handsome. A wide receiver is down-and-out. The middle is left for stalwart tight ends—those gridiron half-breeds—and wandering blocking backs who moonlight at catching afterthought passes that are "dumped off."

But Swann works the middle. And despite being as insubstantial as he is and having only average-sized hands, he works it with rare proficiency. "There is no such thing as Lynn Swann dropping a pass," says Bum Phillips, the Houston coach. Many receivers, like Swann, may regularly be double-teamed, but such coverage is only something to be eluded; going over the middle means that it is all but impossible to catch passes and not be double-tackled. "The licks Lynn takes," says

Sam Davis, Steeler guard, "sometimes he looks like a baton being twirled out there." Tom Moore, the Pittsburgh receiver coach, says, "I'm sure when Lynn goes over the middle that he doesn't let himself see any of the people there. Nobody has an edge on his heart."

Swann himself says, "I just can't ever think about being hurt. In the first game this season, I got hit low while I was jumping for a pass and I came down on my neck and shoulder, and just a little different. . . ." He shrugs; he meant he could have been busted up, maybe paralyzed. "I probably get away with it because of all the little things I have done in my life besides football—ballet, tap, gymnastics, basketball, long-jumping. I'm able somehow to keep my body loose but my hands tight. I'm like the race cars at Indy that aren't built with solid frames any-more, so when they hit the wall, just a portion of the car crumbles. In one of the old rigid cars there would've been a shock through the whole machine. Me, I get my leg hit, I just let the leg fly. I remain limber, and somehow the impact seems to flow out of that leg. Now maybe some-body who knows the laws of physics will say that's all crazy, but it's my body and it works for me."

Swann has been timed in 4.5 for 40 yards. In high school, at 5'10", he could dunk a basketball, and he was the California long-jump cham-pion, doing 25'2", before he relinquished Olympic aspirations to con-centrate on football. He is able, then, to get to the ball and to climb in the air to take it high, away from taller men. He also has great powers of concentration. A gregarious, even voluble man, Swann never chit-chats with the opposition, and only on the rarest of occasions will he approach Terry Bradshaw with a play suggestion. Out there he keeps to himself.

A wide receiver faces a dichotomy in his work, and for Swann, who adores—even milks—the spotlight, it's a painful one. On the one hand, the wide receiver is a dashing individualist, an athletic facsimile of all those Robin Hoods, buccaneers and gunslingers that young Lynn saw himself as. The wide receiver's presence in the huddle is almost *pro forma*. Swann drops in, gets the play, and then ducks out to near the right sideline, where he sets up—stands up—by himself. To the other flank, the Steelers dispatch their other outstanding wide receiver, John Stallworth.

One defensive back aligns himself across from Stallworth, another from Swann. In the Senate, when a Senator of one mind feels it incon-venient to attend a vote, he will ask a colleague who disagrees with him to also skip it, thus "pairing" themselves—the yea vote of one in effect canceling out the nay of the other, though the official record will indicate neither Senator voted. Essentially, this is what happens in pro football, and most plays proceed nine vs. nine.

But while the wide receiver is this glamorous knight errant, he is, conversely, the most dependent figure in football, perhaps in all of sport. Independent? Why, the wide receiver is as independent as an orphan, fulfilled only when he becomes a ward of the quarterback—or the QB, as Swann always refers to his father figure.

Swann was himself a QB during his senior year in high school, and he was even offered a scholarship by Ara Parseghian, with the under-standing that he would be given the opportunity to guide the Notre Dame offense. But Swann was not sure of his arm and felt that his for-tune and fame lay more in catching passes. Through his junior year at Serra High in San Mateo, Swann had been the receiver for a QB named Jesse Freitas, who went on to nearby Stanford, though he would sub-sequently transfer to San Diego State. Now, a principal reason that Swann decided to attend Southern Cal was that he feared that if he went to Stanford and, as expected, Freitas was the QB, then no matter how many passes Swann caught, they would never be his; they would just be balls that Jesse Freitas threw for completions. Swann was a high school All-America as a receiver, but he had grave doubts about his ability. He never considered the pros until after his junior season at USC, when the Trojans won the 1972 national title.

For all Swann's success, all his All-Pro selections, his MVP in the '76 Super Bowl—and for all his good nature, too—it still gnaws at him that he plays a position in which he must always be cast as the back end of the horse. He is certainly not bashful. His manager, Marilyn O'Brien, calls him Ethel, after Ethel Merman, who has never been mistaken for a shrinking violet. "Lynn Swann loves to be onstage, believe me," says his wife, the former Bernadette Robi, who comes from an entertainment family and recognizes the type. So whatever his success between the sideline stripes, Swann is obsessed about making it off the field, visible as a *single*.

"As long as the QB is the star, I'll always be just another guy out there, and that hurts," Swann says. "Now this isn't whining. A wide receiver gets more attention than a lot of other positions. You take Mike Webster [the Steeler center]. He goes one-to-one against every noseguard and defensive tackle in the league, nobody gets past him, and most fans don't even know his name. And it isn't personal. Please. If anything, Bradshaw deserves even more credit, for all the abuse he's taken. But last year, when we won again, it wasn't just the Steelers. For the first time, it was Terry Bradshaw and the Steelers. And it jolted me back to reality. All of a sudden I realized that no matter how good a wide receiver you are, you're always going to be in the QB's shadow. It's just a fact."

And you don't like it?

"I never believe in settling for second best."

And you love the limelight?

"Look, I'm a ham." (*Big, cute smile.*) "If I could sing, I'd be danger-ous." (*Huge, cute smile.*)

Footnote: Bradshaw is also a putative entertainer. He can sing, and not badly. And for something to do with his hands, he plays the guitar while he warbles. But if Swann cannot sing, he has been tap-dancing since the fourth grade, and he does it very well indeed.

Last March, Bradshaw and Swann went to Utah to tape a CBS spe-cial, *The National Cheerleading Competition*, which was co-hosted by an old QB named Joe Namath. The script called for Bradshaw and Namath to banter for a while, and then the two Steelers were to per-form, Bradshaw strumming his guitar as backup to Swann's tapping. Swann was terrific. But when the show was telecast, Swann had been edited into a perfunctory role, and the bit was almost entirely Namath and Bradshaw joking, and Bradshaw playing the guitar, while his pal, the colored fellow, did a few steps in the background. Thus is it always with QBs and wide receivers.

Swann is not, of course, deprived, as we know it. For playing a sec-ond banana, he'll make about $170,000 this year, but because his sub-ordinate position limits him so in football, his greater designs are on the world at large, coast-to-coast. He longs to become the first wide receiver to attain Namathian, Simpsonian status, to become what he and Marilyn O'Brien always refer to as "a national spokesman." Lest conflict of interest endanger any lurking countrywide contract, Swann has already turned down a number of local endorsements for such var-ied merchandise as clothing, soft drinks, canned goods and tires.

It is a measure of Swann's equanimity, as well as of these more tolerant television times—not only of O. J., but of Reggie promoting candy bars and Bill Cosby spokesmanning for every product in Christendom not hawked by Ed McMahon—that he never even men-tions the matter of his race being a deterrent to the household-wordness he desires. Still, the question is: Can a little black wide re-ceiver from an old industrial city go where only backs have ever been?

In this campaign for fame, playing for the Steelers cuts two ways. On the one hand, the champions are so good that nobody, not even the QB, can attract all the attention. Swann himself is often employed more as an implied threat than one realized. His statistics last season—61 catches for 880 yards and 11 TDs—were outstanding and his best, but not the monster numbers that might accrue to a flanker of his talents on a lesser team that doesn't waste a lot of precious time laboring at trench warfare. Significantly, against playoff teams, when the Steelers can't be so bossy, they turn more to Swann. His playoff statistics are well above his regular-season figures, and his best game ever was the '76 Super Bowl.

The presence of the gifted Stallworth on the other wing specifically complicates the issue. They are friendly rivals, sure enough, but the emphasis is often on the latter word. On almost any other club, Stallworth would be the ballyhooed prime receiver. On the Steelers, he is to Swann what Swann is to Bradshaw. The two receivers arrived the same season, too—Swann the pussycat first-round draft choice from USC and the Rose Bowl, Stallworth a fourth-round pick from, uh, Alabama A&M. Swann always goes to the Pro Bowl, Stallworth goes home to Huntsville. Yet this year, Swann has endured a freak injury—a bruised big left toe—and then a hamstring pull. He has missed a great deal of action, and he trails Stallworth in all receiving categories.

"How many did you catch yesterday?" Swann asked Stallworth after a game early this season. The correct answer was six, and had Stallworth wanted to be diplomatic, he would've feigned ignorance of such tacky minutiae. Instead, Stallworth took the opportunity to smile and reply, "Four more than you." And they both laughed, sort of.

Of course, the preeminence of the Steelers lends a luster to Swann's reputation that he could obtain nowhere else, even if he were setting individual records in a more chic metropolis. He has never wanted to play for any other team. Keep in mind that it takes a great deal to raise the ire of Lynn Curtis Swann. It is, then, especially revealing that the one thing that appears to have gotten stuck in Swann's craw is that the Dallas Cowboys, undisputed Super Bowl losers, have anointed themselves as "America's Team." Swann heard this on the P.A. when the Steelers played an exhibition in Dallas, and it irritated him so that he still brings it up regularly.

And certainly he is right to protest the Cowboys' supercilious claim. Even if Dallas were champion, the Cowboys are never perceived as a team, only as an organization. The Steelers, by contrast, are pretty much a collection of personalities who never enjoyed any real fame until they came to Pittsburgh. Swann is the rare Steeler to hail from a glamour campus. But his effervescent nature—"I'm actually envious of his personality," says Pittsburgh Safety Mike Wagner—has endeared him to his more unpretentious teammates. The hard-boiled veterans could not believe it when as a rookie Swann started bringing donuts for the whole damn team every Tuesday. Along with his toothy smile, Swann is also so brimming with quotations, slogans, lyrics, poetry (his own and otherwise) that more worldly observers suspect that he must be putting them on, that perhaps he has caught a touch of something from Steve Garvey. But Swann is so enthusiastic, gets so carried away, that he is literally incapable of recognizing his own exuberant self.

Most weeks during the season, the Steeler receivers meet for dinner, and in an effort to establish even more *esprit de corps*, they started playing an after-dinner game last year. Each man's name was written on a slip of paper, and they were deposited, folded, in a pile. In turn, each receiver would draw a slip and portray the colleague named. Stallworth once drew Swann. "It was easiest of all to play Lynn," Stallworth says. "All I had to do was to get bubbly and keep saying, 'Hey, I've got a great idea, I've got a great idea!'" Swann had no idea whom Stallworth was acting out, although the other receivers all recognized him immediately and broke up.

Unlike so many other hotshot Sunbelt athletes, Swann has adjusted well to his new old-world America address. He makes no bones about preferring Los Angeles—"I like the diversity there, the greater challenges and opportunities it offers me"—but he accepts Pittsburgh for what it is, a real second home. In L.A., Swann drives a Porsche and lives in a condominium near the Pacific; in Pittsburgh, he drives a Jeep and lives in a house in the suburbs.

But now he was downtown, sitting at the edge of Point [State] Park, his legs dangling just above the water at that precise spot where the Monongahela and the Allegheny flow together to form the Ohio. "Each year I look forward to coming back here more," he said. "They're good people, and they make me feel comfortable. In a certain way, I feel that Pittsburgh is more my home.

"It's a pretty place, isn't it?" He swept his arm toward the green backdrop of hills across the rivers from downtown. Unfortunately, Pittsburgh still suffers its shabby old mill image, but it is a solid place, built upon hills and neighborhoods, a heterosexual's San Francisco— for all its sloping topography, straight in most ways. In Pittsburgh, devotion is lavished not only on the game's executives and craftsmen—the QBs, runners and pass catchers—but also on its grubbier wage earners, notably the linebackers. In Pittsburgh you can buy T shirts commemorating the local linebackers.

But then, Pittsburgh has its factory heritage, and linebackers, after all, are the foremen of football. And, too, a football team is really quite like a factory, with each job category—interior linemen, defensive secondary, suicide squad—performing a task on the assembly line. "Football is so specialized that the players are never as close as teammates in other sports," Swann says. "Why, once the season starts, we're only on the road a night at a time a few times a year."

Anyway, in Pittsburgh, in the smelters and boardrooms alike, the Pirates have lost the town to the Steelers. One reason—it is whispered—is that the Pirates field too black a nine, lacking an attractive white star since Dick Groat two decades ago. With Bradshaw and the predominantly white linebackers, this does not seem to be a problem for the Steelers.

Swann himself is, as he declares, "just not race conscious," but he has *not* arrived at this estate by virtue of being what glib Fourth of July orators call "color blind." On the contrary, his evenhanded tolerance derives more from his having been abused by members of both races. Color blindness tends, just like color awareness, to reveal, at best, superficiality in the eye of the beholder. Swann seems to look a bit askance when ingratiating white strangers advertise their goodwill by laying a soul handshake on the famous brother. Having been wounded by "racial games" on both sides, Swann says he is inclined to pay less attention to races and more to persons.

He was born in the segregated South in the company town of Alcoa, Tenn., but Swann never encountered Jim Crow, because his father, Willie, an airplane maintenance worker, moved the family to the Bay Area when Lynn was two.

The Swanns lived a typical lower-middle-class, upwardly mobile existence: they worked, studied and paid the rent. Mrs. Swann, Mildred, went to college and rose from domestic to dental assistant. Lynn's older brother, Brian, has become a dentist. Lynn, a Baptist, won an academic scholarship to Serra High, a Catholic school, where he was one of a handful of blacks. And there, for the first time, he got mousetrapped.

He discovered that a great many of the white classmates who were his bosom pals when he was starring in sports for dear old Serra had little use for him once the season was over. Even more perplexing, Swann found that many black friends wrote him off for going to a white school and for taking on what they considered to be white airs. Even as a young child, his own cousins taunted him for "speaking properly."

It is not, understand, that Swann doesn't talk like an average uneducated ghetto black. He doesn't even talk like an average allegedly educated suburban athlete. Never does a sentence begin with "O.K.," and he has so thoroughly exorcised "you know" from his speech that now it never appears, not even in the most offhand conversation. A great deal of Swann may be described as California Golden Universal—and race is no function of this persona, only style and outlook and eternal youth. If there are two athletes Swann most brings to mind, they would be Tom Seaver and Bruce Jenner, who share with him both orderliness and panache, which rarely go together in handsome young men.

But it is not always smooth for Swann. In the NFL, it has been the prize macho black toughs who have gone out of their way to bust up and bring down the fashionable kid who moves so effortlessly in the white world. And before that, at Southern Cal, where Swann says he "made a conscious effort to get some black racial identity back," he was castigated by many black students for his speech and for choosing to room with a white, Tom McBreen. A childhood friend, McBreen, now a doctor, was an Olympic swimmer who subsequently was Swann's best man. Swann also shares, in common with Bradshaw, Pete Rozelle, Donnie Osmond, Catfish Hunter and Senator John Warner, that most typical of all things American: a white mother-in-law. His father-in-law is Paul Robi, arranger and lead singer with the Platters.

"What am I supposed to do?" Swann says. "I just happen to feel comfortable wherever I go in the world. But it's hard to win. The American dream is to succeed, to move on to higher economic levels, but if you're black and you succeed, then you can be sure that some blacks will claim that you are turning your back on your black roots."

And worse yet, some whites . . . . On the night of Jan. 31, 1974, when Swann was celebrating his selection as the top Steeler draft choice, he was arrested and jailed by the San Francisco Police Department—largely, he feels, for committing the crime of being black. Charged with resisting arrest and battery, Swann was acquitted by a jury in July 1974. Swann—and his two brothers and a cousin, who were likewise charged—sued the city for $2 million for false arrest; the four policemen involved filed a countersuit against the Swanns and their cousin for $200,000 in damages. The case finally reached the courts last summer, and the three Swanns and their cousin ultimately received a total of $143,090. The policemen were awarded a total of $15,000.

Just as Swann cannot understand why the arresting officers, as Swann reportedly claimed in court, destroyed a college All-Star wristwatch and rapped him repeatedly about the knees with nightsticks when they learned he was a football player, so he is genuinely baffled by the casual brutality in his sport. When in 1976 he publicly protested against what he characterizes as "intentional acts of violence," many in football came down on him not only for being a sissy but also for breaking the unwritten code that gentlemen of the gridiron should always settle up like jungle animals. Defensive Back George Atkinson of the Raiders, who twice gave Swann concussions, derided him as "gutless."

The second Atkinson hit, the one that led Steeler Coach Chuck Noll to refer to Atkinson as part of a "criminal element" in football, very nearly drove Swann from the NFL after only two seasons. "It was bad enough earlier in that game," he says. "At one point Jack Tatum came up behind me in the end zone. The officials didn't see it because I wasn't anywhere near the ball, but Tatum left his feet so he could hit me full force in the back of the head. I was still dazed from that in the second half when I caught a pass over the middle, and Atkinson tackled me around the head.

"That put me in the hospital, but what was really frightening was that this time what Atkinson did to me was a quote-unquote *legal* hit. After that, I thought to myself, "Whoa, this is not what I came here for.'"

Swann came out of the hospital to be named MVP in the '76 Super Bowl, in which the Steelers beat the Cowboys, but the euphoria of that triumph did not erase the harsh memory of the Oakland ferocity. In the months that followed, Swann all but made up his mind to retire. In explaining why he finally decided to come back, he employs one of his Norman Vincent Peale sermonettes:

"That thing about Atkinson and my thinking about retiring was the biggest thing I've had to overcome in my life. For once, things just didn't go right for me. But I was traveling in Europe, and I ended up skiing in Innsbruck. I wasn't doing very well at it and I decided to go home. But then, all of a sudden, I said *no*. I bought some new equipment and I decided to stay until I beat that mountain. And it took me four or five more days, but I did, and that's when I decided to meet football head on, too, so I came back to play." He pauses. "But the mountain is still there. For someone else. And there's no mountain in life that someone else hasn't climbed."

He talks that way. He really does. It's the gorilla in him. Around his neck he wears a gold pendant with a swan etched on one side, and on the other, his words: MY FRIENDS ARE MY LIFE, SHARE MY LOVE. He gave duplicates of it to his family and closest friends. At his wedding in June, before 500 guests, he interrupted the traditional service to read love vows he had composed himself to his bride, culminating : "My soul is your soul, and time is our instrument to build life upon love." Even his signature is lyrical, almost carved with painstaking care.

One girl friend broke up with him because, in this unlettered, narcissistic age, she could not deal with a man who poured out mushy love paeans to her. Bernadette and Lynn drink seldom, but when they do, it must be champagne. "With Lynn, it's roses and champagne, all the time," she says. And donuts, with love. He will latch on to any excuse to wear tails; last year he gave a Halloween party and came as Dracula. He would not live with Bernadette before they were married, fearful that it would spoil his vision: "Marriage is something you should do just once, and you ought to do it right."

It is not a matter of Swann being a different sort of football player. It is more the other way 'round, that the strangest aspect to his being is that he plays this fierce, tumultuous war sport. In his childhood, his heroes were not athletes but just entertainers and swashbucklers. When he learned he had been drafted by Pittsburgh, all he knew about the Steelers was that there was a black guy on the team with an Italian name and they had "nice looking uniforms."

Just as his agent says that Swann "transcends" race, so in many of the right ways is the manly Swann temperamentally androgynous. Indeed, his mother longed that he, the last of her three children, would be a girl, and hoping that wishing would make it so, she had no boy's names on tap. So she named the baby after Dr. Lynn Curtis, because she like the obstetrician and his name. So does the recipient. He has been advised that Lynn means a love of life, Curtis refers to courtesy, and Swann signifies beauty and grace. The superfluous double letter at the end of his surname—shades of old Jimmy Foxx—indicates, Swann has been told, some kind of special extra power. Has any athlete ever carried a name so befitting? Stripteasers lie awake at night trying to dream up apt stage names. Even Swann's number is appropriate: double eights to match the double *n*s. Eight beats is a base number for dance; 88 keys on the piano. "I've always seen myself as put to music," Swann says.

His mother introduced him to dance, his older brother Calvin to sports. He was a natural at both, and he would tag after Calvin and try whatever games his brother was playing. So, from the first, Lynn was invariably among the smallest players and he learned to play the bigger boys' game and not be intimidated by foolish size. Oh yes, he does too see everybody waiting for him over the middle, but if fate has made you a baton, then twirl yourself onto center stage. "Whenever I come to the huddle late in a game," Swann says, "I want my team to know, 'Hey, I may have been out there alone all day, doing nothing, but I'll be ready for you when you need me for the big play.'"

Significantly, he then finds a showbusiness metaphor to explain this better, saying, "If I ever have my own TV special, I know exactly how I'm going to open—with *The Ugly Duckling* from Hans Christian Andersen: 'There once was an ugly duckling, with feathers all dirty and brown.' That's me."

But you were never ugly. "Yeah, but I was always the smallest, so I had to learn to play a smarter game. It's the same sort of thing. And I'll come out in this feathery costume and stumble all around, and then I'll break out of that and I'll be dancing in white tie and tails."

When Swann showed up at the Steelers' camp this summer, a couple weeks late because of the trial in San Francisco, an adoring fan was waiting there for his return. She watched him run extra sprints after practice. Chuck Noll is a football coach, and this *player* was late reporting; don't tell me about trials, plagues, famines, earthquakes, nuclear holocausts, we have a football camp to run here. The coach had Swann running laps till he dropped. And Swann did as he was bid, smiling after the pain. He loves football. He really does. It's part of his life, isn't it?

The lady watched him, and she said, "Now it's sunny and 88 again in Pittsburgh."

TRANSITIONS

A Death in the Family

Art Rooney had very little to do with the day-to-day affairs of the Steelers by the 1980s, but he still served as the emotional and spiritual heart of the franchise, its link to both the dark days and the glory days. His passing touched off a wave of grief, sympathy, and nostalgia that spilled beyond the borders of Pittsburgh and affected football fans across the country. He was one of the true gentlemen of the NFL, a man whose handshake was his word, and his death seemed to symbolize the league's transformation from a close-knit group of family-owned teams into an impersonal agglomeration of franchises that were fixated on the bottom line. A brief and appropriately generous obituary from the Pittsburgh Press *summed up what Art Rooney meant to the city and the sport to which he devoted his long life. In another article,* Press *sportswriter Bill Utterback captured the mood of Rooney's beloved Steelers as news of his demise spread. Utterback included a touching tribute from assistant coach Joe Greene, the first number-one draft pick of the Noll era, the most vivid personality of the Steel Curtain defense, and one of the only links between the teams of the 1970s and the 1980s. Finally, an emotion-filled Terry Bradshaw remembered Art Rooney as an owner, a friend, a man, and in Bradshaw's words, a legend.*

REMEMBERING "THE CHIEF"

Editorial

There are a lot of things to be said for Art Rooney, founder and owner of the Steelers, who died this morning at the age of 87:

Mostly, he was a local institution—"The Chief" who established the Steelers franchise here in 1933, who stuck with it through many lean and lamentable years, and who finally saw the team emerge as the powerhouse of the NFL in the 1970s, winning four Super Bowl trophies.

He was the father figure of an entire region. Rich but unassuming, he was a workingman's millionaire.

Known throughout the country, he held to his roots and made it obvious he preferred the atmosphere on Western Avenue in Pittsburgh's North Side to, say, Fifth Avenue in Manhattan.

What isn't so easy to say, what isn't so easy to figure out, what isn't so well delineated is what there was about Art Rooney that made him seem like a dear friend, no matter whether one ever met him.

It may have been his integrity; he certainly had enough of that to spread it around the entire NFL. It may have been his generosity; his efforts on the part of the poor and the downtrodden are as much of history as he is himself. It may have been his love for Pittsburgh and Pittsburghers; the reciprocal love affair endured for nearly a century.

It may have been a lot of things, all of them difficult to express. And then again it may have been one thing and it just seemed like a lot. It may have been what Supreme Court Justice Byron White, a former Steeler, said about him:

"He's the finest man I've ever known."

A lot of people would say that.

GREENE MOURNS . . .
WITH A CIGAR

Bill Utterback

Joe Greene clutched a cigar as warm memories and bitter news clutched at his throat and tugged at his tear ducts. Moments earlier, Greene had learned of the death of Steelers owner Art Rooney Sr.

Greene, a Steelers Hall of Famer and assistant coach, sat rigid on his bed in a dormitory room at St. Vincent College. He stared straight ahead, quietly projecting 20 years of personal memories on a blank cement wall, oblivious to the voice on the television reporting Rooney's death.

Other coaches huddled in a meeting room, but Greene needed to be alone with his memories and his cigar.

"I can't talk now. I just can't."

Hours later he explained why he reached for the cigar.

"The first time I met Mr. Rooney was at the end of a long contract negotiation in my rookie year. Dan Rooney told his father that we were $10,000 apart. Mr. Rooney said, 'Is that all? Give it to him.' Then he gave me a cigar."

From the *Pittsburgh Press*, August 26, 1988. Copyright/*Pittsburgh Post-Gazette*, 2001. All rights reserved. Reprinted with permission.

And so, in the minutes after learning of Rooney's death, Greene reached for another cigar. The memories came quickly to him.

"The first one I conjured up, my favorite one, is after Super Bowl IX when Mr. Rooney stood up on the podium and accepted that cherished trophy. That one means the most to me."

There were quieter moments as well.

"I used to love sitting in Mr. Rooney's office, listening to him talk about the early days of the National Football League. He shared things with me that probably no other person could, and probably no other person would. He loved to talk about George Halas, Bert Bell and his old friends from the infancy of the NFL."

Greene smiled.

"I'm sad personally because he was truly one of the finest people I've ever met. I'm also sad for all the people whose lives he touched."

"But I'm happy for Mr. Rooney because I know he's with his beloved wife again, and he'll get to talk to all his old friends again, and that makes me feel good."

The news of Mr. Rooney's death hit the Steelers camp at 8:30 A.M. Coaches heard it while in their morning meeting. Greene and backfield coach Dick Hoak, a Steeler since 1961, went to their rooms to grieve in private. [Others] stayed and commiserated as a group.

"I feel fortunate to have known him in my life," Hoak said.

Players heard the news from the television or radio. Some received calls from home. Several gathered in Mike Webster's room to share memories. Others met in Walter Abercrombie's room.

"The Chief left us all with a lot of wonderful memories," Webster said. "He really made everybody feel special. He had a very unique ability to make people feel special.

"My favorite memory is when The Chief allowed my daughter to interview him for a school project. He made an 11-year-old girl feel very comfortable and very important."

Guard John Rienstra, who has struggled with stress problems for the past year and missed two weeks of camp earlier this month, said Rooney had been a comfort to him.

"We talked pretty often and he helped me out a lot. He was the most positive man I've ever met, and he taught me to be more positive about life. He thought life could be wonderful and he made me feel that way."

A regularly scheduled team meeting was held at 9:30 A.M.

"I think everybody was a little numb in the meeting," cornerback

Dwayne Woodruff said. "Chuck (Noll) announced that The Chief had passed away. He said we would visit the funeral home before we go to New Orleans, and then there was just a lot of quiet. Not much was said."

"It was a very somber meeting," defensive coordinator Tony Dungy said. "We kind of knew it was coming, but still, when it happens, it's not a very pleasant thing to accept."

"It wasn't so much shock as sadness," Webster said, "sadness that he won't be part of our everyday lives anymore."

After the meeting, it was business as usual for everybody. The players went into meetings with their position coaches at 10 and practiced from 3 to 4:30 P.M.

There was never any hesitation about practicing, or playing tomorrow's game in New Orleans.

"It's something I think he would expect us to do," Noll said. "He would want us to go down and play, and play well."

Because yesterday was the last day of training camp, players spent the early afternoon hours packing their cars. Their luggage was weighed down by memories of The Chief.

"I'll always remember him on the day of a game, going from one locker to the next, shaking everybody's hand and wishing us luck," receiver Weegie Thompson said as he tossed his bags in the back of his Bronco.

"I remember the day I made the team (in 1979), he came and congratulated me in the locker room," Woodruff said. "I was a lowly rookie but he already knew my name and recognized my face."

"I remember just sitting and chatting with him about the old days, talking about all the old fights and old friends he had," tackle Tunch Ilkin said.

"I remember him coming in the locker room after church every morning, walking (for health reasons) around the room, saying his rosary and holding his rosary (beads)," equipment manager Tony Parasi said. "If he couldn't walk outside, he walked inside. And he would always stop to talk to me and ask me about my family. And he always called on Easter and Christmas to wish us a happy holiday.

"I've been with the team for 24 years, and I can't imagine The Chief not being there anymore."

Dick Haley, director of player personnel and a former player, has the same problem.

"I've been around 27 years and he's always been there. And he's always brought people to the office with him. It could be a guy he met on a North Side street, or the vice president of a big company. It could be the wealthiest guy in the city, or the most average guy. Either way, they were friends of his and he loved having them around.

"I got to talk to him for about a half hour last Wednesday. He was still sharp, asking me how the team looked. I'm glad I got to spend some time with him. I'll never meet another man like him."

Dungy, also a former Steelers player, will best remember Rooney's relationship with two former players.

"Out of our group (defensive backs), I think his two favorite players were Mel Blount and Harvey Clayton. One is a Hall of Famer. The other is a guy the fans couldn't get out of town fast enough. But Mr. Rooney loved them both. That says a lot about Mr. Rooney. He didn't care if you were the best player or the 45th guy on the team.

Dungy said Rooney's relationship with Blount grew out of their shared love for horses. His relationship with Clayton probably developed because Clayton—a struggling cornerback often abused by fans, media, and coaches—needed a friend.

"Harvey had some hard times, but The Chief was always his No. 1 booster. He took Harvey to baseball games. He had Harvey over to his house for dinner. To The Chief, Harvey was just a baby-faced kid who lived on the North Side."

Dungy also has a more personal memory of Rooney.

"When I got traded to San Francisco, he sent a letter to my mom saying how proud he was to have had me on the team. I was only a backup here for a short time, but that letter was a thrill for my parents. He did that kind of stuff all the time."

When practice ended, players rushed off the field and headed home. They were not moving as quickly as they have in past years. Usually, the day camp breaks is their favorite day of the summer. Yesterday, it became the worst.

"It's been a very sad day for all of us," kicker Gary Anderson said.

Greene still had his cigar when the day ended. It was clenched in his teeth as he drove away from St. Vincent.

MR. ROONEY: THE ONLY
LEGEND I EVER KNEW

Terry Bradshaw

Maybe it was the warmth of Art Rooney that made so many people think they knew him better than anyone else did. He was special to so many of us, and he is unquestionably one of my all-time favorite people. When I was drafted by the Steelers, most of the talk when I got to Pittsburgh was about The Old Man. I didn't know who The Old Man was, except that he smoked big, long cigars, and they said he owned the team. I remember bumping into him one day my rookie season, back when he was a mere pup of sixty-nine, and one of the first things that struck me about him was the sunshine of his personality. He was always so happy and jovial; a man with a very gracious personality and many flattering comments. The full impact didn't hit me then, but soon I would grow to realize that I'd never meet another person like Mr. Rooney.

I think Mr. Rooney felt sorry for me and took me under his wing. He may have even enjoyed my innocence and naiveté—I was just thrilled to be playing in the NFL. Maybe he liked my enthusiasm, my aggressiveness. Or maybe I was just his kind of guy and he knew I genuinely liked him. I think he liked me in a way that he didn't other players. But each player was unique to him. What's special to me today about Art Rooney is the collection of his handwritten letters and the memories of our dinners together. He probably wrote me a hundred letters while I was playing, most of them encouraging me through the bad times. He would write something like this: "Dear Terry: I'm over here in Ireland and boy, they think I'm a big shot over here! You guys won the Super Bowl, but I'm the big star this year. I'm getting all these awards—boy, oh boy, oh boy, you've really got to go some now to catch up with me! I hope everything is going well with you. We'll be over here another few days, and then we're heading for New York. Call me when you get back and we'll go to the farm. Be sure and tell your mom and dad hi, and that I wish them the very best. They are such wonderful people. Sincerely, Art."

Every letter he wrote always included that line: "Be sure and tell your mom and dad hi, . . . they are such wonderful people."

We would either have dinner at his house or we'd go to an Italian

From *Looking Deep* by Terry Bradshaw with Buddy Martin (Chicago: Contemporary Books, 1989). Reprinted by permission of Terry Bradshaw.

restaurant that he liked. Mostly we made small talk, but he made it a point to invite me to dinner when times were bad for me. When I was depressed and down, or the press was on my back after a bad game or two, he would call and invite me out. Even after I retired, when I was publicly critical of Chuck on my TV show at KDKA, Mr. Rooney would call me and say, "You were great! You're right, they did play lousy! Tell it like it is!" And then he would laugh. I think he kind of got a kick out of my maverick style.

I always tried to get Mr. Rooney to talk about the old days of football, but he'd steer the conversation over to horses or family. Or we'd talk about problems the league was having. He would tell me things that were going to happen. He knew I'd never break his confidence. In turn, he was my sounding board. He always left me brimming with confidence. He would tell me how great I was going to be someday. He would compare me to Sammy Baugh, one of his favorite old-time quarterbacks, because Sammy could kick it and run it and throw it.

I'd often visit him at his office. We'd puff on cigars until the air was blue with smoke. Sometimes I'd go into his office when he wasn't there, take the morning paper, help myself to one of his fat cigars, and sit there behind his desk smoking it. The first time I went in there and took a cigar, I left him a dollar. He kept that dollar until the day he died; to my knowledge it's still on his desk. I don't know how many times he caught me going through his cigar box. I felt like a kid with his hand in the cookie jar, but he told me to help myself. I could walk in there without saying a word to his secretary and have the run of the place. Usually I'd read his thoroughbred magazines.

Sometimes Mr. Rooney would walk in while I was there, pull up a chair, and sit on the other side of the desk. I always jumped up to move, but he'd insist I stay there. He'd say, "You look good in that chair! That's where you ought to be sitting! You're a big shot and I'm a nobody." He, of course, was as big a shot as the game ever knew.

Mr. Rooney wasn't a real hands-on type owner; mostly his sons ran the team. But he *was* the team and he didn't have to do anything but be Art Rooney, Sr. He had people hired to take care of the rest. Besides, he was too busy being a legend. After all, he helped found the NFL. I've said this before and I'm not sure people understand it, but Mr. Rooney was a first, an original. For those of us who had the privilege of knowing him, it was pure joy. I knew only one legend in my entire life and that was Art Rooney. I can't even name you another one.

We usually dealt with Dan Rooney, who was extremely tough. But

I always assumed that Art, Sr., had the final say when it got right down to it. After all, it was his football team—a team he had first purchased in 1933 for twenty-five hundred dollars. They were called the Pirates in those days and through a complicated maneuver in which he sold majority interest to a New York City cosmetics heiress, bought into the Philadelphia Eagles, and then persuaded owners of both teams to swap franchises, Mr. Rooney wound up with a minority ownership in the Steelers. Later they would be merged with the Eagles during World War II and become the Steagles, then with the Chicago Cardinals as the PittCards. But finally Mr. Rooney gained control right after the war ended. He would delight in calling himself "a Pittsburgh guy." He was a champion of the little people and would stop on the street to speak with a steelworker, a taxi driver, a doorman. They, like me, felt there was a special part of Art Rooney, Sr., that belonged to them. In victory or defeat, his personality never changed. Among Americans, that is a rarity.

Nobody ever spoke a bad word about Art Rooney and even his competitors respected him. If he beat you, he would send over a bottle of Dom Perignon—it wasn't always just the winning—he enjoyed the fight.

I began to realize that Mr. Rooney wasn't like the rest of the owners when we'd get together with other players. It wasn't until I heard them discuss their owners in real defiant terms that I realized how lucky I was to be working for a person who genuinely cared about his players. One of the Steelers would mention that hot meals were served to us in the Allegheny Club at Three Rivers every Wednesday and Thursday. And the players from the other team would say, in disbelief: "You get *what?*"

"Doesn't everybody get hot meals on Wednesday and Thursday?"
"Nah, man, we bring a sandwich."

Mr. Rooney went out of his way to make the Steelers feel they were appreciated and respected—like buying a corner lot near Three Rivers Stadium so we could practice on a dirt field and not ruin our legs on artificial turf. The more we won, the more good things he did for us.

Art Rooney was a tough character from the mining town of Coulterville, Pennsylvania, the oldest of eight children and the son of a saloon keeper. He almost drowned as a boy on his way to school. His canoe tipped over while he was trying to cross the Allegheny River during a flood. Art went down twice before finally grabbing the post of a grandstand at old Exposition Park, the original home of the Pirates. Art and his brother, Dan, were great athletes who played virtually every sport, including football, well enough to receive scholarship offers from Knute Rockne at Notre Dame. As brash young kids, Art and Dan would go to the carnivals, accept the challenge of the house fighter, and earn three bucks for every round they could last in the ring with him. Art made the United States Olympic boxing team as a 135-pounder, but decided not to compete overseas. He was a player-manager for a minor-league baseball team in Wheeling, West Virginia—Dan was also on the team—and hit .369, second best in the Middle Atlantic League. And the Rooneys got into the football business early when they started a semipro team called Hope-Harvey; among the teams they played were the Canton Bulldogs, who had a player named Jim Thorpe.

There are volumes of interesting stories about The Old Man. But perhaps the most famous story is about how he became wealthy over a long weekend at two New York race tracks. Nobody knows exactly how much he won, but in 1936 Mr. Rooney experienced one of those hot streaks every gambler dreams about. His reputed earnings were easily equivalent to more than a million of today's dollars at a now-defunct track called Empire City one day and at Saratoga the next week. He said he bet twenty bucks with a bookie in the Empire City grandstand (back when that was allowed) and wound up winning seven hundred bucks. Typically, he felt sorry for the bookie and kept betting with him to give him a chance to get even. "I had three or four winners and broke the guy," he said, almost shamefully. That following Monday, Mr. Rooney went to Saratoga with a couple of guys, including a famous sportswriter named Bill Corum, and kept his streak going. Corum even wrote a column about his incredible run of luck.

When he was inducted into the Pro Football Hall of Fame in 1964, Mr. Rooney said: "I am lucky." He would go to any extreme to avoid taking credit for anything.

Art Rooney died on August 25, 1988; he was eighty-seven years old. I couldn't bring myself to fly to Pittsburgh for his funeral. I knew it would be attended by hundreds; but our relationship was private, not meant to be shared by all those people. Someday I will go to Pittsburgh by myself. Then I will go to his graveside and shed my tears.

Mr. Rooney was the only thread that held me to the Steelers after my retirement. No one in the organization can ever take his place. He treated me like a human being—I love and respect people who treat me the way they want to be treated. There is nothing I wouldn't have done for him. Yet he never asked me to do a single thing. That's why it was so special when we won Super Bowl IX. I used to joke about winning all those Super Bowls for Mr. Rooney. In my speeches I'd say: "We won one for Mr. Rooney! God bless Mr. Rooney!" And then, "We won two for Mr. Rooney, what a wonderful man!" And when we won three: "I'm getting sick and tired of winning Super Bowls for that old buzzard." Truthfully, he was the kind of guy who could have won ten Super Bowls in a row and never change.

Isn't it funny that you don't hear players today saying they want to win the Super Bowl for their owners?

Gene Collier of the *Pittsburgh Press*, on the day after Mr. Rooney's death, wrote a touching paragraph which sort of summarized my feelings: "It was a beautiful August day of majestic clarity when the sky was mammoth, and when the breeze dusted it hard, we could smell autumn start its long approach. And here comes autumn with a big hole in it."

His death left a big hole in the lives of many people.

The Steelers' Legacy

In the late 1980s journalist Sam Toperoff went looking for the meaning of the Pittsburgh Steelers. What was the appeal of this team, which had fallen far from its halcyon days of the 1970s? What accounted for the hold it had on Pittsburgh? Why did it matter, and why would it continue to matter? What he discovered was a team that both reflected the image of the city and fulfilled a psychic need of its residents. And most of all he met the fans, the people for whom football was more than a game. For them, the Steelers came close to being religious icons.

THE SPIRIT OF PLACE

Sam Toperoff

Most professional sports franchises have the local loyalties of a multinational corporation. They will move wherever the veins run deepest and the residual checks have the most zeroes. There are, however, some notable exceptions, teams and places that are so bound together by bonds of history, identity, and mystique that tearing them apart is as improbable as improbable gets. ("Impossible" is just not applicable where human greed is concerned.) Pittsburgh and its Steelers have formed such a bond, and it's a pretty intense affair.

If you want to learn about the "Stillers" (as the team is known in local dialect), talk to Pittsburghers about their city. If you want to know the city, talk about the "Stillers." You'll discover you've learned about the bond as well. Of course, what you learn depends on who you talk to. And it depends mostly on how long they've lived in Pittsburgh and how closely they've identified with the team. Chances are, if they say "Stillers," you'll learn a lot.

Ahiro Okawa does not say "Stillers"; in fact, he has trouble saying the word in any recognizable way. Mr. Okawa was not born in Pittsburgh. He was born in Nagasaki, Japan, in 1945—a year when more Japanese were dying than were being born, especially in Nagasaki. In 1980 he moved to Sewickley, a wooded, fancy middle-class suburb west of Pittsburgh. Mr. Okawa is a representative of a Japanese industrial monolith that is producing small amounts of "specialty" steel in

From *Lost Sundays: A Season in the Life of Pittsburgh and the Steelers* (New York, Random House, 1989). © Sam Toperoff. Reprinted by permission.

a Monongahela River minimill. Allegheny-Ludlum is the sole American firm operating here in the same capacity. Just about the only kind of steel still being made in Pittsburgh on a regular basis, "specialty" is produced by a handful of Pittsburgh workers. Mr. Okawa's company employs 120 men in a mill town upriver that once employed over 9,000 steelworkers

In a sense, Mr. Okawa is the enemy here. The Japanese, most prominently but not exclusively, have subsidized their own steel industries for a long while, but they began to do so heavily in the early 1970s. The French and Germans and British and Swedes and Koreans do the same. Over the years and for a variety of reasons, the American steel giants found it harder and harder to compete, and the Rust Belt was born. Pittsburgh—Steeltown, U.S.A.—was emasculated in little more than a decade.

In Pittsburgh, a Japanese national is a lot more visible than other foreigners, and more obviously connected to a heavy manufacturing firm—electronics being the only other possibility—but Mr. Okawa stands up bravely to the occasional stares he gets. They are only occasional because where he lives and travels, he meets very few unemployed steelworkers. His neighbors are upper-echelon managers like himself, but from the service industries that arose when foreign competitors helped knock out large-scale steelmaking.

Even as steel was starting to go down for the count in the late seventies, the Steelers were unquestionably one of the best damn teams ever to kick ass on NFL turf, real or artificial. If you look at the entire decade, they were *the* best. There was, of course, something wonderful about a team named after an industry, taking for its insignia the U.S. Steel trademark, representing a hard-bitten, smoky, one-industry town. But if the Steelers were a true reflection of what was going on in the steel industry at the end of the decade, with its massive layoffs, they would have put only six men on the field. Either that, or played with eleven and called themselves the Rising Suns.

Okawa is not at all the stereotypic Japanese businessman operating in America, not the silent, unobtrusive observer, hiding behind a deadpan game face. He is tall, around six feet, and appears to have learned his English from an eccentric tutor, because he is refreshingly slangy, direct, and borderline outrageous in his conversation.

I noticed him for the first time knotting and reknotting his tie on a very public shuttle bus. "Red," Okawa said to me across the aisle, pointing to his wild paisley. "Red tie is power symbol. Said so on TV.

Red is power. Crazy American idea. What the heck, I say to myself, here need all the power I can get." What made the power-tie theory even more absurd was that Okawa's tie ended just below his sternum.

Although he gets offers of free tickets to Steelers games, Okawa has gone to Three Rivers Stadium only twice, with his teenaged son. "Terrible team, terrible team. Lose both times. Both times blowout. Team so bad, embarrassing to witness. Good in seventies, everyone say. Super Bowl all the time. No more, no more. Maybe year 2000. My son will have son before Steelers good team again."

I asked Mr. Okawa if he knew how or why a team that was so incredibly good could turn mediocre and then bad so quickly.

He did, sort of. "Football like war. War like being in steel business. If successful, win, win, win, win. But lose too, sometimes. Nobody win all the time. Is matter of cycles. History, business, football, everything. Even great general, great coach like Chuck Noll, must lose to learn from losing. Noll like Japanese emperor. He learn to lose, learn he is not a god, not perfect. Maybe Steelers lose because Noll not perfect anymore, not a god. Perhaps has been emperor of Pittsburgh too long. He should be the last emperor, get it? Har-har-har."

Frank Krupka, Jr., is in his early forties, a Stillers season ticket holder since 1971, eyewitness to Franco Harris's "Immaculate Reception" at Three Rivers that beat the Oakland Raiders in the AFC playoff game two days before Christmas, 1972. That lucky deflection and touchdown run coincided with the Steelers' coming of age: They were becoming a very, very good football team; the luck just made the birth of their inevitable success slightly premature. Frank Krupka, Jr., was there for all the great years. "If I never have another shot at a Super Bowl, at least I've had the seventies Stillers," he'll tell you over every odd round of beer.

My meeting with Frank junior was arranged by his father, another season ticket holder. (We're going to meet Frank senior later. He's an important character in this tale of Pittsburgh.)

Frank Krupka, Jr., tells me he comes from Aliquippa, a mill town without a mill these days. Aliquippa sits along the Ohio River twenty-five miles west of Pittsburgh. But he doesn't *come* from Aliquippa, he *came* from Aliquippa. He has lived in Coraopolis, a suburban town closer to the city proper, since 1978. Frank junior and his first marriage were early victims of the first round of layoffs from the big LTV steel plant in Aliquippa. His father, who had much more seniority, hung on till the bitter end in 1983.

The younger Krupka held things together on unemployment checks and by doing small repairs on old houses. That eventually became Krup's Home Improvement Company. With success and stability came a second wife, a large house in Coraopolis, and financial security. So why does he tell me he's from Aliquippa?

Because, for the purposes of a book on the Steelers, Frank Krupka, Jr., wants to be identified with the gritty cobblestone streets and the work boots that trudged over them to and from the mill. He loved those good times as a mill-town man: an "Imp and an Iron"—a shot of Imperial whiskey and Iron City beer—with the boys in the tavern on the way home from work; shooting the bull about sex that didn't happen and football that did, but not exactly the way it was remembered; and at the heart of things, football, always football—Aliquippa High School games up on the hill Friday nights, college games on TV Saturdays, the Stillers at Three Rivers on Sunday.

Frank junior says he played linebacker his senior year at Aliquippa. In this region, that's the only credential a man needs. Aliquippa's Aschman Stadium is one of the sacred places. Mike Ditka wore the red and black of the Aliquippa "Fighting Quips." In the minds of most old-timers, Ditka plays there still. Frank junior chooses to represent Aliquippa as home. It is his spiritual place.

"Sure," he admits, "the Stillers have come on hard times, but they're gonna pass. They get a few decent draft picks, there'll be no stopping them." Doesn't Krupka see that's just about the equivalent of saying the mills will open again, the sky will glow red at night, the air quality will plummet, and Frank Krupka, Jr., will move back to Aliquippa and take a job as a mill hand? In his fantasy, he might even remarry his first wife.

When the layoffs began, a lot of other things were happening at once, all of them bad. The aftermath of Vietnam reverberated still. The civil rights movement and the murder of Dr. King left a legacy of racial antagonism for years in a city where competition for a declining number of jobs was predictably bitter. All the social disruption was intensified by economic hardship and dislocation. Very bad times in Steeltown.

"At least the Stillers are winning" is what men, fearing that steelmaking was finished in Pittsburgh, said to each other. Black players and white players, meshing well for three hours on a football field, won football games, won championships, and did it in a way that reflected how lots of Pittsburghers were feeling. Sick and tired of getting booted around, they wanted *their* team not just to win, but to take *their* pound of flesh on Sunday. At Three Rivers, that was usually what happened. No team had ever been asked to fulfill so many human needs as those Steelers.

Those needs were met remarkably: 1974, 10 wins, 3 losses, 1 tie, victory in Super Bowl IX; 1975, 12 wins, 2 losses, victory in Super Bowl X; 1976, 10 wins, 4 losses; 1977, 9 wins, 5 losses; 1978, 14 wins, 2 losses, victory in Super Bowl XIII; 1979, 12 wins, 4 losses, victory in Super Bowl XIV.

Unlike so many of the ingrate fans of Krupka's age, whose anger over the latest Steelers team is a full pendulum swing from their pleasure over the seventies Steelers, part of Frank junior remains forever grateful. "What all the Stiller players, the Rooneys, and Chuck Noll gave this town for so many years, we were lucky to get. No other town ever had anything like it. Just to have lived through it once was enough. To see Lambert and Rocky and Brad, Franco and Swann and Stallworth, Joe Greene, Mel Blount, Jack Ham, all those guys—Jesus, that was more than anyone had a right to deserve. I guess a lot of us got spoiled, thought teams like that were our due, but at least we had that. We were the pinnacle of professional football, and no one can ever take that away—ever." Krupka's voice quivers; his eyes fill.

But what of the future? Must future Pittsburghers be content with other men's memories? "No, no, we'll be back eventually. We have to be. It's common sense. Chuck came in 1969, and his first team won only one game. But he built through the draft and just five years later, the boys won their first Super Bowl. We just have to be patient."

Very few of Krupka's contemporaries are as patient and trusting of Noll and the Steelers organization. "Maybe," said a tailgater pulling on a green bottle of Rolling Rock in the parking lot after a miserable Steelers performance, "that kind of bullshit football might be tolerated in Tampa Bay or Atlanta or Kansas City. It won't be tolerated here. This is Pittsburgh." And his friends pumped fists into the crisp air and shouted, "Yeeaargh."

Arthur McEnery has a perspective shared by very few Steelers fans, by very few Pittsburghers. McEnery is seventy-eight. He lives in Oakland, a small city within the confines of the larger city. Civilized, decorous, home to the University of Pittsburgh and the renowned Children's Hospital—all symbolized by the university's towering Cathedral of Learning—Oakland has always been atypical of Pittsburgh. A touch of refinement among the working-class enclaves.

Arthur McEnery graduated from Pitt in 1934 with a degree in history, which he says served him no useful good when he took a temporary job in the university's business office. He stayed only fifty-one years. McEnery never married. "No room in my heart," he supposes. "My passion for football, and slightly less for baseball, consumed me. I spent my youth on the Forbes Avenue trolley and in the bleachers at Forbes Field watching the Pirates. The sporting life in Pittsburgh in those days got divided up neatly by seasons. Baseball all summer. College football in the fall. Hot-stove league in the winter. Spring training in the spring."

In 1933, Arthur Joseph Rooney brought a professional football franchise in the National Football League to Pittsburgh. It was the fifth franchise in the new league, and Mr. Rooney called his team the Pittsburgh Pirates. "I suppose he did that to create an association with the baseball team, which was already well established," McEnery says. "Art Rooney was already a well-known character around town, an excellent athlete in many sports in his youth, then a sports promoter, and always a gambler. Legend was that he bought the football franchise with twenty-five hundred dollars he won at the races in Saratoga. It's a nice romantic legend."

The football Pirates looked like a very bad bet for Art Rooney. McEnery recollects, "When I'd go out to Forbes Field to see the football Pirates play the Chicago Cardinals and the Bears, the Packers and the Giants, there were often more players in the stadium than spectators, surely more than any actual paying customers. I must admit, I slipped in myself without paying some of the time. Rooney's Pirates were dreadful."

So dreadful, in fact, that they started playing some of their "home" games in Youngstown, Ohio, as well as in Louisville and New Orleans. And they stayed dreadful even when Mr. Rooney signed Byron "Whizzer" White, the present Supreme Court Justice, in 1939 for the then largest salary in pro ball—a truly astounding Depression-era $15,800.

"Whizzer drew a few people," says McEnery, "because he was the league's leading rusher, one of its biggest stars." But he didn't help win games; they won only one his first season. They won only two games when Mr. Rooney changed the team's name to the Steelers in 1940.

During World War II, to conserve manpower and fuel, the Steelers combined their roster with that of the Philadelphia Eagles in 1943 and the Chicago Cardinals the following year. Collectively they won five and lost fourteen. You might say the actual Steelers were only 2½-7. Arthur McEnery still wonders at that: "Can you imagine a team representing two cities with two head coaches? I must have had a perverse streak in those days. I always went back, even though sometimes it was hard to find where the team was playing—sometimes it was at Pitt Stadium, more often at Forbes Field.

"I'd go so far as to say," McEnery offers, "that no professional football team has ever been as bad for as long as the old Stillers and Pirates and Steagles and Stardinals were." It is a lovely touch that as well educated and devoid of the local accent as Arthur McEnery has attempted to be, he still can't help but say "Stillers."

The record supports McEnery's memory of all those teams. Wherever their home, whatever their name, they won 162 games and lost 272 in the NFL from 1933 until Chuck Noll arrived as head coach in 1969.

Arthur McEnery appreciates the Steelers in the long term. "I'm sure the experts will analyze the latest fall of the team down to the nub and come up with dozens of esoteric explanations. Well, I don't think it's a very complicated matter. I subscribe to the luck-of-the-draw theory. Chuck Noll was there when the Stillers drafted magnificent players in the seventies. He was still there when the drafts failed in the eighties. Either Noll was smart in the seventies and got extremely dumb in the eighties, or it's all a matter of the luck of the draw. Luck plays such a great part in life in general and sports in particular, that it's as good an explanation for me as any."

McEnery sees the 1988 season as a throwback to Mr. Rooney's old Pittsburgh Pirates and appreciates them for that: "I watched every game to the bitter end on TV. I'm beyond 'win or lose' now, I'm just happy to see the Stillers play. We've won more than our share of Super Bowls. It's time to give some of these other cities a chance. They've been deprived."

With Steelers history, as with history in general, there is a price to pay for ignorance. Plenty of contemporary Steelers fans, without Arthur McEnery's perspective, are paying it now. "I didn't realize," says Judith Klein, an industrial psychologist with her own consulting firm, "how important the Steelers have been to the men of Pittsburgh. I was working on a project in Johnstown after the mills there shut down in the early eighties. Things were extremely bad in town. The entire region was severely depressed. It didn't look as if the people would be able to survive. Our intention was to find among the laid-off workers those with potential entrepreneurial ability, retrain them, and start them off in small businesses. Not much, I'm sorry to say, ever came of our search. But during my interviews it hit me what the Steelers really meant to these men. One phrase kept coming up over and over again— 'Things are so bad around here, even the Stillers are doing lousy.'"

The "even" was the giveaway. It meant that, when all was said and done, their bedrock belief, their psychological underpinning—the seventies Steelers—could crumble. *Even* they. Pittsburgh steel, the men who produced it, and, yes, *even* the Steelers had become irrelevant. Nothing was forever.

McEnery knew that. Anyone with a knowledge of history knew that. Permanence was pure illusion, impermanence was life's rule. Dynasties rose, dynasties fell. They didn't rise very often, but those that did, fell certainly.

A psychologist could see quite clearly that these men, especially the macho blue-collar types who were losing their personal effectiveness, had attached themselves emotionally to an intimidating football team that was still the scourge of the league. Everyone around the league feared the Steelers of the seventies. They were rough, they were borderline dirty, they were effective. For these fans, the association was psychological projection. But it was more than that. It was myth—that is, factual history transformed into legend and stamped with timelessness.

Though the current team is a poor one, the myth of the team that once was shines through in spite of everything. You hear it whenever men get together to drink beer and talk football. It's nostalgic stuff, but it is a very real and very powerful emotion as well.

Not surprisingly, you can see the mythology of old Pittsburgh most clearly in the local beer commercials. Rolling Rock and Iron City beers run ads that tap into the Pittsburgh of the golden age. Prominently featured in sepia or hazy focus are the old ethnic neighborhoods, the taverns, throngs of hard-hatted workers carrying lunch pails coming from the mill—their bonding and camaraderie almost palpable—shots of football games, a gritty running play by a team that can only be the old Stillers.

Yes, it's cynical—tapping a myth to peddle the beer—and, yes, it trivializes the real lives behind the images, but once again, you can't miss the power and intensity of what those days were to those men. The Rolling Rock spot ends with the poignant, untrue refrain "Same as it ever was . . ."

Arthur McEnery has always believed football was the important basis for Pittsburgh's mythology. "Years ago, back when the Stillers were a municipal embarrassment, the Pirates were a darned respectable major league baseball team. Many a Saturday and Sunday afternoon I'd pay my quarter, take the sun out in the bleachers, and watch the old Dutchman, Honus Wagner, and Pie Traynor and the Waner brothers and Arky Vaughan. But in its basic temperament, in its soul of souls, Pittsburgh is a football town, always was.

"I can't prove it, but football speaks more to the fiber of the people in this city than anything else. Even if the Stillers revert to the old days and become the league's doormat, this will stay a football town. Baseball, fine. But football *means* something here. Why? Darned if I know. Sometimes I swear I think it just comes right up out of the soil here."

In 1988, the baseball Pirates had their finest season in a decade. They finished second to the Mets in the National League East, with a young and improving team. They sold more tickets than ever before in their history, over two million. The 1988 Steelers, as noted, were abysmal. Yet every game at Three Rivers Stadium was sold out. They had, in fact, sold out for 119 consecutive games until the 1987 strike games broke the string. The Steelers have a request list for season tickets that will ensure sellouts for at least six more seasons.

The Pirates have proved that winning draws fans; the Steelers draw through winning and losing seasons. Of course, winning matters, but basically, it is the game itself that draws people in this place. If you doubt it, when Aliquippa plays archrival Ambridge, ten thousand spectators overflow a high school stadium with a capacity of eight thousand.

I've come to the same mysterious conclusion as Arthur McEnery: I honestly believe the football madness in western Pennsylvania really does "come right up out of the soil." Perhaps that's because I believe in the "Spirit of Place." The phrase belongs to the British novelist D. H. Lawrence, who came to America to search for the source of the power he admired in our literature. He wrote: ". . . different places on the face of the earth have different vital effluence, different vibrations . . . different polarity, call it what you like. But Spirit of Place is a great reality." There is something strangely physical and compelling in this western Pennsylvania landscape. Football does indeed come right up out of this ground.

My God, do they play football here. They have always played football here, or at least ever since there was football. The spirits of this place insist on it.

When America threw her gates wide open to immigrants at the end of the last century, it was because she needed strong shoulders to carry her to industrial prominence. The central furnace of her industrial greatness was hotly forged here of coal and iron and steel in a blessed conjunction of people and geography. The people came from the mining regions in Poland, Germany, France, and all the Balkan countries. Irish, Italians, and Ukrainians came. There was hard work to be done here and payment for that work.

Two insights captured the essence of the place and the people. British writer James Parton described the place as "Hell with the lid off." Teddy Roosevelt said, "Pittsburgh has not been built up by talking about it. . . . There is not a Pittsburgh man who did not earn his success through his deeds."

When the damnable work was over, the sport those men played was soccer. They played it under the stacks, they played it under the coal tipples, they played it in fields behind their churches, they played it on cobblestone streets. But their kids played football. It was new and daring, like America. The kids wanted to be American kids. They were big, heavy-thighed kids who were better at blocking and tackling than at the nimble-footed moves of European soccer. Football, as they first played it, was a bruising running game of courage and will, the style that was the hallmark of football in this region until the great quarterbacks began to develop in the towns along the rivers.

Kids shoot hoops from long range on playgrounds all over Indiana, and they bang the boards viciously in ghetto schoolyards of all the East Coast cities. Up in Minnesota, important high school hockey games draw more than eighteen thousand. Baseball, well, they play that everywhere, but more of it where the weather's better. They play all those sports in western Pennsylvania, but not the way they play football.

Last season in the NFL there were sixty players who hailed from an area within one hundred miles of Pittsburgh. No other region produces so much football talent in so concentrated a space. College scouts call it the "fertile crescent."

Football is not a sport here. It is a human ritual with a variety of crucial functions. Drive through a town like Jeannette, twenty miles east of Pittsburgh, and you see high school booster signs in every store on the main street, which becomes a lonely place on Friday night as soon as the lights flash on up at the field. The town is overwhelmingly Italian, and the men coming off the 5 P.M. shift at the glass factories will have a few drinks at the bar and talk about the great Italian players who have done Jeannette proud, foremost among whom is Dick Hoak, a Steelers running back for ten years and Noll's backfield coach for almost twenty.

They'll eventually walk up to the stadium, where about seven thousand parents and children and friends have already gathered. People other people have known all their lives are here. For those unfortunates working the night shift in the glass factories, the game is piped in over the loudspeaker system.

Football is a rite of passage, a trial by ordeal that comes at a time when boys are required to put aside the silliness of childish things and begin to act out the warrior ways of the men. Sacrifice and pain and courage, it is thought, will teach them to live better in their new, manly bodies. Football requires all those things.

It is a bonding rite, in the sense that every man-child on a high school team is not only joined to his teammates by valiant deed, but bound forever to all the boys who ever played on high school fields in western Pennsylvania on Friday night. More important, football links generations of men. A boy with a strong body doesn't have the choice of not playing football. A Pittsburgh man I know, reluctant to go out for the team when he was a boy, remembers telling his father, "If I was from some other place, I wouldn't have to play football." He still recalls his father's exact response: "You are not *from* some other place. You are from *this* place. My father played football. I played football. You will play football. And your sons will play football." He did indeed play. And so will his sons.

Football is also a rite of worship. The exceptional ones live in memory precisely as Alexander was remembered by the Macedonians; a blending of history and fable is absorbed into the haze of legend in the steel-mill towns along the rivers. The great ones are still immortal, their football deeds passed along by generations of fathers and sons. Not an accident, then, that Frank "Tiger" Walton and his boy, Joe, from up in Beaver Falls, became the first father and son to play in the National Football League. Joe coaches the New York Jets these days. And yes, that's the same town where Joe Willie Namath was the high school centerpiece on Friday nights, a place where no other quarterback seemed to exist.

In the cafés and saloons of the river towns, the feats of Johnny Lujack, from Connellsville, and Leon Hart, from Turtle Creek, have been reshaped and embellished since the late forties. Mike Ditka remains for the Slavic population in Aliquippa the closest thing to Hercules on the face of the earth. John Unitas played quarterback at St. Justin's High in Mount Washington, a huge bluff that overlooks downtown Pittsburgh.

Har-Brack High School had a man-child running back in the early fifties who didn't even bother playing college ball: Cookie Gilchrist went right to the Cleveland Browns. His legend didn't blossom in Cleveland, but with the Buffalo Bills in the AFL. Cookie Gilchrist is the John Henry of western Pennsylvania.

Har-Brack was the same school that offered the NFL the Modzelewski brothers—Big Mo and Little Mo. Tony Dorsett may be at the end of a great NFL career, but don't dare say that in any bar in Hopewell. Not unless you want to get levitated right out the door by the glares of large men.

The legends live. Kids are weaned on them. Through oral history, the torch is passed. We play football here; we play great football here. And the process continues. Dan Marino, from Pittsburgh Central Catholic, Jim Kelly, from East Brady High, Joe Montana, from Monongahela, and Bernie Kosar, from just over the Ohio border in Youngstown, have inherited and enhanced the Lujack and Unitas and Namath quarterback legacies. They are already the models for ten-year-olds, whose fathers teach them to finger the laces of the ball with their eyes closed. Great football re-creates itself continually here, as ritual is layered upon myth.

Football is the rite of autumn that begins when the air turns chill in mid-September and intensifies when it is frigid in November. The greens turn to yellow and then to rust and wine, the dark earth blackens. The smell of decaying leaves hangs in the thin air, its odor so close to burning you look around for the smoke. The big boys come home from school, do their chores, and get ready to face their futures—and their pasts—on football fields, doing what boys have done here since the turn of the century. All the rituals come together on Friday nights in all the old mill towns along the Allegheny and Monongahela rivers, along the Ohio even after it crosses out of Pennsylvania and into the foothills of Ohio and West Virginia.

Usually the Steelers have a number of players from the region, but in '88 there was only one, and he wasn't really a local boy. Chuck Lanza, a rookie third-round draft choice from Notre Dame, didn't get to play very much because he was Mike Webster's backup at center. Although Lanza played junior-high football in Coraopolis and would certainly have played in high school, where his father had played before him, his family moved to Tennessee in 1977 when he was thirteen. "My dad's business went bankrupt because the economy here was so bad back then," Chuck says, "and we had to move away. I'd have loved to have played around Pittsburgh." Chuck Lanza never got to live the rituals he'd heard so much about.

There is a new mythology being manufactured in Pittsburgh these days, one that is trying to exorcise the ghosts of the gritty past. Its refrain might be: "Forget what it ever was," and it is sung persistently by the Pittsburgh Chamber of Commerce, which proclaims the city completely transformed, a model for the nation on how to handle the wrenching economic changeover from ugly mill town to service-industry metropolis. From unpleasant to lovely. From dirty to clean. From granite to glass. From union to nonunion. From male to female. And, in a very elemental way, from the power of myth to the effectiveness of images.

The economic miracle, proudly called the "Pittsburgh Renaissance" in municipal literature, is projected most dramatically in the futuristic architecture of the downtown commercial towers that are clustered at the confluence of the Allegheny and Monongahela rivers and are known as the golden triangle. Yet another startling change—from rust to gold.

The brave new Pittsburgh proclaims itself in lots of other unmistakable ways as well. Arrive at Greater Pittsburgh International Airport and you're hit by a large sign boasting, THE MOST LIVABLE CITY IN AMERICA. Pick up your bags and there's another. And another at the taxi stand, and on and on.

Yes, Rand McNally has voted Pittsburgh "most livable," but why the never-ending self-aggrandizement? Sure, she's proud, but doesn't she proclaim too much?

Nevertheless, it is a pleasure to see that the sky above western

Pennsylvania really is azure and to know that you can breathe the air without developing a regional wheeze. The rivers are cleaner—not clean, clean*er*—and the line of ugly ore and coal barges has stopped. Probably forever.

It is fair to say that no industrial city in America reflects the Old Gipper's Reaganomics as directly as Pittsburgh does. The loss of the industrial lifeblood, in the form of jobs going to places in the world where labor costs are significantly lower (and profits that much higher), has not been staunched in the eighties; quite to the contrary, the bleeding has been encouraged. Pittsburgh was given no choice; it had to make a change or die. It is branded a "renaissance," an "economic miracle," and its result is clean, modern, "livable" Pittsburgh. Look at the "miracle" closely, however, and you'll see it is really sleight of hand, more illusion than substance, far more illusion.

The unemployment rate topped out at 16 percent in 1982 and began to fall to what passes for acceptable these days, but the figures deceive, as service-industry figures usually do. The new clerical jobs at banks, investment firms, and insurance companies were filled mostly by women at salaries only slightly above the minimum wage.

The younger laid-off mill hands tried to retrain themselves; those who found jobs felt fortunate, even though they were poorly paid. The older men collected unemployment for a while and eventually went to the reduced pension benefits of early retirement. Both groups remain bitter. The fast-food industry—among the top ten employers in Pittsburgh now—pays teenagers and some older women the minimum wage, and these jobs, too, are considered "employment," and they bear the same statistical weight as that of coal miner or open-hearth worker.

The employment figures for the city look respectable because one-job families became two- and three-job families, although together husband, wife, and kid barely make as much as a single steelworker used to. The figures do not measure the pride and sense of dignity that actually go with bringing something tangible and useful into being, as opposed to moving paper around, tapping on a computer keyboard, sending smooth signals over a telephone line, or flipping a quarter-pounder. "Most livable" came at an invisible cost that hasn't been totaled yet.

Bt the greatest deception has been the redefinition of what constitutes Pittsburgh itself. Pittsburgh of the steelmaking days was a region. Wherever the steel was made, that was Pittsburgh. The central city of the neighborhoods was supplemented by steel towns up and down the Allegheny, the Monongahela, the Ohio, and all the smaller tributaries, the ethnic towns that climbed sharply up the hills from the river mills—towns like Homestead, McKeesport, Duquesne, Braddock, Clairton, McKees Rocks, Frank Krupka's Aliquippa, Ambridge, and Beaver Falls, among dozens of others.

Conditions in these towns are every bit as bad as they were in the Great Depression, maybe worse. On the streets at midday, you see forlorn men—black or white, depending on which town or section of town—leaning up against boarded-up storefronts. They have become invisible, no longer even unemployment statistics because their benefits have run out. Since they won't just go away, they are overlooked in the upbeat focus on "renaissance" and "most livable."

Aliquippa, Frank Krupka, Jr.'s original home, is one of the most devastated towns, and it has one of the most devastating high school teams. There is a connection: Football excellence and aggressiveness constitute a ticket out of the dead-end despair that stalks these desolate streets, and the boys who play football here grab at that ticket.

I drove through town early one Sunday morning before a Steelers game. The high school stadium and the houses on the hill nearby displayed red-and-black placards and large Quips schedules showing that the team was undefeated and was ranked number one in its class statewide. At the other end of town, just before the underpass that led to the all but abandoned steel mill, dozens of picket signs stood against the wall. A particularly large one, also in red and black, carried the Polish word for "Solidarity." The next sign said, WE ARE SOLIDARITY!

An intense and precise young man who reveres traditional Pittsburgh, Vic Ketchman, a local football writer, was my guide through the city and the Steelers' 1998 season, and I could not have been more fortunate. Born in the city thirty-seven years before, Ketchman has covered the Steelers since 1972, when the team became one of the league's elite squads.

Ketchman is very aware of the invisible forces that shaped this region and this football franchise. For him, the real Pittsburgh remains a ghostly spirit, not the golden triangle or gentrified neighborhoods with lovely boutiques.

"This is not basically a friendly town," he insists. "It's a good town with good people, but for the old-timers friendship was a slow thing.

Distrust had to be overcome. They're trying to sell the easy smile and 'Have a Nice Day' around here, but it comes from elsewhere, not from this place."

Once I asked him to reduce Pittsburgh to its absolute essence. We were in the Steelers' press box. Ketchman considered for a long time and said, "I'll bet you own the land your house sits on, but that's not the way it is in Pittsburgh. This town is different. You own the square footage but you only own the ground six feet down. The state retains the mineral rights to everything below that. Lots of these houses are built right over mine shafts. Hell, everyone knows his house could begin to disappear tomorrow night. We even have a name for a house sinking—we call it 'subsidence.' Think of living in a place like that!"

D. H. Lawrence and Arthur McEnery would have understood perfectly. Dynasties rise and dynasties fall. Egypt, Persia, Greece, Rome, the Pittsburgh "Stillers." Why not the homes of the people who once made this city, this region, so remarkably productive? They sink back into the spirit world below the earth, the very earth from which all power here had once emanated.

Steelers and Steroids

Steve Courson's autobiography, False Glory, *represented a change in the tenor of American sports reporting that began in the 1970s. The first instance of this new genre was the publication of New York Yankees pitcher Jim Bouton's* Ball Four *(1970), the original tell-all sports autobiography. A few years later, when* Washington Post *reporters Bob Woodward and Carl Bernstein cracked open the Watergate scandal, they inspired a trend toward investigative journalism that continues unabated to this day. Imitating Woodward, Bernstein, and Bouton, journalists and athletes increasingly focused on the seamy underside of sports. Sex, drugs, internal bickering, unlikable and bizarre personalities—all was now fair game. In this selection, Courson, a Steelers offensive guard from 1978 to 1983, plunged readers into the dark side of life in the NFL. Courson's own alcohol and steroid abuse left him with a heart condition that he battled for years. He talked to hundreds of youth groups about the dangers of drugs before he passed away in 2005.*

ROCK AND ROLL, SEX AND DRUGS
Steve Courson

I can probably say with some surety that offensive linemen were—and are—more likely to use steroids to enhance (football) performance than players at other positions. The reasons are simple: Your job relies more on physical strength than any other. Your basic purpose is to push someone in a direction that he doesn't want to go. And when these reluctant someones are 270, 280, even 300 pounds of speed and muscle, you've got a real occupational hazard.

Technique may keep you around for awhile. Knowledge of tactics is essential. Certainly quickness is an asset. But you cannot last in the National Football League as an effective run or pass blocker without brute, out-of-this-world strength. And there are two main ways to build strength: weightlifting and steroids. If you combine the two, the results will be extraordinary.

Without naming names, I can state unequivocally that during my time in Pittsburgh 75 percent of the Steeler offensive line took ana-

From *False Glory: Steelers and Steroids, the Steve Courson Story*, by Steve Courson and Lee R. Schreiber (Stamford, Conn.: Longmeadow Press, © 1991). Reprinted by permission of Steve Courson.

bolic-androgenic steroids at one time or another. Disgruntled players throughout the league called us the "Steroid Team," as if performance-enhancing drugs were the sole reason for our success.

The fact is, our AAS usage was the same—give or take—as most of the NFL teams at that time.

Pat Donovan, a Dallas Cowboy offensive lineman who retired in 1983 after nine years in the NFL, has said: "In my last five or six years [steroid use] ran as high as 60 to 70 percent on the Cowboys' offensive and defensive lines." And in 1985, while playing for the Raiders, defensive end Lyle Alzado said, "On some teams, between 75 and 90 percent of all [players] use steroids."

What the Steelers had was one of the most advanced strength programs under Lou Rickey, and some of the most dedicated, hard-working athletes in or out of football. When the NFL began its Strongest Man Competition in 1980, the Steelers dominated it: Mike Webster won it in 1980, with Jon Kolb and Steve Furness second and sixth; in 1981, Kolbie won, and I came in third; and in 1982, Rick Donnalley won, with me in second and Craig Wolfley in fourth.

While I would estimate that about 50 percent of the team in the power positions experimented with anabolic-androgenic steroids, an even greater number took amphetamines on Sunday before a game. The use of amphetamines was much more open during the early years of pro football; there are confirmed stories of cups or cookie jars in several locker rooms, sitting out for all to see, from which interested players could scoop up however many pills they wanted.

Since the offensive line on the Steelers were so close, we discussed anything and everything. Among ourselves—away from the coaches and the media—we talked about our feminine conquests, our jobs, and about our drug use.

It was like group therapy. Most of us were just learning about anabolic-androgenic steroids. They seemed like wonderful new toys, and if one of us discovered a more effective drug, we were eager to share it with the others.

Some of my Steeler teammates and other serious weightlifting friends would occasionally gather around my kitchen table and discuss our mood swings or our latest 'roid attacks. Most of us agreed that the juice made us more sexually aware men, though the levels of arousal varied among us.

There was considerably less variance, however, when it came to aggression. In all cases, when we took steroids our aggressiveness got turned way up. Which, of course, is another reason why coaches choose to look the other way. They're constantly yelling at the players to "hit harder!" Or: "Be more aggressive!" And here is that magical pill (or injection) that could do just that.

Anabolic-androgenic steroids and amphetamines definitely increased our levels of aggression. Some of us, myself included, would use marijuana to take the edge off of the 'roid rage and/or the speed rush we might experience; it also tended to smooth out the gladiator mentality, which might not be appropriate in a social setting. Other than the occasional joint, however, I was not really an ardent recreational drug user.

Like many of my generation, I did experiment with most drugs— usually once, out of curiosity—including mushrooms, acid, quaaludes, opium, ecstasy, and cocaine. Some I enjoyed more than others, but I never did any of them regularly. I was too focused on football and didn't want any additional distractions.

The one drug that left me especially cold was cocaine. It didn't do much other than make my heart race and my nose burn. Many of my teammates—some at Pittsburgh, more at Tampa Bay—were into coke fairly heavily. The combination of cocaine and steroids would have most of these guys bouncing off of walls, barstools, bar patrons—you name it. Needless to say, it was not the most peaceable union.

As for amphetamines, which can make you hyper and aggressive all by their lonesome, I used them maybe three times in my entire pro career. The first time was in 1978, my second year with the Steelers, when my basic function was that of a messenger guard—ferrying the plays in from Chuck Noll to Terry Bradshaw.

It was a Monday night game against the Oilers, and I wanted a little extra fuel for the national TV audience—in this case, two black beauties. Sometime in the second quarter, Chuck yelled the play in my ear, "1-84 Trap Pass," and I eagerly trotted out onto the field to inform my teammates. Which I did, of course. All except one.

It seemed that I had told the play to everyone except our quarterback, Bradshaw, who instead calls out, "Flow-37." We're about to break huddle when it dawned on me—even in my "beaned out" state—that something was amiss. I leaned over and whispered to Brad, "That's not the play." He laughed and called a time out. You can be sure, however, that Chuck Noll was not laughing.

As you may guess from that episode, amphetamines—speed, beauties, beenies, beanies, greenies—made me goofy. I couldn't think straight. If they had worked for me, like they did for many players throughout the league, I probably would've taken them more frequently.

As I mentioned, a speed or 'roid rush was perceived by most of us as a positive thing, a belief tacitly shared by our coaches. The way I figured, I was getting paid to explode on the line of scrimmage, and if I occasionally exploded in my car out of rage—often, when caught in rush-hour traffic, I'd feel like ripping the steering wheel off its column—I shouldn't take the ups and downs too seriously.

Passing the Torch

The 1980s saw the Steelers struggling to maintain their position as one of the NFL's premiere teams. One by one, the stalwarts of the Super Bowl-era squadrons retired, leaving Chuck Noll to make do and rebuild. Great players—Gary Anderson, Louis Lipps, Rod Woodson, Dwayne Woodruff—still came to Pittsburgh, but they could not replace the departing stars. The Steelers remained competitive during the early 1980s, maintaining a .500 or better record from 1980 to 1984, but failed to return to the big game. With mediocre quarterbacks like Mark Malone and Bubby Brister at the helm, they slumped from 1985 until 1991, never winning more than nine games in a season and making the playoffs only once. After their 7-9 season in 1991, Noll's 23rd as head coach, Dan Rooney decided to reshuffle the organization and reduce Noll's control over the team's affairs. Four days after the season ended, however, Noll decided to retire. His departure caught many by surprise, and the always-reticent coach did little to explain his move. He left a city that revered him but, as Ron Cook suggested in the Pittsburgh Post-Gazette, *did not ever really know or understand him. "As Chuck Noll came on this scene something of an enigma, so did he leave it," wrote* Pittsburgh Press *scribe Phil Musick. With Noll and Art Rooney no longer on the scene, the Steelers seemed poised to shed the burdens of their triumphant past and rebuild for the future.*

The hiring of Bill Cowher to replace the man known as "the Emperor" exemplified the club's fresh approach. At 34, Cowher was the second-youngest head coach in the league. He was a local boy who played linebacker for the Browns and the Eagles, studied under coach Marty Schottenheimer in Cleveland and Kansas City, and showed proper reverence for the Steelers and their history. The city of Pittsburgh eagerly embraced its new coach and wondered if he might be the next . . . Chuck Noll. Cowher has become a fixture in Pittsburgh over the past fourteen years. He has led the Steelers to ten postseasons (including playoff appearances in his first six seasons, a feat only matched by the legendary Paul Brown), six AFC conference championship games, and two Super Bowls. He may well surpass Noll's mark of 206 career wins. He became the face of the team, and the Steelers have consistently reflected his own tough and gritty persona.

Ron Cook captured the franchise in its moment of transition from a current legend to a future hero. His glowing report of Cowher's introduction to the media was indicative of the lofty expectations thrust upon the first-time head coach.

NOLL MAY HAVE CHECKED OUT EARLIER THAN HE WANTED TO

Ron Cook

Every sportscast in America led with the news last night. *"Chuck Noll, the only man to win four Super Bowls, retired today as coach of the Pittsburgh Steelers after 23 seasons."*

Some showed red-eyed Steelers President Dan Rooney, reading from a piece of yellow legal paper, thanking Noll for being a great coach and better person. "The best compliment that I know is what my wife said a long time ago. 'If anything happens to us, I would like Chuck Noll to raise my kids.'"

Others showed the typically stoic Noll, sitting in the front of the same room where he addressed his team hundreds of times, saying, simply, it was time to quit. "The only thing I can say is thank you. I mean this to everybody, to the city of Pittsburgh, to the coaches that I've been associated with through the years, to the players. Especially to the players."

What the cameras didn't catch was Noll's long-time secretary, Pam Morocco, sobbing at her desk. Moments earlier, Noll had called her in to tell her he was leaving. She broke down. More telling, he broke down.

"You don't have any idea how hard this is for him," Morocco said through the tears. "People seem to think he's some cold piece of stone with no feelings. But he cares. He's a very emotional man. He has feelings. Believe me, he has feelings."

I believe. Now, I believe.

Noll gave us a glimpse of his human side yesterday, maybe our first real glimpse in 23 years, certainly our most instructive glimpse. It was no fun to see.

There is a pall over a large portion of our city today because the legendary coach has called it quits. The sadness has nothing to do with Noll as a person. He never allowed us to really know him, not the way Jim Leyland has or Bob Johnson did. No, there is sadness because we remember Noll's tremendous accomplishments, because we were comfortable with him, because we all tend to be a little afraid when it comes to change and the unknown.

I'm sad for all that even though I'm convinced it's in the Steelers' best interest for Noll to step aside. But I'm also sad for another reason. I can't shake the feeling Noll isn't ready for the easy life on his boat. I think he's going to miss his job terribly, miss the satisfaction of teaching, the challenge of building a winning team. I think he's retiring against his best judgment.

That bothers me.

I tried to temper that feeling. You work 39 years in one profession, the final 23 at the same job, it's tough to pull the plug. Of course, it's tough.

But I never knew Noll to be uncertain about a decision, any decision, even the hard ones. He would make up his mind and live with the consequences. His resolve—some people call it his stubbornness—was his greatest strength as a coach and maybe his greatest weakness.

I saw a lot of uncertainty yesterday.

Maybe Noll, a loyal man, quit because he couldn't tolerate the expected changes on his coaching staff. Rooney said the subject never came up at their meeting, but that doesn't mean Noll didn't know it was coming. There had been widespread speculation that offensive coordinator Joe Walton would be fired and defensive coordinator David Brazil would be demoted.

Or maybe Noll quit because he couldn't accept a reduction in his authority. That subject also wasn't addressed, but Noll had to know it was planned. The Steelers went through the entire season without a qualified long snapper because Noll refused to sign one. That's inexcusable for a professional football team, and Rooney won't stand for that sort of thing again. He's going to give more personnel power to someone—maybe Director of Football Development Tom Donahoe—which would have meant less for Noll.

No matter the reason, it just didn't seem like Noll was quitting because he plain wanted to quit.

At one point, he admitted vacillating between retiring and coaching. He said he didn't make his final decision until yesterday morning.

At another point, he left the door open to coaching another team. Can you imagine that? Noll as coach of any other team?

At no point did he give any real indication he was content with his decision or relieved he had made it. In charge, as usual, at the start of his press conference, he quickly lost control of his emotions. He isn't one to expose so much of himself—he plainly was uncomfortable in the bright lights—so he ended the briefing prematurely. He grabbed his coat and bolted for his car, off into the cold, gray afternoon. I'll bet anything he cried the whole time on his drive home to Upper St. Clair.

The next time we see Noll publicly might be at the Hall of Fame induction ceremonies in Canton, Ohio, in August 1993. That's where he will end up, you know? That's where he belongs.

You can make the argument Noll had a greater impact on Pittsburgh's self-image than any man. In my lifetime, I would put only the late Mayor Richard Caliguiri on the same short list.

Noll came to a football town in 1969 and made a winner out of the pro team after 36 years of losing. He gave Pittsburgh people something about which they could boast. He gave them something to look forward to at the end of the long work week in the fall.

I made it a point to walk the Steelers' side of the field at Three Rivers Stadium after Noll's announcement. The place was empty, but I could see Noll at the 50, hands in his coat pockets, a stocking cap protecting his head from a freezing rain. I could see Franco Harris making The Immaculate Reception against the Oakland Raiders. I could see the Mike Renfro non-catch in the far corner of the end zone, and little Donnie Shell kicking out big Earl Campbell. I could see Lynn Swann's grace and Jack Ham's perfect technique. I could see Jack Lambert's legs churning like pistons.

Those were the days you were proud to say you were from Pittsburgh. Those were Noll's days.

But that was the 1970s. This is the '90s. The past decade hasn't been kind to the Steelers. They had a 51-60 record the past seven seasons. They failed to make the playoffs six times.

I have no doubt Noll made the right decision for the football team. It's time for a change, a fresh start, a new approach.

I just hope he made the right decision for himself. After bringing so much joy to so many people, he deserves to be happy, now more than ever.

HERE WE GO, STILLERS: COWHER WINS HIS FIRST

Ron Cook

You knew it was going to be big, the day R Stillers introduced a new coach for the first time in 23 years. But this was ridiculous. There wasn't so much commotion when Pittsburgh said hello to a new mayor a few years ago.

Do we have priorities or what?

You should have seen the chaos yesterday when Dan Rooney led the procession up the hall at team headquarters for the big press conference. Beside him were The Chosen One, Bill Cowher, and The Chosen One's wife, Kaye. Around them, on all sides, every step of the way, were the cameramen and photographers. Rooney and the Cowhers needed help getting through the mob.

If you didn't know better, you would have thought somebody really important was in your presence. Madonna, maybe. Is it any wonder everybody hates the *paparazzi*?

You should have seen The Talking Heads jockeying for the best position inside the conference room. Sam, an old hand at this sort of thing, had the wisdom (pomposity?) to block off his space with tape. It was a good lesson for Alby and John. Maybe they, too, can become Ted Baxter when they grow up.

You should have seen the panic when Rooney stepped toward the podium at 11:58 A.M., two minutes ahead of schedule. "We've still got a minute-and-a-half if we want to go live," Sam bleated. "You can't start yet." Rooney dutifully sat down.

The photographers took that as a green light to swarm around the Cowhers, who appeared petrified. You would be petrified, too, if a dozen strangers were popping flashes, oh, maybe six inches from your face. All you can do is smile the same stupid, forced smile and try not to scratch your nose under any circumstances. If you do, the picture is going to pop up in somebody's newspaper tomorrow and somebody will get the wrong idea.

The Cowhers should have been used to this treatment. In the previous 48 hours, since word leaked Cowher was The Man, their lives had been scrutinized and analyzed, put on display for all of Pittsburgh to see. You know everything about Cowher with the possible exception of which side of the bed he prefers. We're happy to report he's a right-side man.

Who ever gets used to that treatment?

That's why Cowher was relieved when it finally was time for Patrice back in the studio to throw it to John, who threw it to Rooney, who threw it to him. He got off to a strong start by introducing his family. The family thing always plays well in Pittsburgh.

Cowher pointed out his parents, Laird and Dorothy (she was the one in the black-and-gold outfit), who never dared to dream that when their son left their Crafton home in search of a career in football he might one day come home to coach the Stillers. He pointed out his brothers Dale and Doug. And he pointed out Doug's wife, Janet (she was the one in the black-and-gold outfit).

Do you think maybe Kaye (she was the one in the black-and-gold outfit) said something to him last night about whom he forgot?

Nerves.

It's true—that oversight was a major error. But that's the only one Cowher made. He was at his best politely answering all the questions about Chuck Noll. There must have been 30 or 40. A guy loses count after a while. At different times, Cowher called Noll "a legend" and "one of the all-time greats."

"Chuck Noll brought tradition and pride to this city. That's the thing I want to do in my own way. No, I have no reservations about following Chuck Noll."

Cowher laughed when asked if Pittsburgh could expect him to be a soft-spoken, low-key kind of guy, in the Noll mold. More telling, his family laughed. They know better. "I'm just going to be me," Cowher said. This is a guy who used to sprint 60 yards along the sideline exhorting his kickoff team when he was the Cleveland Browns' special teams coach.

Cowher showed a nice sense of humor, unforced and relaxed. Like when he was asked about his high school pictures that appeared on these pages yesterday. "The moral of that story is to always keep your parents updated with recent pictures." Or when he was asked about coming home to coach. "It's nice that we're not going to have to fly in anymore for visits. That will save us some money."

The players started showing up about then, hanging on the fringe of the throng. David Johnson was first. Then, Gerald Williams. And

Eric Green and Beltin' Delton Hall. It's always good to be seen by the new boss on his first day. It's considered especially good schmoozing form to be seen in shorts with that just-sweated look, as Bubby Brister was.

Hey, Coach, I've been working out since about 6 this morning. Can't get started on next season soon enough, ya know?

"I like 'um," The Bubster said, even before meeting Cowher. If sucking up is going to win that quarterback job next summer, Bub has a head start on Neil O'Donnell.

"He has a lot of enthusiasm," Johnson said of Cowher. "A lot of flair. Almost like a college, we're-going-to-get-it-done flair. I think he has a lot of what Dick MacPherson brought to the New England Patriots. That's going to be good for us."

"I like what he had to say."

That pretty much was the consensus.

None of what Cowher said meant anything when it comes to winning games on Sunday afternoons. And there's still absolutely no way of knowing if he'll be able to keep the job for 23 years or 23 months.

But if the rest of Cowher's days with the Stillers go as well as the first, he'll do fine.

Playing in the Long Shadow

It has become popular to criticize athletes for failing to show proper reverence for the history of their sport. Fans wail in anguish when present-day stars affirm that they don't know Otto Graham from an ottoman. Perhaps it is for the best that players do not dwell upon bygone days, for the triumphs of seasons long ago can provide heavy burdens for those who follow. This onus is especially crushing in Pittsburgh, where memories of the glory days of the 1970s overshadow the achievements and failures of the teams that have followed—where every new player is inevitably compared to Blount, Bradshaw, Greene, Ham, Harris, or Stallworth. In this selection, veteran Pittsburgh Post-Gazette *sportswriter Ed Bouchette looked at the 1992 Steelers and discussed the challenges of playing in a city with one eye eternally cocked toward the past. New coach Bill Cowher guided the Black and Gold to a promising 11-5 record that year, leading some to believe that the franchise had finally shed the yoke of the past and was ready to embark upon a new Golden Age.*

NO STEEL CURTAIN CALL

Ed Bouchette

It had been building all season—for several, really—but after the Steelers crunched the Cincinnati Bengals, 21-9, on November 29 to forge a 9-3 record, the time was ripe for them to get out the spade, dig a six-foot hole, and bury the 1970s in it.

Pittsburgh football fans had lived in the '70s for more than a dozen years. They compared each Steelers team to the four-time Super Bowl champs, sized up each player against Hall of Famers who erected that dynasty.

Everywhere the contemporary player turned, the 1970s smacked him in the face. Few active Steelers received endorsements or television commercials, but there was Jack Lambert or Franco Harris or L. C. Greenwood or Joe Greene or Rocky Bleier selling something or other. During a span in the '80s, Terry Bradshaw critiqued them on

From *Dawn of a New Steel Age: Bill Cowher's Steelers Forge into the 90s* (Champaign, Ill.: Sagamore Publishing, 1993). Reprinted by permission of Ed Bouchette.

KDKA-TV every Monday night. Writers who covered the Steelers of the '70s and were still on the beat in the '90s sometimes contrasted the two. When modern Steelers would get hot, broadcaster Myron Cope would on occasion whistle for the Terrible Towel to come out of the bullpen.

It was natural, but finally on November 29, 1992, the young generation screamed for it to stop. On that chilly afternoon in Cincinnati, Barry Foster broke Franco Harris's rushing record of 1,246 yards, set in 1975, and the Steelers established a one-game team record with 10 sacks of rookie quarterback David Klingler in his black-and-blue NFL debut. Afterward, someone mentioned to linebacker Greg Lloyd that the defense looked like the old Steel Curtain that afternoon.

"I don't like to be compared to those guys," Lloyd huffed. "We're the Steelers of 1992. We don't want to be compared to the Steel Curtain. We'd appreciate it if you guys would quit doing that. I know I would."

Foster rang up 102 yards to give him the NFL lead with 1,319. For the past several weeks he had been swamped with questions about Franco, and the inevitable comparisons followed. No, he said, he had never met Franco. Yes, he had seen him on TV as a kid romp all over his favorite team, the Cowboys, in a couple of Super Bowls. And what did it mean to him to break this Hall of Famer's record?

"It means to me, it's a new era starting," Foster answered unexpectedly. "We've been trying to shed the image of the Steelers and the '70s for quite some time now. I think that the fall of Franco's records are just the beginning of a new era coming in."

It wasn't arrogant, and it wasn't selfish, and Foster did not want to demean Harris or the Steelers' Super Bowl teams. But ENOUGH ALREADY!

"We realize who we're following," Foster said. "They had a great team and it's hard to live that down. So until we actually get there, we're not going to live that down. We all realize that. The fans in Pittsburgh were very spoiled throughout the Bradshaw and Greene era. Sometimes, they can be very hard on us, which is not fair. But when you follow a great team [like] those guys had, it's very tough."

Lloyd, reflecting on it later, added to the debate. He thinks today's players are better than they were 15–20 years ago.

"People can't get those four Super Bowls out of their minds," he said. "I know that's hard. But some of those guys couldn't play today because the game has gotten faster. I respect those guys and everything they did back then. Hell, they were the best back then. But nowadays it's a different ball game."

Foster and Lloyd made it clear how the new Steelers felt, and others began to pick up on it.

"I'm glad he said that," Tom Donahoe [then director of football operations] said. "This is the Steelers of the '90s. That's not saying tradition is not important here. You see the tradition's important every day you walk into this place because the first thing that hits you are four Super Bowl trophies, and that's a heck of a tradition to try to live up to."

"Your players have to say, 'Hey, we have to make our own mark,' and that's what some of our guys are starting to do. That in no way is being disrespectful to Chuck, to Franco, to Bradshaw, to Joe Greene. No way at all. But it's difficult. I thought that was one of the ways we did a disservice to our players. We were always talking about the '70s and the players of the '70s and it's very, very difficult for guys to live up to that. They have to find their own niche."

Mel Blount congratulated them for doing so. He was a vital member of the Steel Curtain, performing at cornerback better than anyone else before him, and was swept into the Hall of Fame. But when he joined the Steelers in 1970, the players were trying to live down a reputation that preceded them, too.

"People were saying the Same Old Steelers, guys who went out in the streets and drank and fought in the bars," Blount said. "We had the same attitude that these guys have: Don't tell us about what the Steelers did back when we were in high school or college. That's a different group of guys.

"I respect what these guys are saying: 'We want to make our own niche in Steelers history, we want our own destiny.' To me, that's a mark of a champion. 'Hey, don't tell me anything about what guys did in the '70s. This is the '90s. We're going to make our own history.'

"I think to be a great athlete, you have to have a certain amount of confidence and you have to have a certain amount of arrogance about you. Those guys have a point. They're saying, 'We respect what those guys did, but don't keep bringing it up to me.' I can relate to that."

Rocky Bleier, the little halfback who could in the '70s, also endorsed those feelings. He heard Bill Cowher's wife, Kaye, say in a meeting: "The Steelers start NOW."

"As bold as that might seem to be, that's important," Bleier said.

"I thought one of the transitional problems that had taken place through the '80s was there was no clear cut break or identity with the old and the new. The old was around for so long that an identity always was with the old. The fans and the mentality of the organization didn't allow new blood to create their own identity. There was always a holdover. It wasn't Mark Malone's team because some of the guys were still there—Stallworth, Webby, Shell. No one really created that until that ended.

"So a clean break has taken place—a great coaching staff, not a whole lot of egos involved, a mesh of experience. They adapted the system to the personnel rather than the other way around. They got rid of some deadwood in training camp that the other staff might not have and that sets a tone for everybody."

Chuck Noll also thought it was good to bury the past.

"When I came here in '69 that's all I heard about—SOS, Same Old Steelers. We tried to get rid of the past and focus on the present and the future. That's your whole thing. You spend a lot of time trying to do that because that's important. What you've done in the past doesn't matter. It's today and what you're going to do.

"It's a distraction, whether it's good or bad. It's no different now than it was in '69 and '70 when we were trying to erase not a very good recollection of the past. A very good recollection of the past can get in the way, too."

The new Steelers actually gave Noll, Blount, Bleier, and many of their former teammates something with which to relate. They excited them. Many of the Steelers from the Super Bowl years live in the Pittsburgh area: Dwight White, L. C. Greenwood, Bleier, Harris, Andy Russell, Lambert, Lynn Swann, Jack Ham, Mike Wagner, Jon Kolb, Blount, J. T. Thomas, Larry Brown, and others. They suffered through the 1980s with all the other Pittsburgh fans, probably more so. It had been a long time in coming, but they enjoyed the 1992 season as both fans and alumni. Many of them met Bill Cowher, his coaching staff, and the players at a party for the new team and alumni before the season.

Instead of talking about the 1970s, the stars of those years prefer to speak about the new Steelers.

"This year for the first time, maybe I got caught up in the Bill Cowher thing," said Ham, the ex-linebacker who is in the coal and gas business as well as the Pro Football Hall of Fame, and broadcasts a weekly NFL game on the Mutual Radio Network. "I mean, you see guys out there busting their butt. I see Barry Foster running his butt off out there and just knocking defensive backs down and just delivering a blow rather than accepting one. I got caught up in it and I'm really pulling for these guys, more so than in the past. For the first time in a lot of years it's exciting."

Ham believes the difference was the exit of [offensive coordinator] Joe Walton and the introduction of Cowher.

"It had been a team on the rise, getting better. It was a confident Bubby Brister after that 1989 season and everyone was looking forward to the following year. I think that offense not only set back the offense but after a point it even had an effect on the defense as well and the whole thing started to break down.

"That took its toll on this team, and I think now it's starting to fight its way back."

Bleier thought the clean break might have happened in 1990 had Noll done some things differently. Instead, Noll became part of the clean break that ultimately led to the success in '92.

"There's always a death and a rebirth that has to take place in the cyclical world of life, the same within an organization. The Steelers had a birth when Chuck Noll came in and it went through that whole cycle of birth and growth and excitement, and it started to die off again. It needed to have some outside regeneration again.

"I think Chuck Noll started to do that with some outside personnel, but it really didn't catch. Maybe it was the wrong personnel to give it the infusion that it needed from the coaching staff. The unfortunate thing that happened in the last couple of years is that Chuck's infusion of a new influence was the wrong guy. So it was the prime time for the right person to come in."

Dwight White, a dominating defensive end of the Steel Curtain, once knocked the Steelers defense in the mid-1980s as "soft and cheesy," words that will live in team infamy.

"Those guys got very upset with me over that," said White, an investment banker in Pittsburgh. "But it was damn true. Tunch Ilkin and Gary Dunn and all those guys got pissed off at me. Hey, I'm retired. Mine is history; you guys got to do it on the field. Don't get pissed off at me, get pissed off at the guy on the other side of the line, OK?

"After I did say that, guess what? They lived right up to it because they got worse. Go look at the record. They lived right up to what I said. You were soft and cheesy, and that was putting it nicely."

White said the new Steelers don't play so nicely. He likes that.

"Playing defense is not a popularity contest. You have to be a little nasty. You got some people over there who will bring sparks on people—Greg Lloyd, Woodson. Those guys are real, sharp-edged competitors. They're not taking any prisoners. They aren't just playing the game to be a good sport.

"I understand all that sportsmanship stuff; I try to teach it to my daughter and all that. But at that level, if you have a white hat on and are a nice guy, that's not going to get you squat.

"People who win and are successful are the ones who get people down, put their foot on their neck and kick them in their ass. And then you say, 'Next?'

"You get a lot of respect that way and, guess what? You win a lot of football games that way, too. You get a few penalties, too, personal fouls and stuff. But that's all right."

Franco Harris is still running. He chases down clients, pushing products in his various business ventures. Based in Pittsburgh, he runs through more airports than O. J. Simpson ever did, representing, among other things, his Super Donut, a nutritious breakfast food; his professional bike racing team, the Pittsburgh Power; and Score trading cards, of which he's a part owner.

He periodically watches a Steelers game and got caught up in the excitement of 1992. He became part of the story, also, as Foster snapped his records, bringing the Harris name alive again, 20 years after the Immaculate Reception presented the franchise with its first playoff victory.

"People remember more about the Super Bowls and us winning than if you were a leading ground gainer or something like that," Harris said as Foster was about to break his single-season rushing record. "If you can do both, it's even better, which is great and how I look at the Steelers right now. As great as Barry's doing, the team is doing great, too. So when you have that combination, that's the best of everything. There has to be a lot of momentum and a lot of enthusiasm. That seems to be contagious. I think that's going to propel and drive them to keep this going."

Andy Russell, the linebacker who witnessed the lows of the '60s and the highs of the '70s, believes Cowher had a major influence on the 1992 team.

"I'm a big Chuck Noll fan, so no way would I suggest anything negative about his abilities. On the other hand, I'm very impressed with what Cowher's accomplished. I'm excited about the whole thing. I think it's terrific. I'm impressed with what they've accomplished this year and I'm a big fan."

Russell thinks Noll might have done the same thing had he stuck around for '92 because "sometimes the raw talent needs to just age, like a wine, and they might have matured exactly the same way under Chuck."

Dwight White doesn't hold that opinion.

"I really think Cowher relates better to the players. You have talent, but it's a different day, a different generation. With us, Chuck was more of an administrator. He was not, in my opinion, a great motivator. We were the self-starters. We were very much individuals and had very strong personalities. We had, if you will, a bunch of characters on the team. If you could keep them all on the same page, you had harnessed lightning.

"And that's pretty much what Chuck was able to do. Every Sunday he would just take the muzzle off and say, 'Go get 'em, guys.'

"It worked, but I think you had a whole different demeanor of player in the '70s who didn't need to be motivated. Cowher's a little bit different. He's more current. I've always felt the best coach is the one who can get the players to feel that they don't want to let the coach down. It's not about their job, not about the win and loss. The players who go and reach down and give you that extra UNNNGGH for the coach. I think Cowher's that way. Chuck was a little different, very efficient, but it was a different personality, a different time, a different set of players."

A new era, Barry Foster called it. New, but while the players of the '90s don't want to be compared to those of the '70s, they no longer are intimidated by them, either.

A priest from Ireland told his friend, Dan Rooney, that the Steelers would forevermore have trouble winning. Rooney asked him why.

"You've got these young guys coming in here and they have to pass that deity every day," the priest revealed. "Every day they walk past those trophies. They can't overcome that."

At one point, Rooney thought about moving the four Vince Lombardi trophies from the lobby to someplace where they wouldn't be so imposing. Then he thought, why? His father founded the team in 1933 and it took him 43 seasons to win the first one. If those trophies intimidated the players, maybe they were not the kind of players who could win another one.

Bleier played at Notre Dame. He knows all about rich tradition and deities. Stashing those trophies wasn't the answer.

"Organizations, like anything else, have cultures and backgrounds. There is a certain culture the Steelers have developed, and those Super Bowls are part of that culture. So if it's an intimidating factor, it's a bullshit team. You have to look at them and say, 'Either we duplicate it and that has to be the goal or here is the precedent that has been set and the standard that has been set and we as a team and a culture will live up to it.'

"So you use that and guys who come in and see that should say, 'Hey, I'm proud of being a Steeler,' not, 'Oh, shit, I don't know if I'll ever be able to do that.'"

After their ninth victory of the season in Cincinnati, the players walked back into the Steelers' executive offices, where lunch is spread out for them each Monday. A new interior design struck them.

A mural along the wall in the lunchroom for years depicted a collage of photos from the '70s—Art Rooney holding the first Super Bowl trophy, players carrying the first trophy through the airport, photos of Blount, Ham, Greene. Now, after years there, the old mural vanished. In its place was a full-color photo of Rod Woodson bursting through a big hole while returning a kickoff against Houston in Three Rivers Stadium on November 1, 1992.

It was as if someone had heard Foster and Lloyd talking in the locker room in Cincinnati a day earlier.

The four Super Bowl trophies, all that silver like lead weights around the necks of the '80s Steelers, still whack you in the eyes when you enter the Steelers' lobby. But those who work there no longer talk about One for the Thumb anymore.

"People talk about One for the Thumb," cornerback Rod Woodson says. "We're trying to get one for any finger."

"We don't want people trying to live up to a tradition; we want them to carry it on," Rooney said. "If they win a Super Bowl, it won't be a fifth ring or this or that. It's going to be their Super Bowl trophy. They'll be carrying on the tradition."

As Barry Foster said, it's a new era. Dan Rooney has a plan for that fifth Lombardi trophy, whenever it arrives. At that time, he will remove the large Plexiglas case that protects the original four and order five separate ones. Each trophy would stand on its own.

And when future generations talk about the Super Bowl Steelers, no one will assume they mean the ones from the 1970s.

The Steelers performed well under Bill Cowher, making it to the play-offs in his first three years. After a heartbreaking 17-13 loss to the San Diego Chargers in the 1994 AFC Championship game, the Black and Gold regrouped in 1995 and returned to the Super Bowl, extracting a measure of revenge along the way by defeating the Chargers 31-16 in the regular season. Super Bowl XXX once again matched up the Steelers and the Cowboys, their third meeting in the big game. Neil O'Donnell, Pittsburgh's starting quarterback during the early 1990s, discussed the pre-game hype that surrounded the Super Bowl, his team's game plan, and the disappointment he felt when they failed to win their fifth Super Bowl title. In closing, O'Donnell implied that this was not the beginning of a new Steelers dynasty, but rather the last gasp of a team that would soon be dismantled by free agency. O'Donnell himself left for the New York Jets after the season.

SUPER BOWL XXX

Neil O'Donnell

Finally we had made it to the Super Bowl, which was going to be played for the first time in Tempe, Arizona. Dallas had made it back to the Super Bowl for the third time in four years by beating Green Bay in the NFC Championship Game. The press wrote about the Steelers and Cowboys resuming their Super Bowl rivalry, but the players really didn't get into that, because Super Bowl X and Super Bowl XIII had been played back in the seventies and the game had changed so much since then. The media was playing up how both teams had won four Super Bowls and were going for a fifth, but that didn't put any extra pressure on me. Everyone was saying, "Win one for the thumb," but I just wanted one ring for my finger. I didn't care which finger I put it on; I just wanted one for myself.

Was the week leading up to the Super Bowl fun? No. That week was both pressure-filled and uncomfortable. There's so much build up to the game. It's unbelievable how big an event the Super Bowl is, how much revenue there is, how much money changes hands—it's really something. I was kind of prepared for how big the Super Bowl was from talking to other quarterbacks about how the media was going to be all

From *Superbowl: The Game of Their Lives*, Danny Peary, ed. (New York: Macmillan, 1997).

over me. And it was. I was ready for it but I hadn't learned to just say no. There are too many people who think you're their best friend and who want your time. Everybody wants your time. I really didn't get a chance to enjoy my family with all that was going on around there. It was really hard just to be yourself and take time to reflect. You have in the back of your head that you have a game to play on Sunday and it's hard to focus. I'm not blaming anything on the week prior to the game, but it was overwhelming at first. I told myself that I wanted to return to the Super Bowl as soon as possible because I would do things differently.

The players stayed at a chain hotel. It was away from our families, and to tell you the truth, it wasn't the nicest accommodation. I thought it would be a lot more secluded. So the most relaxing thing turned out to be going to practice. It would take us away from everything. We'd go to this junior college field and there'd be mountains around us and we'd sit there and stretch, and there'd be times when I'd be saying, "I'd rather just stay right here." It really is beautiful there. It's no wonder that we had very good practices.

I'm sure the Cowboys knew better how to handle the hoopla. Even when the media tried to come up with some negative stories, it didn't bother them. It didn't matter to them because they'd been there before. They knew what it was all about. They knew what they were doing. If they didn't have curfews, that was fine. They could do whatever they wanted because they'd been going there almost every year. The Steelers hadn't been there since Super Bowl XIV, so it was all new to us.

I don't think the media had much regard for the Steelers. I know they were giving the Cowboys the win the whole week. All you kept hearing was "blowout, blowout, blowout." I think the spread was around 13 points. Sure it angered us that we weren't given a chance. We put it on the same as everyone else and we deserved to be there as much as the Cowboys did. When you worked as hard as we did and had been playing this game for so long, you want to get respect. I don't think we got it.

Bill Cowher had a lot of respect for his team. He didn't tell us that we had to overachieve or play mistake-free to beat the Cowboys. He told us, "Go out there and play the way you've been playing the past year and we should be fine. Don't be uptight, play loose, go out there and have fun." He had that open attitude, that open spirit, the whole week.

In preparing for the Cowboys, I think we had every game of theirs cut up. You could drive yourself crazy because there was so much film, so I just really focused on what they did in the playoffs and in beating the Packers. Ron Erhardt gave me a chance to look at his game plan to see if I liked it. He would always say, "I'm not married to anything." Ron gave me a lot of freedom to call plays and also to throw some things out that maybe they thought would work better than I did. I'd have to have the confidence in a play. I'd have to know that this guy is going to run the correct route and things like that. I'm a strong believer in: You put a game plan in and then the players have to execute it. I was satisfied with the game plan. I'd never hold a loss against our game plan. Because you never know; some days our running game may not be going well and we'd throw the ball a lot, or vice versa. The Steelers believed in seeing how games unwound. We didn't go into the game with the attitude: Okay, we're going to run the ball today. You can't do that. Especially against a team as strong as Dallas. You looked at their guys up front. Leon Lett, Tony Tolbert, Russell Maryland, Charles Haley—those guys could bring a lot of heat. I saw that their defense was very talented and confident in their ability and played well together. There really wasn't a weakness. What we had to do was not get caught up in all the hoopla early on and stay in the game. We knew that if the score was close in the third quarter, we could make it an interesting game.

I was asked a lot if we were nervous before the game. It really wasn't *nervous*, it was *anxious*. You want to get out there and play. You want the first snap. In the locker room at Sun Devil Stadium, the players were focused, not loud, there was nobody jumping up and down. Mostly it was people minding their own business and just waiting. That's the tough part, just waiting, all the way through the introductions. They really leave you there for a while. We did our normal routine and Bill Cowher spoke about what we had to do, then we just said our prayers and went out there. There really weren't pep talks or anybody taking control of the locker room and voicing his opinions. That late in the year, everybody knew what it took to win.

The pregame ceremonies were very exciting. There was "the Circle of MVPs" from the previous 29 Super Bowls, the tribute to the *Challenger* with the planes, Vanessa Williams singing the national anthem, the long player introductions. . . . Sure, it was emotional. I'm standing there thinking, "Wow, this is what it's all about, it really is." The Super Bowl is what you really work for. You get to a point in your career where you say, "Okay, I've done everything else. I've broken seven

Steelers records; I've played in the playoffs four times; I've played in two AFC Championship Games; I played in the Pro Bowl in '93; I won a Quarterback Challenge. Now I'm just trying to win the Big One." As you stand there you reflect on how hard it was to get there. If the ball bounced one way instead of the other, then you aren't there. I thought about all the great quarterbacks who had never played in the Super Bowl, so I wanted to make the most of my opportunity. You are focused on the game ahead but you think of many things. I lost my father two years before and he would have been a big part of that day. I wished he could have been there in person to really experience it all, because you still play for your father in a lot of ways. So that was hard. But I had 37 other people there from my family and I had plenty of support. What also made it special is that the Super Bowl turned 30 only a few months before my own thirtieth birthday.

The Cowboys got the ball first and I stood on the sidelines watching our defense. Dallas had two big plays on its first possession. Troy Aikman completed a pass to Michael Irvin on the right side for about 20 yards and then Emmitt Smith ran to the left for another 20–25 yards. It would be his only long run of the game. Those two big plays back-to-back didn't shock me. It was early and we had to settle our feet, too. I was thinking, "Okay, stop them for three and let's get some points." I think our defense had a bend-but-not-break mentality. I had the confidence in our defense that they would adjust and stop them. They did hold them after Smith's run and Dallas ended up with only a field goal by Chris Boniol.

So we were down only 3-0 when we got the ball. The field looked beautiful, but it did give a lot. It was a fast track, but it was cut too short and there was some slipping. I don't know how much it affected receivers on pass routes. When you're under the gun, you think about so many other things. After the first play, you stop thinking, "I'm in the Super Bowl." It's out of your system. There's so much more going on than what's happening in the stands or what happened the prior week. You're focused only on what's happening on the field.

On our first possession, we ran Erric Pegram a couple of plays up the middle and then threw a short pass to Hastings. We didn't get a first down and had to punt, but we did get to feel out Dallas's defense a bit. The plan was to go out and see how Dallas would react. They had a lot of talent on that defensive line with guys like Leon Lett and Russell Maryland, and we wanted to see how well we could protect the passer and how we could run the ball early in the game, and just go from there.

We wanted to mix it up and see how our one-on-one match-ups would be. When we passed, we were not going to make an effort to stay away from Deion Sanders, as people said we would, and go only to Larry Brown's side. Brown was a good corner, too. We would take our chances with Deion. He was a great athlete—everyone knew that—but you have to use the whole field.

When Dallas got the ball back, they put together their one touchdown drive of the game. Their big play was a long completion to Deion, who also played some wide receiver. It was a concern that he would be playing on offense because when Deion's in there you've got to watch him. I think Willie Williams almost made a pretty good defensive play, but Deion somehow came up with it. Deion made a great play and they got almost 50 yards. Then they scored their first touchdown on a short pass to Jay Novacek. I know people were complaining about the block that picked off our linebacker in the end zone. They were saying it was an illegal pick, but what can you do about it when it's all said and done?

We had led the AFC in time of possession, but we were already down 10-0 and couldn't do ball control. We had to get some points. We started to move the ball, but then we were faced with fourth-and-1 close to midfield. We didn't want to give up the ball, so I wasn't surprised when they didn't send in the punter. Instead Kordell Stewart took the snap. Prior to the game, Bill told us, "We will have to take our chances. We didn't come here just to play close; we've come here to win this thing." So we all thought, "Let's go for it and try to make something happen." Kordell ran for the first down and we continued to put together a good drive by mixing it up. But then there was a bad snap way over my head. I was fortunate to recover it because if I'd fumbled it, they would have gotten the ball on our 40. We kept the ball but lost about 13 yards on the play. That killed our drive, and after Rohn Stark punted into the end zone, the Cowboys put together another drive of their own.

Troy Aikman completed several passes in a row and took the Cowboys all the way down the field. But then they had a touchdown pass to Michael Irvin called back because Irvin was called for interference. Everyone who followed football knew that Irvin used his hands on defenders. He was a physical player and did a good job of getting away with it, but that time he got caught pushing off Carnell Lake. That was a big play because instead of going up 17-0, they had to settle for another field goal by Boniol and went up only 13-0. So we didn't have to go to a totally different hurry-up offense. I felt that if we fell 17 points behind, we'd be in real trouble. I knew that when the Cowboys were ahead by a lot of points, they played their best. They were very cocky and would go out and show all their attributes and really hurt you. But if we stayed close, it could be interesting. Keep them to three and hopefully we'll go out and get something.

With the score 13-0 everything was pretty quiet. The Steelers fans had watched us move the ball, but we weren't executing the way we wanted to on third downs. We said we had to get points on the board before halftime and we snuck one in there right before the gun. I was even sacked a couple of times and we still made it downfield. Bam Morris started to run the ball well, Kordell had another fourth-down run, and Hastings, Mills, and Thigpen made some great catches. It was one of those times when we had timing and rhythm in our passing game, and once we got things going, completing a few passes felt pretty good. I wasn't trying to compete against Troy, because the only numbers I care about are wins and losses. All I was trying to do was run our offense and do what I had to do. Mills made a terrific catch inside the 10, and then with only about 13 seconds left in the half, we scored when Thigpen cut inside of Sanders on the right side and I quickly completed it to him just over the goal line. Yancey wasn't the prime receiver on that play—it was just a read that I got and I took a chance and fired a slant in down to him. That was a big, big touchdown for us because we were right back in the game at 13-7. That made our fans cheer. We went in at halftime feeling pretty good and knowing we were going to get the ball back to begin the second half.

Bill felt good at halftime. He was glad that Dallas had scored only one touchdown and had to kick field goals the other two times they'd gotten close to our end zone. He thought we'd been jittery at first but had settled down. Our defense was playing well and we'd finally put some points on the board. He wanted us to keep the momentum going because if we were close in the fourth quarter anything could happen. We talked about what we had to do to keep drives going. We didn't go into details, like how many passes we were completing on first or second or third down, or what our stats were using the shotgun. We were aware we were doing well with our hurry-up offense, because that's when we were moving the football.

We got the ball into Dallas territory on our first possession of the second half. Then we stalled. Instead of trying a long field goal, we had Rohn Stark punt, and for the second time he kicked the ball into the end zone. That he again failed to knock it out of bounds had to frustrate us. If you put the Cowboys at their 10-yard line at a time our defense was getting settled, that could have made a big difference in the game. There were a ton of Steelers fans there—in fact, the majority of the crowd was rooting for us—so if we backed the Cowboys up near their end zone, the fans could have been very loud and made it difficult for them. It could have changed things around. But we couldn't get mad at Rohn. We didn't get caught in blaming anyone for anything because we were out there as a team. I'm sure Rohn didn't want the ball to sail into the end zone. He had been punting for 14 or 15 years and knew we wanted him to angle it in the corner. It just didn't work out that way.

The Cowboys got the ball on their 20, but got only one first down before our defense held them. This was a different defense than the one that had started the game. That Dallas had played in two recent Super Bowls had definitely been a factor in their favor early in the game. Oh, yeah, their experience helped them jump to that early lead. But once we calmed down, I think we did fine. I wouldn't say our defense had solved all its problems, but after Dallas had those big plays in their first two drives of the game, they didn't have much luck. The goal of our defense coming into the game was to stop Emmitt Smith. Stop the running game first, because that's what Dallas did best—when they were successful at it, they were at their best. I think our defense did a great job doing just that. Emmitt had the one big run in the first drive and that was it. We had strong linebackers with Greg Lloyd, Kevin Greene, and Levon Kirkland, a big kid, and they were making big plays, but I think it has to start up front. Our defensive line was doing a great job, too. Dallas had Nate Newton, Larry Allen, and all those other 330-pound offensive linemen against our much smaller linemen, and I think our guys held in there pretty good. The entire defense was playing great. Even Rod Woodson played some on third downs after having come back from surgery. The media played up how inspired our team would be if Rod played. I don't think the players got caught up in that. It was great to see Rod come back because it really was a miracle that he was able to step on the field. But was his presence inspiring? I would have to say yes and no. Rod was a great talent and had been there for many years, but we had gotten to the Super Bowl with him on the sidelines.

Dallas's defense was also playing a very good game. A very physical game. The Cowboys were bringing some pressure from their down linemen, and on third downs they were throwing a lot of zone blitzes at me. They were mixing it up pretty good. They didn't show much of that prior to this game, but they did a pretty good job doing those things. I felt pressure and got sacked a few times—Charles Haley had a sack, Tony Tolbert . . . But I'd give our linemen a lot of credit for hanging in there, especially when they were outnumbered on passing plays. For the most part I was well protected. We had good players on the line, including the best center in the business, Dermontti Dawson, who was someone I had a very close relationship with. He was such a great athlete and did wonderful things. As always I could rely on him.

On our second possession of the half, I was intercepted for the first time. The Cowboys might have blitzed, but I had time. On that play I believe I had three receivers over on the right side. They cut to the middle, but the throw went to the sideline, and Larry Brown picked it off at the Cowboys' 40 and had a long runback. Then Troy hit Irvin on a pass at about their 2 and Emmitt ran it in for a touchdown to make the score 20-7 in Dallas's favor. On that interception, it just wasn't a good throw on my part. I just lost the ball out of my hand. Of course, you're frustrated by a play like that, but you tell yourself to get it out of your mind in a hurry. Because there was still a long way to go in the game and we were only down by 13 points.

Even though the score didn't change by the end of the third quarter, we didn't feel we were out of the game. There were times during the season when we'd struggle in the first half and then in the second half we would get it rolling, and come fourth quarter, we knew we would win the game. I don't care if we were down or not, we believed, "Hey, fellahs, this is ours. Let's play the last quarter the way we are capable of doing it and we'll come out with a win."

We narrowed the score to 20-10 early in the fourth quarter on a long field goal by Norm Johnson, one of the best kickers in the league. Then we got it right back. I didn't know that Johnson would then try an onside kick. I was probably off getting something to drink and talking to Erhardt. So it was a big surprise, a nice present to learn we had tried an onside kick and had recovered the ball. That gave us some momentum.

When we took the field we were businesslike rather than emotional. And once again we had a great drive. It seemed that the whole game we had great drives and great catches by Mills and Hastings and

Thigpen, and some good running, but we had trouble scoring. This time we knew we had to get it done. I had great confidence in my receivers and they had great confidence in me. We knew what we had to do. We had some big receptions over the middle, but it wasn't like, hey let's go across the middle every time we pass. We were going to mix it up and do whatever we could against their defense. Mills hurt his knee that drive, but Hastings and Thigpen made some big catches that took us inside the Cowboys' 5. Then I handed the ball to Bam Morris. Sometimes you didn't know if he'd turn it on during a game. But he ran extremely hard that day, as he had throughout the playoffs. He wouldn't go down. Morris scored on one of our basic short-yardage plays to the right. He went in untouched. So with the extra point we had cut the Cowboys' lead to only three, 20-17, and there was still a lot of time on the clock.

When I came off the field I sent a kiss into the stands to my mom. That was as good as we felt all day. At that point we thought we could win. But from Day One, we thought we could win. We had stepped on the field to win, not just make it close.

Unfortunately, when we got the ball back with still over four minutes remaining and started a drive that could have put us ahead, I was intercepted again. There was a blitz on third down and I threw it to the sideline and Larry Brown ran it back again. That second interception was a total . . . there was a miscommunication between Andre Hastings and myself. I can't blame anyone. I will never ever sell anyone down the river because that's not my style. It was just too bad because we were still right in it. It was very frustrating. I made the tackle on Brown on that play. But then Emmitt Smith had his second short touchdown run. That made the score 27-17 and put the game away. Later, all I could do was throw Hail Mary passes. You just let it go and take a shot.

I don't remember what Troy Aikman said to me after the game. It wasn't a blur, but you're frustrated by the loss and just want to get off the field and reflect on everything. In our locker room there was a lot of disappointment. Dallas had played a good game, but everyone knew we had a chance to beat them. We had them right where we wanted them, but in the end, things didn't happen the way we wanted.

I have a lot of pride about our performance in the game. I have a lot of great memories of that game. It was exciting; it really was. When it was over, people said the Steelers really did play a good game and then they started giving us a few accolades. Of course, you'd still hear crap about a couple of plays here and there. That's what they like to write about. But would the Pittsburgh Steelers have been better off getting blown out as everyone predicted, or making it an interesting game, one of the best Super Bowls? I didn't get caught up in all the negative headlines and newspaper stories. After you watch the tape of the game and see how we lost, you just go on. You have to look at the big picture. We had a great year. I had a great year. It was a great year and it's too bad it ended the way it did, but you get over it and you have a whole new beginning. When I moved on to the Jets after the year, I immediately started thinking of playing in another Super Bowl.

During the 1995 season and during Super Bowl XXX, I wasn't thinking about the fact that I'd be a free agent after the game. That was so far out of the picture that it didn't cross my mind. But I knew how it was with free agency. I looked around our locker room and knew that the team wouldn't be the same the following year. It was kind of tough looking at a lot of the guys and thinking that this may be the last time the team would be together. Sure enough, there were a lot of people there, including myself, who wouldn't be wearing the black and gold in 1996. I never thought that so early in my career I would go to New York, but it happened through free agency. It would be hard leaving Pittsburgh after six years. I would miss my teammates. We'd been through a lot and we all played extremely well together and we all really cared for each other. We were really a close group. It's too bad we couldn't all stick together.

Kordell

With the departure of Neil O'Donnell after the 1995 season, much of the hope for 1996 and the more-distant future fell upon the shoulders of second-year quarterback Kordell Stewart. Stewart was something new to Steeler fans. On any given play, the flashy "Slash" might connect on a long bomb, tuck the ball and dash for twenty yards, or confound secondaries by making a catch downfield. The NFL had not seen anyone like Stewart since John Elway, whom the Denver Broncos occasionally used as a rusher, a receiver, and even a kicker, and the Steeler faithful embraced the budding star as the franchise's salvation. Stewart proved a frustration for Pittsburgh. He was a microcosm of the teams of the late 1990s: full of talent but unable to perform consistently enough to attain greatness. That he served as a model for multi-tool quarterbacks like Donovan McNabb and Michael Vick meant little to a city that expected winning teams. Stewart left Pittsburgh after the 2002 campaign and never fulfilled the lofty promise he once held. The search for a franchise quarterback continued. In this 1996 article, Rob Ruck, the preeminent historian of Pittsburgh sports, discussed Stewart's background, his impact on the game, and the overwhelming expectations placed upon him by Steeler loyalists.

SEE SLASH RUN, SEE SLASH THROW, SEE SLASH CATCH

Rob Ruck

It's been a summer of incredible highs and one devastating low for Kordell Stewart, arguably the most exciting player in pro football today. After a season in which the young Steeler emerged as the prototype for a new kind of offensive player and an August in which he smiled, smirked or scowled on the covers of a dozen magazines, Kordell went home to Louisiana to bury his sister, Falisha, only days before the regular season began.

It's not the first time that Kordell has lost a family member before her time. But the NFL, which did not stop play when John Kennedy was murdered, leaves little time to grieve—even for a player who injected some much-needed life into the professional game. One week after his sister's death, Kordell was back on the field as the Steelers lost their 1996 opener.

From *Pittsburgh Magazine*, October 1996. Reprinted by permission of Rob Ruck.

Yet expectations regarding Stewart are giddily high, even though it might take months before his role is defined. By October, if the Steelers are not knocking their opponents backward, fans will be calling for Kordell to take over at quarterback. If they're not screaming for that to happen, it's probably because he's already driving them wild again as Slash, the have-ball/do-it-all sensation.

The contrast between Kordell as a traditional quarterback and Kordell as Slash, the quarterback/receiver/running back, is not the only duality shaping the Steelers' 1995 rookie of the year. Stewart wants to play quarterback badly enough to have turned his back on a million dollars, yet he's willing to submerge that desire to do what is best for the team. He's a flashy player at the most egocentric position in the game, but he's quiet and keeps to himself off the field. Few players have received so much attention; few have remained so grounded.

Careers in football can end suddenly, but Kordell's tenure here could be the most engaging this town has seen in some time. Few would have thought that possible only a year ago.

When the Pittsburgh Steelers opened last season, rookie Kordell Stewart stood on the sidelines in street clothes. For the next four games, the fourth-string quarterback was allowed to suit up but not get his uniform dirty. Kordell could only watch, never stepping onto the field as the Steelers stumbled, losing games they were expected to win. "I was just rotting away," the usually sunny 23-year-old recalls.

He had wondered if he would ever see action. But when the Steelers played the Jacksonville Jaguars last October, Kordell went from frustration to a guy who looks at his life today and concludes: "It's just about perfect."

Seven games into the 1995 campaign, the Steelers had won three games and lost four, and were headed nowhere fast. The team desperately needed a jolt to shock its dying offense back to life.

"We had most of the pieces," explains coach Bill Cowher, "but we didn't have a spark plug—a player that constantly keeps the opposition off-balance with his big-play potential." In Stewart, Cowher found his spark plug. The first time he lined up at quarterback, Kordell rushed 16 yards down the field on a quarterback sneak. "That," Kordell said afterward, "was fun!" Such frivolity has been noticeably lacking in the NFL, which many have dubbed the No Fun League.

But fun it was as Kordell began to run, pass and catch the ball. And more to the point, Pittsburgh's season turned around. The Steelers beat the Jaguars, the first of eight wins in a row. During the streak, Kordell became opposing coaches' worst nightmare. Almost every time he stepped onto the field, something good happened, whether he was running, catching or throwing the ball (including the catch that earned the team a spot in the Super Bowl). No longer the forgotten man, he had become Slash, the National Football League's newest phenomenon and the first Steeler to pass, run, catch and kick in a single season in at least four decades.

He was the freshest new twist in the game. In some ways, though, Kordell was more of a throwback to the old days. He was playing football the way kids do, when everybody gets some chance to pass, catch and run with the ball. The difference was that Kordell was doing it in the NFL.

But not even the Steelers knew what they had, until Stewart had to fill in at team practices for injured players. "We had this great athlete sitting on the bench," Cowher reasoned, so "we created a series of sets specifically designed to incorporate him into the offense."

"It came to us out of necessity," he continues, "and it just snowballed." But Cowher did give Stewart his cyber-like handle. He called Stewart "Slash" because he played quarterback *slash* wide receiver *slash* running back.

The sight of Slash running onto the field was enough to send a buzz through the stands and a shudder through the defense, as they could only guess what he was up to. A pass? A run? A decoy? Nobody knew. He was triple-threat trouble. In one game, a defender began yelling "It's a screen" after he lined up at quarterback. "Another one's going, 'Draw, draw,' and another said, 'Going deep,'" Kordell says with a chuckle. "It's crazy. I could tell they were confused."

A fairly predictable Steeler offense that had relied mostly on ramming the ball downfield now had other teams guessing. Opponents spent extra time in practice getting ready for Slash, but few could solve the challenges he presented. Of the 36 times he threw, caught or ran with the ball during the regular season, 30 resulted in first downs or touchdowns. He never once fumbled, threw an interception or committed a penalty.

However, Stewart isn't eager to pioneer a new position, even one whose versatility gives it the potential to be the NFL's most revolutionary innovation in years. He just wants to play quarterback. Always has—probably always will. It's *the* position in football.

In Pittsburgh, Stewart is already the people's choice, and if the Steelers' quarterback derby were to become a fan popularity contest, he would win in a landslide. Fans campaigned for Stewart even though he played little more than half of last season.

Until Stewart becomes a full-time QB, both Cowher and offensive coordinator Chan Gailey say that he will play more at that position than he did last year, but neither is willing to ditch what might be their most potent offensive weapon.

"He's made great strides," says Gailey, "and we want to give him as much as he can handle." And more, he hopes, than any opposing defense can prepare for.

Stewart even has a ringing endorsement from a most unlikely source. Momentarily forgetting himself in the pre-Super Bowl hype, Dallas Cowboy superstar Deion Sanders called Kordell the "most exciting player in the game." After meeting Stewart before the Super Bowl, Sanders told reporters that Slash was a great guy personally and a great guy for the regimented league: "The NFL has gotten a little boring in the last few years. It needs guys like Kordell Stewart who do everything, guys who are versatile, guys who have a little more freedom to be themselves."

Stewart has had that freedom, at least within the boundaries defined by his family, because he was a young boy who had little choice but to grow up fast. His parents separated when he was 6, and his mom, Florence, died of liver cancer six years later. But Kordell had his family, the church and football to fall back on.

It's hard to imagine anything worse when you're 12 than your mother dying. "Kordell was so young," his brother Robert Jr. recalls. "He was suffering severely." But Florence Stewart, working as a nurse and finishing college when she became ill, had prepared her children for life without her. Sick for a year, she made sure her three children—Kordell, Falisha and Robert Jr.—knew what being a family meant.

"Her death drew us even closer together" Robert Jr. explains. "That's all we ever knew, to stick together."

"No one," Kordell said earlier this summer, "comes before my brother, my sister and my father. No one."

After his mother died, Kordell lived with his father in Marrero, across the Mississippi River from New Orleans. "Marrero will always be home," he smiles. "Those are the people that I know will be there for me, regardless of what happens."

The three children also had the church, where they sang gospel on Sundays at Nineveh Baptist, and to which they turned for help in facing their loss. "I was brought up in the church." Kordell says quietly, "where there's a saying that things happen for a reason. That's the way I always look at it.

"I think that it made me a stronger person."

His father made Kordell stronger, too. Besides barbering, Robert Stewart Sr. laid tile *slash* did carpentry work *slash* and still played hoops with his son. "Look at all Daddy does," Kordell exclaims. "He's Slash Senior. I'm Junior."

Robert Stewart, 54, gave his young son responsibilities—going to the public laundry, managing his own money, often cooking for himself—and showed him how to cut hair, a trade he practiced on teammates in high school and college. "He began turning me into a man from the time my mother passed on," Kordell says.

Robert Stewart taught Kordell how to stand on his own and avoid trouble. "Things got pretty rough down where I live," Kordell explains. A cousin was shot to death when Kordell was in college. "I have to thank Daddy for keeping me in line."

Kordell grew up a few blocks from Marrero's housing projects, but his family's compass helped him navigate through both a tough adolescence and neighborhood. "I know everybody around there," Kordell notes. "It's not bad. When you grow up around them, you don't see them as projects, you see it as home. I go out on the street and don't worry about anything at all."

To prevent Kordell from tearing up the house as a kid, his brother, Robert Jr., schooled him in sport. "He was Slash from the time he was 5," Robert Jr. declares. "He could catch. He could run with the ball, shaking and baking the guys. He could pass and punt, too." The brothers played a game where 5-year-old Kordell would try to run through the living room with the football and make it into the hallway before Robert, eight years older and twice his size, tackled him. "I would never stop trying to get by him even though I never could," Kordell remembers. "But I just had to." Robert now 31, laughs while recalling those games. "He would try so hard he would almost be crying to get that ball past me."

Even when playing against bigger kids, Robert Jr. says, "Kordell had no fear." Playing defense in Biddie Football as a 7-year-old, "He'd hit the other guys so hard that their parents would plead with me to calm him down. 'He'll kill my son!' they'd say."

"I was always the tiny one in the crew," remembers Kordell, now 6-foot-1½, and a solid 212 pounds. He never put any of his young contemporaries on the injured list; and by playing with big brother and his peers, he absorbed more punishment than he dished out. "I wanted to do whatever my brother Robert was doing." he says. "I've always wanted to compete, to run the quickest sprints, to bench press or squat the most weight, to do agility drills the fastest."

Most of all, he wanted to play quarterback. Kordell "broke" his way into the starting line-up as a quarterback his sophomore year at John Ehret High School. He accidentally fractured the hand of the starting quarterback, who was holding the ball while Kordell place-kicked it. Before he left high school, Stewart made All State and led his team to division championships his junior and senior years. He then went west to the University of Colorado.

At Colorado, Stewart broke most of the team's passing records. A communications major, he is one course short of graduating. He would have returned to finish up this summer but the commercial opportunities were too good to pass up. "I want to go back to Colorado and do it right," Stewart says. "I want to have my gown on and graduate where I started." He intends to turn that major into a post-football career as a commentator. "I want to get on the tube and talk. That's my cup of tea."

His senior year, Colorado went 11-1 and contended for the national championship. In one game, Colorado trailed Michigan 26-21 with six seconds left in the game and the ball on its 36-yard-line. As his receivers sprinted for the end zone, Kordell dropped back to pass and threw the football as far as he could. The ball traveled 73 yards in the air and remained airborne for five full seconds before it landed in the grasp of teammate Michael Westbrook for the game-winning touchdown.

After the catch, Stewart said. "I kissed the end zone, I licked the grass, I kissed my teammates on the lips." His Hail Mary heave was one of [the] longest last-play, game-winning touchdowns in NCAA history. You'll see it on college highlights for the rest of your life.

In the pre-season, Stewart connected on two more of these last-second desperation heaves. Is there a pattern here? The Steelers, who selected him in the second round as the 60th player overall in the draft, certainly hope so.

Ironically, when NFL clubs came to size up Stewart for the college player draft, few teams were interested in him as a quarterback. Instead, they wanted him to show what he could do catching or running the ball. Stewart declined.

"I knew I could do it—running and catching the ball—but if I did it for them at the workouts," he recalls, "they would have gotten excited and wanted me to play those positions. But I wanted to pass the football."

Instead of being a top pick at another position, Stewart lasted until the second round. "I knew in my heart I should have been in the top picks," he says. Not being one cost him more than a million dollars. Instead of the more lucrative contracts first-rounders are offered, he played for $240,000 last season and received a signing bonus of $132,500. That puts Stewart in the bargain-with-great-potential category—one of the few categories that you can actually put him in.

One person who knows that potential is Steeler receiver Charles Johnson, who caught Stewart's passes for three years in college and worked out with him during the off-season. "He was a take-charge guy at Colorado who made everybody around him better," says his teammate and friend. "And he's better now. Kordell hasn't even shown us what he can do at quarterback yet. We've just got a taste of it. He just has to have his hands on the ball."

Stewart admits that he wasn't 100 percent happy with how he was used last season. "But I realized what a wonderful thing was happening to me. Without doing those things as Slash, I wouldn't have had the opportunity to meet Shaq [Los Angeles Lakers center and megadollar marketer Shaquille O'Neal], see Patrick Ewing play basketball, and do commercials."

In fact, Stewart has been turning Slash into cash. He did a spot for FootAction, a national footware company, that spoofs his Slash role. In the ad, he is seen working out at Steelers training camp. A football falls from the sky, hitting coach Cowher on the head and giving him triple vision—of Stewart running, throwing and catching. Kordell looks into the camera with a shocked expression: "You want me to play *what*?" The spot ends with Cowher again getting knocked in the noggin and saying, "Kordell, get in there and punt."'

Despite poking fun at his image, Stewart was very serious in the off-season. He stayed in Pittsburgh, working out four or five hours a day three or four times a week in between jetting around the country to take advantage of his newfound marketing clout. "I can't settle for where I'm at now," Stewart contends. He says he needs to develop both physically and mentally in order to do the job on the field.

Meanwhile, the phone never stops ringing. It's been the most exciting off-season of his life. "I just love having the attention," he admits, "but it's hectic." He welcomes the chance to become bigger in a marketing sense and recognizes that Slash gives him a cachet that few players ever achieve.

"But it's hard to be comfortable with all that stuff. It's why I stay to myself. It's the way I've always been. I like to stay as focused as possible. I want to control my own destiny."

Though he's single, good-looking and much sought-after, Stewart stays focused on football and its spin-offs. He doesn't drink or smoke and, other than video games, has few apparent vices. He says he can't leave his apartment without the bed made and the place in order, and confesses that, unlike his free-wheeling nature on the field, "I'm close to being anal. I like things nice and in place."

Also in contrast to his football persona, he says he would rather be out of the spotlight, alone with Dice, his Akita dog, banging away on his drums, or just hanging with his friends. "I kid around with friends, but I don't hit the clubs. Maybe once in a pink moon, like at the Super Bowl, when some of the guys said, 'Let's go out and meet Deion.'" Stewart is closest to Charles Johnson, the Steelers' first draft pick in 1994 and their fellow Colorado teammates, Chad Brown, Joel Steed and Deon Figures.

"I'm a private person," Stewart explains. "I want to stay Kordell Stewart, a normal guy. I've been brought up in the church. Just because you have a lot of money doesn't mean you need to wear a lot of gold around your neck. I'm just as normal as the guy walking down the street.

"On the field, I control the team. Off the field, I control myself."

But Kordell couldn't control his sister's illness. Falisha Stewart-Dase succumbed to respiratory disease the last Sunday in August, only months before her 30th birthday. During the summer, while Falisha battled her illness, Kordell said that the best advice he ever got was from his sister.

"She told me, 'Be yourself and never change,'" he recalls. Falisha's absence will create another void in Kordell's life, one he'll probably fill, at least in part, with football.

And he wants to fill it as the Steelers' regular quarterback. "I want to be the man here and get us to the Super Bowl as many times as I can."

Because Neil O'Donnell now plays in New York, the job was up for grabs during training camp.

Although he outplayed Jim Miller and Mike Tomczak, the other quarterbacks on the team, Stewart was not chosen to start. He was prepared for that. Earlier in the summer, Stewart predicted: "Unless I have a stellar pre-season, I'm bound to be Slash again. I'll do that. I'm a team-oriented guy. I've been taught to work within a system."

That system has tremendous potential. Other teams might try to develop a Slash position, coach Gailey speculates, "But only one team has Kordell. I don't think he will ever be a traditional quarterback. He's got unique abilities, and he'll be a unique player in this league.'"

Stewart could wind up as the Steelers' quarterback before the season is over. Until then, he just might have to settle for being Slash, the guy who gets to do everything, the most creative player to hit the NFL in recent memory.

Three Rivers

Just like old ballplayers, there inevitably comes a time when old stadiums have to retire. Conceived as part of Pittsburgh's revitalization plan in the 1960s and opened in 1970, Three Rivers Stadium was the site of some of the best baseball and football ever played. It never became a national treasure like Chicago's Wrigley Field or Green Bay's Lambeau Field, but Pittsburgh's rabid fans imbued it with an atmosphere unlike any other stadium in the country. Many cities launched urban renewal programs during the 1990s that included new sports facilities. The multipurpose, "cookie-cutter" stadiums that had appeared in Pittsburgh, Cincinnati, Philadelphia, and St. Louis during the 1960s had fallen out of favor. Now, team owners and city officials envisioned separate buildings for baseball and football and emphasized the importance of lucrative luxury suites that catered to wealthy individuals and corporations. Pittsburgh launched its own $850 million makeover in the mid-1990s. Groundbreaking on a new football stadium took place on June 18, 1999, prompting a thoughtful article from Pittsburgh Post-Gazette *sportswriter Bob Smizik. Smizik accepted the need for a new stadium, but lamented that the end was near for a potent symbol of Pittsburgh's glory years. The winning Pirates and Steelers teams of the 1970s had served notice to the country that Pittsburgh had been reborn, and Three Rivers had been their home. Would the new stadium provide the setting for new heroes, new legends, and new levels of fame for the city? As the new stadium rose nearby, the Steelers managed only a pedestrian 4-4 record at home in 2000. But they did close the place with style, blowing out the Washington Redskins 24-3 in the final home game of the season, giving the franchise an all-time mark of 182-73 in the thirty-one-year-old building. After the game, Steelers past and present gathered together for one last Three Rivers celebration with their fans. The* Post-Gazette's *Robert Dvorchak captured the joy and the sorrow of Pittsburgh's last Sunday in Three Rivers, poignantly articulating how much a "concrete bowl" can mean to a city built of steel.*

LET'S NOT FORGET THE GREAT TIMES AT THREE RIVERS

Bob Smizik

They put shovel to earth on the North Side the other day, which means it's only a matter of time before they put wrecking ball to concrete.

They're building a new football stadium in town, to be ready for the 2001 season of the Steelers and Pitt, and the politicians and business leaders got together the other day to pat each other on the back and sing the praises of the new building.

While that celebration, which lasted into the night, went on, in other parts of the region grown men living so far in the past they can't see the future were mourning the loss of Pitt Stadium.

Exactly what they were mourning was hard to figure.

- Was it a 74-year-old structure that has been outdated for at least 20 years and that is so user unfriendly it keeps prospective customers away by the thousands?

- Was it the 23-56 record Pitt has compiled over the last seven seasons playing in this dilapidated facility?

- Was it the four winning seasons in the past 15?

- Maybe it was that for the better part of the last 50 years Pitt has had one of the worst football programs in the country?

But this isn't about that small group of Pitt whiners who can't recognize how beneficial playing in the new stadium will be for their downtrodden program.

This is about an old friend, almost 29 and not long for the world. This is about a place no one is mourning when, in this case, there is good reason to do so. This is about Three Rivers Stadium, which won't make it to 31. This is about the much-maligned structure whose outer reaches hosted the festivities Friday and, if truth be told, still looks pretty good.

Behind the temporary stands set up for the groundbreaking, heavy construction machinery lurked, including the one that swings the wrecking ball. It was a sad reminder that when the new building goes up, the old one comes down. Three Rivers is in its final seasons.

This, folks, is a stadium to mourn, a stadium that brought us a life-time of thrills and memories. It's an oft-ridiculed ballpark that we never took to our hearts, but should have. It was too hard to get to and harder still to leave. And it housed baseball and football and so wasn't really right for either. But, oh, the memories, oh, the thrills.

It hasn't stood for three decades, but it has given us remembrances we can pass on to the grandkids, stories we'll tell as long as we live.

True, its time might be near, but dress it up and you can bring any-one to see it—be it AFC championship or baseball's All-Star Game. The old place looked pretty good for those recent major events.

They mourn ramshackle Pitt Stadium and are ready to bid a quick goodbye to this good friend. It doesn't make sense.

Franco Harris took a bow at the ground-breaking ceremonies. Noth-ing more need be said to bring to mind the most famous play in NFL history—The Immaculate Reception. It will be talked about as long as they play the game and it happened at Three Rivers.

Think about it: Four Super Bowl champions, arguably the greatest teams in NFL history, played on this turf. So did two World Series winners. The division titles compiled by the Pirates and Steelers are too many to even recount.

This is the place that enabled Pittsburgh to be called the City of Champions in the 1970s. This is the place that Joe Greene and Roberto Clemente graced.

Clemente's 3,000th hit happened at Three Rivers one cool Septem-ber afternoon. Willie Stargell launched shots into the upper deck in this structure. Jack Ham played here. So did Mel Blount and Jack Lam-bert, Terry Bradshaw and Lynn Swann, Mike Webster and Ron Woodson. Chuck Noll coached here. The Steeler Nation was born here. So was Franco's Italian Army and the Terrible Towel.

Yet no one is saying a word about its demise. No one is demanding a stay of execution.

Nor should anyone. Time marches on. It's time for new stadiums, one for football, one for baseball. They'll be places with great good looks, views of the city and amenities the old place never had.

But if [they guarantee] us half the thrills, half the memories, and half the hall-of-fame cast that wonderful old Three Rivers did, well, we'd take that right now.

BLAST FROM THE PAST

Robert Dvorchak

The place had never been harder to get to or harder to leave. The Steeler Nation assembled from the far reaches of the empire on a dreary, drizzly, December day to bid a glowing farewell—one for the place where dreams were made and another to the heroes, past and present, who made those dreams come true.

The game summary will show that Richard Huntley scored the final touchdown in the 31st and last season of the concrete bowl, but Franco Harris crossed the goal line last, recreating the Immaculate Reception with Frenchy Fuqua. Terry Bradshaw, unable to attend, took part with a bit enacted on the big screen.

Harris was one of the last players to leave, posing for pictures and signing autographs in the end zone. Like the fans, he wanted to savor every last moment of the greatest single moment in stadium history and the most dramatic play ever in the NFL.

"Pittsburgh Steeler fans were always the best. Always the best. Special people," said Harris, trying to explain how a play that happened 28 years ago has gotten more miraculous with time.

It was a tough day to handle, but the fans did themselves proud, letting the house that had treated them to so many thrills go with dignity. That surprised those who stereotype all Steeler fans as beery louts who use the North Shore as an outdoor urinal.

The boisterous crowd was on its best behavior. A few seats were dismantled and removed by souvenir hunters, and a number of restroom signs were pilfered, whatever that says.

But no one was arrested. Five patrons were ejected, and three fights broke out—which is fewer than a normal game. One man was hospitalized after falling 25 feet from a walkway ramp near Gate C. He suffered head and spine injuries.

It was a time of good cheer, and more than a few tears. Maybe there's no crying in baseball, but there were plenty of teary eyes among the steely tough football multitudes, 58,813 in all.

"I always thought of Three Rivers as a first home. Think of all the firsts that happen in your first home that can never happen ever again," said Maureen Cole, a nurse at Children's Hospital and a season ticket holder for 25 years.

"I'm excited about the new stadium, and that will be our new house. But home is where the heart is, and this will always be my home," she said.

Using her Terrible Towel as a crying towel, she was among the last to head for the exits. "I didn't want to leave," she said.

Just getting to this final game was a challenge, what with the construction of the new ballpark, football stadium and road network going on. Fans had to negotiate a maze set up like an obstacle course, wending their way around barriers, fences, orange cones and mud puddles.

But for this occasion, Steeler fans probably would have swam the rivers to bring down the curtain on a stage that provided glory, greatness, and its share of disappointments.

The construction zone squeezed tailgating spots—some fired up their grill as far away as the Mon wharf—but didn't stop the party. Thunder and lightning were greeted with cheers. When the rain fell, fans figured the heavens were crying with them. This was Steeler weather; the only thing better would be if it had been snowing.

The mood was uniquely Pittsburgh. Where else could Hank Williams Jr. sing the National Anthem and a country tune, then be followed by the polka fight song they used to play in the '70s?

With the sky the color of the bruises the old Steel Curtain used to lay on opposing quarterbacks, Washington actually had a 3-0 lead. But the Bus got his 100 yards, Hank Poteat returned a punt for a touchdown and Earl Holmes recovered a fumble for the final defensive gem of a 24-3 win.

But it was almost anti-climactic. Maybe the final game should have been the 21-20 win over Oakland rather than a win over a team with the league's highest payroll and a billionaire owner who charges his fans to watch Redskin practices. No matter.

Even the Steelers of today were into it. During the pre-game introductions, they ran the length of the field to commune with fans in the far end zone.

"They gave the fans everything they were looking for," said Lynn Swann, the former wide receiver who was among dozens of players who returned for a swan song.

Some of the old banners were hung in the rain, from the Steel Curtain to Dobre Shunka (Good Ham). But there were others appropriate to the finale, from Farewell Old Friend to We're Moving Out, See Yinz Next Door.

After being energized by a victory, the festivities reached a new level when the Steelers of old, like gladiators returning to the arena, took the field. Even if the Steelers by some miracle make the playoffs, their wild-card game would be on the road.

While players like Mean Joe Greene couldn't attend, they took part by videotape.

Bradshaw was off doing network duties aboard a Navy ship, but he got a big cheer when he appeared on the Jumbotron. It seems like only yesterday that as a rookie playing the first game at Three Rivers, he was so nervous he threw up on tight end Bob Adams' shoe and Ray Mansfield had to call a play. Now he's a Hall of Famer with four Super Bowl rings who gets paid to talk football for Fox.

"It's hard for me to imagine that 30 years later, they're going to tear it down," Bradshaw said. He also provided a Bradshaw moment, suggesting that the unnamed new place be called Bradshaw stadium.

That got a laugh from Dan Rooney. But the team president also got a lump in his throat when an NFL Films production resurrected clips of his father, team founder Art Rooney. Laughter mixed with tears, just like an Irish wake.

"I think The Chief was here in spirit with us," said Rocky Bleier. "He would have approved of moving forward. So now we start the new era."

What a thrill it was for former players to hear the roar one last time, six levels of sound focused onto the turf. To a man, players pumped their fists in the air and raised their index fingers as they crossed a walkway leading to midfield.

The loudest roars were reserved for those who played on all four Super Bowl winners in the '70s, which coupled with two World Series trophies in the same stadium provided the greatest sports high this city has ever known.

The cheers for Jack Lambert reached such decibel levels that he doffed his beret, although the ovation for former coach Chuck Noll was a close second on the noise meter.

L. C. Greenwood wore a Christmas cap, proving that red and white coordinates with the gold and black shoes he wore. His neon models were light years brighter than the old high-tops he once wore.

The post-game show, complete with fireworks, was so spectacular that Dermontti Dawson captured it all on his camcorder, the graybeards of yesteryear and the players of today circling the field for one last victory lap.

The strains of "Auld Lang Syne" and Sara McLachlan's "I Will Remember You" tugged at heartstrings.

Some fans had gone as far to call talk radio to announce what size wrenches were needed to remove seats, but the mounted police that took the field after the game weren't needed. Neither were the security guards who surrounded the Steelers logo at midfield.

When fans did file out, search lights were shining on the new stadium rising just 65 feet away from the outer edge of Three Rivers. The fans are the lifeblood of this franchise, and while some question the wisdom of leaving a stadium on which $26 million is still owed, it is the fans who paid the charter seat licenses to help pay for new construction.

Many re-lit the fires to tailgate into the night, a time-worn ritual of the Steeler Nation. Those who walked home on the Fort Duquesne Bridge paused to take one last picture or just grab one last glimpse over their shoulders.

Unless they return for the January auction, they had left Three Rivers for the last time.

ONE FOR THE
THUMB

A New Stadium, A New World

It was almost perfect. On October 7, 2001, the Steelers celebrated Heinz Field's regular-season debut with a 16-7 win against the Cincinnati Bengals. The victory also saw running back Jerome Bettis become the fourteenth player in the history of the National Football League to rush for ten thousand yards. But the milestones occurred in an atmosphere that teetered on the edge of surreal. Less than a month before the game, on September 11, 2001, Al Qaeda terrorists attacked the United States by crashing hijacked commercial planes into the World Trade Center and the Pentagon. The Steelers' original home opener, scheduled for September 16 against the Browns, had, like all NFL games that week, been postponed.

Shortly before the start of the Steelers-Bengals game, President George W. Bush ordered bombing assaults against terrorist targets in Taliban-controlled Afghanistan. Bush's speech was televised live on the giant screen in the south end of the stadium. When he said, "Now the Taliban will pay the price," the 62,335 fans in Heinz Field cheered wildly in the biggest outburst of the day. Never had sports, entertainment, and war been so thoroughly intertwined.

THE BIG PICTURE: HOME OPENER ALMOST NORMAL

Chuck Finder

At game's start, at a time to celebrate Heinz Field's regular-season debut, the radio broadcasters were watching television. They were concerned. They were confused. They were feeling a grocery list of emotions, the last being festive.

"It was, like, kind of weird," Tunch Ilkin said. "We could see that we started the bombing. We're having a football game here, and we're having a war there. We were wondering, 'Are they going to start the game?'"

The games went on. President Bush—last seen around a Sunday afternoon kickoff a month earlier handling the coin toss—interrupted the first 10 minutes of network NFL broadcasts so he could tell the nation about the start of the war on terrorism. His new secretary for Homeland Security, former Gov. Tom Ridge, was standing in the lush

Heinz Field grass for a pregame ceremony. It was an odd juxtaposition.

The games went on. The Steelers toppled the Bengals, Myron Cope went "pish and tush," and Bill Hillgrove accidentally referred to it as Three Rivers Stadium. The first official football Sunday on the North Shore sounded like most others. During the Steelers Radio Network broadcast, however, regular host Guy Junker of Fox Sports Net Pittsburgh and the newsroom from flagship WDVE-FM provided updates from the real world.

The games went on, and maybe half the Heinz Field patrons knew about the news outside the building's walls, and 150 of them huddled in the Great Hall afterward to be entertained by Ilkin and Cope.

Nothing like the diversions of football and Mahrn.

At game's end, Cope dragged his suitcase on wheels to the Steelers locker room for the postgame interview show, when Jerome Bettis criticized the Heinz Field patrons: "The fans never even stood up. They looked like they were just watching the game." Bettis couldn't have known that their minds were likely elsewhere.

At postgame show's end, Cope dragged himself to the Great Hall, where cold bleachers and a record crowd faced his personal stage. It's a Hawaiian chuppah, a Polynesian porch, or however you'd identify the thatch canopy that covers the craniums of Ilkin and the Steelers' colorful commentator of the past 32 seasons. The radio folks simply call it Cope's Cabana, and they start the show with the star crooning a borrowed theme to it. (And how do you identify that song, Barry *Marhn*ilow?)

Terrible Towels waved and fans exulted as the Cabana's man hitched his pants and hunkered into his seat. For the next hour, he talked about the "love-ah-lee" crowd there, Aaron Smith's amazing one-handed sack, a caller watching his language ("we run a clean show here"), the quiet fans, the winter chill in the airy Great Hall. "Would somebody close the door on that darn tunnel? . . . Or build a door and close it fast?" Y-y-y-y-y-yoi.

One female questioner asked Cope to "never, ever, *ever* retire." Ilkin responded, "I think she has a crush on you." To which Cope replied emphatically, "She should."

At show's end, off the air and back in the real world, Cope said he could hardly take any more of the terrorism news. "It depresses the heck out of me. I was in the Depression. . . . World War II. . . . At my age, I don't seem to have the mental resilience anymore. But, when the game started, yes, we were into it just like the fans."

For a while, the games went on and broadcasters entertained.

Hmm hah, we needed that.

A Franchise Quarterback

Midway through the 2004 season a local eatery named a calorie-infused sandwich after him: the Ben Roethlis-Burger—a grilled beef patty, bacon, barbecue sauce, ranch dressing, and melted cheddar and provolone cheese between two buns. The rookie quarterback from Findlay, Ohio, and Miami University of Ohio had captured the heart of the city and was leading the Steelers to victory after victory. But five months earlier, when the Steelers drafted Roethlisberger in the first round, many experts and fans questioned the wisdom of the choice. In 1970 the Steelers drafted Terry Bradshaw, another quarterback from a smaller school, in the first round, and he eventually vindicated the selection. No one could have guessed how soon Roethlisberger would turn the Steelers draft team into a collection of savants.

SIGNAL OF CHANGE: STEELERS MAKE QB TOP PICK FOR FIRST TIME IN 24 YEARS

Ed Bouchette

The Steelers made a large down payment on the future and placed the destiny of Tommy Maddox in question when they broke a 24-year silence and drafted a quarterback in the first round yesterday.

Ben Roethlisberger, a 6-foot-5, 240-pounder with immense stature and talent, became the first quarterback drafted by the Steelers in the first round in 24 years and only the fourth in 50 years. By taking Roethlisberger from Miami of Ohio with the 11th overall choice, he became the highest quarterback draft pick by the Steelers since they selected Terry Bradshaw No. 1 overall in 1970.

Cornerback Ricardo Colclough of obscure Tusculum College in Tennessee became their second-round pick. The Steelers fulfilled one of their goals of replenishing their fading cornerback position by trading a fourth-round choice to Indianapolis to move up six spots in order to draft Colclough with the 38th overall pick.

"We thought it was reasonable to do," defensive coordinator Dick

LeBeau said. "He was attractive enough to us to make the commitment."

In the third round, the Steelers drafted for another obvious need, offensive tackle with their choice of 6-foot-7, 343-pound Max Starks of Florida, a three-year starter. Starks will get an opportunity to win the starting job at right tackle, a problem area for the Steelers last season that they did not address until yesterday.

"It's good to get players at two positions where we need young depth," Steelers director of football operations Kevin Colbert said of the picks after Roethlisberger, "and both Ricardo and Max filled that for us."

While the Steelers missed out on the quarterback they wanted first, Philip Rivers of North Carolina State, the Steelers did not miss out on Roethlisberger because Jacksonville and Houston rebuffed trade offers made by Buffalo that would have allowed the Bills to draft the quarterback just in front of the Steelers.

The Steelers, whose fans cheered the pick at a special Heinz Field draft gathering, were not a bit disappointed.

"We're excited," Colbert said. "We think this kid's potential is unlimited. I don't even think he's scratched the surface yet. . . . He hasn't peaked yet. We're excited when he does peak, he's going to be a Steeler."

They plan to have Roethlisberger spend one year behind Maddox and/or Charlie Batch and then move into the starting job in 2005, similar to what Cincinnati has done with the No. 1 overall pick last year, Carson Palmer.

"This is a good situation to be in because of the veterans we have in front of him," coach Bill Cowher said, "because of the veterans we have on our offensive football team.

"If there is a situation for a young quarterback to not come in and feel the pressures of having to turn a football team around, we think this is one of those situations that exists."

Roethlisberger, dressed in Steelers colors (black suit, gold tie) at the NFL draft headquarters at Madison Square Garden in New York, said he is willing to follow whatever timetable his new employers want.

"I am more than willing to do whatever it is that coach asks of me that is best for the team," said Roethlisberger, a native of Findlay, Ohio, "whether that is coming in and play right now or learn behind Tommy for a little while."

The questions now turn toward Maddox, 32, their starter the past two seasons who has been trying to get more money. The Steelers also have Brian St. Pierre, their fifth-round draft choice last year, on the roster, so one must go. Could it be Maddox through a trade? "You can never have . . . enough good players at any one position," Colbert said without answering the question, "especially at this one, because this is the most important."

Maddox and Vann McElroy, his agent, have said Dan Rooney promised to talk to them about restructuring the veteran quarterback's contract after the draft.

"Tommy will visit with them and we'll go from there," McElroy said.

But how much more money will or even can they give Maddox? Roethlisberger, represented by agent Leigh Steinberg, will command a signing bonus anywhere between $7 million and $9 million on a six-year contract. The Steelers have little salary cap room left as it is, and Maddox does not have nearly the kind of bargaining leverage today as he would had they not drafted a quarterback.

Maddox has three more years left on a contract he signed before the 2002 season, when he was the backup to Kordell Stewart. It calls for him to be paid $750,000 in salary plus incentives based on the number of games he plays, yards passing, completion percentage, etc. He earned about $400,000 in extra pay in each of the past two seasons by reaching those bonuses after he became the starter.

The Steelers preferred to draft Rivers, but the San Diego Chargers foiled that early. They drafted Eli Manning, but had a deal in the works with the Giants that if Rivers lasted until No. 4, New York would draft him and the teams would then swap quarterbacks.

The Giants paid a steep price by shipping their picks in the first and fifth rounds next year and a No. 3 this year to San Diego.

As the first round unfolded, the Steelers knew one team could prevent them from getting Roethlisberger—Buffalo, which wanted a quarterback to succeed a fading Drew Bledsoe.

Tom Donahoe, the Bills president and general manager, rated Roethlisberger higher than Rivers and talked with the Jacksonville Jaguars at No. 9 and the Houston Texans at 10 about making a trade to move from No. 13.

The Jaguars and Texans, though, declined the offer. The Jaguars felt they weren't offered enough. The Texans wanted to draft cornerback

Dunta Robinson and knew if they traded with Buffalo, the Jets would draft Robinson at No. 12.

"One thing you have to remember," Donahoe said of his failed bid to get Roethlisberger, "it always takes two to tango."

Thus, Roethlisberger fell to the Steelers, and Donahoe traded with Dallas to draft quarterback J. P. Losman at No. 22.

"A lot of people have talked about, athletically, he may have a lot better attributes than some of the other two picked in front of him," Cowher said. He said the only questions scouts had of Roethlisberger were his experience and the level of college football he played.

Those reports seemed to rile Roethlisberger. He started three seasons at Miami University after playing only one year at quarterback in high school because, he said, the coach preferred to play his son there. He opted for the draft after his junior year at Miami, where he was the Mid-American Conference offensive player of the year, completing 69.1 percent of his passes for 4,486 yards, 37 touchdowns and 10 interceptions.

"People knocked me for the time that I played and the level of competition," Roethlisberger said, "but I have played there for three years. I have been in school for four. Randy Moss, Chad Pennington and Byron Leftwich came out of the MAC; they are not doing too badly right now in the NFL."

Colclough was projected as a late pick in the first round or early in the second. He visited the Steelers two weeks ago, and Tuesday he ran a 4.4 in the 40 for NFL scouts. He was finally over a nagging hamstring injury that had prevented him from sprinting earlier in the year.

"I don't know too much about their depth at corner," Colclough said, "but if I get an opportunity to show my talent, and if I get an opportunity to come in and play, I should make a big impact."

LeBeau expected him to at least be part of a group of three or four cornerbacks who play in their dime passing defense. "I definitely think he's going to help us."

Colclough, a Sumter, S.C., native, is the first player from Tusculum to be drafted by an NFL team.

"I never heard of the place," LeBeau said. "I don't know where it is. I say that unashamedly because I don't think anyone in the building knew where it was."

Colbert said Starks played the past two seasons with a high ankle sprain that has since healed, and the Steelers expect him to be better.

"Do I think I was playing at 100 percent? I would say no," Starks said.

Steelers offensive line coach Russ Grimm said Starks got better as the season went on, culminating with physical play in the Senior Bowl.

"You need a cab to get around this guy," Grimm said.

The Tasmanian Devil

Troy Polamalu is the poster boy for the paradoxes of modern America—laid back and intense, cooperative and competitive, a team player with a heavy dose of individuality, symbolized, in some ways, by his trademark long hair. Polamalu's way of playing football exemplifies opposites, too: blistering speed and punishing power, poetic grace and sudden violence. He once commented, "I have developed the Samoan mentality—you have to be a gentleman everywhere but on the field." His hair, then, is not so much a trademark as a focal point. It announces to everyone watching the game, "Fix your eyes on me. I'll take you to the action."

THE MANE MAN

Nunyo Demasio

He's soft-spoken and self-effacing off the field, but when Steelers safety Troy Polamalu hits the gridiron, his hair comes down and the rampage begins

His hair wrapped in a white towel, turban-style, Troy Polamalu sits in the Pittsburgh Steelers' locker room after a spirited practice, quietly watching an impromptu competition among teammates. Spurred by trash talking, several players—some shirtless and barefoot, with baggy, gray sweatpants—are trying to touch the 12-foot ceiling. Polamalu smiles slightly as 6'3" linebacker Joey Porter takes a running start and grazes the ceiling after whiffing on his first attempt. When 6'1" receiver Nate Washington crouches and then swats the tiles to emphatically end the contest, Polamalu grins. Despite a vertical leap that has been measured at more than 40 inches, Polamalu has stayed out of the fray. "I've always been the observer who learns from other people," he says in a near whisper.

That reticence disappears on game days, when Polamalu unbundles his long locks and is transformed from a shy, self-effacing 24-year-old into one of the league's fiercest players, known for a hyperactive style and haymaker hits. Taking center stage as the strong safety in Pittsburgh's miserly 3-4 defense, the 16th pick in the 2003 draft is at the forefront of a new breed that is changing the way defense is played in the NFL. Says Steelers wide receiver Hines Ward, "When [Troy] lets his hair down, he becomes a warrior."

What distinguishes Polamalu—aside from the hair—is the multitude of roles he plays in the Steelers' defense. At times he ambles to the line of scrimmage, then sprints back before the snap to become a third cornerback. Other times he'll jog up from his safety spot to become a fifth linebacker. But his most exotic role is as a pass-rushing end, in essence giving Pittsburgh a 4-4 formation; he'll even occasionally execute a stunt with a defensive lineman. In a Sept. 18 victory over the Houston Texans, Polamalu came at quarterback David Carr from all angles, tying an NFL record for a safety with three sacks. Only linebackers Porter and Clark Haggans have more for the Steelers this season.

The 2004 Pro Bowler's play at the line compels opposing coaches to pay special attention to him in their game plan, often using motion and shifts to force him to stay deep, where he has a tendency to bite on play-action. "If you don't know where he is, he'll kill you," says Patriots coach Bill Belichick. "He's all over the field." The Packers got a firsthand look on Sunday, when Polamalu made six tackles and recovered two fumbles, returning one for a 77-yard touchdown in a 20-10 Steelers victory.

Polamalu so effectively masks his intentions that keeping track of him is a challenge. The quirkiest disguise is when he moves up, faking a blitz, then turns his back to the offense as if he's about to return to the secondary. At the snap Polamalu will suddenly whirl back around and rush the quarterback. "The thing that puts teeth into those moves is the fact that he can [do so many things]," says Steelers defensive coordinator Dick LeBeau. "So when he's at the line of scrimmage, the offense has to say, 'He may be coming.' If he turns his back to go deep, they're saying, 'Oh, no, he's going deep.' And then he wheels from that and blitzes. So you're dealing with the element of surprise."

Polamalu's frantic movement and ravenous appetite for ballcarriers earned him the nickname Tasmanian Devil from fellow starting safety Chris Hope last season. "It goes with the way his hair goes all over the place and the way he runs," Hope says. "He's always into something. If you look at our film, he's always diving, scratching, clawing under a pile. He's always full speed, going 125 miles per hour."

Once the whistle blows, though, Polamalu appears to be the most serene person on the field. He often helps up an opponent he just walloped, then saunters back to the huddle, head down, saying a silent prayer. He hardly chats with teammates and never talks trash. Porter has heard the safety curse on the field only twice, both times shocking his teammates.

Defensive end Kimo von Oelhoffen noticed Polamalu's idiosyncrasies during the safety's first NFL preseason game, in 2003. "I love to watch him," says von Oelhoffen, a 12-year veteran. "He [just] smiles between plays. Then it's *Bing! Bing! Bing!* He's all over the place."

At times Polamalu's untamed play can go over the edge—he has picked up three personal fouls this season, including two in the space of four snaps against Jacksonville on Oct. 16. "I'm passionate about everything I do," Polamalu says. "You have to play so aggressively, and it's hard to find the fine line."

While Polamalu's physical tools are apparent—he was timed at 4.35 seconds in the 40-yard dash at a predraft workout and has exceptional strength for his size—it's his cerebral approach to the game that has helped him master his multiple roles. Not long after last season ended, he watched more than 20 hours of game film over a two-week stretch at Pittsburgh's practice facility, studying the league's top safeties. He viewed every defensive play in the 2004 season for the Broncos (John Lynch), Cowboys (Roy Williams), Eagles (Brian Dawkins and Michael Lewis), Patriots (Rodney Harrison), Ravens (Ed Reed) and Redskins (Sean Taylor), compiling a three-hour DVD of their highlights and mistakes. "In a game with a lot of great athletes the mental edge is what you [have to] have," says Polamalu, who led the Steelers in interceptions (five) last season and tied for second in tackles (97). "I need to get better because all these [other] people are getting better."

Polamalu grew up in Santa Ana, Calif., the youngest of five children (he has a brother and three older sisters) in a household headed by his divorced mother, Suila. During the summer of 1989, when Troy was eight, the family took a trip to tiny Tenmile, Ore., where his Uncle Salu and Aunt Shelley lived with their three sons, one of whom, Joe Polamalu, played football at Oregon State. Troy was struck by the pastoral setting. "This was a complete contrast to my life in L.A.," Polamalu says. "I saw horses in the field, sheep, cows, beautiful green trees. I'm thinking: Dang, this is awesome."

After a week Suila was ready to drive back to California, but Troy asked to stay behind for a while. His mother agreed, and when she called a few days later, Troy cried and pleaded for more time. Realizing that rural Oregon was a better environment for her child, Suila allowed him to remain with his aunt, uncle and cousins. Troy grew into a star running back and defensive back at nearby Douglas High in Winston, and didn't return to Southern California until 1999, as a highly prized freshman for the USC Trojans. At USC, Polamalu embraced his Samoan heritage, joining Polynesian dance clubs and learning the Samoan language from friends. After his freshman year he took his first trip to American Samoa to visit his mother, who had moved there in 1996 after remarrying.

Success in football was also part of his heritage. His brother, Kaio Aumua, played at Texas–El Paso; his cousin Nicky Sualua was a tailback for the Cincinnati Bengals and the Dallas Cowboys; and Troy's uncle Kennedy Pola played fullback at USC from 1982 to '85 and is now the running backs coach for the Jacksonville Jaguars. Polamalu maintained the family tradition at USC, where he was a two-time All-American and one of three finalists for the 2002 Thorpe Award.

It was at USC, too, that he had his last haircut—in 2000, when as a sophomore he was told to do so by a coach. Polamalu's mane is now so long that it obscures the name on the back of his jersey, revealing only the first and last letters, but he has no plans to cut it again unless his wife, Theodora, insists. "It's a part of you," he says. "It just feels like an appendage. I guess I'd save a lot of money on shampoo and conditioner, rubber bands. . . . "

After he speaks, Polamalu ties his locks up into a bun, the way he keeps it when not playing. But come Sunday he can't wait to let his hair down.

Voice of a Generation

Players came and players went. Dynasties rose and crumbled. Only the voice stayed the same. Myron Cope was the soundtrack of Sunday afternoons. He was the ultimate Steelers fan. The only difference between us and him was that he had a microphone. In an age when slick, handsome young broadcasters and retired jocks jostle for time in the booth, Cope stood out as one of the most natural, one of the most real men ever to work the airwaves. "Hum-hah!" "Feh!" "Okel Dokel" "Yoi!" No one else talked like that. No one else cheered and cried for his team the way Cope did. In his thirty-five years behind the microphone—he was there for 326 wins—he invented the language of the Pittsburgh Steelers. "The Bus," "Slash," "The Cincinnati Bungles"—that was Cope. The Terrible Towel—that was Cope too. His retirement in 2005 marked the passing of an era. Here, Pittsburgh Post-Gazette writer Bob Smizik captures some of the shock and sorrow that surrounded Cope's decision to leave. Sundays would never be the same.

ENOUGH TO SILENCE HIS ONE OF A KIND VOICE

Bob Smizik

As befitting so momentous an occasion, eight television cameras lined the back of the Steelers' media room, almost going wall to wall. In front of them, 30 or so men and women, armed with notebooks, pens and tape recorders, stood poised to chronicle what they had been all but promised was a major news event.

The making of this monster media scene began about 18 hours earlier when the Steelers quietly sent out word they would have an announcement of serious import the next morning.

Literally within minutes, speculation within the media was out of control. Included among the more obvious scenarios worth investigating were:

- The long-awaited signing of Hines Ward.
- The coming to terms of No. 1 draft choice Heath Miller.

By early evening, serious reporting proved that neither of those were the story in question. Which meant the speculation took a giant step forward to these fairly far-fetched scenarios:

- Dan Rooney was retiring.
- Jerome Bettis was retiring.
- The Rooney family was selling the team.

By 11 a.m. yesterday, no one knew anything, which is almost unheard of when there is nearly a full day to work a story.

At which point, a short, balding, pot-bellied man with a gnarled ear walked into the media room, and in an instant everyone knew.

This was bigger than Hines Ward, bigger than Heath Miller.

The word legend is tossed around much too casually in the sports business. It's often used to describe men whose accomplishments don't begin to merit it. But this was one time where the word fit. So did all the clichés.

A legend in his own time was retiring, and this truly was the end of an era.

Myron Cope, the most recognizable man in Pittsburgh and probably the most popular, was taking the final step in a series of cutbacks in his working life that began with the closing down of his famously successful, extraordinarily entertaining, one-of-a-kind talk show in April 1995. He was retiring as color analyst for the Steelers, a position he had held since 1970 and was his last link to an adoring public.

This was the end, and truth be known it was time—a point Cope did not attempt to hide.

He easily could have cited ill health. His voice was a raspy whisper yesterday, barely audible. His inability to hear, always a shortcoming, obviously was more pronounced. He also has been beset with a multitude of injuries and illnesses which, for a time, deprived him of the rich quality of life he loved so much.

But he was confident he would regain his voice and his health in time to broadcast another season.

What he could not regain was his competence.

Cope had a long-standing agreement with Joe Gordon, the former Steelers public relations boss and his good friend. If Cope was slipping, Gordon should tell him.

It was a task that could challenge any friendship and one Gordon did not relish.

Instead of citing Cope's competence, Gordon urged his friend to retire for the sake of his health.

Gordon said, "When I tried to persuade him to give it up because it was too much of a burden, he said, 'My voice will come back and I can get better.'"

A few days later, June 10, Gordon told Cope the truth. He wasn't his old self. He was making too many mistakes, mistakes he had never made in the past.

That's all Cope needed to hear. He knew it was time. There was nothing to think about. If Gordon had said it, it must be true.

He also knew it wouldn't be easy.

"It's my whole life," Cope told Gordon.

"It was my whole life and it was Chuck [Noll's] whole life, too," answered Gordon.

"You'll get another life."

The first day of that life began yesterday.

Cope likes nothing better than being the center of attention, but that might have been particularly so yesterday because it could have been for the final time. This was his chance to officially and formally say goodbye to the millions he had entertained over the years and to whom he was the main link to their team.

Befitting the old-school gentleman he is, he came immaculately attired in a Seersucker sport coat, dark slacks and shoes, a white shirt and a blue tie with faint design.

Art Rooney II was there representing the Steelers and his dad, Dan, was on the phone from Ireland wishing his best.

Cope, despite the voice, was his usual sharp self. If he has slowed in the broadcasting booth—and he acknowledged as much—he remains a master on his feet. It was always a strength and it still remains one.

Since he was sitting where Bill Cowher usually sits for his news conferences, Cope drew a laugh by imitating the coach at those sessions. "Jerome with a quad; he's probable."

He also had a word for the Steelers' motorcycle-riding quarterback.

"Ben with a cracked head. He's out."

He later pleaded with quarterbacks Ben Roethlisberger and Tommy Maddox to give up their motorcycle riding for the sake of their teammates.

It's well known, despite his immense success in broadcasting, that

Cope's passion has been his writing. It's what he always wanted to do, what he was educated and trained to do and what he did so brilliantly in the 1950s and '60s.

"That's what I had a gift for. I'd like to be remembered as a pretty decent writer," he said.

Then he told a story—which he admitted was boastful—about the time he went to his boss at *Sports Illustrated*, where he did free-lance work under contract, and asked for a raise.

"I was told I already made as much as any of the contract writers, and that included George Plimpton."

It's true, he was up there with them all, even the widely acclaimed Plimpton, a darling of the literary set and a best-selling author.

That was a lifetime ago. He chose another path, one he might have found somewhat less fulfilling but one that was so much more enriching for Steelers fans throughout the region and across the country.

A Playoff Run Like No Other

Since Heinz Field had opened in 2001, the Steelers had gone to the divisional playoffs three times and the AFC championship game twice (once, in 2004, with a regular-season record of 15-1). Each time, the season had ended in heartbreak for the Steeler Nation, and renewed hope for the following season. But the 2005–2006 season belonged to Peyton Manning and the Indianapolis Colts. National Football League announcers and the national press had virtually scripted the outcome: a run for a perfect season and a Super Bowl victory in a domed stadium. For most of the season the Colts followed the script. They won with offense and defense. They seemed more all-American than the Brady Bunch. Yes, they slipped a bit on the home stretch, but journalists offered a variety of reasons why the last month of the Colts' season didn't really mean squat. In the playoffs, they assured the nation, the Colts would use all their troops and Peyton would be Peyton once more. This was where the number six–seeded Steelers were supposed to exit—again. Take a bow. Leave the stage. Better luck next year. But someone forgot to tell the Steelers that they were supposed to play the patsy for Peyton's Colts. The result was one of the greatest games in Steelers' history, with an ending as improbable as Franco's most famous reception.

WHEW! STEELERS HANG ON FOR VICTORY

Ed Bouchette

Move over Immaculate Reception, you have some company.

The Steelers head to Denver for the AFC championship Sunday after their most improbable ending to a playoff game since Franco Harris ran into history in 1972.

They survived the Indianapolis Colts, 21-18, yesterday because quarterback Ben Roethlisberger made a game-saving tackle and Mike Vanderjagt, the most accurate field-goal kicker in NFL history, missed badly from 46 yards with 17 seconds left.

"I don't need too many more of those feelings," receiver Hines Ward said, "but it's good to come out on the right side. You thought the game was over, your season was over and then the guy missed the field goal."

The game appeared over when linebacker Joey Porter sacked quarterback Peyton Manning on fourth down at the Colts' 2 with 1:20 left and the Steelers ahead by three, the fifth sack of the NFL's leading passer yesterday.

Because the Colts had three timeouts left to stop the clock, the Steelers sent Jerome Bettis off right guard to try to put it away.

"We score there, and the game's over," coach Bill Cowher said.

But linebacker Gary Brackett slammed into Bettis and put his helmet on the ball. The man who rarely fumbles fumbled for the first time this season.

The ball popped backward. Cornerback Nick Harper, playing with three stitches in his right knee where his wife allegedly stabbed him Saturday, picked it up. He had one man to beat to run 93 yards for the go-ahead touchdown—Roethlisberger.

"It's one of those things that once in a blue moon Jerome fumbles, and once in a blue moon I'm going to make that tackle," Roethlisberger said.

The quarterback who had not made a tackle in two NFL seasons got in front of Harper, wrestled with him a little and then tackled him by the foot as tight end Jerame Tuman came in to finish him off. For all the punishment the Steelers dealt to Manning and the Colts' offense yesterday, a tackle by their quarterback was the most important of all.

"That might be the biggest play ever in his career," linebacker Larry Foote said. "My heart was going to my feet and back up."

Still, the Colts and Manning had the ball at their 42 with 1:01 left. They reached the Steelers' 28, where rookie cornerback Bryant McFadden broke up a pass in the end zone to Reggie Wayne on second down and knocked away another for Wayne on third.

Vanderjagt came on to do what he does better than anyone: Convert a field goal and send it to overtime.

"Not today," Foote said.

Vanderjagt's attempt was long enough, but looked to be 20 feet wide, and the Steelers became the first No. 6 playoff seed to knock off a No. 1 seed.

"That was one of the craziest games I have been in," Porter said. "It feels good for the ball to actually bounce our way one time."

The Steelers, winning for the sixth consecutive time, overcame 10-point odds to a team that beat them, 26-7, here Nov. 28. The Colts were favorites to win the Super Bowl.

"A day ago, nobody wanted to give us a chance," Ward said. "We came out and we did what we had to do. We knew it would be tough to come into Indianapolis, and they beat us pretty good the last time. This is kind of redemption for us."

The Steelers stunned the Colts and the noisy RCA Dome crowd when they took a 14-0 lead in the first quarter on Roethlisberger's touchdown passes of 6 yards to Antwaan Randle El and 7 to rookie Heath Miller.

Roethlisberger was hot, hitting 6 of 7 on the first scoring drive and connecting with Ward for a 45-yard pass on third-down that set up the second touchdown. He would throw only five times in the second half, completing 14 of 24 on the day for 197 yards.

"We knew we wanted to do that early on and establish at that point that we were going to throw the ball on our own terms," Miller said.

When many expected the Steelers to run and control the clock, they came out throwing. They ran 13 times in the first half, and Roethlisberger threw 19 times and completed 12 in the first two quarters as the Colts dropped one safety back and kept everyone else but their cornerbacks close to the line of scrimmage.

"I knew they were going to give us eight guys in the box," coordinator Ken Whisenhunt said, "and they were going to play to stop the run. And our quarterback is really maturing, and he's understanding what we're trying to do."

Roethlisberger threw his only interception, in the first half, when he was hit by Dwight Freeney. But the Colts did nothing with that, much the way they spent the first three quarters. Manning (22 of 38, 290) threw off target, his passes sailing on him. The Steelers seemed to rattle him with both their blitzes and their disguised non-blitzes. Indianapolis managed only Vanderjagt's 20-yard field goal in the first half.

"I think we pressured them a lot more," Foote said. "Coach [Dick] LeBeau whipped up some new magic, gave them something nobody's seen yet."

The Steelers seemed poised to put the game away after linebacker James Farrior's booming sack on a blitz of Manning put the ball on the Colts' 1 on fourth down. The Steelers took over on the Indianapolis 30 after the punt and ran six times in a row—Willie Parker on an 11-yard scoot to start it and then Bettis five times for the other 19, including the final one up the middle for a touchdown that bounced them in front, 21-3.

Cowher's record is 100-1-1 in the regular season when his team leads at any point by more than 10. That did not seem to be in jeopardy even when Manning threw a 50-yard touchdown pass to Dallas Clark early in the fourth quarter.

And safety Troy Polamalu appeared to settle matters when he made a diving interception of Manning at the Steelers' 48 with 5:26 left.

But Colts coach Tony Dungy challenged it, and referee Pete Morelli overturned it, saying Polamalu dropped it, even though he did not drop it until he stood up after making the catch and before a Colts player touched him.

The Steelers were incensed by the call.

"The world wanted Indy to win so bad, they were going to do whatever they had to do, man," Porter claimed. "It was like the 9-1-1 year, when they wanted the [New England] Patriots to win it for the world. . . . At a point, I didn't think the refs were going to let us get out of here with a victory."

The Colts, given new life, continued on the series that ended with Edgerrin James' running 3 yards for a touchdown. Manning's pass to Wayne for the two-point conversion drew the Colts to within three with 4:24 left, and the Dome rocked again.

When Porter sacked Manning twice in three plays, dropping him at the 2 on fourth down, it was all over. Except for a few plays at the end.

"I know a couple of times our players were ready to celebrate prematurely," Cowher said.

That they finally got to do so was a wonder in itself.

Dreams Fulfilled

In the 1970s the greatest rivalry in the National Football League was between the Pittsburgh Steelers and the Dallas Cowboys. Dallas was a city on the move. Its team had a millionaire owner, a fast-talking linebacker, and . . . well, cheerleaders who looked like they belonged on Charlie's Angels. The Steelers had less money, less glitz, and fewer cheerleaders. Super Bowl XL was another game of contrasts. The Seattle Seahawks are the "new economy" in pads. Business-like, efficient, sometimes a touch passionless, the players do their jobs well and say the right things. Bill Cowher's Steelers play with a sense of joy, almost as if they were engaging in a neighborhood pick-up game. Watching Cowher talk with Ben Roethlisberger on sidelines you can imagine him saying, "Tell Ward to buttonhook behind the blue Chevy and have Randle El hit him with a bullet." Super Bowl XL went something like that. Passionate and inspired play, infectious smiles, and at the end of the day, one for the thumb. Perhaps Pittsburgh and Seattle can do it again in the near future. The league needs a new rivalry.

SUPER BOWL XL: ONE FOR THE AGES

Robert Dvorchak

Some will call it one for the thumb, but it was truly one for the ages.

No team had ever won three playoff games on the road and then won a Super Bowl, but the Steelers last night completed a magical ride with a 21-10 victory over the Seahawks, igniting celebrations throughout the far-flung Steeler Nation.

Their Super Bowl triumph was the team's first in 26 years and the fifth in franchise history, putting the Steelers in company with Dallas and San Francisco with five Super Bowl wins.

"We were proud of the team of the '70s, but we have our own little niche right now," said Coach Bill Cowher, who won his first title in 14 years and is the first coach other than Chuck Noll to bring home a championship. "It's a special team."

Although the Super Bowl is supposed to be a neutral site, the week and the game were dominated by towel-twirling Steelers fans who made the game and the on-field trophy presentation a Pittsburgh event.

From the *Pittsburgh Post-Gazette*, February 6, 2006, Copyright/*Pittsburgh Post-Gazette*, 2006. All rights reserved. Reprinted with permission.

The championship marked the end of the line for Jerome Bettis, who announced his retirement while clutching the silver Vince Lombardi Trophy in his hands. He completed a journey of 13 NFL seasons in his hometown, in front of family, friends and adoring fans.

"My teammates put me on their backs and wouldn't let me down," said Bettis, a large reason why the city of Detroit adopted the Steelers this week as their own. "I played this game to win a championship. I'm a champion. The last stop was here in Detroit

"It's been an incredible ride. Mission accomplished. With that, I have to bid farewell," Bettis said. "I'm the happiest person in the world right now. . . . It's better than I ever thought it would be."

Confetti fell like flurries from the rafters of Ford Field as NFL Commissioner Paul Tagliabue presented the championship trophy—a silver football to go with the other four in the Steelers offices—to Dan Rooney and his family.

The storyline was all about The Bus, but the real motoring in Motown was by a Parker. That's Willie Parker, whose 75-yard touchdown run 22 seconds into the third quarter put the Steelers in the lead for keeps. It was the longest running play in Super Bowl history.

The score that clinched it was a bit of trickery to Hines Ward, who caught a 43-yard touchdown pass from wide receiver Antwaan Randle El, an ex-quarterback, after he took a handoff from Parker. Ward, named the game's Most Valuable Player, had 123 receiving yards on five catches and ran once for 18 yards.

"I am at a loss for words," Ward said. "There have been a lot of great MVP's who won the Super Bowl. I am speechless right now. This is truly a dream come true."

Dan Rooney, accompanied by his son Art Rooney II, accepted the prize on a special stage wheeled onto the artificial surface of Ford Field, an indoor stadium with an ear-splitting noise level.

"It's wonderful. It belongs to those right out here," Rooney said. "We're so thrilled to bring that back to Pittsburgh."

This was the 40th edition of the Super Bowl, an event now seen by a billion people around the world, but it had special meaning to a new generation of Steelers fans who had never experienced a football championship.

The changing of the guard occurred on a night that Baby Boomer favorites dominated the entertainment. After Motown's Stevie Wonder provided the pre-game music and Aretha Franklin teamed with Aaron Neville to sing the National Anthem, the Rolling Stones provided the signature moment. Keith Richards strummed the famous guitar riff to "Satisfaction" as Mick Jagger gyrated around the stage.

Franco Harris, MVP of the Steelers' first Super Bowl win and holder of four rings, whipped the crowd of 68,206 into a frenzy by waving a Terrible Towel during the introductions of Super Bowl greats.

The game didn't have the kind of start the Steelers wanted, and there were several anxious moments. The Seahawks had the better of the play in the first quarter and led 3-0 on a 49-yard field goal by Josh Brown.

The Steelers finally clicked on their fifth possession. A 21-yard shovel pass from Ben Roethlisberger to Ward got the drive started. Then facing third down with 28 yards to go, Roethlisberger connected with Ward again on a 37-yard pass that put the Steelers three yards from the goal line. Roethlisberger dove for the final yard, and referee Bill Levy upheld the call after reviewing the play.

The touchdown came with 1 minute, 55 seconds remaining in the half, and the Steelers never trailed.

"We played a terrible half. We knew it was a matter of time for us to get going," Bettis said.

The big electricity came on Parker's touchdown to open the second half. The Steelers had a total of 113 yards to that point, and Parker boosted that total by 75 more yards with a sprint.

"Once Willie gets through a hole, there's no way anyone is going to catch him. He's too fast," Roethlisberger said. "He broke loose and there was no one even close to him."

On their next possession, the Steelers were on the doorstep, seemingly assured of at least a field goal when Roethlisberger threw his second interception of the game. Kelly Herndon stepped in front of a pass intended for Cedric Wilson and returned it 77 yards. Three plays later, the Seahawks made it 14-10 on a 16-yard pass from Hasselbeck to Jerramy Stevens.

But Ward's touchdown catch—on a play called "X Reverse" that Roethlisberger said was the "perfect call at the perfect time"—put the game out of reach and brought the trophy back to Pittsburgh.

"It was a big touchdown for us," Ward said. "It really sealed the thing for us."

Seattle's last offensive play was a pass that clanked off the hands of tight end Jerramy Stevens, who had engaged in a war of words with linebacker Joey Porter during the week. Stevens did catch a touchdown pass, but had several drops.

"It leaves you speechless," said linebacker Clark Haggans. "Everybody's face says it all. You can see the sweat with tears of joy coming out. It's the best feeling in all the world."

Roethlisberger, the youngest quarterback to win a Super Bowl, knelt down to kill the final three seconds.

"We got the win, and that's all that matters. Boy, it feels so good," Roethlisberger said.

In the dying seconds, Cowher took the obligatory Gatorade bath on the sideline. He raised both arms to the roof with clenched fists, then hugged his wife and daughters. Known for his fierce demeanor on the sideline, Cowher was reduced to wiping tears from his eyes after the Super Bowl win.

After Rooney handed the trophy to Cowher, the coach handed it back.

"I've been waiting a long time to do this. This is yours," Cowher said.

Later, in the locker room, Cowher tried to let it all sink in.

"It's surreal right now," Cowher said. "It is a rewarding feeling to give that trophy to Mr. Rooney. That's what he brought me here to do. It really does complete a void that's been there. I couldn't be happier for him and the city of Pittsburgh."

It was one for the ages.

Super Bowl XL was a fitting farewell party for Jerome Bettis. More than a model representative of the Pittsburgh Steelers, Bettis was the ideal embodiment of the National Football League. He was a throwback to the earliest days of the league, to a time when big men smacked head-on into other big men, then drank beers together after the game. But Bettis was greater than even his running style and statistics indicate. His smile assured viewers that he enjoyed the game. Yes, it was a billion-dollar game; yes, it was often a painful game. But it was—and is—a game. Super Bowl XL also witnessed the full emergence of Hines Ward as a superstar player. Like Bettis, Ward plays in a way that shows he truly loves the game. Not since Magic Johnson has there been an irrepressible and joyful smile like Ward's. Together, Bettis and Ward represent all that is right about sports.

BETTIS DRIVES OFF IN STYLE

Greg Garber

He pulled himself up onto the interview podium with a slight grimace, but as he sank into the director's chair, his beaming smile quickly returned.

Jerome Bettis gulped bottled water, and the sweat glistened on his round, expressive face. He was talking fast and a good octave higher than his normal register.

"I'm still in a place," he said, shaking his head. "This is amazing."

The record will show that Bettis carried the football only 14 times for 43 yards in Sunday's Super Bowl XL. Despite the best efforts of the Pittsburgh Steelers, he did not score a touchdown. It really didn't matter.

The story line everyone outside of Seattle hoped would come to pass did. Thirty-three years after he was born here in Detroit, "The Bus" became a champion when the Steelers defeated the Seattle Seahawks 21-10.

The story of the NFL's fifth all-time leading rusher is over. Finally, he is at peace. At last, he is home.

"It *is* an end," Bettis said. "It's been an incredible ride. I came back to win a championship, and now I have to bid farewell.

"It's totally, totally a blessing. I'm probably the luckiest football player who ever played."

There were tears on the Steelers' sideline in the waning moments of Pittsburgh's loss in the 2004 AFC Championship Game at home to the New England Patriots. Rookie quarterback Ben Roethlisberger, who threw three interceptions, felt responsible. He told Bettis that if he came back for one more season, he'd get him to the Super Bowl in Detroit.

"I promised Jerome last year that I would get him here—I didn't promise him I would win it," Roethlisberger explained. "Then after the Cincinnati game, I promised him I would get him four game balls.

"I'm just glad I could fulfill the promises that I made to him."

As a team, the Steelers were desperate to win for Bettis. Linebacker Joey Porter, the emotional leader of the team who usually leads them onto the field, asked Bettis to take the field first.

"He said, 'You lead us out there,' so I did," Bettis said. "They gave me a moment I'll never forget."

Said Porter, "It was Jerome's day. It was his time to shine in his hometown."

Bettis said he had been mulling retirement all season long. In the middle of last week back in Pittsburgh—he couldn't remember whether it was Tuesday or Wednesday—Bettis sat down separately with Steelers chairman Dan Rooney and president Arthur Rooney Jr. and told them he planned to retire after the game.

"I let them know this was it," Bettis said. "It was probably going to be my last game, either way. My body's been breaking down. I didn't want to talk to [head coach] Bill [Cowher] and distract him from preparation. Still, he knew this was the last ride."

Cowher, who was within earshot when Bettis said this was his last game, seemed happier for Bettis than for himself.

"He's a special person," Cowher said. "I'm sure we'll talk soon."

Steelers wide receiver Hines Ward was named the game's MVP, but he spent much of his postgame interview talking about Bettis.

"He's touched every player in that locker room in some form," Ward said. "For him to come so close and fall short of the Super Bowl last year, I took it very hard. It's not often you're playing with a Hall of Fame running back. I truly appreciate what he's done for my career.

"Having him come back, winning the Super Bowl, from where it all started, it's a fairy tale come true for him."

Bettis, like John Elway, goes out at the very top. He'll likely be enshrined in Canton, Ohio, as a member of the Class of 2010.

The image that will endure from Super Bowl XL? Jerome Bettis, beaming and clutching the Vince Lombardi Trophy in his pudgy hand.

"You hold the trophy because you've earned it," Bettis said. "I've waited 13 years for that."

So this is it? Super Bowl XL was his last game?

"It's official," Bettis said. "Like the referee's whistle."

WARD A PERFECT SYMBOL OF SELFLESS STEELERS

Len Pasquarelli

Next to future Pro Football Hall of Fame tailback Jerome Bettis, wide receiver Hines Ward is inarguably the player who is most often cited as personifying what it means to be a Pittsburgh Steeler.

And so it was only fitting that, on an evening in which the retiring Bettis was finally able to hoist the Vince Lombardi Trophy as confetti rained down on him, Ward was chosen as the Most Valuable Player in Super Bowl XL. Fitting because Ward, an eight-year veteran, has played for one franchise, one owner and one head coach his entire career, and figures to retire in a black-and-gold uniform.

Fitting, too, because Ward is often noted by teammates as a great team leader, a veteran who exemplifies what the selfless Steelers are all about.

"You know, with the [franchise] records I've been setting the last year or two, people like to keep comparing me to Lynn Swann and John Stallworth," said Ward, conjuring up the names of the Steelers' two Hall of Fame wideouts from Pittsburgh's halcyon days of the 1970s, when the club won four titles in six seasons. "Until tonight, I never really thought I should even be mentioned in the same breath as those two. But you know what? Winning a Super Bowl, being the Most Valuable Player, now I feel like I belong in that club with those two."

This was a season—and a Sunday—that began unevenly for Ward, a four-time Pro Bowl performer who's known almost as much for his down-field blocking as his receiving. Ward missed the first week of training camp in a contract dispute. On Saturday, Ward was so anxious about his first Super Bowl appearance, he missed a good night's sleep.

Ward awoke at 5:30 a.m. Sunday, ready then to play the game. Ironically, once Super Bowl XL kicked off, he felt like he was sleepwalking through the action.

In the second quarter, he missed a touchdown catch when he was wide open in the right corner of the end zone. His feet seemed to get tangled on the play, set up by a nifty pump fake by quarterback Ben Roethlisberger, and he misjudged the ball. At best, it would have been a difficult catch, but it was a catch Ward has made many times before, and felt he should have made on Sunday night, too.

"I don't know, for as anxious as I was to play this game, it took me a long time to really get into it," Ward said. "I think it was maybe the second quarter when I woke up and thought to myself, 'Hey, man, you're playing in a Super Bowl. Snap out of it.' Once I got through that, I think I was fine."

Finer than fine, in fact, was Ward, who finished with five catches for 123 yards, and a 43-yard touchdown grab from fellow wide receiver Antwaan Randle El on a well-executed reverse in the fourth quarter. Ward also added 18 yards on a second-quarter reverse. On the touchdown pass, Ward and Randle El switched positions, with the latter moving into the "X" receiver spot. Ward sold the reverse well, and when backup safety Etric Pruitt bit and moved up into the intermediate zone area, Ward burst past both he and cornerback Marcus Trufant and into the open. The touchdown was critical, given that the Steelers had squandered some promising scoring opportunities, and it boosted Pittsburgh into an insurmountable 21-10 advantage.

"At times like that," wide receiver Cedrick Wilson said, "you want your premier guys to step up for you. You want athletes to do athletic things to win the game. And we put the game into the hands of two of our best athletes. And you see what happened, right?"

Ward, 29, hasn't always been recognized by those outside the game as one of the NFL's great wide receivers, but don't try telling that to his teammates or to most opponents who appreciate the diversity of his skills. The former University of Georgia standout, who played five positions during his Bulldogs' career and wasn't selected until the third round of the 1998 draft, catches, runs and blocks.

He has posted a 112-catch season, four 1,000-yard campaigns, and once again led the Steelers in receptions (69), receiving yards (975) and touchdown catches (11) in 2005. But he also, characteristically, subjugated elements of his game for the common good. Talk to opponents and they generally rave about him.

Said Seahawks cornerback Kelly Herndon late Sunday night: "I don't know anyone in the league who ever underrates the guy. He's a player's player, you know? He does all the little stuff well. Guys around the league respect the heck out of him. I know we tried to pay a lot of attention to him."

In becoming the fifth wide receiver to garner MVP honors—Swann, Fred Biletnikoff (Oakland), Jerry Rice (San Francisco) and Deion Branch (New England) are the others—Ward won't have to worry about a lack of attention now. Then again, he never really fretted very much about individual accomplishments, which is why he is so respected by his teammates.

"Doing this with this team, man, it means so much," Ward said. "Honestly, this is what my holdout last summer was all about. I wanted to be with these guys, finish my career with this organization, and be an important part of this franchise's great legacy. Hey, a lot of great players never got this opportunity. Believe me, it's humbling, and it's something I will never forget."

The Rooneys' Legacy

In Pittsburgh it is all about the team. People have talked about Bobby Layne's team, Terry Bradshaw's team, and, now, Ben Roethlisberger's team. They have discussed Buddy Parker's teams, Chuck Noll's teams, and Bill Cowher's teams. Outsiders might even mention Art Rooney's teams and Dan Rooney's teams. But neither Rooney would have any truck with such loose references. For them it was all about—and always about—not a person, but a collection of people; not an organization, but a group of individuals. And, of course, it is all about the city. In an era of globalization, where the idea of an NFL franchise relocating to Tokyo does not seem like a stretch, the Steelers are rooted in a town with a history. The Steelers are part of that history, inseparable and permanent. And although he would never admit it, Dan Rooney is an indispensable part of both the town and the team.

STABILITY KEY TO STEELERS' SUCCESS

Len Pasquarelli

Given his status as the seventh-wealthiest man in the world, with a personal net fortune exceeding $21 billion and, according to Seattle center Robbie Tobeck, "richer than some countries," Seahawks owner Paul Allen could literally buy up almost the entire NFL, based on the current valuations of the other 31 franchises.

Apprised of that fact, and asked how it compared to his view of Pittsburgh owner Dan Rooney, Steelers wide receiver Hines Ward didn't blink.

"Oh, I doubt that matters to Mr. Rooney," said Ward, a Steelers employee for the past eight seasons. "This team is more than enough for him. Heck, he basically owns the city of Pittsburgh, people love him so much. I'm sure that if you asked him how he feels this week, he'll tell you he feels like the richest man in the world. People talk about how we want to win this game for [Jerome] Bettis. But, hey, the feeling we all have for this team and this franchise starts at the top. Wanting to play hard for (the Rooney) family comes easy, because they're just such fundamentally good people. They treat us like family."

There is a certain stability that has contributed to bringing both these franchises here for Super Bowl XL on Sunday evening. Allen, after all, spent a lot of money (albeit not by his business standards) to lure coach Mike Holmgren to Seattle, and then retained him during some tough times when the return on his investment was dubious at best. But nothing compares to the continuity the Rooney family has forged in Pittsburgh, where the clan has been anointed with a level of beatification usually associated with sainthood.

And why not?

After all, the Rooney family has never threatened to relocate the team, and probably couldn't anyway, their Pittsburgh roots are sunk so deep. A lot of fans love their teams. Pittsburgh fans live and die with the Steelers, a team whose fortunes didn't turn until the 1970s, but whose rough-and-tumble history made them beloved. And that feeling, which transcends mere passion, certainly extends to Steelers ownership.

No league official will discuss it, few league owners will acknowledge it, but Super Bowl XL represents teams whose proprietors are at opposite ends of the spectrum. The Steelers are decidedly "old guard," a franchise not only trying to make history, but also trying to add to a tapestry that dates back to the first *day* of NFL history. Seattle, on the other hand, is clearly new-age.

The parable which suggests Steelers founder Art Rooney, a notorious railbird in his youth, purchased the franchise with the proceeds from a big day at Saratoga (N.Y.) Racetrack, probably is more apocryphal than accurate. But he plunked down his $2,500 franchise fee along with guys named Halas and Mara to get the league started. When he bought the Seahawks in 1997, Allen probably just cashed in some Microsoft stock.

Reporters here for the run-up to the Super Bowl have waited breathlessly all week for the much-anticipated arrival of Allen, who made his fortune as co-founder of Microsoft, and who seems to exist in some mystical cocoon. Allen was scheduled to arrive, according to the latest rumors, on Saturday, maybe on one of the huge jets he owns. Dan Rooney, who pilots his own single-engine Bonanza A36 (and was forced to crash land it a couple years ago when he couldn't get the landing gear to deploy), has been here all week.

He has moved unobtrusively through the media hordes, never quite comfortable with the attention granted him, but always accommodating to those seeking a few minutes of his very valuable time. He is, after all, a man of the people. In keeping with a tradition that his father began, there is no biography of Dan Rooney in the Pittsburgh media guide. None, either of his son, Art II, the club president, who now runs most of the team's day-to-day affairs.

The Rooney family doesn't like calling attention to itself—Dan Rooney sat at the back of the room during commissioner Paul Tagliabue's "state of the league" address on Friday and slipped quietly out, after visiting with some media well-wishers—but, given its many and varied accomplishments, doesn't necessarily have to.

"One of the absolute rocks of this league," allowed New England Patriots owner Bob Kraft. "How could anyone not be thrilled for Dan and his family to be here this week? What he means to the league, the contributions he's made, you can't put into words. A great family and a great legacy, certainly."

If the city fathers in Pittsburgh ever wanted to carve out their own version of Mount Rushmore on Mount Washington, the craggy South Side cliff that overlooks the town, some legendary silhouettes would be included. Candidates for such an honor might be some of the city's early business leaders with very familiar names: Mellon, Heinz, Carnegie, Westinghouse and Scaife.

But dyed-in-the-wool 'burghers who bleed black and gold would probably petition, too, for Steelers founder Art Rooney, so beloved is he even 17 years after his death. And his family, led by Dan Rooney, is regarded with that same level of affection. Why so? Part of the reason is that they define unpretentiousness. Mostly, however, it's because of their loyalty, a commodity that in a blue-collar town is seen as gold, that they exude.

"There's just sort of a commonness about them that draws you in," center Jeff Hartings said. "I mean, I played in Detroit, for the Ford family, and they were good people, don't get me wrong. But I don't know that, when I was in the company of Mr. [William] Ford, I ever got completely comfortable. Mr. [Dan] Rooney walks in and the last thing he wants is for people to treat him like he's a big shot, you know?"

Think about this: Since 1969, the Steelers have employed just two head coaches, Pro Football Hall of Fame member Chuck Noll, who led the franchise to four Super Bowl victories in a six-season span of the '70s, and Bill Cowher. Over the same period, the 31 other teams in the NFL have averaged 9.2 head coaches, and that's counting even the expansion franchises that joined the league over the last three dozen seasons. Nine franchises have had 12 or more head coaches in that stretch.

Ward will almost certainly finish his career having played in one uniform and for just one coach, a rarity in the age of free agency and the salary cap. And he'll have played it, he acknowledged, having worked for an owner and a family without whose surname the history of the NFL could not be written.

Not even the Rooney family can operate their team with the mom-and-pop philosophy that the late franchise patriarch Art Rooney practiced. A man who loved walking through the locker room on a daily basis, and who savored his conversations with players nearly as much as he did the fat stogies he chain-smoked, Art Rooney would probably blanch at the game's current intricacies.

But the Steelers' founder, who died in 1988, left his heirs a simple, three-word credo that has grown into a mantra for eldest son Dan Rooney and his own children.

"Treat people right," said Dan Rooney this week, when asked about the success of the Steelers, a franchise seemingly embraced this week by most football fans outside of the Pacific Northwest. "That's probably the biggest lesson my dad [imparted]. And I think we do a good job of practicing it. We don't see our employees as employees. They're part of what we do and who we are. We try to hire good people, get out of their way, and let them do their jobs. I don't think [the formula] is all that complicated."

That formula, and his own modesty aside, Dan Rooney during his tenure as owner, and actually even before the death of his father, has been universally regarded as among the most powerful and influential men in the league. A centrist thinker, who has never lost sight of the fact that football is his family's primary undertaking even as the Rooney clan has expanded its horizons, he played a key role in ending two work stoppages. Rooney has a knack for typically placing the good of the league ahead of all else. At a time when some of his peers are more concerned with individual revenues, Rooney clings to the all-for-one-and-one-for-all concept that became the underpinnings of the league's success.

"How can I not be proud of what my grandfather and father have meant to the league?" said Art Rooney II. "It's been very gratifying to see the way my father has been received here this week. It means a lot to us."

It will mean a lot, as well, if Dan Rooney exits Ford Field on Sunday evening with a fifth Vince Lombardi Trophy to adorn the lobby of the team's offices.

Cowher has reiterated several times this week, and often eloquently, what it would mean for him to secure a Super Bowl title for his boss. And as much as the Bettis story seems to supersede everything else this week, it's actually the strong feelings that the Steelers have for Dan Rooney and his family that has provided at least equal impetus.

"To see Mr. Rooney with that trophy, it would be great, really," said defensive end Kimo von Oelhoffen. "I mean, it would be just like one of us standing there holding it, because he really is just one of us. He's family, and we're like family to him, and that's a pretty rare thing anymore in any business relationship. But, then again, he's a rare man."